Restoration and
Eighteenth-century Poetry
1660–1780

The Routledge History of English Poetry

General Editor

R. A. Foakes
Professor of English
The University of Kent at Canterbury

The Routledge History of English Poetry

Volume 3

Restoration and Eighteenth-Century Poetry 1660–1780

Eric Rothstein

Professor of English
University of Wisconsin

Routledge & Kegan Paul
Boston, London and Henley

TO LOUIS LANDA
in lieu of a panegyric ode

First published in 1981
by Routledge & Kegan Paul Ltd
9 Park Street, Boston, Mass. 02108, USA, and
39 Store Street, London WCIE 7DD,
Broadway House, Newtown Road,
Henley-on-Thames, Oxon RG9 1EN
Photosetting by Thomson Press (India) Ltd., New Delhi
and printed in the United States of America by
Vail Ballou Press, Inc.,
Binghamton, New York

British Library Cataloguing in Publication Data

Rothstein, Eric

Restoration and eighteenth-century poetry, 1660–
1780. – (The Routledge history of English poetry;
vol. 3).
1. English poetry – Early modern, 1500–1700 –
History and criticism
2. English poetry – 18th century – History and
criticism
I. Title   II. Series
821'.009   PR561   80–41728

ISBN 0–7100–0660–8

Contents

General editor's preface

The last major history of English poetry was that published in six volumes by W. J. Courthope between 1895 and 1910. In this century there have been some discoveries, some major shifts of critical opinion, and many revaluations of particular authors or periods. Twentieth-century poets have both added an exciting new chapter to the story and in doing so altered perspectives on the nineteenth and earlier centuries. In addition, there has been a massive growth in the publication of works of criticism and scholarship, many of which have helped to provide a better context for understanding what poets at various periods were trying to do, and for appreciating their achievement. Courthope's principal interest was in poetry as an aspect of intellectual history, as related to ideas, culture and political institutions. It is time for a fresh appraisal, and one of a rather different kind.

This new critical history of English poetry is planned to extend through six volumes, each written by a different author. Each author, a specialist in his period, has been encouraged to develop his own argument about the poetry he deals with, and to select his own historical emphases. The volumes will be uniform in appearance, but each will reflect in style, presentation, critical perspectives, and historical emphases, one person's viewpoint, and, no doubt, his own intellectual background; for, as is appropriate at a time when so much of the best criticism of English literature is being produced outside England, the authors are drawn from the USA and Canada, as well as Britain. The aim of the volumes is not to provide merely another account of the major figures, but to reassess the development of English poetry. The authors have been asked to take into account poetry that seemed important when it was published, and to set what now seems important in the context of the views held at the time it was written. The volumes are not necessarily separated in terms of a strict chronological division, and some poets may figure in different aspects in more than one of them, for a degree of overlapping has been encouraged where it seems appropriate.

Above all, each volume represents its author's personal testimony about a range of poets and poetry in the light of current knowledge, and taking into account, so far as this is helpful, current modes of criticism. In the present volume, the author

John Gay, *Poetry and Prose*, 2 vols, ed. Vinton Dearing and Charles Beckwith (1974)

Oliver Goldsmith, text as for Collins above

Thomas Gray, text as for Collins above

Matthew Green, text as for Dyer above

Samuel Johnson, *Poems*, ed. E. L. McAdam, Jr, with George Milne (1964)

James Macpherson, *The Poems of Ossian*, 2 vols, ed. Malcolm Laing (1805)

John Norris, *Poems*, ed. A. B. Grosart (1871)

John Oldham, text as for Dorset above

Thomas Otway, *Works*, 2 vols, ed. J. C. Ghosh (1932)

Alexander Pope, *Poems* (Twickenham edition), 11 vols (1939–69)

Thomas Purney, *Works*, ed. H. O. White (1933)

the Earl of Rochester (John Wilmot), *The Complete Poems*, ed. David Vieth (1968)

Sir Charles Sedley, *The Poetical and Dramatic Works*, 2 vols, ed. V. de Sola Pinto (1928)

Christopher Smart, *Collected Poems*, 2 vols, ed. Norman Callan (1949)

Jonathan Swift, *Poems*, 3 vols, ed. Harold Williams (1937)

James Thomson, *Complete Poetical Works*, ed. James Logie Robertson (1908)

Thomas Traherne, *Centuries, Poems, and Thanksgivings*, 2 vols, ed. H. M. Margoliouth (1958)

Edmund Waller, *Poems*, 2 vols, ed. G. Thorn Drury (1901)

Introduction

'Why will not my subjects write in prose?' grumbled King George II. A hundred and fifty years later, in 'The Study of Poetry,' Matthew Arnold told assenting Victorians that effectually George II's subjects had: 'Though they may write in verse, though they may in a certain sense be masters of the art of versification, Dryden and Pope are not classics of our poetry, they are classics of our prose.' Today, I suspect, Arnold's blandly malign judgment would have few open defenders. From the 1920s on, admiration for 'metaphysical' wit and allusive poetry has made regard grow for the wit and allusiveness of Dryden and Pope. The close analysis sponsored by the 'new criticism' long ago dislodged the method of 'touchstones' by which Arnold assayed 'our age of prose and reason' as fool's gold. Through historical and philosophical techniques, too, scholars of the 1930s and later started to rediscover the depth and complexity of the poetry to which Arnold condescended. As a result, Dryden and Pope have regained their old prestige, with only rare dissent now and again heard from a mystical critic or an anthology-monger. Better still, a wide audience reads their poetry, enjoys it, sometimes cherishes it. Arnold's words, after the work and care of the last half-century and more, should by all rights have followed the career of the doves in Dryden's *The Hind and the Panther*:

> sunk in credit, they decreased in power:
> Like snows in warmth that mildly pass away,
> Dissolving in the silence of decay.

Yet here and there the Arnoldian doves linger on, or at least their dovecote of consensus does, in barely recognizable shape but still itself. Even those who might be expected to discard the clichés of the 1880s sometimes endorse them. For example, a venerable scholar's still-used introduction to eighteenth-century poetry implies, as one reviewer protested, that beguiling as it may be, 'eighteenth-century verse fails to challenge comparison with first-class poetry.' From this book one learns that eighteenth-century poetry was polite, discreet, safe, shunning 'what was too subtle, or too complex, or what involved too difficult a reconciliation of opposites.' More recently, a young scholar's article claimed that the period (in which he specializes) was a 'relative wasteland of great imaginative literature, especially in England' because creative men turned from poetry to science – here is the age of prose and reason with a vengeance! – and a science, moreover, that 'actually forced the human spirit into a strait-jacket.' With men like this teaching and writing about eighteenth-century literature, one is tempted to adapt Ferenc Molnar's famous comment that someone who has a Hungarian for a friend doesn't need an enemy. 'Hungarian friends' and enemies alike will not find my history congenial. I believe that the poetry of the 120 years from 1660 to 1780 is overall as distinguished as that of any 120 consecutive years before 1660 or after 1780 in English literature. Writing this book has strengthened this belief; I hope that reading it will help others see why.

The assumptions behind the Arnoldian consensus have created more than occasional disdain: they have created a myth, the pervasive myth of the cloven century. In much modern writing about eighteenth-century literature (and art and music as well), a long, jagged fissure divides two camps, often called 'classicists' and 'romantics.' Sometimes one finds 'neoclassic' or the now outmoded 'pseudo-classic' for the first group. They make up part of 'the Age of Reason' or exemplify 'Augustanism' (usually desirable) or 'Augustan humanism' (almost always desirable), the last strain of 'Renaissance Christian humanism.' Under this placard stand Dryden, Pope, and Johnson. Across the fissure mill Thomson, Gray, Collins, the Wartons, and Chatterton (Young and Smart are double agents). This second group has the sign 'Age of Sensibility' or some other substitute for 'preromanticism,' now discredited for its hint that poets before 1798 were mere unwitting heralds of the half-revolution, half-revelation of the early nineteenth century. Whatever the labels of the groups, though, the two camps have become folklore, criticism's equivalents of York and Lancaster, Montague and Capulet, Hatfield and McCoy. As such they provide literary historians with all-too-handy tags, at times used simply for convenience and at times given credence. The more credence in the minds of scholars or of their often unwary and unsure readers, the worse. Such divisions, taken seriously, have often damaged the study of eighteenth-century poetry by imposing false categories on a complex continuum, and exaggerating or engulfing certain similarities and differences in all kinds of poetry from the time of Milton and Marvell to the time of Byron and Keats.

The myth of the cloven century has also created scholarly camps. Poets like Collins and Young enjoyed some favor from nineteenth-century critics who found in their lines a bit of the spontaneity, feeling, and love of external nature so much prized in the 'Romantic' movement. Dryden and Pope then lay at their Arnoldian ebb. With the revival of certain forms of 'classicism' in this century, typified and to some extent led by the criticism of T. S. Eliot, poets of the second group lost ground to those of the first, the 'neoclassicists.' For the most part, present-day scholars have been attracted to eighteenth-century poetry by the 'classicists' in vogue, and have been eager, by argumentative necessity as well as by temperament, to stress the continuity from the 'humanism' of the 'Renaissance' to the 'Augustans.' This has been extremely desirable, but some such scholars fail to go on stressing continuity. In their literary histories, 'humanism' gutters out with Pope, Johnson, or perhaps Crabbe, depending on which version of it one reads about. As over against old-fashioned enthusiasts for glimmerings of Wordsworths to come, we now have enthusiasts for the rich, mellow sunset of Miltonic ideals, tories who lament the falling dust and dew of later sensibility. I recall a colleague of mine, then devoted to the eighteenth century but now distinguished for his work in the early seventeenth, who said to me mournfully, 'Do you realize that it was in *our* century that everything started going to pot?' As an expression of taste, this lament – or its opposite – is perfectly fine. But taste has an odd way of commandeering seemingly objective arguments in its behalf. From among those scholars who have faith in the myth of the cloven century, with dawning and darkening on either side, have sometimes come special pleading instead of analysis, and elaborate diagnoses of what went wrong (e.g., creative men turned from sonnets to science) when nothing did go wrong.

As I have been implying, this history is meant to aid those scholars who have been trying to dispel old myths. I have also tried to avoid starting new ones. T. S. Ashton, in the preface to his eighteenth-century volume (1955) of *An Economic History of England*, boasts of banning all words ending in 'ism' (except 'baptism') from his book. I have not been able to match him, but as in the preceding paragraphs, I have tried to handle 'isms' and the like only with the tongs of inverted commas. For the vague, established categories that the 'isms' represent, I have had to substitute some other generalizations – a short book on 120 years of poetry needs them – but mine, I hope, are typically hedged, mainly testable by someone who knows the major works of the period, and whenever possible centered on specific examples of clearly described models. Whenever I could present the poets' rationale for doing what they did, I have, and have tried to suggest how a given practice might produce poetic complexity. Occasionally I have speculated about historical changes. None the less, I have tried to remember that not all changes have reasons. Wide lapels, beards, carved and gilded picture frames – these have gone in and out of fashion without learned disputes about underlying causes. Shifting taste in the arts bows to rational discourse only a bit better than does shifting taste in haberdashery.

Because *literary* history starts from and returns to specific works, I have devoted more space to analyses of texts than books like this usually do. When one deals with objects of value, like poems, one must understand the formal elements – conceptual and structural as well as historical – on which judgments of value might be based; and I do not think that understanding can come from the mixture of chronicle and impressionism which typically marks broad, standard literary histories. More such analyses occur in the first chapter than later in the book – if the analyses are suggestive beyond individual cases, they need not be multiplied. Generally the poems discussed in detail are familiar, anthologized ones, which I would expect to be at hand to anyone interested enough in the period to read this book. I hope that this familiarity will enable readers to confirm or dispute particulars and, by extension, to weigh the opinions that I have been liberal in voicing. Familiar poems, of course, are likely to be the best ones, but more or less discussion of a given text should not be taken as a sign of my own preferences: for one reason or another, I devote more space to passages by James Cawthorn and Richard Jago than to Dryden's or Gay's *Fables*, *An Essay on Man*, and *The Deserted Village*. (Each of these victims of my selectivity has a place in the chronology at the end of the volume.)

The organization of the history responds to some of the concerns I have mentioned. The two chapters that survey the poetry (Chapter 1 and Chapter 4) take 1720 as their dividing point (1660–1720, 1720–80) simply because that year is the middle of the period the book covers: the date is arbitrary so as to avoid imposing any groupings of my own contrivance. These two chapters are basically organized in terms of genres rather than favored authors (to avoid 'the school of' groupings). Chapter 1 touches in passing on matters of style and the uses of the past; Chapters 2 and 3 take up these topics in detail from 1660 to 1780. They do not, that is, break at 1720, so that that date does not seem in any way canonical. Historically, these two topics – style and the uses of the past – have been perhaps the most troublesome for readers of Restoration and eighteenth-century poetry. Stylistic touchstones assured Arnold that Pope wrote prose and have assured some later critics that Thomson wrote no language. And Pope's and Thomson's indebtedness to the past, to different pasts, have prompted much of the sorting of poems into 'classical' and 'romantic' cabinets. In some sense, these chapters might have come first so that the survey of poetry could draw upon them. I thought, though, that an orientation for the reader, through descriptions of genres and their formal elements, had priority. For that reason, Chapter 1 tries to present such an orientation in its discussion of poetry to 1720; Chapters 2 and 3 then deal with style and the uses of the past; and Chapter 4, on poetry from 1720 to 1780, draws on all three preceding chapters.

Each kind of discussion, incidentally, claims its own pattern of historical change. 'The uses of the past' presents an essentially linear movement: the growth and decline of classical models and their partial replacement by native English and 'primitive' ones. Stylistic change was much less linear. The classically described high, middle, and low styles all changed contemporaneously but at different rates of speed and for different purposes, and their variants enjoyed different kinds of prestige, depending on genres in vogue from decade to decade. Still a third pattern of historical change informs the two chapters that survey the history of poetry as a whole. My argument is that one here finds a movement from a concern of one type to another of a different type. From 1660 to roughly the 1690s, what is most distinctive about poetry – the poetry to which the most interesting poets, in the judgment of posterity, turned their energies – is its focus on a theme, the theme of power. From the 1690s to roughly the 1740s, however, what is most distinctive is a focus not on a theme but on an operating principle, that of interaction, interconnectedness. From the 1740s to 1780, finally, what is most distinctive is a focus on neither a theme nor an operating principle but on an attitude, that of fellow-feeling. Chapter 1 details the poetic modes involved in the change from the first of these concerns (the theme of power) to the second (the principle of interaction), and Chapter 4 from the second of these concerns to the third, the attitude of sympathy or fellow-feeling. As a whole, the history tries to give the period it covers a coherence based on linear and non-linear patterns of change and development playing off against (and with) one another. I do not pretend, however, that I could not just as well have started at 1625 or 1675 or any other time, or ended in 1760 or 1800 instead of 1780: there is no magic in dates if one believes, as I do, that literary history is continuous.

Finally, I should add that despite any impressions I may have given to the contrary, and despite my idiosyncrasies of selection and opinion, most of this history is hardly pioneering. No one can be more conscious than I of my debt to, and admiration for a great amount of fine, penetrating analysis and synthesis by previous scholars, especially those who have written on Dryden and Pope. A main function of a history like this is to bring together, so far as one can, the best that has been thought about its subject; and in this book I have much more often retailed others' insights than had to contrive my own. Perhaps ungratefully, I have usually not entered into discourse with other scholars with whom I differ; and I have not acknowledged my piracies from others in footnotes. Readers should please assume that I am not simply dismissing previous studies, and should credit to others any theories or insights that occur in work published earlier than this book. Any howlers, of course, must howl on my doorstep.

I have debts of a more personal sort, which it is a pleasure to acknowledge. The American Council of Learned Societies awarded me a grant for the basic research for this book. A trip to the British Library was made easier by a grant from the American Philosophical Society. The University of Wisconsin, always bountiful, has again been so in helping with this project. Such generosity creates an obligation that I hope this book begins to repay. My discussion of *The Rape of the Lock* has profited by advice from Maureen Mulvihill. Three friends have read the manuscript closely and scrupulously: Reg Foakes, who has shown me how to clarify many points; Howard Weinbrot, on whose learning, rigor, and acumen I have as so often before been able to rely; and my best of friends, my wife Marian. Finally I must thank the man to whom the book is dedicated, Louis Landa, who started me on all this nearly twenty-five years ago.

1 Restoration and early eighteenth-century poetry 1660–1720

'In the seventeenth century men killed, tortured, and executed each other for political beliefs; they sacked towns and brutalized the countryside. They were subjected to conspiracy, plot, and invasion. This uncertain political world lasted until 1715, and then began rapidly to vanish.' As members of the society drawn here by J. H. Plumb (*The Growth of Political Stability in England 1675–1725*, p. 13), poets, like politicians, were fascinated with power. The special savor of Restoration verse comes largely from this fascination. I say this as one might say that Indian cuisine gets its special savor from curry, knowing that 'curry' covers a range of blended spices, mixed in different proportions, typically and flexibly used but neither inevitable nor self-sufficient. 'Power' is at least as various. Moreover, a vast quantity of Restoration verse – many epistles, pastorals, kinds of religious verse, 'Anacreontic' (light, convivial) odes, narratives, prologues and epilogues – has other concerns. But these are, so to speak, side dishes. Almost all the Restoration poetry that posterity has judged worth reading, from 1660 to about 1690, has power as its center, and the most talented poets of the age, as well as many dreary ones, worked and thought under the sign inscribed in the intellectual sky by Hobbes in the eleventh chapter of his *Leviathan*: 'In the first place, I put for a general inclination of all mankind a perpetual and restless desire of power after power, that ceaseth only in death.' When Hobbes wrote that at mid-century, Englishmen had already seen the great source of virtual power, the king (Charles I), destroyed in the Civil Wars by an army that made itself lawful by victory, and had seen glory won for their country by the man whom traditional values taught them most to despise, the regicide usurper Cromwell. After the Restoration, the egocentric roistering of Charles II and his court scandalized the virtuous and seemed, once more, to disjoin might and right. Men whose ancestral values and loyalties were so muddied by history turned to the inescapably real, to relationships of power. The poems of Milton and Marvell, who bridge the earlier and later seventeenth century, show the growth of this dominant theme; and no one can miss it in the poems of the major figures whose important work comes after 1660, Butler, Dryden, and Rochester.

Four postures that a writer of verse can take toward power define four of the most common groups of Restoration poems. First, the poet can celebrate the power of others, typically in odes, elegies, panegyrics, and dedicatory poems. Second, he can demonstrate his own power, typically as a satirist who scourges the public enemy and reclaims the corrigible. He may lash or ridicule others for his own private ends (malice, vengeance) or for the public good, in accord with the three purposes of legal punishment listed by the great eighteenth-century jurist Blackstone: amendment, deterrence, and 'depriving the party injuring of the power to do future mischief' (*Commentaries*, IV, 1); in either case the poet models himself upon the observable actions of the mighty. Third, he can express human relationships in terms of assertions of sexual and emotional power, as in seduction poems about the willful, amoral imperiousness of beauty. Finally, the poet can make a show of distaste for the restless greed for power. He can assert an alternative, the power of self-sufficiency, as in the poetry of rural retirement.

Each of these four modes combines praise and blame: panegyric uses negative examples as foils and satire uses positive ones, love poetry mingles pleasure and suffering, and pastoral often praises the country by disparaging the court. Each has as a principal task to express an emotional attitude toward an ideal; and because emotional, therefore to some extent personal, psychological. In considering these four related modes, I will take the celebration of power in panegyric as basic, the one most likely to be serious, lofty, generally social, and demanding of assent. Satire inverts it, love poetry and pastoral replace its values with more individual ones. Panegyric too, with love poetry following behind it, most sensitively registered the change in climate as the seventeenth century moved to an end and gave way to the eighteenth. By 1720, poems devoted to gilding men in power had been left to hacks and party writers, while poets of talent looked elsewhere for their themes.

Panegyric and patriotism

Factions during the Civil Wars prompted panegyrics (like satires), as did Cromwell's dubious welding of right and might, and finally as did the return of a hereditary monarch, Charles II. Some of the panegyrists wrote for love, some for money, but both refined for the occasion the techniques of praise developed for other rulers in other times. In particular these techniques included the heroic narrative and the grand ode. The heroic narrative suited the heroic illusions of the Commonwealth years. Edmund Waller, for example, used the heroic narrative in 'Of a War with Spain, and a Fight at Sea' (1657?), a poem written (like many others during the Commonwealth) to urge Cromwell to reunite authority and monarchy by taking the royal title himself. Although the hereditary line would be broken, Cromwell thus could, it was argued, reconcile social position, personal achievement, and inner greatness. Waller deals with all three, by making Cromwell's reign the source of England's military and moral strength. In the poem, the bold English navy assaults the fleet of the Spanish plutocrats who sway the Old World with gold they ferry from the New. So well do the English succeed that 'victorious Montague' returns 'with laurels in his hand, and half Peru.' The poem ends by awarding laurels and Incan gold to 'our great Protector':

His conquering head has no more room for bays.
Then let it be as the glad nation prays:
Let the rich ore be melted down
And the state fixed by making him a crown;
With ermine clad, and purple, let him hold
A royal sceptre made of Spanish gold.   (ll. 105–10)

Waller doubly exploits his fellow Englishmen's rejoicing over the victory – public thanksgiving was declared in all the churches after the battle in late 1656 – and their desire to see in it an emblem of British supremacy. Having gained their sympathy by speaking as a patriot, he hopes to keep it by his patriotic suggestion to Cromwell. Having satisfied the public desire to treat the victory at sea as an emblem, he hopes that by analogy his readers will want to extend the emblematic process to Cromwell. The forceful Lord Protector should take on the consecrated, ceremonial role of king and thereby cause the flux of the state to be 'fixed.'

Persuasive analogies give the poem whatever structure the narrative sequence does not. The motifs of gold, reign, and virtue converge in Cromwell, as we have seen, whereas by contrast the Spanish have a mere material solidity, a 'gilded majesty' whose 'sinews are of coin,' rather than the spiritually 'solid virtue' of the English. Spain supplies venal prelates, who rule without Protestant virtue over tempestuous 'troublers of the world's repose,' and who are natural enemies of an English navy that can 'tread on billows with a steady foot' and an England whose past unsteadiness a royal Cromwell could 'fix.' In the British victory, spirit regains precedence over matter. Waller stresses this subordination by juxtaposing spirit and matter just before the lines to Cromwell. Much of the gold (material 'seeds of luxury, debate, and pride') sinks while a Spanish Marquis puts his sons to sea in a lifeboat and resigns himself and his wife to a fiery death. His courage and paternal care, analogues of the virtues about to be ascribed to Cromwell, demand from his foes a generous solidarity. The brave English 'suspend the fight, and silence all [their] guns,' so that in the narrative movement the discords of gold and battle are purged before the final tribute to the Protector.

In more formal terms, Waller gives us three movements, each composed of two contrasting sections and a coda. His first thirty lines set the stage, with a dozen lines about Spain, a dozen about England's countervailing siege by which 'They that the whole world's monarchy designed/Are to their ports by our bold fleet confined,' and a half-dozen lines of patriotic coda. In the second movement (ll. 31–64), the rich galleons arrive, discharging their guns as a signal, only to meet the English, whose more serious guns mean war; these contrasting sections lead to four lines of mythological and patriotic coda. The final movement includes the sinking of some of the gold and the death of the Marquis (ll. 65–110), with the paean to Cromwell as its coda. These sections and movements are not measured out with poetic calipers and have no mystic numerological value, nor, I think, do they add to one's sense of Waller's poetic control. They are a means of presentation. They govern rhythms and tell us what to expect, as do the couplet form, the iambs, and the level of diction. Together with the system of imagery, they

3

bring the poem to a satisfying resolution, and compensate for the lack of a tense, angular, argumentative structure such as one finds in Donne or the earlier poems of Marvell. Waller's panegyric has a rightness but not an inevitability about it, firmness but not poetic urgency.

In fact, the restoration of Charles II made Waller tactfully dock his Cromwellian coda. Throughout most of Charles's reign the poem stood simply as a tribute, in which all patriotic hearts could share, to the British navy. The ease with which Waller could convert his poem suggests why heroic narrative soon lagged behind its rival in Restoration panegyric, the great ode. Such narratives must glorify corporate action to glorify individuals; they are either tributes to leadership or pay oblique, symbolic compliments by attributing social achievements (like England's sea victory) to one person (like Cromwell). Restoration panegyric, however, drives toward magnifying the individual, toward whom society more often acts as a foil or grateful client than a supporting phalanx. The poem goes beyond tribute to something more rapt, more spontaneously eloquent. Under these circumstances, heroic narratives seemed more fit for panegyrics of the nation's rather than persons' power. From Waller's 'Instructions to a Painter' (1665) and Dryden's *Annus Mirabilis* (1667) to Defoe's 'The Spanish Descent' (1702) and John Philips's *Blenheim* (1705), the exploits of individual heroes are points of focus within the poem, not the point of the poem itself. Some later narratives did center on individuals, like Addison's *Campaign* (1705; to Marlborough) or two poems of 1707 to the Earl of Peterborough, Aaron Hill's *Camillus* and George Farquhar's *Barcellona*. As a rule, though, panegyrists of individuals turned to the ode and left heroic narratives about individuals to flatterers and, inverted, to satirists. The ode, in a spanking new form loosely imitative of Pindar, had just been developed (1656) by Waller's contemporary Abraham Cowley. With it, unlike narrative, poets could choose whether or not to build on any historical event. Fashion and practicality declared for it. So did the ode's ability to absorb the methods of the heroic narrative: emblems (symbolic images with commentary), persuasive analogy, some degree of narrative sequence, running motifs, and division into sections of discourse (like the three movements of Waller's 'Of a War with Spain').

Cowley's slightly later 'Ode upon His Majesty's Restoration and Return' (1660) shows how his Pindaric mode worked. The most distinguished of the poetic bouquets for Charles, this poem has five movements, each developed in three or four stanzas with intertwined images and a constant pressure of divine reference. Peaceful, auspicious stars for Charles, disease and venom for Cromwell – these two motifs (sts 1–7) lead to a third movement about Charles as divine martyr's son (sts 8–11; with another contrasting glance at Cromwell (st. 10) through a return to the star and serpent imagery of the first two movements), and then a fourth, looking to the glorious future rather than the spotted past (sts 12–14). The coda gives the new king his train of brothers (st. 15), a rejoicing populace (st. 16), his 'royal mother' (st. 17), the attentive General Monck, whose army effected the Restoration (st. 18), and finally the 'great patriots' within Parliament who have 'redeemed' its 'once venerable name' (st. 19).

Cowley launches this sequence with the star which appeared at noon on the day of Charles's birth in 1630, precisely thirty years before his arrival in London at the Restoration. Connotations of the star – peace, light, (re)birth, divine annunciation – form the ground of topic and image for the ode, as Waller's setting of the political and naval scene forms his poem's ground of topic and narrative. As Waller uses analogy for coherence, so does Cowley. England is reborn like Charles; the comet or *ignis fatuus* of Cromwell is outshone by Charles's steady, guiding star; the fire of adversity makes way for the bonfires of England's joy, a joy so radiant that 'the starry worlds which shine to us afar,/Take ours at this time for a star' (st. 16). Through the analogies, Charles gains the extraordinary power that translates him from man or hero, bold and tested by adversity, to the role of healing king. Reborn to his realm by God's justice, he becomes for that diseased and guilty land the surprising sign of God's mercy. A martyr's son, tried like Daniel in the fiery furnace, having suffered 'the bleeding mark of grace,' Charles is a type of Christ:

> As a choice medal for Heaven's treasury
> God did stamp first upon one side of thee
> The image of his suffering humanity;
> On th'other side, turned now to sight, does shine
> The glorious image of his power divine.   (st. 12)

The traditional topics for panegyric, such as the hero's ancestry, his deportment, his tribulations, his companions, and his destiny, all are developed in this poem to display the new king as an embodiment of 'power divine.'

Besides their similarities of method in their different poetic forms, Waller and Cowley draw on similar funds of imagery. Both had at their disposal images of power and fortitude: predators (eagles, lions), massive natural objects (mountains, seas, trees like the cedar and the oak), natural objects of force (storms, floods), riches (gold, treasure), and the divine absolutes of Heaven and Hell. If one looks at Homer's example, one can see why these should be his descendants' common portion. Pope's translation of the *Iliad* ends with a 'poetical index,' including Homeric similes. The vast majority come from animals (Pope's categories of 'beasts,' lions, birds, serpents, insects) or powerful natural phenomena (fires, trees, the sea, the heavens, storms, and 'heavenly appearances'). Even some similes that Pope puts in other categories like 'rural arts' and 'miscellaneous' fit one or the other of these groups: a thick mist on the mountains, two bulls plowing, a mound dividing the course of a river, a fragment of rock falling. These images have a kinship of ideology as well as of feeling. Through them, human action appears fated and, in heroes' hands, irresistible. As a result, reasoned analysis merely adds to one's consciousness of the unalterable, for moral decisions emerge from the compulsion of a man's nature and role. This force of likening human acts to natural movements, seen and admired from without, suits Homer's tragic irony and the tough ironic politics of the Restoration poem. In Waller's and Cowley's panegyrics Cromwell and Charles do not choose; they are what they are,

5

and through their acceptance of self earn the right to the diction proper for both their epic roles in art and their ineluctable, objective greatness in the world of nature.

The difference between the way in which Waller and Cowley draw on their common fund of images depends on a difference of genre. A narrative includes images of the action it presents, and therefore needs fewer figures of speech to make it vivid, to provide a context of feelings, or to mark the speaker's involvement. Waller uses more figures of speech than his narrative genre demands: he prefers not to stress elaborately presented action for fear of blurring the clear moral balance between noble deeds (the battle) and noble sentiment (contempt for the gold, compassion for the Marquis) which permits his paean to Cromwell at the end. He still uses figures much less than Cowley, however, whose genre, a version of the Greek celebratory ode, demands that the speaker's fervor bubble up through irregular meter, jumps of thought, exclamations, and the profusion of imagery that a heated imagination naturally employs. The form, like so many seventeenth-century forms of verse, is dramatic, with ultimate allegiance not to an object or action but to a speaker's way of seeing that object, that action. Waller's 'us' and 'our' establish the speaker as a patriot who can call forth from his countrymen a sense of national solidarity, but Cowley's first-person pronouns imply direct mental participation in the great event. Enraptured by what confronts him, its splendor and complexity, the poet examines it from all sides in the logical and chronological disorder that – the Cowleyans argued – is the truest order of the excited mind.

The Cowleyan or Pindaric ode therefore tends to be additive in form, with repeated interconnected imagery. Its elaboration of the heroic images listed above falls into groups suggested by the connotations of the phoenix and the fountain, both recurrent in the lyrical panegyric. Thomas Shipman's praise of the Countess of Rutland calls her 'rare . . . in life and death' like 'the phoenix, who with closing eyes/Mounts on her spicy pile and dies.' Rarity gives us, connotatively, treasure, gold, silver, ore, mine, crystal, and by contrast, debt; 'spicy pile' connotatively gives us spice and balm; the conflagration of the phoenix gives us fire, sun, light, Heaven, and Apollo; the phoenix itself gives us bird imagery and imagery of mounting and flying, aether, and celestial music. From the fountain we get springs, Helicon and Hippocrene, and fertile Nile; wine and liquors; snow, sometimes melting, sometimes binding in the form of frost, with its cold chains. The two connotative groups come together in images of turbulence related to Heaven and water (sea, storm) and of disease related to fire and water or ice (fever, ague, pestilence – this last often tied to malign heavenly forces). The resurrection of the phoenix makes it kin to the seasonal connotations I have assigned to the fountain, and the metaphor of the fountain for poetic inspiration makes it kin to certain connotations – rarity, Apollo, music – that I have listed under the phoenix.

All these images share a voluptuous grandeur commonly called 'baroque.' Like the Homeric types they elaborate, their job is to aggrandize rather than strictly to compare, so that their sensory strength, which gives them the greatest impact as images, has little to do with their fitness for the specific objects, events, or feelings to which the poem attaches them. The speaker acts only as rapt bard, excitedly disordered but free of private associations and idiosyncratic fondnesses. His images are, and are meant to be, strictly conventional testimony to value. For the poet and his subject, a kind of anonymity is the price of glory. The same deliberate imprecision and simplification of feeling, one might add, mark most classical and biblical allusions, what Pope's Homeric index calls 'similes exalting the characters of men by comparing them to gods.' In general, Restoration odes treat Hercules, Achilles, Samson, and Horatius as interchangeable, except for differences in the sound and meter of their names. The odes are hardly more about individual persons than the Nelson Column or the Washington Monument is 'about' the human being it commemorates. What the memorial and ode most require is directed sensory excitement and a capacity to lead the mind to noble reflections. Everything else is sheer bonus.

For thirty or forty years, the great and the worthy found themselves, their deaths, their estates, and their societies praised in the irregular, enthusiastic, emotive form invented by Pindar to praise Olympic athletes – or, as John Oldham has it in 'Spenser's Ghost' (1683), 'for praising jockeys' – and refurbished by Cowley for exploiting analogy and psychology in the service of national panegyric. (Humbler folk, like friends, kinsmen, teachers, and squires, usually received a humbler mode, the familiar epistle, spruced with some borrowings from the emblematic and analogical techniques that grander modes popularized.) As Waller's heroic narrative proved too narrow for Restoration panegyric, however, Cowley's Pindarics proved too broad. Writers seized on irregular odes for so many purposes that the genre lost its specific force and meaning. This was not the fault of the critics, who kept insisting that the irregularity of the ode was plausible only to express sublime rapture. John Norris of Bemerton, discussing in the 1680s his Pindaric 'The Passion of Our Blessed Saviour', held that the ode was 'the highest and most magnificent kind of writing in verse; and consequently fit only for great and noble subjects; such as are boundless as its own numbers, the nature of which is to be loose and free, and not to keep one settled pace, but sometimes (like a gentle stream) to glide peaceably within its own channel, and sometimes (like an impetuous torrent) to roll on extravagantly, and carry all before it.' From the time of Cowley until well into the eighteenth century, critics proposed this theory. Poets continued to do as they themselves pleased.

John Pomfret's 'Pindaric essays' (1690), for instance, deal with great subjects like death and divine judgment, but their praise of God's power is written as ornamented rational discourse, like a sermon, not poetic ecstasy. In 1691 Thomas Heyrick wrote Pindarics on angling and – at great length – a 'Submarine Voyage,' in which the poet becomes a dolphin and provides a moralized underwater survey of nature and nations. (Heyrick suggests elsewhere in this volume that the Pindaric form is useful to spare the poet the task of making his poems coherent.) John Hopkins (1700) uses the Pindaric, in 'To the God of Love,' to prefer – at least for himself – love and lowness to the great stature of Congreve, Wycherley, Dryden, and King William III. In the hands of Robert Gould (*To the*

7

Society of the Beaux Esprits) and John Tutchin (*A Pindaric Ode in the Praise of Folly and Knavery*), the Pindaric sprouts satire (1687, 1696). Even the Pindaric of continued praise, like Mary Chudleigh's tribute (1703) to Dryden's translation of Virgil, can unrapturously maintain a single, consistent argument rather than leap about; Chudleigh, like Heyrick, sensibly explains that she has used the Pindaric 'because it allows me the liberty of running into large digressions, gives a great scope to the fancy, and frees me from the trouble of tying myself up to the stricter rules of other poetry.' Even if these comments are taken at face value instead of being discounted as cynical or deprecatory, they do not mean that the Pindaric, more than other kinds of verse, became the poetic equivalent of an unbuttoned day at the beach: one can loll on holiday in tetrameter couplets or Spenserian stanzas just as easily, perhaps more so, as a glance at light verse or casual verse will confirm. The poets' comments and practice do mean that the Pindaric lost specific meaning as a genre, as policemen's uniforms would if everyone wore them. For this reason and others, early in the eighteenth century the ceremonial ode of Cowley was moribund.

Before that, though, some distinguished Pindarics had been written, especially by Dryden, far and away the greatest creative writer of his age and the most versatile of his century. England before 1700 produced no one to equal Dryden in writing literary criticism, heroic plays, verse translation, theatre songs, prologues and epilogues, satire, poems of religious controversy, verse epistles, or political verse; no one matched him in the grand ode. Dryden's six odes, written 1685–7 and 1695–6, reflect his mature genius and an understanding of the form no doubt sharpened by the attempts of Cowley and a generation of successors. Each of the odes rejoices in the union of power and order. If one compares even the most potentially gloomy of them, the funerary pieces for Charles II, Anne Killigrew, and Henry Purcell, with, for example, the funerary odes of his contemporary Thomas Flatman, a specialist in such things, one is struck by Dryden's exuberance, his refusal to dwell on loss and transience as Flatman does. Flatman's opening lines tell a glum story: 'No more! Alas, the bitter word, "No more"!' (Ossory), 'A long adieu to all that's bright' (Katherine Philips), 'Unhappy Muse! employed so oft/On melancholy thoughts of death' (Richard Flatman), and so on through the odes for the Duke of Albemarle, Prince Rupert, John Oldham, and Charles II. In his ode on Charles, Dryden does claim to have been struck dumb with grief at the King's death, but the five-hundred odd lines of *Threnodia Augustalis* prove how briefly dumb: throughout, his subject is as much the gained excellence of the new King, James, as the lost excellence of Charles. The dead King's virtues, celebrated in the middle stanzas of the poem, are largely temperate (majestic mildness, 'clemency and love,' bounty, culture) while the live King's, as mentioned in the early stanzas and celebrated in the late ones, are powerful, a profound grief at his brother's death and a warrior's fire that will rouse the land to conquest. Implicitly, Charles's virtues and death equally enable the loftier virtues of James to flourish. The power of Providence justifies the rise and fall (or – st. 13 – phoenix-like resurrection) of the mighty.

Divine power and order govern the mighty, too, in the odes for Henry Purcell and Anne Killigrew. The great composer, who is fit to teach 'the heavenly quire,' rises in death to an audience fit for him, thus letting earthly musicians sigh in relief at the loss of a masterful rival, a man who now will so preempt the gods' attention that they need not kill other musicians to play for them. Even Hell, happy in its preferred disharmony, benefits from Purcell's being installed above. There are three words of grief, no more, in the poem. Anne Killigrew's death loses her the 'mighty government' of the Muses, but we learn immediately that she is more than compensated by having won a place in Heaven. Dryden's rehearsal of her virtues and powers upon earth brings not eventual lamentation but a magnificent final stanza about the Last Judgment, with its golden trump, its resurrection of 'rattling bones . . . from the four corners of the sky,' and, amid this show of celestial power, Anne herself leading the choir of ascending spirits to Heaven. The sense of magnificent bounty in *Anne Killigrew* makes it more similar in timbre to Dryden's nuptial ode, 'On the Marriage of . . . Anastasia Stafford,' than to the crape-hung lines of a Flatman.

Such a celebratory tone suits the ode historically and in its Restoration embodiment. As I have said, Restoration odes, and indeed most of the major poems of the Restoration, treat the speaker largely as a member of society and the subject largely as an emblem of something, not (or not principally) as a person. Dryden, perhaps more than any other poet in English, knew how to exploit the extroversion of the public voice. For a certain class of readers, the loss of what might be called 'spiritual intimacy' or, tartly, the reader's right of trespass on others' feelings, makes poetry of this sort into mere show. Dryden's odes, however, provide virtues deeper than the dazzle and crackle that invigorates their surfaces: the speaking voice and the passage from one idea or image to the next give us a contact with a live intelligence, a live imagination, that makes up for any lack of 'spiritual intimacy,' while the person celebrated – Anne, Charles II, Anastasia Stafford, Purcell – transcends individuality (as Flatman's subjects, for example, do not) to become part of a grander order.

The ode to Anne Killigrew will show what I mean. Like the two sumptuous odes to music and *Threnodia Augustalis*, this poem expounds a dynamic order that governs the flux of antithetical ideas, of dying and creation, of historical process, and of personal feeling. Specifically, the subjects of these poems – Anne, music, the royal brothers – embody this ordering energy, whether it is the divine creation that Anne's art recreates, the divine harmony and control of the passions that music exemplifies, or the self of a great nation symbolized by its kings. As a virginal poet and painter, Anne imitates the pure creativity of the divine. After a stanza of introduction, Dryden traces her lineage from earth to Heaven (st. 2), from Heaven to earth (st. 3). Through this temporal lineage and linkage, she can reject present earthly corruption (sts 4–5) and remake in her art another linked series, the Great Chain of Being from landscape to animals to the highest humans (sts 6–7). Dryden then returns to poetic and personal lineage (sts 8–9), expressed now in terms of death and mourning, not as earlier in those of birth; but just as he has previously seized on an element of the divine in Anne's living, recreative art, he now seizes on another in her earthly death. At the Resurrection of the Dead, he tells us, she will rise like a mounting lark, a 'harbinger of Heaven, the way to show,/The way which

9

thou so well hast learned below' (st. 10). The dead Anne thus lives on in, and unifies, five different kinds of time: (i) that of her art, (ii) that of her soul's passage through the bodies of great poets (Sappho and other classic poets in st. 2, Pindar – not, as sometimes thought, Plato – in the bee image of st. 3, Katherine Philips in st. 8), (iii) that of earthly remembrance (of which her mourning brother, st. 9, and Dryden's poem are tokens), (iv) that of a probationer in Heaven (st. 1), and finally (v) that of the future moment when the power of God awakens all the dead at the Apocalypse:

> When in mid-air the Golden Trump shall sound
>   To raise the nations under ground;
> When in the Valley of Jehosaphat
>   The judging God shall close the Book of Fate
>   And there the last assizes keep
>   For those who wake and those who sleep;
> When rattling bones together fly
>   From the four corners of the sky;
> When sinews o'er the skeletons are spread,
>   Those clothed with flesh, and life inspires the dead:
> The sacred poets first shall hear the sound.   (ll. 178–88)

This last order of time at once negates and yet confirms the four prior orders – art, spiritual inheritance, earthly remembrance, and probationary joys. Through allusions to classical poets, to Anne's patriotic family (her father, st. 2, and brother), and to martial power (st. 7), Dryden also brings ideas of cultural and social order to converge on her. The ode is not a poem about art and the artist, but rather about a human imitation of the divine, a human pattern for us less pure mortals. Dryden's tone, genial rather than exalted when writing of Anne's actual poems and paintings, places the achievement of art on earth in its proper place beneath the genuinely exalted, the spiritual achievement of someone who provides in art and life an imperfect historical manifestation of pure creativity. Anne's conquest of the arts that mirror nature is a type of her winning her place in the greater process of divine order.

The decline of the Pindaric through the reign of William III (d. 1702) meant that other forms rose to take its place. One of these was the Horatian ode, less high-flown than the Pindaric and more contained within Horace's pre-established patterns. Matthew Prior, for instance, dropped Pindar after 'On his Majesty's Birthday' (1690) in favor of Horace in 1692 (an imitation of *Odes* 3:2), an ode in quatrains in 1695 (for Queen Mary's death), Horace in 1699 *Carmen seculare*), Horace in 1704 (for George Villiers), and Spenserian stanzas in 1706 (for the Battle of Ramillies). Congreve took another tack. In 1695 he had written a Cowleyan Pindaric on the Battle of Namur, but turned in 1706 to an imitation of what he now perceived as Pindar's own regularity and coherence: he prefaced his 'Pindaric Ode Humbly Offered to the Queen' with a condemnation of the Cowleyan type, 'a bundle of rambling, incoherent thoughts, expressed in a like parcel of irregular stanzas, which also consist of another such complication of disproportioned, uncertain, and perplexed verses and rhymes.' Congreve's charges, and his and Prior's practice, look like part of a campaign for neatness. In fact they are evidence that the Cowleyan ode was no longer justified in the psychological terms Cowley set down, the 'enthusiastical manner' which dignified its subject and created a bond between poet and hero. This bond of rapturous awe was not to grow strong again in the eighteenth century – not among poets whose work anyone now cares to read – except as a bond between poet and his country. Kings, peers, generals, and their families had to be content with verse that was more stiffly formal or less adoring than had been true in the Restoration. But England and her resources enjoyed praise in poetic forms like the epistle and the topographical poem, in which the 'rambling' of the individual mind, with all its lack of neatness, was still more important than in Cowleyan odes.

Three poems which exemplify the possibilities of this sort of patriotic poem in the Restoration and early eighteenth century are John Denham's *Cooper's Hill* (1642–68), Dryden's 'To My Honoured Kinsman' (1700), and Pope's *Windsor Forest* (1713). In each of the three an English pattern – the scenes one can see from Cooper's Hill, the life of an English country gentleman, the royal forest – becomes an emblem (portrait with commentary) of the uses of power and of the need for equipoise among constantly changing sources of power or weakness. The emblem gives the poem its base of experience, its means of merging the abstract and the concrete. It also helps organizing the poem as discourse, through association of related ideas. Each of the three poems, then, needs and has a single speaking voice behind it, a speaker who is at once individual and a spokesman for his fellow Englishmen in his musings.

Cooper's Hill, published in two versions during the Civil Wars and a third during the Restoration, was perhaps the most influential and admired shorter poem of the mid-seventeenth century. As Denham's speaker, standing on Cooper's Hill, surveys two seats of present power (London and Windsor) and two reminders of power used or abused (Chertsey Abbey, ruined by Henry VIII, and Runnymede), he sees that the great norm for the use of power should be the order of nature itself, which renounces excess. A bit less than the first half of the poem (ll. 1–156 of 358 lines in the final text) shows us four promontories, St Paul's in distant London, the hill crowned by Windsor Castle, another once crowned by Chertsey Abbey, and Cooper's Hill itself. Each of the four presents a reciprocity between man and nature. The poet's 'parnassus,' Cooper's Hill, gives him vantage over the sweep of the Thames Valley and he in turn gives it poetic distinction, spiritual sight repaying physical sight (ll. 1–12). St Paul's, which partakes of earth and sky, milling businessmen and the King as head of the Church (ll. 13–38); Windsor, where eternal pattern comprises years of royal magnificence (ll. 39–110); St Anne's Hill, despoiled of the Abbey by a Defender of the Faith (Henry VIII) who greedily seized the gold of monks sunk in 'empty, airy contemplations' (ll. 111–56) – these variants of the spiritual and the physical, the active and the contemplative lives, man employing or ignoring nature, establish the first movement of the poem. Here the English poet adapts Parnassus to his own time, as

11

his contemporaries Milton and Butler did, and moves through the pictorial energy of the mind to blend past and present, considered under the general heading of power – the power of the martyred soldier-king Charles I, of the London crowd in the Interregnum, of Edward III and Henry VIII, and so on. His scanning eye prompts his reflections, and analogies between things he sees prompt him to form analogies in interpreting them.

In this first movement of the poem, the poet's eye repeatedly recoils from what he perceives: in 1655, Puritans had evicted God from St Paul's in favor of horses, and the King (except as a corpse) from rifled Windsor. From these spectacles and the despoiled abbey, Denham turns, to let his eye descend to the Thames and the order of nature. He finds an analogue to, and an inversion of, human vicissitudes in the river that 'hast[es] to pay his tribute to the sea,/Like mortal life to meet eternity,' enriching fields and commerce with a continuing life and loss of self in the ocean. Beneath the wind-beaten mountain flows this symbol of natural harmony, an ideal for poetry (ll. 189–92) and the England its waters nourish. With the rest of nature, forest and mountain and sky, the Thames participates in a wider harmony of discords that repeats, but makes positive, the balancing of polar qualities in the first movement of the poem. There the mob tarnishes St Paul's and Windsor, the ruin of Chertsey Abbey dims the glow of England's religious and royal past; here the harmony of discords gives us a vital creative tension:

> Here Nature, whether more intent to please
> Us or herself with strange varieties
> (For things of wonder give no less delight
> To the wise Maker's than beholders' sight;
> Though these delights from several causes move,
> For so our children, thus our friends we love),
> Wisely she knew, the harmony of things,
> As well as that of sounds, from discords springs.
> Such was the discord which did first disperse
> Form, order, beauty through the universe:
> While dryness moisture, coldness heat resists,
> All that we have and that we are subsists. (ll. 197–208)

Physical nature, synthesized by the poet's eye, leads to spiritual knowledge.

The second movement of *Cooper's Hill*, in reaffirming the course of nature, offers a large context to accommodate the stresses of abused power and conflicting wills. Man therefore can be reinstated cautiously in the poem's final movement, which begins with the King's stag hunt. The ritual of the hunt, where man within nature sublimates in sport his will to power, seems to give order to the violent energies in the first movement of the poem, the energies whose basic forms are the cruelty, zeal, ambition, and aggressiveness which have debased St Paul's, Windsor, and Chertsey Abbey. The royal hunt has mixed success, however. It is a thing of the past now that Charles himself has been hunted to death. The chase, seen through the eyes of the anthropomorphized stag, shows us more anguish than ritual or justice; and the explicit comparison of the stag and 'a declining statesman' (l. 273) shows us not only how much better deer hunts are than man hunts, but also how much danger there is in drawing too firm a line between them. The chase, with its doubleness of tone, leads plausibly to an analogue suggested by the speaker's glimpsing Runnymede, where King John's hunt of his subjects was suddenly reversed in the confrontation that produced Magna Carta. As power meets power, tensions are resolved by law, a human version of the harmony of discords seen in the landscape. Yet as the tensions resolved in the landscape remain in the stag hunt, so the tensions resolved by law remain in the kingdom, where King and subjects keep at the pursuit of power that made Magna Carta necessary. The poem ends, as it began, with the motif of man's cooperating with nature. One can embank a high river, Denham says, thus amplifying nature, but to dam or reroute it is fatal: 'Stronger and fiercer by restraint he roars,/And knows no bounds, but makes his power his shores.' Human power depends on channeling the 'perpetual and restless desire of power after power, that ceaseth only in death,' of which Hobbes had recently written.

When he wrote his epistle to his cousin John Driden of Chesterton, John Dryden saw his King in exile, as Denham had nearly a half-century earlier; his notions of power were conditioned by the Revolution of 1689 as Denham's were by the wars of the 1640s, and his opening lines might have appeared as a warm aside in *Cooper's Hill*: 'How blessed is he who leads a country life,/Unvexed with anxious cares and void of strife!' Like Denham, Dryden employs the emblem (not allegory in either poem) of the hunt, as a version of social order (ll. 50–61) and of predatory politics (the princes of ll. 67–70 who, 'chasing, sigh to think themselves are chased'). The method of analogy, implicit in the use of emblems, gives Dryden's epistle its structure, as with *Cooper's Hill* and almost every other serious poem we will consider. Thus the first half of the poem (116 of 210 lines) treats cousin Driden's life pattern of individual and social order: justice in settling others' conflicts (ll. 7–16) but peace in his own celibate life (ll. 17–35), benevolent generosity to his fellow men (ll. 36–49) but zeal, 'industrious of the common good,' to hunt down 'the wily fox' who murders 'the firstlings of the flocks' (ll. 50–61). Engaged in mortality like the hare, Driden avoids being engaged in political dangers like those of the hunted hunters on 'slippery thrones' (ll. 62–70); his keeping his health through tried-and-true methods, energy and temperance, frees him from blind, greedy doctors (ll. 71–116), whose incompetence contrasts with his shrewd judgment, whose self-seeking opposes his charity, and whose butchery parodies his just and useful hunt. We have, then, a poem about equipoise in which the first half has two parts—Driden's characteristics (ll. 7–61) and the doctors' (ll. 71–116)—connected by a bridge. In Driden's life, virtues balance virtues; in the doctors' practice, virtues balance vices. The social range also widens, with the doctors, from Chesterton to the nation. Ethically and socially the poem has brought us to the concerns of its second half, on the political and military power of England.

The second half emerges from the individual values of the first, of course, in that cousin Driden needs as an MP the same independence, even-handedness, love of peace, and just use of martial skill that he needs as a gentleman of Chesterton. In

13

addition, the values of the second half of the poem are country, not court values: liberty, dispersion of power, disinterested service. From the peace about which the poem is eloquent come freedom and order, for in peacetime the King has no cause to demand special prerogatives. So one country value begets others. 'Patriot,' a word repeated in the first lines of three verse paragraphs within the last forty lines of the poem, refers us to its etymology, to both *patria* (native land) and *pater* (father, ancestor), ideas in which the first part of the epistle is rooted. If England has a foreign King (William III) committed to wars on foreign soil, and – so satirists claimed – to beggaring England to pay for them, Driden's attributes must stand as an emblem of implied resistance. By keeping to the strenuous life of 'our sires,' he keeps free of the murderous meddling of doctors; by imitating his 'generous Grandsire's' 'noble stubbornness resisting might,' he keeps his country safe from England's claimed healer, William the warlike interventionist. The analogical structure holds together a poem that seems, as verse epistles often do, to ramble spontaneously.

Spontaneity in epistles arises from association of ideas, as I have said, a process given direction in an epistle with a topic (like the pattern of Driden's life as private and public man) by what one might call the pressure of the excluded. As with the panegyric ode, the poet has certain traditional matters that wait impatiently for places in the poem, e.g., in panegyric, the lineage or the deeds of the person being praised. The topographical poet has a responsibility to a locale, so that he feels the same pressures, though they mostly (not all) come from the outside – the sight of St Anne's Hill denuded – rather than from within – the realization that Driden's celibacy may seem selfish, which makes the mind move quickly to his deeds of generosity. For both Dryden and Denham the process of composition, or at least the process of utterance, enforces a process of balance and modification: the royal heroes and victims of Windsor are balanced by, and our idea of royal power modified by, King Henry's depredations on St Anne's Hill. Driden's independence is balanced by, and our evaluation of it modified by, his 'feed[ing] with manna [his] own Israel-host.' 'The pressure of the excluded' can also produce a simple additive structure, as it often does in the panegyric ode, rather than a balanced, modifying structure, as in Denham and Dryden; but a merely additive structure leaches so much sense of mental process from the poem that only a highly ornamental mode, like the Cowleyan Pindaric, can use it with any success. Balance, analogy, and modification tell us about a mind at work; they are also, of course, the processes that define the political ideology of *Cooper's Hill* and Dryden's epistle.

Pope's *Windsor Forest* elaborates the techniques of Denham and Dryden. Sounding with classical and biblical echoes, the poem celebrates Queen Anne's ordered England, where balance and analogy make a world cohere. Grand pageants, unlike anything in Dryden and far less subjective than Denham's scene of the hunted stag, form the basic units which Pope arranges in terms of past, present, and myth (the equivalents of the lineage, deeds, and transcendence typical of panegyric). The first half of the poem (210 of 434 lines) has to do with that familiar Restoration theme, power, expressed through that familiar metaphor, the hunt. After an introduction about the opulence and ordered variety of the forest under Anne (ll. 1–42), Pope presents the land in times past as 'a dreary desert and a gloomy waste' under William I and II (and tacitly, by extension, William III), despots whose 'prey was man' (ll. 43–84); then, after a bridging passage (ll. 85–92), he moves to the present with a hunt as a sublimation of war (ll. 93–164); and after a second bridging passage (ll. 165–70), he tells the myth of the nymph Lodona, lustfully pursued by Pan and metamorphosed into a 'soft, silver stream,' the river Loddon. A short passage about the Loddon and the Thames (ll. 211–34) brings us, along with those waters, from reflections of Windsor to England, her navy, her poets, and her women. In the enlarged context of the second half of *Windsor Forest*, Pope turns again to past, present, and myth. He begins with the contemplative life (ll. 235–58) and a mingling of poets past (ll. 259–80), and present (as heir of the past, ll. 281–98). England's discordant past (ll. 299–328), as sung by a poet, stops with the fiat of the present, Anne's quasi-divine 'Let Discord cease!' The final section of the poem is a long visionary prophecy from Father Thames, who mingles present and future as the section on contemplation and poetry has mingled present and past. An allegorical panorama gives the second half of the poem a rather gaudy public myth to balance the individual myth of Lodona at the end of the first half:

> In brazen bonds, shall barb'rous Discord dwell:
> Gigantic Pride, pale Terror, gloomy Care,
> And mad Ambition shall attend her there.
> There purple Vengeance bathed in gore retires,
> Her weapons blunted and extinct her fires:
> There hateful Envy her own snakes shall feel,
> And Persecution mourn her broken wheel.   (ll. 414–20)

Pope articulates the argument of the poem through the relationship of the two halves. In the first half, devoted to the aggressiveness of the hunt, each of the three analogous episodes contains its own principle of modification: the despotic William II 'bleeds in the forest, like a wounded hart'; the 'vig'rous swains' who hunt birds create the pathos of the pheasant and 'the mounting larks' who 'leave their little lives in air'; the pursued Lodona defeats the swifter Pan by becoming a constantly weeping stream. The pattern of blunted violence changes in the second half of the poem, devoted to Queen Anne's peace. Both the poetic and the royal lines survive the assaults of war and death. Granville's poetic mistress, Myra, succeeds Surrey's Geraldine to reaffirm one pattern, and Anne succeeds her discordant ancestors to redeem the other. The stage is set for Father Thames's pageant, which begins 'in that blest moment' of Stuart peace and shows us the creation of victory from that peace: at Whitehall, 'mighty nations shall inquire their doom' and 'suppliant states' bend before Anne. As the quotation above suggests, Father Thames's final allegorical vision sees peace in a guise proper to the violence of war, with binding, blood, torment, and mourning: peace encompasses its opposite. *Windsor Forest* ends with a pattern like those of the hunter hunted or left without booty in the first half of the poem. For the reader and presumably the

15

speaker, an act of patriotic imagination sublimates the drive to power, resolving the poem in the sphere of contemplation more fully than the sphere of action ('arms employed on birds and beasts' (1. 374)) allows. As in *Cooper's Hill* and 'To My Honoured Kinsman,' perceived pattern supplies an ideal that the world will not achieve.

More than in either Dryden or Denham, *Windsor Forest* joins the order of nature (an emblem in *Cooper's Hill*) and the order of human will (the focus of 'To My Honoured Kinsman'). Pope writes in the tradition of the country house poem, like Ben Jonson's 'To Penshurst' and Marvell's *Upon Nun Appleton House*, where nature is at once itself and the sign of a controlling mind; he broadens these individual panegyrics to include Queen Anne's microcosmic estate, Windsor Forest itself, and her great estate of England. In addition, taking a cue from the opening of *Cooper's Hill*, he adds another controlling mind to the poem, that of the poet. Although he follows Denham in making landscape a metaphor and theater for his imagination, he does not let the roaming of his eye set the order of the topics he treats. Instead, he raises his deliberateness and conscious choice into an element of the poetic effect. Throughout *Windsor Forest*, he speaks as the poet of a nation, a position inherited from the practice of Waller and Cowley, of Dryden's political poems under Queen Anne's uncle and father; but more than any of these, Pope here makes the order of the poem part of the order that the poem describes. He makes the responsive, controlling intelligence of the speaker, as a national British poet, part of the evidence for the richness and stability of the land under its Stuart queen. That is why the section on contemplation and poetry opens the second half of *Windsor Forest*. It includes a plea to the Muses for visionary inspiration and rehearses the speaker's poetic lineage in songs of love and patriotism. Appropriately, this section is flanked by the tale of Lodona, a song of mythic British love, and the visionary, patriotic prophecy of Father Thames: the poet is integral to the meaning of the British landscape. The tale of Lodona, moreover, is a deliberate imitation, anglicization of a classical poet, Ovid; much of Father Thames's speech draws on the poetry of messianic prophecy in *Isaiah*. Such allusions call attention to the poem as poetry and to England as a source for poetry and a land of eloquent poets. *Windsor Forest* itself helps prove the argument that Pope puts forth.

I hesitate to leap to historical generalizations based on the sequence of Denham, Dryden, and Pope. The differences in genres and historical circumstances behind their respective poems make that unsafe. Correspondingly the marked similarities in handling have a strong claim to be taken as typical of widespread practice, precisely because the three men wrote at such different times. Besides the generally allusive, subdivided, analogical, associative, and emblematic techniques that the discussions of these poems have emphasized, one should note that all three men look for patterns in natural processes, including those of human nature. None of the three gives the Bible or the classics sanctified status, although they draw on sacred and classical texts with respect. I said earlier that the ode treats most classical and biblical allusions with a deliberate imprecision and simplification of feeling, so that except for sound and meter Hercules, Achilles, Samson, and Horatius are interchangeable. Poems less devoted to extremes of praise and blame

16

probably discriminate among these honorifics more, but then the comparisons themselves are more peripheral. No doubt in the enthusiasm of the Commonwealth, patterns of biblical history looked especially apropos for righteous England, but after the Restoration such delusions marched in the heads only of pamphleteering Cassandras and clerical doomsayers. One can see how a sophisticated, empirical poet employed this sort of messianic reading by looking at Dryden's masterpiece, *Absalom and Achitophel* (1681).

From those who gave scripture a privileged role in making analogies about English politics – the practice, that is, of serious biblical typology – Dryden took his plot, in which the events surrounding the Exclusion Crisis are described in terms of Absalom's rebellion against his father David. By using this fiction, *Absalom and Achitophel* alludes to the terms of discourse in which some were treating the Exclusion Crisis: Dryden alludes, that is, to the rhetoric of his own time as well as (perhaps rather more than) to the Bible. The biblical fiction also allows Dryden's thunderous ending in the triumph of divine right. Yet he does not follow the biblical chronicle of actual revolt; he selects names for his English figures from Scripture even on the basis of puns and anagrams (Jonas = Sir William Jones, Caleb = Arthur Capel), indifferent as to who does or does not appear in the biblical story of Absalom; and he flaunts his playfulness by using the parallel with David to construct an outrageous and amusing apology for Charles's whoring at the very opening of the poem. In short, even when biblical patterns have been awarded a privilege by others, Dryden simply exploits them as material serendipitously at hand.

If Dryden, like every other significant poet of his time, uses the Bible (and the classics) as a quarry rather than a coercive model, he does so to build the most complex and superb panegyric of the years from the Restoration to 1720 (or, I suspect, any other date one might care to choose). Critics from Dryden himself to those of our time have properly stressed the satire in this epic narrative; by no means does a simple panegyric intent dominate it. *Absalom and Achitophel* begins and ends, however, with Charles II, and all the figures attacked are shadow kings of his splendor. Dryden assaults the Earl of Shaftesbury and his train for their planned usurpation of the kingship (the plot of the poem) and for their grotesque usurpation of the King's normative nature (the characterization in the poem). *Absalom* contains far more wit, blame, and qualification than panegyrics by Waller and Cowley, but in technique we find the heroic narrative combined with the analogical glorification of a Cowleyan ode. Dryden's hero Charles ('David' in the poem) imitates divine bounty like a patriarch, as literal begetter of his people, 'scatter[ing] his Maker's image through the land,' and he ends by exercising a restorative, ordering power through his voice alone – the Word made Act to the tune of heavenly thunder. As Anne Killigrew has a double lineage, physical and spiritual, through her family and past poets, so Charles joins the physical line of the Stuarts and the divinely anointed line of David; as Anne defines her public, emblematic self through her conquest of God's world through art, so Charles defines his through his imitation of God the Father, in mercy and power, over the moral polity of England.

17

As with Anne once more, these traits of Charles's are – before the time of crisis – humanly imperfect, recounted with geniality, even fond irony, perhaps endearing more than ennobling. Dryden gives them their full value, though, by letting us see their parodies in the two main villains of the poem. Monmouth (Absalom), in his self-indulgence, parodies his father's mercy and indulgence to others. Despite his inherited grace, he is clearly a bastard son. Shaftesbury (Achitophel), with his politicking, parodies the King's power. Both villains are egoists, unlike Charles, whose fault is uncritical love – of women, of his son, of the land he rules so mildly. Dryden also introduces three subsidiary villains, also egoists. They parody Charles by composing a triptych like the Charles his enemies were painting: an inconstant libertine, a looter of the public purse, a fraudulent seeker for power. Buckingham (Zimri) is a model of inconstancy, Bethel (Shimei) of grasping, and Oates (Corah) of perjury in the usurpers' cause. To define Charles as Dryden partly does, by scattering his alleged faults among his satirized enemies, is to make a principle of mirroring central within the poem and also within the world to which the poem refers. Since England is the King's public body, Charles is in a sense purified by the shadow kings' localizing in themselves the selfish, degenerate, or inverted reflections of the royal ideal.

Dryden's static portraits focus our attention on character rather than action. The rebels can gain power only through action; Charles keeps it through his royal character, through the brilliant revelation of his self, previously clouded by his human warmth. In the movement of the poem, therefore, the action keeps slowing: till the introduction of Achitophel (l. 150), Dryden sets the scene for the drama of Absalom's seduction, which in turn takes up the first half of the poem; the portraits of Zimri, Shimei, and Corah follow, in which the earlier energy of psychological conflict is converted into satiric energy, emotional conflict between narrator and object. The action resumes with a speech by Absalom and an account of its success (ll. 682–752), whereupon the narrator offers his own speech, longer and more logical, which stops the action and leads to another group of portraits, prefatory to 'Godlike David's' mighty assertion of power. The biblical tags – 'David,' 'Absalom,' 'Achitophel' for Charles, Monmouth, Shaftesbury – also make one stress character by providing historical roles into which the men of 1680 seem to slip, and a pattern of historical action which the men of 1680 do not fulfill. In *II Samuel* there is suffering, the revolt goes well beyond orations, and force breeds force. Dryden instead brings before us a tableau of non-confrontation. The uprisen multitude, charmed and duped, idolizes Absalom; Charles's right remains upheld by the virtuous caryatids (Barzillai, Zadoc, *et al.*) who do not, need not, act. Nor can the narrator's voice, which has progressively darkened, act within the poem except by tone. The darkening raises the sense of crisis so that David can re-enter at a new level of divine imitation, a manifestation not now in terms of becoming (begetting, giving) but of being, the immutable law. Like the end of the ode to Anne Killigrew, with its apocalyptic vision, *Absalom and Achitophel* ends with a historical moment that repeals past history:

He said. The Almighty, nodding, gave consent,
And peals of thunder shook the firmament.
Henceforth a series of new time began;
The mighty years in long procession ran;
Once more the Godlike David was restored
And willing nations knew their lawful Lord.   (ll. 1026–31)

Through the power of the self, the Restoration takes place again, spiritually. 'Willing nations' know 'their lawful Lord': 'lawful' because rightful and also because the repository of law, the ambiguous 'Lord' because the one in Heaven and the one in Whitehall have for the moment merged in the polity of the poem. Next to this David, the conspirators and their crew shrink, hardly worth the satiric energy that has etched them. No greater panegyric for King Charles could be conceived, and the more so because he seems to grow into his greatness.   .

Satire

The panegyrist bows to others; the writer of preceptive verse and the satirist require others to bow to them. In discussing the poet as judge and legislator, I shall give the lion's share of attention to satire, since even the best authors' preceptive verse – Dryden's *Religio Laici* or Pope's *Essay on Criticism*, for instance, has less poetic interest, I think, than the satire of the same men or their subalterns. Furthermore, before 1720 preceptive verse has a much shorter, more limited career than does satire: that fact itself is perhaps the most intriguing thing about it. Between 1660 and 1680, no significant preceptive verse was published; Mulgrave's *Essay upon Satire* (1679), which is a cousin to the genre, turns out in fact to be a satire itself, part of court battles in which Rochester was central. In 1680 and 1681 respectively, Roscommon and Oldham produced translations of Horace's *Ars poetica*, and the next two years saw Thomas Creech's translation of Lucretius' *De rerum natura* and Dryden's (with Sir William Soame, who began work on it in 1680) of Boileau's *L'Art poétique*. Dryden's two poems of religious controversy, both with strong political overtones, date from the same general period, *Religio Laici* in 1682, *The Hind and the Panther* five years later. Also at about the same time we get two Horatian 'essays,' Mulgrave's upon poetry (1682) and Roscommon's on translated verse (1684). A lull of fifteen to twenty years follows, till the eighteenth century itself begins. During the first decade, several poets wrote prescriptive verse about the two subjects of the 1680s, poetry and politics. Then, between 1710 and 1720, greater variety crept in, till such verse became abundant in the 1730s and later. *An Essay on Criticism* (1711) can be grouped with several other such 'essays': the elder Samuel Wesley's *Epistle to a Friend concerning Poetry* (1700), Granville's *Essay upon Unnatural Flights in Poetry* (1701), William Coward's *Licentia Poetica Discussed* (1709), and Thomas Parnell's *Essay on the Different Styles of Poetry* (1713). With a dose of georgic conventions in John Phillips's *Cyder*

(1708) and Gay's *Trivia* (1716), and of religious-philosophical didacticism in Prior's hilarious *Alma* and sober *Solomon* (1718), poets were ready to regale readers of the 1720s with advice on honesty (Giles Jacob's 'Human Happiness' (1721)), the art of shooting birds (George Markland's *Pteryplegia* (1727)), physiology and physics (Richard Collins's *Nature Displayed* (1727)), and other subjects on which poetic advice would earlier have been withheld.

One can invent reasons for this pattern: growing confidence in a growing body of English criticism; desire for law and system in times of political turmoil, like the Exclusion Crisis and the later years of Anne's reign; the prestige of Newton's and Locke's systems, starting in the 1690s; fascination and rivalry with the French and the classics, especially Boileau in the 1680s, Horace and other Augustan poets in the early eighteenth century. Speculating about historical reasons is probably idle here; less so, I think, is remarking poets' movement toward being socially helpful, first about their own art, then – surrendering the privileged position of poet giving dicta about poetry – about other kinds of issues. Horace, after all, had written the *Ars poetica* as a friend of the Piso family; Virgil, the *Georgics* as a good Roman citizen. The relative retreat from power or advance toward being a corporate citizen fits the development we have seen in the panegyric.

With preceptive poems still more than panegyric, though, the poet must have a central voice, perhaps even a 'central intelligence,' to save the verse from being a vending machine for bromides. Dryden openly dramatizes himself in his controversial religious poems, as a benevolent, bright, candid man who legislates by appealing for our suffrage. To do so is good Aristotelian practice and also a rhetorical necessity at a time of religious violence and furor. Whatever the circumstances, Dryden's method lulls combativeness without lessening the importance of the subject, and allows a wide emotional range which enables one to look from different angles on what otherwise might be platitudes or mere assertions of will. Pope, in *An Essay on Criticism*, does not dramatize himself, much less combine himself and dramatized beasts in the manner of *The Hind and the Panther*, but he puts on such a virtuoso performance that we yield to his critical intelligence. The *Essay* offers not a battery of rules but the practical and theoretical understanding within which the rules can be sensed to cohere, an understanding that lives in the star performer Pope and that he proves by his adroitness with threadbare precepts and ambiguous terms of reference ('wit,' 'nature'). Dryden argues toward common ground, if not agreement then sympathy; Pope argues from common ground, by and large using materials that none would challenge and creating from them a complex, delicate equipoise. His brilliance makes one grant assent long enough to enter into the poised structure as the speaker has, assess its counterweighting and tensile strength, and so learn to adopt it as one's own. This kind of goal, or Dryden's of a sympathy that goes beyond simple tolerance, lies beyond the conceptual talents of other doctrinal poets in the period, even those who had the talent of writing forceful, charming, racy verse. Gay's *Trivia* and Prior's *Alma* are rhetorically as complex, but neither is a preceptive poem – though both use its conventions – like Dryden's and Pope's.

Satire too required a central voice. Typically it is one of three sorts: the man with the lash, a punitive expert in invective and sarcasm; the good, bright man of principle, at times a naive victim, scandalized citizen, or public benefactor; and the self-deluder, who is at once the central intelligence of the satire and its butt. Relative to earlier satire, satiric poems of the Restoration and early eighteenth century made more use of the most powerful figure of these three, the man with the lash, and the psychologically most complex figure, the self-deluder; when the good, bright man appeared, he often was a lone man of principle, a kind of hero (as the man with the lash is and as the self-deluder fancies himself to be). Satirists did not keep these divisions crisp and final, as in logic they are not. The man with the lash may be the scandalized citizen driven to rage. The self-deluder may reveal himself fully only with a good, bright man to prompt and comment on his actions, so that a seeming agent for the boastful fool (the Aristotelian *alazon*) turns out to be an *eiron*, who has been belittling himself, or a pungent ironist sprung from ambush. Within the mock-heroic, the period's greatest poetic discovery, the mixed central intelligence and mixed emotions – anger, scorn, amusement, malice, righteousness – had their full play.

Samuel Garth's *The Dispensary* (1699) shows us the simplest kind of mock-heroic. This is not to say that the poem is simple to read, for its couplets are crowded with special draughts for each of Garth's medical enemies, and need as much deciphering as the most cryptic prescription. Garth also compounds a system of allusions, the bulk of which near the beginning of the poem come from Boileau's *Le Lutrin* (1674–83), a mock-heroic about squabbling clerics as *The Dispensary* is about squabbling doctors. Besides the extra layer of distancing Garth gets through alluding to another mock-heroic instead of directly to Homer, he tars his enemies economically with Boileau's brush, made blacker for Englishmen by entailing a comparison to Frenchmen. Sections in the first two (of six) cantos praise British martial virtue (mocking the doctors' battle still more) and invert Boileau's panegyric of Louis XIV into one for Louis's greatest foe, William III (see 1: 137–44): in this context, to make the doctors exact parallels with Boileau's fatuous clerics is particularly rude. Later, having made his point, Garth does draw on Homer and Virgil, but also on epics by one of the men he is attacking, Sir Richard Blackmore, whose turgid doggerel at once justifies and contributes to the mock-heroic assault. Since the wit of the verse matches the wit of the allusions, *The Dispensary* (despite its muddy plot and need for annotation) is a considerable poetic achievement. My calling it the simplest kind of mock-heroic refers to its working assumption, that the traditional heroic represents an ideal that can be consistently applied to shrink a subject by contrast or make it (or him) grotesquely menacing.

Dr Horoscope's prayer to the goddess Disease in Canto 3 is in the fundamental mock-heroic mode:

> Disease! thou ever most propitious power,
> Whose soft indulgence we perceive each hour;
> Thou that wouldst lay whole states and regions waste,
> Sooner than we thy cormorants should fast,

21

If in return all diligence we pay
T'extend your empire and confirm your sway
Far as the weekly bills can reach around,
From Kent-street end to famed St. Giles's Pound –
Behold this poor libation with a smile
And let auspicious light break through the pile.   (ll. 91–100)

The inflation of the style and the grandeur of the genre become ironic concessions to the subject's notion of himself. They are no less than he seems to think he deserves. In testing this opinion, the poet may flank the fundamental mode, as I have called it, with genuine heroic passages (or passages that would be heroic in another context) and epic, Juvenalian satire. Garth, for instance, presents the epic figure of Envy with her 'hissing snakes, 'lying on her bed of ravens' plumes and 'breath[ing] a blue eruption' 'like Aetna with metallic steams oppressed' (2: 1–50). Alternatively, in describing Covent Garden (Canto 4), he drops into satire:

The country dames drive to Hippolito's,
First find a spark, and after lose a nose.
The lawyer for laced coat the robe does quit,
He grows a madman and then turns a wit.   (ll. 25–8)

Only two or three times does Garth drop still further into low burlesque, as in his comparison of the angry doctors to brawling watermen (5:239–44), and then always to end a canto, summing up the action in a contemptuous simile. This essential consistency allows him to dramatize a state of mind through an allegorical action (some of the events of which come, of course, from real actions taken by the doctors whose state of mind, self-important anger, fear, and indignation, is being allegorized). The personified abstractions, like Envy and Disease, fit perfectly not only with the conventions of epic but also with the allegorical tenor of the poem as a whole.

A variant of the mock-heroic mode Garth uses also accepts a traditional heroic ideal to be applied consistently to an unheroic subject, but does not make the subject a self-important fool and the speaker his tongue-in-cheek agent. Instead the speaker uses mock-heroic as a gesture of affectionate condescension, a way of chucking the subject under the chin, or even a gesture of affectionate respect, an admission of having been gracefully charmed. In John Gay's *The Fan* (1713), for example, three books, 650 lines in all, burden the invention of the fan with mythological machinery, moral comment, and stately diction. Here mock-heroic indicates the attitude of the speaker alone, as he flatters a trifle by gilding it with majesty. The satire grows playful, and plays, moreover, claws in. A little such poetry is amusing; the very late Restoration and the early eighteenth century produced a lot of it. Bowling greens and kites, cork-screws and patches, fans and shoes, snuff, tea, hoopskirts, the mousetrap and the lousetrap all were crowned with this kind of wit by 1725. Obviously the method does not work well with

22

people, who are not likely to enjoy being teased in miniature epic style, though they may accept having their household pets treated that way, as some were. With these limitations, the affectionate mock-heroic faded as a mode for independent poems by 1730 or so. It reappears in other kinds of poetry and invades much prose, where Fielding, above all, gave it real artistic stature.

Dryden's *MacFlecknoe* (1682) may look like a poem of the same sort as *The Dispensary*. Shadwell's literary pretensions cry out to be measured by the epic, and his political agitation on behalf of Shaftesbury's populism makes him a perfect candidate for becoming a common king among ale mugs, brothels, hack writers, and floating dung. Like Garth, Dryden takes traditional heroic ideals as norms. Those norms give *The Dispensary* its structure, a tight narrative with continuous reference to the heroic, and its characterizations, versions of the doctors' real thoughts exaggerated and cast into the heroic idiom. Dryden produces a much looser, more fantasy-like poem by avoiding any model for *MacFlecknoe* and creating a kingdom, the realms of Nonsense, whose panegyrists might write a poem like this. The ideals invoked in Dryden's kind of mock-heroic come (as they do, for instance, in the Cowleyan ode) not only from epic but from a variety of other sources too, classical and Christian, without much consistency. Shadwell seems to be a Christ, with Flecknoe his John the Baptist, but he is also a prophet from the Old and New Testaments (ll. 29–34, 216–17), an Ascanius but also a Hannibal, 'a mortal foe to Rome' (ll. 108–13). Since the epic coronation does not follow a set pattern (Garth's narrative method) but feeds on heroic allusions by analogy (the method of the ode), Dryden can allow Flecknoe to show his own taste, and Shadwell's, by simply expanding analogies till all discrimination is lost. Shadwell is like Heywood and Shirley (l. 29), the dancing-master St André (l. 53), Ogilby the mangler of Virgil (l. 174), and Flecknoe himself, as well as like messianic heroes. Whereas the doctors of *The Dispensary* assert heroic values while distorting them, Flecknoe and his spiritual son pick their willful way through a chaos of values. Kingship loses its cultural referent and turns into arbitrary self-exaltation, made less arbitrary only inasmuch as the best credentials for reigning over Nonsense are the very brazenness and indiscriminate egoism needed for such self-coronation – for father and son are 'perfect images' (l. 15) of each other. In keeping with this characterization of Flecknoe, the narrator of the poem pretty well keeps to heroic tone (ll. 1–12, 60–138) while Flecknoe, who speaks almost all the other lines, often veers from it for want of taste and chronic itch for originality, the artistic assertion of self.

MacFlecknoe, by analogy with Flecknoe's indiscriminate praise, jumbles the typical heroic theme of expressing spirit through body. It presents a harmony of body and spirit in making a spiritual son (Shadwell) into a real son (MacFlecknoe), and also in alluding to prophets, King David the Lord's anointed (by allusion to Cowley's epic *Davideis*), and Virgilian bearers of divine will (Augustus, Ascanius). But the logic of this harmony between body and spirit makes physical creativity parallel to, and also equivalent in value to, that of the mind. Poems and excrement turn out to be the same, sometimes overtly as with the authors whose works serve for toilet paper (l. 101), sometimes hardly less so as with

23

spelling 'Shadwell' as 'Sh – ' or having the boat pass by 'Pissing-Alley' and 'A – Hall.' Similarly, Flecknoe defends his son from charges of copying Ben Jonson, a giant of both wit and belly (ll. 193–4) whom the real Shadwell claimed as his artistic model, by insisting that his, MacFlecknoe's, talents lie not in the Jonsonian modes of tragedy, comedy, and satire, but in those forms of creativity ('spirit') that depend on appearance ('body') alone, like the anagram, acrostic, picture poem, and pun (ll. 195–208). Flecknoe's final fall through a trapdoor, a theatrical inversion of Elijah's flight to Heaven, concludes not only the prophetic motif but also that of body and spirit, as his dull, inertial matter is given sudden movement (by stage characters as *dei ex machina*), and descends with a flatulent burst (playing on the identity of wind and soul, as in Latin *anima*). Dryden's ingenious pursuit of these themes confirms the notion that the capacity for creative analogy – more in the manner of the ode than in that of the heroic narrative, like Garth's – is one of the greatest virtues of *MacFlecknoe's* mock-heroic. The analogical method displays Flecknoe's lack of discrimination, but it also allows Dryden to give an insultingly elegant turn to a number of common, discrete insults, like scatological comparisons, accusations of dullness, and mockery of one's person.

In still a third type of mock-heroic, Garth's and Dryden's greatest predecessor, Samuel Butler, captures a protagonist's idea of himself in *Hudibras* (1663–4, 1678). The Puritans whom Butler attacks and of whom Hudibras is one, thought of themselves as militant messiahs. Numerous topical allusions in *Hudibras* remind us of that. They justify Butler's use of the mock-heroic form, in the same way that allusions also justify Garth's and Dryden's, and in the early 1660s they made the poem seem wonderfully apropos to Butler's readers, loyalists who had endured under Cromwell the leaden edicts of Hudibras's real forbears. The self-praise of self-righteous Puritans, windy, rambling, and larded with misapplied learning, begged to be inverted. That is what Butler's windy, rambling, absurdly learned poem does. Succeeding generations of readers, lucky enough to miss the originals, have unluckily therefore missed the witty inversions of *Hudibras*. Perhaps to compensate for this, perhaps because modern readers like to think of poems as wholes, critics have tried to smooth the convoluted texture of *Hudibras* by reading it as a coherent narrative. I think the narrative form of Butler's poem is misleading, in that – like *MacFlecknoe*, with its analogical method – the poem does not develop. Instead, it repeats a program of solemn Punch-and-Judy episodes, a puppet imitation of life under Puritan rule, filled with energy and directedness, lacking intelligence and direction. Narrative in *Hudibras* exists to provide showcases for self-display.

If Butler resembles Garth and Dryden in the allusiveness and psychological force of his mock-heroic, and Dryden in his fundamentally static treatment of narrative, he deviates sharply from both in his hostility to any sort of heroics. In *Hudibras* the wars of religion become willful squabbles for a whore. A lover is better off if he 'has two strings t'his bow,/And burns for love and money too': emboldened by greed, he has 'all his flames and raptures double,/And hangs or drowns with half the trouble': (3: 1.3–8). As for steadfast heroic virtue.

> th'ancient stoics in their porch
> With fierce dispute maintained their church,
> Beat out their brains in fight and study
> To prove that Virtue is a body,
> That Bonum is an animal,
> Made good with stout polemic brawl
> In which some hundreds on the place
> Were slain outright, and many a face
> Retrenched of nose and eyes and beard
> To maintain what their sect averred.   (2 : 2. 15–24)

Heroism is a form of pretension, mingling delusion and hypocrisy. Butler brings down the hard heel of his contempt upon it as an evil below hatred, like a troop of cockroaches, and thus stamps his way through thousands of epigrammatic lines. Only when heroism and power come together, as in the Puritans of Part 3, does the evil earn Butler's hatred. Power, of course, is beyond the clumsy dwarf Hudibras, who has to prove by logic that he is no gelding (2 : 1. 705–20) and whom women defeat in the knightly endeavors of war and love. The incongruity between the knight's heroic claims and his actual ignominy or low pragmatic cunning, a source of Butler's humor, makes him easier to endure than his historical counterparts whose 'heroism' was more consistent; Hudibras, unlike the doctors of *The Dispensary* or Sh – , improves on his real-life models.

The 'low pragmatic cunning,' in fact, faintly suggests Butler's main positive norm, common sense. A similar scheme of values marks the style of the poem, where lofty allusions to the Muse or Homer (1 : 1.639–58, 2.781–5) jostle foolishly against the catch-as-catch-can of doggerel and homely reference. As rarely happens after Butler, the heroic is presented as an imposition on a homely norm, just as the Puritans had clamped their clanging laws on normal English life. In any mock-heroic, the poetry makes the usual and the spontaneous stiffen into forms of ceremony, a stiffening that Dryden and Garth use to give added strength to the poem as a work of art. Butler makes us feel how superficial the ceremony is, and draws on the 'low' for nearly all the vitality of *Hudibras*. Laws and categories, of which ceremony is the outward symbol, form the butt of his satire. The laws of the heroic poem, of chivalry, of the state, of courtship and love, and of the heavens are mocked as Hudibras appears as knight, lawgiver, battler, lover, and astrologer's client, even as disputant over divine law with his equally rigid and addled man Ralph. Butler ends his poem with his hero in a lawyer's office after glancing at popular law (the skimmington, a mock-triumph for a cuckold, 2 : 2) and the center of law under Cromwell (the Rump Parliament, 3 : 2). In developing this pervasive theme, Butler no doubt drew on his own legal experience, but he went beyond the personal to what was to be a central concern of Restoration and early eighteenth-century poetry, the interplay between codes of behavior (usually social or deterministic) and individual nature. In this, as in his choice of mock-heroic and distrust of fine professions, Butler was a spiritual patron for his successors. Most of them did not follow him, however, in his radical reduction of ideals to egoistic passion and mechanical reaction or in his redefining law as rationalization or mindless routine. And none, I think, created so great a gap between story, which Butler keeps at the level of simple romance, and surface, where the tortuous ingenuity of the characters and the poet's learned inventiveness give us a wonderfully elaborated poetic texture of arcane references, metaphysical conceits, and plays on words. For Butler, verbal artifice is the only kind of cunning and bustle that one can enjoy without fear of damage to the common peace.

The fourth mode of mock-heroic, that of Pope's *Rape of the Lock*, differs from Garth's and Dryden's, and almost turns Butler's upside-down. Butler scorns real and pretended heroes; Pope treats both kinds with real and ironic admiration. Butler bristles with allusions, learned and historical, in presenting his series of deliberately pointless episodes; Pope sets forth a single, well-paced narrative with few allusions, except for running references to heroic conventions and to one classical poem, Catullus's *De coma Berenices* (Of Berenice's Lock). Butler's righteous characters disrupt society, but Pope's shelter themselves within it. Because Butler treats motives as basically irrelevant, he flattens his characters, unlike Pope, who rounds his with delicate, shrewdly sympathetic explorations of the heart. The two men do share a theme, the interplay of individual nature and codes of behavior, as well as the common pattern of the mock-heroic: power-seeking protagonists who 'deserve' to be treated mock-heroically, a historical referent, and a skepticism to go with the irony of the style.

The first version of *The Rape of the Lock*, in two cantos, tries to tease two feuding families, the Petres and the Fermors, back into good humor with each other: Bella Fermor becomes Belinda, the 'gentle Belle' who (quite understandably) grows furious when the Baron, Lord Petre, mischievously snips her hair, but who ought not – the playful, civilized tone of the poem tells her – hold a grudge. In elaborating the poem and its epic 'machinery,' such as the sylphs and the Cave of Spleen, for the five-canto version, Pope also moralized his song through deepening his exploration of motives. He seems to have taken a cue from Catullus's *De coma Berenices*, to which he had alluded near the end of his first version (2 : 174–5) when Belinda's lock, like Berenice's, turns into a star. Queen Berenice in Catullus gives her locks as votive offerings to Venus for her beloved husband's safe return from war. Since her husband was her brother, Catullus stresses the purity of her love, fraternal rather than sexual (ll. 21–2). Pope's modern version of the myth, of course, makes the loss of the lock unwilled, even if it is a sort of votive offering to Venus, and hints a bit more openly than is polite of Belinda's and other women's sexual longings. His reigning heroine battles her lover at cards rather than praying for his victory, rejects the ideal of marriage that Catullus's poem celebrates, and earns her hair a place in the skies only through the kindness of a poetic muse. Appropriately enough, Belinda's lock becomes a comet, a long-haired but eccentric and portentous 'sudden star,' unlike the constellation Coma Berenices. Appropriately too, her gods are not the classical pantheon, but a troop of sylphs from Rosicrucian fantasy, a 'light militia of the lower sky,' fragile spirits devoted to vanities and appearances.

Belinda too is devoted to appearances, the painted surfaces of her face that let her triumph in love as a cruel coquette, the other painted surfaces of cards that give her her triumph, in war, at ombre. In response, Pope uses various syntactical forms to link together heterogeneous elements in a way, he suggests, that Belinda and her society approve: appearances become as important as deeper values. Just as his use of heroics offers Belinda the kind of stature she thinks she deserves, so his syntax imitates her state of mind. It makes equivalent a stained honor and stained brocade (2:105–10) or 'Puffs, powders, patches, Bibles, billets-doux' (1:138). Appearances are honored because they are psychologically convenient. They locate a person within a social order that exists for the ego, for power and pleasure. Even Clarissa's counsel for 'good sense' and 'good humor' (5:9–34) relies on the ego, on individual prudence, not morality or social virtue. In her speech she appeals not even to ideals of manners, only to self-interest. One must sometimes stoop to keep one's conquest, since beauty is transient, but 'virtue' and 'merit' remain strategies, like holding back one's hearts in ombre. Belinda, at once the type and flower of her society, must worship appearances, then, as part of a radical individualism.

The first two cantos present symbols of this worship, her toilette (physical appearance) and her sylphs (the appearance of emotional freedom – real love baffles the sylphs' magic). The third canto, logically, shows her at the summit of power, at once woman and man (ombre = Sp. *hombre*, man) complete unto herself; the painted cards symbolize the appearance of power, a triumph of and by surfaces. Suddenly comes the peripateia. Cropped, tear-swollen, and sylphless, Belinda sinks, in Canto 4, impotent. No thematic conclusion is possible for the poem. Belinda cannot follow Clarissa's advice in the last canto, and surrender her illusions of beauty and freedom as sustaining values. If she did she would change character and invalidate Pope's mock-heroic form which those illusions alone justify. But in rejecting Clarissa and battling as Thalestris urges, she reaffirms values that have played her false. *The Rape of the Lock*, like *MacFlecknoe*, ends its narrative with a *deus ex machina*, abandoning the central character in mid-act. The teasing resolution of the plot is one of those poetically painted surfaces that Belinda so admires:

> But trust the Muse – she saw it [the lock] upward rise,
> Though marked by none but quick poetic eyes
> (So Rome's great founder to the heavens withdrew,
> To Proculus alone confessed in view):
> A sudden star, it shot through liquid air
> And drew behind a radiant trail of hair.
> Not Berenice's locks first rose so bright,
> The heavens bespangling with dishevelled light.
> The sylphs behold it kindling as it flies,
> And pleased pursue its progress through the skies.
> This the *beau monde* shall from the Mall survey
> And hail with music its propitious ray.   (5:123–34)

From this summary of *The Rape of the Lock*, one might guess that Pope censured Belinda or at least her society sharply. One would be wrong. Like his contemporaries who wrote playful mock-heroic about fans and cork-screws, Pope works from an affectionate, indulgent tone, almost never veering far toward the sardonic and often (as Garth alone had done before him, and then sparingly) creating a reduced heroic of considerable beauty. The sylphs, who represent Belinda's fascination with her glamourous sway, appear on the Thames in some of the loveliest lines in eighteenth-century poetry (2 : 47–68). The more positive our feelings toward fragile, iridescent beauty, the more we think of real Homeric heroics as like a garlanded bull in a Spode shop. Clarissa's counsel of moderation and good sense, moreover, based on a speech from the *Iliad* that Pope translated in 1709 ('The Episode of Sarpedon'), reverses the glory-seeking message of its Homeric original. The allusion reminds us that Homer's egoistic warriors fixed their eyes as firmly on victory and reputation as Belinda does. Her ideals, unlike those of Garth's doctors and Dryden's dunces, parallel the Greeks' – with the appropriate social adjustment – and her success in carrying them out, unlike Hudibras's, is admirable, if the ideals themselves are. The only explicit counter to Homeric and modern egoism in the poem comes from Clarissa, a comfort- rather than glory-seeking egoist, whose motives have been darkened by her having given the Baron the scissors – 'So ladies in romance assist their knight' (3 : 129) – to mar Belinda's 'radiant lock[s].' In short, Pope has done his best to keep us from the sort of judgments that Garth, Dryden, and Butler have done their best to encourage. They had used the form for intensity, but he uses it for complexity of feeling; they had taken certain norms for granted, including heroic norms in *The Dispensary* and *MacFlecknoe*, but he makes his norms joust on equal terms.

Other than imitators like Giles Jacob, almost no one else wrote mock-heroic in the manner of *The Rape of the Lock*, but Pope's tone helped the vogue of the playful mock-heroic, and his manner appears in the nonheroic poems of Gay. *The Shepherd's Week* (1714) parodies the yokel 'realism' of the pastoral school of Ambrose Philips, opposed to the dandified pastoral of Pope; its Grubbinol, Blowzalinda, and Bumkinet spend their time 'fat[ting] the guzzling hogs with foods of whey,' and such like, when they are not engaging in pastoral dialogues. Much of this is very funny, but at the same time that Gay saps the pastoral norm by parody, he also supports it by his pleasure in its materials, like proverbs and popular superstitions, and ends up creating rather engaging bumpkins. One has only to set *The Shepherd's Week* beside Swift's murderous parody of the same mode, 'A Pastoral Dialogue,' to see the difference between intense attack and an amused, emotionally equivocal exploration, perhaps exploitation, of a style. *Trivia* (1716), in which Gay comically adapts the georgic to London, does the same sort of thing, and even his 'The Toilette. A Town Eclogue' (1716) approaches it, though too brief to achieve complexity of feeling. Other poems in the same decade as *The Rape of the Lock* which keep us from making simple judgments on the basis of genre are Lady Winchilsea's playful Miltonic praise of beggars, 'Fanscomb Barn' (1713), and Pope's own *Eloisa to Abelard* (1717), where the form of the poem – an Ovidian epistle from a new nun to the priest who is her castrated ex-lover – makes one expect either a moral or a pagan reading, and where Pope exploits both, creating his poem from the unresolved play of values.

This sketch of contexts for *The Rape of the Lock* suggests that the attitudes behind the fourth of the mock-heroic modes flourished during the second decade of the eighteenth century. We have seen that the 'playful' variant of Garth's mode thrived only during the first quarter of the century. The other three mock-heroic modes, those of Garth, Dryden, and Butler, occur more generally, often in poems that are not mock-heroic but that use deluded central characters. For example, Garth's mode of simple inversion appears in the first and third of John Oldham's four violent *Satires on the Jesuits* (1678–81). The ghosts of dead Jesuits, in heroic oratory, invoke their living brothers to treason, poisoning, hypocrisy, and unremitting zeal. Black is simply made white. By contrast, practically everything is spattered with dark grey in the poems of Swift, who often used Butler's mode, attack on the subject and on the supposed norm as well. *Baucis and Philemon*, for instance, perhaps Swift's best early poem (1709), squashes not only its central characters, dull rustics who stand for a dully material spiritual landscape, but also the miracle-ridden, sometimes sentimental version of the world Ovid's *Metamorphoses* depict. One can find Dryden's mode, finally, in mock panegyrics, such as were common in political satire or literary jibing like Dorset's compliments to Edward Howard's poem *The British Princes*:

Come on, ye critics! Find one fault who dare,
For, read it backward like a witch's prayer,
'Twill do as well. Throw not away your jests
On solid nonsense that abides all tests.
Wit, like terse claret, when't begins to pall,
Neglected lies and's of no use at all,
But in its full perfection of decay
Turns vinegar and comes again in play.
This simile shall stand in thy defence
'Gainst such dull rogues as now and then write sense. (ll. 5–10)

The inversion and shrinking, the fertility of metaphor through the thirty-four lines of the poem, and the use of the rather loose form of commendatory verses to stimulate such an abundance of wit – these mark Dorset's poem as in the same mode as *MacFlecknoe*, to come ten years or so later. While 'prayer,' 'solid . . . abides all tests,' 'full perfection' keep up the panegyric ring, 'dull rogues' supplies a hint of the sulky defiance that the real Ned Howard might adopt, and the helpful speaker adds to this psychological realism by offering his friend some encouraging, brazen poetic defenses, as in the simile about vinegar or the later remark that 'the dull eel moves nimbler in the mud/Than all the swift-finned racers of the flood' (ll. 28–9).

The treatment of the self-deluded 'central intelligence,' in burlesque or not, seems to me the greatest satiric achievement of the Restoration and of early eighteenth-century poetry, both conceptually and in terms of individual poems that posterity has prized. Many more poets, however, relished the heft of a

29

whiphandle. Bitterness during the Commonwealth years had taught English verse to make the lash of invective and sarcasm bite; John Cleveland (1613–58) was the patron saint, or patron imp, of this style. In general, the wittier and more flexible in tone, the more successful the invective, and the less successful the more the writer embraced Oldham's dangerous maxim, in the 'Prologue' to his *Satires on the Jesuits*, 'Nor needs there art or genius here to use,/Where indignation can create a muse' (ll. 28–9). One can see why this cheap muse fails by looking at a satire like Robert Gould's 'The Playhouse' (1689), which calls on 'scorpions with inveterate spite' to teach the poet how 'to stab with every word.' Gould then flails with the wooden dagger of his talents at victims grouped at the playhouse – prostitutes, quacks, lecherous noblewomen, fops, witty debauchees, and bullies – before he strikes critics, authors, and actors:

> Thus sighs the sot, thus tells his amorous tale
> And thinks his florid nonsense must prevail;
> Bows and withdraws, and next to prove his love,
> Steals up and courts the fulsome punks above.
> Meanwhile the nymph, proud of her conquest, looks
> Big as wreathed poets in the front of books,
> Surveys the pit with a majestic grace
> To see who falls a victim to her face,
> Does in her glass herself with wonder view
> And fancies all the coxcomb said was true.
> Hence 'tis the whiffling, vain, fantastic chit
> Is the fair ladies' only man of wit:
> With servile flattery sleeking his address,
> Where'er he goes, he's certain of success.
> Speak truth to our fine women and you'll find
> Of all things, that the least can make 'em kind.
> Nor can we blame 'em, for it calls 'em plain,
> Deceitful, idle, foolish, fond, and vain.
> Wit in a lover more than death they fear,
> For only witty men can tell what trash they are.   (ll. 217–36)

'The Playhouse' has several vigorous passages with cumulative weight. Even a wooden dagger leaves bruises and splinters behind it. None the less, the poem lacks form and focus, because Gould's 'indignation' requires that he give us a sense of spontaneous feeling, and he buys this at the cost of control. In letting 'The Playhouse' sprawl, Gould forfeits intellectual and moral authority both: since he never makes us believe that the playhouse vices are symptoms of general corruption (as his model, Juvenal, could), he has too many separate targets for us to agree that he can be indignant about them all. His attempt at piquant documentation by lampooning the greatest actor and actress of his time, Betterton and Barry, fails because he has no pattern within which their supposed vices fit. One suspects either sensationalism or self-interest behind the attacks, rightly with

Gould, as it happens; but satirists must be above such suspicions. In poems where the suspicions start hardening into certainties, like the wretched Thomas Shadwell's attacks on the author of *MacFlecknoe*, a loss of intellectual control in favor of fuming indignation saps moral authority still further: the vengeful poet is left bobbing at the level of one's contempt as his verse sinks farther beneath it.

The most successful practitioner of the broad social satire that Gould tries in 'The Playhouse' was the Earl of Rochester. He was a master of witty invective within the wide range of tones inherent in civilized discourse. Like most of the court wits' poems, his profited from their intended audience. Circulated in manuscript (through a clearing house of sorts, run by one Robert Julian), the poems found their way to men of some esthetic refinement who prided themselves as skillful judges. Most of all, perhaps, Rochester was a great mimic, with a penetration beyond any other poet of the period, even Swift, in making verse capture colloquial speech and the movement of a persona's mind. Within the dramatic situations Rochester creates, different voices find precise form. Compare, for example, (1) the swashbuckling of a fictive Rochester who demands of a post boy, 'Son of a whore, God damn thee, canst thou tell/A peerless peer the readiest way to Hell?'; (2) the conversational ease of the speaker in 'An Allusion to Horace,' who begins,

> 'Well, sir 'tis granted,' I said, 'Dryden's rhymes
> Were stolen, unequal, nay dull, many times:
> What foolish patron is there found of his
> So blindly partial to deny me this?';

and (3) the clumsy bluster of the wit in 'Tunbridge Wells' who cries

>   'Madam, egad,
> Your luck last night at cards was mighty bad;
> At cribbage, fifty-nine, and the next show
> To make your game, and yet to want those two:
> God damn me, madam, I'm the son of a whore
> If ever in my life I saw the like before.'   (ll. 104–9)

The psychological force of the profanity in (1) and (3) differs sharply, as sharply as the rhythms of the two; the crucial rhymes (tell/Hell) that shock from the first speaker carry far less weight from the negligent second and none at all from the oafish third. Such local control, based more on proper imitation than on ideals of polish, carries over to the creation of patterns of thought – Rochester's or a fictive speaker's – which give his social satire, unlike Gould's, a personal voice.

'A Satire against Reason and Mankind' and 'A Letter from Artemisia in the Town to Chloe in the Country' are the best of Rochester's sustained poems, and illustrate two different but powerful kinds of social satire. Rochester shapes his 'Satire' as a formal argument, following the rhetorical parts of an Aristotelian oration (*Rhetoric* 1414a–b): an introduction, a narration of facts in the case with the points of contention made clear, a proof of one side of the case with refutation of the other, and a conclusion. The declamatory style of much satire, and other poetic forms as well, led many poems to be set up this way. Rochester introduces a paradox, that one is better off a beast than a man. His narration of facts gives epistemological and ethical reasons, in terms of personal happiness, why this should be (ll. 8–30, 31–45) : men destroy themselves by self-delusion and destroy others from fear. In a third section of about the same length (ll. 46–71) an idealistic adversary tries to dispute the paradox through name-calling bad and good ('your degenerate mind,' 'blest, glorious man'); his generalizations bring forth two fifty-line refutations, one upon epistemology (ll. 72–122) and one on ethics (ll. 123–73). These developments of the sections following the introduction, now couched as a dispute with the adversary, produce a mock concession in the near-fifty-line conclusion (ll. 174–221). If there is a good man at court unknown to Rochester – and of course no one at court is unknown to Rochester – the initial paradox will be withdrawn as a universal claim, but a new one will be substituted, that 'Man differs more from man, than man from beast' (l. 221). In other words, the line between humans and animals, a chasm for Christians and for the adversary whom the poet rebuts, matters less than that between one man and another. Rochester thus substitutes the criterion of behavior for one from divine plan. This substitution logically allows the preference for beasts over men, first stated as a matter of personal rhetoric, of explosive disgust, to be argued instead with philosophic weight. Overall, the order of this extraordinary satire permits the invective to accumulate meaning for the speaker as he moves from the simply personal to the mingling of personal and general, fueled by the adversary's idle slogans.

Rochester used the same dynamic in several poems, to different effects. The process of argument strengthens the speaker of the 'Satire,' but it demolishes another debater, the braggart Bajazet in 'A Very Heroical Epistle in Answer to Ephelia.' His self-assertions of unchanging egoism near the start of the poem falter as he argues for his value and finds he must readjust two metaphors of glory, sun and gold, which Bajazet has claimed for his own but which turn out to fit a godlike sultan much better. Elaborating his boasts, he drops into envy of the sultan and finally to a confession of his own anxiety while the 'injured kinsman' holds the 'threatening blade' and rivals lay 'midnight ambushes.' Eventually, through redefining images, Bajazet ends the poem as a mock king and sycophant, a Damocles. In another of Rochester's dramatic monologues, the titular Disabled Debauchee starts his poems as a jovial warrior of love, but as he goes on reveals that he has been a contriver of 'handsome ills' (l. 35) and a sodomite. By now he has slipped to being the malicious and contemptible advisor for someone who would 'fire' 'some ancient church' and 'fear no lewdness he's called to by wine' (ll. 43–4). His manly imagery for himself grows increasingly ironic. In still another poem, the acridly self-conscious Rochester of 'To a Postboy' deliberately and scornfully flaunts the paradox of 'peerless peer' – socially a peer, privately peerless in his vices – and of the play of the aristocrat's casual oath 'God damn thee' and the private traveller's obviously parallel but hardly casual command, 'tell me the readiest way to Hell.' The offhand abuse, 'son of a whore,' coming from a lord to a working boy, also changes meaning when a few lines later the lord announces that he himself is a great whoremaster. Here the process by which the set phrases take on genuine meaning gives us a sense of the speaker's increasing moral awareness, so that we take the end of the poem as his own logical, savage conclusion, though the actual line is spoken by the boy asked the readiest way to Hell: 'Ne'er stir./The readiest way, my lord, 's by Rochester.'

'Artemisia to Chloe,' probably written in the same twelve or eighteen months (in 1675–6) as the other poems just discussed, uses the same dynamic, but makes the process of discovery the reader's alone. In Greek, 'Chloe' is tender shoot or young verdure; 'Artemisia,' in Latin, is wormwood; and the letter showers the bitter medicine of urban vice on sheltered innocence. Or so it might seem: in fact Chloe lusts for the game of gossip, asking Artemisia to turn scandal into pure fun by putting it in verse, and Artemisia complies, after thirty lines on how she 'stands on thorns' to try this kind of masculine wit. Within this frame, the poem presents three analogous women – Artemisia, the 'fine lady' who visits her, and Corinna, the subject of the fine lady's anecdote. As a whole, the letter is an essay on the natural and social characters of women, each of them a victim of society and of herself, from Artemisia who is free, to the fine lady who disencumbers herself of her foolish husband by giving him 'the perfect joy of being well deceived' (l. 115), and finally to Corinna who gets rid of her lover with poison after securing his money. All three make morality serve wit (or outwitting), sometimes because they are 'pleased with the contradiction and the sin' (l. 30) of asserting dominance, sometimes because they have to. As wits, all three practice moral satire for their own ends, accurate moral satire that gives their actions a context and makes them both critics and typical members of society.

To suggest this double function of critic and exemplar for each woman, Rochester divides the presentation of each into halves, one of being attacked and the other of attack. Thus Artemisia first expects to be cursed or scorned by the town for writing verse (ll. 1–31), and then scorns the town for formalism in love (ll. 32–72); the fine lady satirizes fools (ll. 101–35) and is satirized by Artemisia as 'an ass through choice, not want of wit' (ll. 135–68); Corinna first lies 'diseased, decayed,' and deserted by her lovers (ll. 189–208), then murderously retaliates (ll. 209–51). The darkening of events and the moral analogues make no impression, of course, on Artemisia, who promises Chloe more infamous gossip by the next post; they make an impression on us, who have morally explored – as in 'The Disabled Debauchee' or 'To a Postboy' – what Artemisia has playfully recounted. Even the women's moral blindness has its advantages. By surrendering their awareness of their own follies, Rochester has left them a sense of their own superiority and security, precisely the confidence they need to launch their tart or disdainful accounts of everyone else. The spottiness of their vision insures the breadth of ours.

As one might expect, there was only one Rochester to join wit, control, and a deep (if narrow) sense of human nature. Most social satire was more like Gould's or like Dorset's scabrous 'A Faithful Catalogue of . . . Ninnies' (written 1688), or else – in the early eighteenth century – unpretentiously sportive. Swift's 'Mrs. Harris's Petition' (written 1700) and Prior's 'Jinny the Just' (written 1708) are well-known poems which, if they are satires at all, fit in this latter group. Exceptions include Swift's two acid 'progresses' written in 1719, 'The Progress of Love' and 'The Progress of Beauty,' and two mock-panegyrics by Butler, *To the Memory of the Most Renowned Du Val* (1671) and 'The Elephant in the Moon' (written 1676?). In the first, Butler hymns a doughty man of adventure, in fact a foreign bandit lionized by romantic women, in Cowleyan Pindarics. The second employs narrative panegyric, such as we have seen in Waller, to relate a great astronomical discovery which turns out to be a fraud, the result of a mouse trapped in the telescope. Of Butler's numerous followers in Hudibrastic verse – iambic tetrameter doggerel – Edward ('Ned') Ward was the best, except of course for Swift, and a rapid reader can still take pleasure in such rambling social satires of his as *A Journey to Hell* (1700) or *A Walk to Islington* (1701). Finally, if one were to count a gigantic swaddling of prose notes as part of the short poem they gloss, Bernard Mandeville would demand long discussion, for his *Fable of the Bees* (1705, 1714) is the most slyly devastating of English social satires. Unfortunately 'The Grumbling Hive,' the poem that in theory elicits the notes, is not a very good poem.

Feminist social satire sometimes is good poetry. Moreover, I should like to pause over it because its concerns are important and illuminating to a history of poetry. The legal status of women in the Restoration remained static; their social status moved forward; their literary status took an enormous leap. For the first time in English history, a good-sized number of women wrote and published what they wrote. Male reaction was predictable. Of women authors of any note, only Katherine Phillips, the 'Orinda' or 'Matchless Orinda' (1631–64) who ran a literary salon and wrote modest (in all senses) verse, escaped the sort of male censure typified by Robert Gould's, 'If any vain, lewd, loose-writ thing you see,/You may be sure the author is a she' ('Prologue Designed for a Play of Mine' in *Poems*, 1689). This sort of attack, mentioned in the mid-1670s by Rochester's Artemisia, joined the old misogynistic armory supplied by Juvenal's Sixth Satire (tr. Dryden, 1693) and glosses on Scripture. In response to the renewal of anti-feminism, some women tried to prove their intellectual capacities by writing learned verse, for example in Mary Chudleigh's use of Thomas Burnet's cosmogonic theories in 'The Song of the Three Children Paraphrased' (*Poems on Several Occasions*, 1703) or Sarah Fyge Egerton's entering into philosophical commendations of Boyle's and John Norris's theological ideas (*Poems on Several Occasions*, 1706). More to the point I have been stressing in this chapter, though, is a less oblique self-defense: satire that not only asserts the power of the satirical poet but also analyzes social relationships in terms of power.

Egerton complains sarcastically that 'our sex is confined to so narrow a sphere of action' (Preface), and refuses the confinement at the beginning of her angry 'The Liberty': 'Shall I be one of those obsequious fools/That square their lives by custom's scanty rules?' Her retort, in 'The Emulation,' is that 'Wit's empire . . . shall know a female reign.' The author of 'Wedlock a Paradise' (1701) also uses anger and exhortation:

Stand up, fair ladies, and your rights maintain,
Heaven gives you equal liberty with man:
Woman is born by nature full as free
And is, if learn'd, as wise and brave as he.   (p. 13)

If women and men are natively equal, a theory given added color by Locke's principle of the mind as *tabula rasa*, then women's inferior social position results from male unfairness and love of domination. This becomes the point of satiric protest for Mary Chudleigh ('The Ladies' Defence') or Elizabeth Thomas, for instance, whose *Miscellany Poems* (1722) charges that the 'servile heavy chain' that women drag comes from men's 'brutal rage' and 'thirst of rule' (p. 146). In 'On Sir J—S—,' she insists that men who are 'conscious of our native worth/. . . dread to make it more' (p. 186). Characteristic of the period are both the shrewdness of the observation about the politics of domestic power and the voicing of it from the assertive stance of the satirist.

I should add that with the relative retreat from power or advance toward the corporate citizen as material for poetry, this sort of satire dwindled after the first quarter of the eighteenth century. One possible exception comes in the vigorous 'Hypatia' of the learned Elizabeth Tollet (1694–1754); since her *Poems on Several Occasions* was posthumous (1755), one does not know when she wrote her eight-page attack, with charges that men, 'As barbarous as tyrants, to secure their sway,/Conclude that ignorance will best obey' (p. 67). Other women did not go further than the philosopher Catherine Cockburn, who merely called upon the Queen to patronize women as redress for their being denied education (1732). By the time of Mary Collier, whose *Poems on Several Occasions* appeared in 1762, attack has declined to defensive grumbling that if women had the education 'which justly is our due,' many of them 'might fairly vie with' men. Even this reaction stands out by the 1760s. The poem, 'An Epistolary Answer to an Excise-man,' may well have been written much earlier, or perhaps Collier's assertion has to do with her having had, as a washerwoman, the experience of a whole class, men and women alike, denied education and probably given to a social life in which women's roles were bitterly restrictive—or at least, so she suggests in another poem, 'The Woman's Labor.' As one can see from, for example, J. M.'s 'The Scale, or, Woman Weighed with Man' (1752), some women poets felt themselves victims, but at least in verse they made no angry accusations of the sort given weight by the Restoration's concern with power.

From 1678, the start of the Popish Plot, to the end of the reign of Anne in 1714, political satire absorbed poets' attention. No earlier period could have had popular, topical collections called 'Poems on Affairs of State,' and no later period either, except for the mid-eighteenth-century of Walpole, Pitt, and Bute. Between the arrival of William III (1689) and the early years of George I, who succeeded Anne, some thirty such collections were published, with about twelve hundred poems; and more than double that number of political satires survive in manuscript. By the calculation of George de F. Lord (editor of the modern edition of *Poems on Affairs of State*), the collections hold about 40 per cent of the published satirical verse from 1660 to 1714 (*POAS* 1 : xxvi). Some of the forms this verse took, like the mock-heroic (or mock-panegyric or discommendatory verses) and the lampoon of an individual were shared with other kinds of satire; the satiric dream (or vision or prophecy), the ballad, and the advice-to-a-painter poem (in which a hypothetical painter is told how to depict certain people and events) were peculiarly, if not wholly, political forms. Obviously, a great deal of passion and ingenuity was poured into this verse, more than we now can extract from it. Much of it is popular in style – ballads, doggerel, snatches of parody – and commensurately simple in meaning. Much of it is visible chunks of a lost running commentary, scenes from a discourse on a subject we do not, and can not, know deeply enough to note exquisite deftness where it exists. Much of it shrewdly and legitimately counted on its readers' cooperative anger to give shape to what now seems like a mere swarm of stinging lines.

These difficulties afflict the political satires of even the best such Restoration poets, apart from Dryden: Andrew Marvell, who wrote in various popular and parodic modes, and John Oldham, whose stream of invective comes sometimes from his own mouth, sometimes from that of a villainous Jesuit persona. Marvell's technique is essentially external commentary, for instance in his *Last Instructions to a Painter* (written 1667), which parodies the genre of Waller's *Instructions to a Painter* (1665) about how a great English naval victory should be portrayed. In visual detail, Marvell sets forth the vices and stupidities of his subject, sometimes with irony, sometimes with rancor, sometimes with fury shuddering behind a cloak of lyricism. Although in his lyrics he had once used the visual as the setting for inner reflections, Marvell now refuses to share in the minds of those he attacks, and simply shows us empty actions from which a depravity of spirit can be inferred. The outward behavior of the powerful is crucial, and so his satires intersperse public history with glances at shameful, unnatural, back-alley chronicle and, for contrast, normative scenes of natural English countryside. He raises lampoon to the level of patriotic feeling by conceiving of his subject as a chaos of personalities within a context, as an England frayed into a mass of separately twitching threads. This expressive strategy has its costs. The reader must supply the focus through shared feeling if the poems are to cohere, and even then they lack the subtleties of touch which cumulative structure makes possible. Oldham, in his *Satires on the Jesuits* (but not in such fine non-political satires as 'Spenser's Ghost' and his various imitations), tries to imitate the thrashings of mind and feeling without creating real human beings in the manner of Rochester. He depends on popular fears and the crackle of his own poetic energy to translate cardboard villains into flesh-and-blood ones; in the fever of the Popish Plot, this translation succeeded, but not – if that matters – by poetic means.

Most of the poems that did succeed by poetic means were short, less than a hundred lines. Swift contributed several, including some Horatian imitations and a devastating attack on Marlborough, *The Fable of Midas* (1712). Arthur Maynwaring, a seventeenth-century Jacobite turned eighteenth-century Whig, proved a master of invective in poems like *Suum Cuique* (1689). And Defoe, whose prose style is neither economical nor pointed enough to make one think he could write good satiric verse, did write some, including his long, eloquent *Hymn to the Pillory* (1703). It is no derogation to Defoe or to Marvell and Oldham, though, to say that by far the most successful ambitious political satire of the period was Dryden's *The Medal*, a denunciation of the Earl of Shaftesbury (prompted by his acquittal from charges of treason) and of Shaftesbury's London allies, who honored the occasion with a gold medal. The speaker's vehemence makes the poem look formless, but if it were, it would suffer like other poems of the same vituperative type: first it would fascinate, then overwhelm, then (as a consequence) grow boring and distasteful. *The Medal* fascinates at first and throughout. Its form comes from the golden medal itself, with Shaftesbury's head on the obverse, and on the reverse a scene of the Thames and the London skyline from St Paul's to the Tower beneath the sun breaking from clouds. Almost exactly in the center of the circle is the tip of the Monument, as a reminder (so the inscription on its plinth once read) of the 'treachery and malice of the Popish faction' who had tried to burn down 'this Protestant city.' Dryden imitates the medal by dwelling on the Earl and the city both. A narrative of Shaftesbury's career (ll. 26–82) and a discourse on his demagogy (ll. 83–144) precede two sections of about the same length as the first two, one on the character of London (ll. 145–204) and the other on its readiness for Shaftesbury's demagogy (ll. 205–55). These four sections give us a rectified version of the medal, 'so golden to the sight,/So base within, so counterfeit and light.' The poem then ends with a double conclusion, half a quasi-religious curse on the Earl (ll. 255–86), half a prophetic vision of an England in agony (ll. 287–322).

Dryden's imagery comes from the medal too, a golden, two-sided, counterfeit coin (or so Dryden treats it), in which Shaftesbury's head replaces Charles's and the scene of London replaces the figure of Britannia or – depending on the coin – the shields of Charles's realms. The medal is the coin of self-aggrandizing fantasies in which the rebellious Earl and City usurp the King's material position ('Rex Mag. Bri. Fr. et Hib.') and his spiritual right ('Dei Gratia'). From both royal fact and divine right comes law, which Shaftesbury and London have counterfeited already, in acquitting the Earl of treason. Shaftesbury has jesuitically turned law to self-interest (ll. 82–90), as has the 'great emporium' (l. 167) of London, which makes weight of numbers into the measure of justice, matter into what passes for spirit. The greedy, quantitative deceits of both reduce everything to the level proper for gold coin, so that images of cheating, whoring, forcible possession, and doctored wine crowd into the later parts of *The Medal*. The two-sidedness of the medal, finally, gives Dryden a pretext for developing parallelism in his treatment of the worldly and the godly, a parallelism between the Earl and the city that becomes, as so often in Dryden's work, a meeting of extremes. Shaftesbury the self-seeking loner sees eye to eye with London's robber horde where 'All hands unite of every jarring sect;/They cheat the country first, and then infect' (ll. 197–8). His 'jolly God' who 'winks at crimes' in ease brings him to the same point as their 'tyrant' in 'a Heaven, like Bedlam, slovenly and sad' (ll. 279, 285). Obviously, however, parallels based on radical egoism necessarily bear the seeds of division, and as the poem proceeds, those seeds grow. Disruption in the world (stormy weather) and body (disease) express this factionalism, as religious imagery joins secular, until the prophetic vision at the end. There Aesopian fable turns the anguish of England into historical pattern. The graven images of pretended public virtue on the medal do yield a genuine public meaning, the destruction of the unity they assert, like the destruction of their Commonwealth ancestors when Englishmen's 'wild labors, wearied into rest,/Reclined us on a rightful monarch's breast' (ll. 321–2).

Pastoral concerns

Modern critics have stressed the 'public' quality of Restoration and early eighteenth-century poetry, its shying from intimacy or confidentiality, and its tone of the forum even when the poem is cast in a more private mode, like a panegyric or satire addressed to a specific person. Most of the poems we have been considering fit this bill. Yet, exclusive of topical ephemera, which are almost all 'public,' more verse appeared in print which – openly or not – rejected assumptions of the 'public' modes than which accepted them. I am thinking of poems in which the speakers either turn from power or assert it only in social relations. No doubt there is a sense in which some of these poems are 'public' too: an epistle or love poem may be conceived as part of a dramatic situation, in which an encounter or plea or song crystalizes the relationship between two typical lovers, and often personality is reduced to poetic essentials so that main figures lack the other traits and untidinesses of character that would make them individual people. But in the Restoration even this degree of 'public' quality has its limits, for epistles and love poems almost all rely on a criterion of 'private' sincerity, a rejection of what writers saw as harmfully 'public' in their predecessors' verse. Restoration poets did print some short conceited ('metaphysical') verse, like Benjamin Hawkshaw's 'On a Fly that Was Drowned in a Lady's Mouth' (1693) and some in John Hopkins's *Amasia* (1700). On the whole, such poems are rare; and almost everyone would have agreed with William Walsh (1692) that love was not to be shown through 'forced conceits, farfetched similes, and shining points; but by a true and lively representation of the pains and thoughts attending such a passion.' Psychological truth, once more, becomes a criterion for poetic truth. This test of validity, rooted in what must be private (even if common to many individuals), complements the embracing of the private life which marks love poems, many epistles, and nearly all poetry of rural retirement.

Through the time of Prior, many poets worked skillfully in the Cavalier mode associated with Herrick (who lived to 1674), Lovelace, and Suckling. How skillfully may be seen, for example, in Sir Charles Sedley's most famous lyric, one simply called 'Song':

> Love still has something of the sea
> From whence his mother rose:
> No time his slaves from doubt can free,
> Nor give their thoughts repose;

They are becalmed in clearest days,
And in rough weather tossed;
They wither under cold delays,
Or are in tempests lost. . . .

By such degrees to joy they come,
And are so long withstood,
So slowly they receive the sum,
It hardly does them good.

'Tis cruel to prolong a pain
And to defer a joy;
Believe me, gentle Celimene
Offends the winged boy.

An hundred thousand oaths your fears
Perhaps would not remove;
And if I gazed a thousand years
I could no deeper love.   (ll, 1–8, 17–28)

The movement of the poem, which explores and then drops the metaphor of the sea, admirably imitates the speaker's psychological movement. He battles nature, growing so weary that he foresees a success drained of its sweetness by fatigue and, perhaps, dull resentment. In this state of mind, the 'joy' of line 17 is ironic and the cruelty of line 21 becomes more than simple tantalizing: to defer joy is to risk destroying it. Having proceeded from the conventional idea of love's torments to the far less conventional one of a joy that can no longer be prized, the speaker drops the metaphor that has led him this far toward truth. He speaks to Celimene first in the third person, gently and with a gentle circumlocution ('the winged boy'), and then, in the last stanza, directly, placing the paradox before her. She is an unmoving slave to her timidity (a psychological variant of the driven, doubting slave of line 3), whom a hundred thousand oaths cannot stir to recognize a millennial love. The exasperated hyperbole of 'hundred thousand' yields to the sincere intensity of 'thousand years,' with the shrinking of the number, oddly, adding to its impact, its demonstration of how wrong is the fearful 'gentleness' of Celimene.

Such psychological accuracy helped satisfy the new demand for 'sincerity,' to which John Oldmixon pays tribute in the preface to his *Poems on Several Occasions* (1696): 'You will find nothing in this little volume, but what was the real sentiments of my heart at the time I writ it.' As a shaping device, the description of states of mind tended to sweep the field it had once shared with poetic argument, for instance in Donne or Marvell. A line of argument may be implicit or explicit, like Sedley's, but the process of reasoning does not guide the poem. Often the line of argument itself simply works to project a mood, a turn of mind. Rochester's 'All my past life is mine no more,' for example, uses the image of life as a 'transitory dream . . . whose images are kept in store/By memory alone' to argue that fidelity

39

must be measured by moments, since Heaven allots a man control of no more than moments. With such a conclusion, the poem is less an argument than the witty evasion of a quarrel: the speaker's sparkle, not his mind, saves the day. Even when the manner seems to be 'metaphysical,' continuity of argument does not govern poetic movement. Philip Ayres's 'Love's New Philosophy' (1683) cultivates a garden of amorous paradoxes, through the polar images (life/death, heat/cold) by which love poems dramatized excesses and extremes of feeling. For Ayres, the water of tears inflames the fire of love, the body moves although the soul has abandoned it for the beloved, the man's heart catches fire from the icy heart of the cruel lady, and so on. The logic behind these Petrarchan alogicalities is one of attitude, not argument: the paradoxes are so complete, so absolute, that they do not admit of sequence, but index a single state of mind. If one is inclined – and one certainly is – to find this kind of poem foolish, the foolishness itself proves that reason has been overwhelmed in the passionate speaker. (The proof does not redeem the poem, but makes claims to sincerity, at least, more plausible.)

The unintellectual nature of 'sincere' love poems and their emphasis on feeling fit well with two themes inherited and much nurtured by the Restoration, though progressively more shunned in the 1690s and later. One is sexual abandonment, the other is pleasure in mental cruelty. In 'Love Defined' (1674), Edward Howard dryly notes that 'Love is a dwarf in giant's clothes,/Wearing the robes which Lust bestows' (*Poems and Essays*, p. 33). Scores of Restoration love lyrics show us, over and over, the robes flying off while, over and over, nymphs and swains 'die' together; as Dryden put it, 'Then often they died, but the more they did so,/The nymph died more quick and the shepherd more slow.' Other poets' Celias, Corinnas, and Sylvias pant for the trembling, sighing, melting joys to which their beautiful womanhood and someone else's ardent manhood persuade them. Thus the illusions of erotic fantasy, the power of ready pleasure, spring from a lack of illusion about the spirituality of human desire. Many delightful poems result, including some where boy and girl make so much haste that they 'die' without the raptures of growing moribund together. This charmed and amused view of sex makes folly of the mystical, the prissy, the tittering, and the melodramatic treatments of the same subject in other ages: a sane, though eventually tedious animalism spares one the pretentiousness and megalomania that sex has historically invited from poets. Although Restoration verse of sensuous pleasure is intentionally slight verse, a good number of the poems enjoy triumphs of tone and turn of phrase. Occasionally, within this context of hedonism, verse of sexual frustration (through premature ejaculation) like Aphra Behn's 'The Disappointment' and Rochester's 'The Imperfect Enjoyment' even develops some psychological complexity.

More often complex and less often agreeable is the love poetry of cruelty. If the sensual poem has analogues with the more frolicsome parts of Restoration comedy and the softer moments of tragedy, the cruel poem reflects willful torments inflicted by some comic heroes and most tragic villains, who entertain themselves with the ingrained passions of their victims. Aphra Behn's best poem moves from emblem to accusation in this mode:

Love in fantastic triumph sat
While bleeding hearts around him flowed,
For whom fresh pains he did create,
And strange tyrannic power showed.
From thy bright eyes he took his fire,
Which round about in sport he hurled;
But 'twas from mine he took desire
Enough to undo the amorous world.
From me he took his sighs and tears,
From thee his pride and cruelty,
From me his languishments and fears,
And every killing dart from thee:
Thus thou and I the God have armed
And set him up a deity,
But my poor heart alone is harmed
Whilst thine the victor is, and free.

This sort of victory recurs in poet after poet, especially the fashionable ones, as a means of expressing the political psychology of everyday life. 'Ephelia' (Joan Philips?) ends her 'The Change or Miracle' (in *Female Poems*, 1679) tamely bending and vainly suing 'To one that takes delight t'increase my pain,/And proudly does me and my love disdain.' John Glanvill's 'Revengeful Courtship' (1685) takes the next step, toward fantasies of retaliation:

Thus to revenge your false disdain,
False love I will employ,
With studied malice work your pain
And then that pain enjoy.   (*Poems*, 1725, p. 151)

Behn, 'Ephelia,' and Glanville obviously have found the rough bust of Hobbes glaring over their Arcadias. If their suffering fails to be short or, perhaps, solitary, it is certainly poor, nasty, and brutish. But one can recognize the same sense of the state of nature, Hobbesian in spirit though of course not necessarily derived from him, in the hedonistic poem, which celebrates 'brutishness' uncontrolled by social or inner restraint. Desire for power, over a body in the hedonistic poem and over a heart in the cruel poem, governs action. The world of panegyric and political satire brings us into the world of law, where shared judgment tries to rein the extremes of will and desire; but love poetry withdraws one from law and shared judgment, and revels in extremes. Its world therefore has certain formal similarities with another we have seen, the corrupt world of Dryden's Shaftesbury or Oldham's Jesuits which triumphs in the satirist's worst fancies. Like satire, love poetry commonly employs polar imagery, such as we have seen in Philip Ayres's paradoxes. Images are paired in two ways, following the paradigms 'health : sickness' and 'fire : ice.' In the first kind of pair, an extreme stands opposite a desirable normal state. Some common examples are 'free : slave,' 'shore : stormy sea,' and 'gold : loss.' I hardly

41

have to mention similar norm/violation pairs in panegyric and satire, which treat publicly, on the level of the state, the opposites that love poetry internalizes as symbols of indwelling affections of passionate women and men. In the second paradigm, extremes are opposed so as to be equated: the tormented lover freezes or burns with equal pain. Again one can easily see the same governing pattern in satire, where zealous faction mirrors zealous faction, where the libertine Shaftesbury shares a coin with roundhead London. Love poetry, then, in one sense rejects but in another sense participates in the temper of the more public poems we have been discussing. If its images seem as stylized or heraldic as those of panegyric, they still can carry conviction by standing for such deeply felt patterns of political understanding.

Rochester's satires show the greatest sensitivity to human relations as functions of the will to power, and his love poems, not surprisingly, explore best the power-seeking in love. The 'Very Heroical Epistle' from Bajazet is one example. Another is the epistle 'Could I but make my wishes insolent,' with its charge that 'My hopes your self contrived with cruel care/Through gentle smiles to lead me to despair.' In 'Caelia, that faithful servant you disown,' a different masochism appears: the lover begs 'leave to glory in my chain,/My fruitless sighs, and my unpitied pain,' so that he can serve as 'th'example of your power and cruelty.' The lover in 'Insulting beauty, you misspend' tells his scornful lady that her punishment and his revenge is that 'I alone, who love you most,/Am killed with your disdain' – the sufferer's death will torment the deprived tormenter. Alternatively, in 'Nothing adds to your fond fire,' the lady must conceal her love for Thyrsis and torment him with scorn so as to keep him hers, for 'You grow constant through despair,/Love returned you would abuse.' Alexis, finally, in 'A Pastoral Dialogue,' wishes he could tyrannize coldly over his lady as she does over him; while in 'A Dialogue between Strephon and Daphne,' the victim does turn the tables: after pleading with Strephon to come back to her, and being met only with his smug advice to follow him in sacrificing faith to pleasure, Daphne reveals or vengefully pretends that she has wanted him only as her doting dupe, to whom she can continue to be false like all 'Womankind, which more joy discovers/Making fools than keeping lovers.'

At first, the fire and ice of Rochester's nymphs and swains might seem to have little to do with more conventional poems of pastoral retirement, where innocence, friendship, and love warble unceasingly. In the Restoration, though, these poems typically present the same division between passion and aloofness: the speaker watches, apart and smug, the miserable rage of the world beyond his country retreat. He does not, of course, glory in its pain, but does glory in his own safety and Epicurean ease. If the retired life had once meant for poets a chance for contemplation, often for piety, the Civil Wars and the skeptical bent of the Restoration poets now made retirement an act of prudence for which one might, and did, congratulate oneself in verse. Like the erotic lyrics we have discussed, retirement poems have a strong air of fantasy – they do not suggest that one save oneself from court and city at the cost of deprivation or hard work. Instead, these poems propose an ideal, an imaginative evasion of pain and luxuriating in ease. As a result, they do not try to give the sense of actual, individual experience.

For example, Thomas Otway's 'Epistle to R[ichard] D[uke]' (1684) gives us an epitome of hostility to power, a court of starving, wriggling courtiers who throng 'for a taste/Of the deceitful, painted, poisoned paste,' eager for 'power, the woefullest state of man,/To be by fools misled, to knaves a prey' (ll. 24–6, 132–3). In the Edenic country, 'cheerful birds' sing 'joyful songs of liberty,' while swallows skim the river and the declining sun 'Kisses and gently warms the gliding streams' (ll. 15–16, 34–6); it is a place for the reading of Virgil and Horace, for friendship, for 'A generous bottle and a lovesome she' in whose company one can feed 'every sense with perfect pleasure,' dissolve in joy, and fall asleep 'With twining limbs that still love's posture keep' (ll. 63, 93–5). Despite the revelling speaker's constant 'I,' one feels that the delights are all typical, aimed at the reader's response rather than welling from the speaker's recollection. Otway is less concerned to convey his own memories than to make someone else desire a personal version of a generally accessible kind of experience, that of a primal and yet not historical Golden Age which the poem propounds through an alluring fantasy. Otway gives us less sententiousness and more sex in presenting his golden age than do some of his contemporaries and most of his predecessors – in general, the poems of the 1660s relax in the arms of morality and those of the 1670s and 1680s in the arms of Chloe or Phyllis. Where Otway makes much of friendship and love, others sometimes praise solitude, 'the soul's best friend,' as Charles Cotton called it ('The Retirement,' 1676). The essential mode, however, is as we have seen, that of a first-class vacation brochure for leisured men and women of somewhat various tastes and habits. One can write, as Restoration poets did, very appealing minor poetry of this sort, made more appealing at the time by Oliver Cromwell, the Dutch Wars, the Popish Plot, Monmouth's Rebellion, and the turbulent, abruptly-shortened reign of James II. I suspect that under these pressures, readers assimilated to the hedonistic mode even those earlier and contemporary retirement poems whose intent was somewhat different.

Some poets, of whom John Norris of Bemerton is the most distinguished example, referred the tranquillity of rural retreat on earth to its prototype in Heaven, looking forward to eternal bliss rather than obscurely backward to Eden or a myth of the Golden Age. In such poems, Heaven becomes the fulfillment of which we get but a taste in the gardens of this world. Hedonism, the pleasure principle, lies behind such imaginings, just as it lies behind the secular joys that charm Otway. Apart from the delights of sex and friendship, therefore, the elements that appear in Otway also find a place in Norris. Like the tradition represented by Otway, but unlike most earlier seventeenth-century poetry of retirement, the kind of poem Norris wrote does not use the garden or farm as a retreat for introspection, but as a refuge from the iron maiden of power; nature is not a mystical veil behind which the divine vision gleams, but the setting for the inner experience of calm, to be enjoyed less for its sensuous beauty – the land and its creatures are not described in rich or personal detail – than for its gift of psychological sweetness. Norris sees the world as a place where man's appetites are 'vex[ed] and cheat[ed]/With real hunger, and fantastic meat' ('The

43

Complaint') while the 'one immense and ever-flowing light of heaven' promises the peak of delight: 'Stop here, my soul: thou canst not bear more bliss,/Nor can thy now raised palate ever relish less' ('The Elevation'). Poem after poem professes indifference or scorn for the dangerous, tantalizing, or cloying prizes of worldly life, but in turn Norris promises exactly the same emotional state these prizes pretend to offer – contentment – without danger or transiency in Heaven. Even knowledge, intellectual power over the world, will come as one nestles at ease in God's bosom. 'And [his] great victory enjoy,/And not, as now, still labour on and die' (The Curiosity'). In that state of liberty (power over oneself) and knowledge, 'There's now no further change, nor need there be,/When one shall be variety' ('The Prospect'). For this reason, a struggle for knowledge on earth is needless as well as frustrating and disruptive of our little sampling of divine peace through the garden. Norris's image is a comfortable version of the practical imagery common in his worldly seventeenth-century predecessors:

> What need I then great sums lay out,
> And that estate with care forestall,
> Which when few years are come about
> Into my hands of course will fall?   ('The Discouragement')

Earlier I said that the Restoration inherited and nurtured the erotic and the cruel love poem; but no one should imagine that those were the only kinds written even by the court wits. Etherege and the graceful Sedley wrote numbers of more conventional love poems, and still others, with weaker court connections, never wrote any but conventional kinds. In singling out the erotic and cruel poems, I am remarking on a change in the relative strengths of various elements in the mixture. Similarly, I do not mean to imply that the lazy, though pure spirituality of John Norris marks all or most Restoration religious poetry, or even – the laziness, that is – all Norris's. His 'Hymn to Darkness,' perhaps his best-known poem, plays in a 'metaphysical' way on paradoxes of physical darkness and spiritual light. In one important respect, though, it resembles Norris's more fully developed religious retirement poetry, and typifies religious poetry of the period: it involves little sense of personal conflict. For an age in which love poetry dwells on pains and anxieties so much, and previous to which religious poetry (Donne, Herbert) had often done the same, the Restoration saw exceptionally little poetic weeping for sins, shivering for fear of damnation, and crying out like a stranded voyager in the night. Some of the religious poems admonished the sinner through emblems, like the utilitarian verse of John Bunyan and the more sophisticated verse of John Rawlet; an extremely popular form, the paraphrased psalm, admonished the sinner through revoicing biblical threats; but poets did little with the sinner's own doubts and struggles. If religious verse did not become an extension of rural retirement, in Norris's manner, it typically (though not invariably) became an extension of panegyric, like the psalms themselves.

As in the psalms, in panegyric, in love poetry, and in the poetry of retirement, argumentation does not offer understanding in religious poetry of the Restoration.

It offers a means of focusing intuitive faith: we go through one sort of process to sight a goal that is to be reached by another process entirely. (Obviously I am not referring here to quasi-political doctrinal poems, like *The Hind and the Panther*.) Intellectual experience can bear no poetic weight because it is so plainly insufficient for achieving bliss, the only thing that counts. That is unfortunate. Even poets cannot easily renounce their cake and eat it too. Not enough is left in religious verse besides exclamations, vapid raptures, and ramblings, such as one finds in Thomas Traherne, nowadays the most studied religious poet of the Restoration. However compelling Traherne's mystic intuition may have been, however cunning he was in transforming theological tradition – and those are the claims scholars have made for him – his poetry remains diffuse and reductive. Like Norris, he makes pleasure ('felicity') his controlling theme, so much that one might almost mistake the ending of 'Desire' for a fragment of Restoration eroticism:

> Sense, feeling, taste, complacency, and sight,
>> These are the true and real joys,
> The living, flowing, inward melting, bright
> And heavenly pleasures (all the rest are toys):
>> All which are founded in desire,
>> As light in flame, and heat in fire. (ll. 60–5)

If Traherne was inwardly melted by this style, no major poet of the period was. In general, the results of late seventeenth-century religious versifying turned out to be tepid at best.

As the seventeenth century moved to an end, so did the overarching value of hedonism. Nature itself began to assume more importance as a stimulus, which 'our souls insensibly does move,/At once to humble piety and love' (Jane Barker, 'The Prospect of a Landscape,' 1688). 'Humble piety' – Barker's moral emphasis marks an ideal quite different from the self-contained and self-centered retirement praised by her predecessors. We have already seen morality settle like a summer haze into the rural world of Dryden's kinsman Driden. It settles too into the modest estate wished for by John Pomfret in the most popular of all poems of rural retirement, *The Choice* (1700). Like Otway in his 'Epistle to R. D.,' Pomfret chooses a garden with a rivulet, reading of classical poetry, a genteel life with food and drink, friends and a woman, and freedom. Unlike Otway, he keeps moral ends in view. He asks for enough 't'oblige a friend,' relieve 'the sons of poverty' and 'objects of true pity,' and 'feed the stranger and the neighboring poor' (ll. 35–46). His friends are to be 'loyal and pious,' his lady reasonable, constant, prudent, wise, brave, regular in conduct, civil, a sort of nubile Girl Scout with whom he retires to an intimacy that compromised him as a clergyman in 1700 but that is far less boldly explicit in its sexuality than Otway's (ll. 98–139). Pomfret also offers 'Whate'er assistance I had power to bring/T'oblige my country or to serve my king,' whether 'My tongue, my pen, my counsel, or my sword' (ll. 142–4); nothing would disgust the Otway of the 'Epistle' more. For him and other writers of the Restoration, the country was sweet as a refuge from aggressive knaves and

45

fools; for Pomfret and other writers of the 1690s and earlier eighteenth century, it was sweet as a place to live. *The Choice* says not a word against city and court, whose exhausting and terrifying rage for power are no longer an issue.

The country's positive value in and of itself, rather than as an escape from the city, is not new, but reminiscent of an attitude common throughout the first half of the seventeenth century. At the end of the century and in the early eighteenth, however, retirement poetry did develop two new emphases. One, connected with the benevolence of ideal country figures like Dryden's honoured kinsman and Pomfret's 'I,' makes the country a revelation of God's benevolence. The other revalues the life of real country people, simple if not wholly innocent, to produce what I earlier unkindly called 'yokel' pastoral. Thomas Purney's Argument to 'Paplet: or Love and Innocence,' the first of Purney's *Pastorals after the Simple Manner of Theocritus* (1717), tells us that 'Cubbin, the writer so called, was acquainted with Paplet and Soflin. All young was Paplet and ignorant of love: Soflin more experienced, but equally tender and innocent.' These two go out at evening 'to a bush of a sweet and pleasant situation, to tattle of love and of Collikin, Soflin's lover'; Cubbin, the hypothesized writer of the poem, overhears them and later tries vainly to ease Paplet's mind about Collikin. This action is delivered, part through dialogue and part through narrative, in a style both simple and deliberately antique, smacking of Spenser's *Shepheardes Calendar* updated; I do not dare quote any of it, for fear of being thought to have chosen passages maliciously. Ambrose Philips, the best poet of this mode, had the lethal misfortune of having his pastorals (1706–10) compared with Pope's, written at about the same time and with a skill that paints credible flowers over barren content. Philips lacked that skill, and remains less successful not only than Pope but also than other writers in Pope's more lacquered and gilded Virgilian style, for instance Elijah Fenton in his 'Florelio' (written 1703?). The chief literary value of Philips's dispute with Pope is that it produced Gay's charming, hedge-straddling *Shepherd's Week*, mentioned earlier. Historically, though, Philips and Purney are of interest for having revived an English (Spenserian) rather than Latin mode, and for their insistence, however awkward the results, on a somewhat more realistic treatment of Arcadians who were English. Their new mode, dignifying the sincere feelings athrob in rustic hearts, also has ideological implications in the eighteenth century and beyond.

Still more important is the emphasis on the country, physical nature, as a display of God's benevolence. If Restoration poets had embraced the Epicurean ease preached by the Roman Lucretius, the next generation preferred a different Lucretian theme: the study of nature as a glorious machine. To most of them, as to the poet Henry Needler in 'A Vernal Hymn in Praise of the Creator,' a 'thinking soul' armed with a 'piercing eye' was sure to 'see the various marks of skill divine/That in each part of Nature's system shine,' and feel impelled 'in grateful lays/To sing his bounteous Maker's solemn praise.' These men did not look for cabalistic signs in natural objects nor did they tremble with mystic communion; their trembling was for joy at the visible, scientific evidence of God's bounty and intelligence in the ordered plenitude of the universe. Here were metaphysical knowledge and promise both. Man's understanding of a world he did not make fell as far short of the Maker's understanding as man's local benevolence fell short of the divine bounty it imitated. In Heaven, as Norris and Mary Chudleigh insisted, some of this darkened vision would grow lighter; on earth, one could do no better than wander in the country, where one was alive to God's creation and its promise.

Sometimes the poet launched into panegyric – which, as I have suggested, was the dominant mode of religious verse – with a rudder of argument that combined both external nature and the mind of the observer. The most ambitious religious poem of the early eighteenth century, Sir Richard Blackmore's widely read *Creation* (1712) 'proves' the wisdom and bounty of God 'from the various marks of wisdom and artful contrivance which are evident to observation in the several parts of the material world and the faculties of the human soul' ('A Summary Account of the Following Poem'). This kind of argument, relating physical nature and metaphysics (and therefore called 'physicotheology'), demanded a great deal of versified scientific description such as was rare in earlier English poetry, but which flourished in the eighteenth century. Less didactic retirement poems, which a freight of science would have overloaded, also celebrated universal design, as does John Gay's otherwise unreligious *Rural Sports* (1713): while 'Her borrowed lustre growing Cynthia lends,' the speaker sees the heavens as planetary systems, 'Millions of worlds. . ./Which round their suns their annual circles steer,' an order that makes 'Sweet contemplation elevate my sense,/While I survey the works of providence' (ll. 109–14).

Morality, a value placed on the country for itself, a focus on nature as visible evidence of divine order – these were the new emphases of the 1690s and the early eighteenth century. At the same time, themes of power, hedonism, and eroticism began to fade, so much so that the eloquent religious poet Isaac Watts (b. 1674) had to apologize for his use of erotic imagery in his earlier work: 'Different ages have their different airs and fashions of writing. It was much more the fashion of the age when these poems were written to treat of divine subjects in the style of Solomon's Song than it is at this day, which will afford some apology for the writer in his younger years' (note to the poems 'peculiarly dedicated to divine love'). Love poetry itself tended toward the gallant style of mid-seventeenth-century courtiers like Waller. Pope's mentor and friend George Granville, Lord Lansdowne, who was commended in his youth by Waller and flattered him by imitation thereafter, offers the best example of this style in his numerous poems to 'Myra'. Like Restoration nymphs, Myra is sometimes unkind but – unlike them – not in order to gloat, sometimes kind but not as a preface to melting in ecstatic embraces. Granville achieves elegance by shortening his emotional range. He keeps, as do his fellow love poets of the early eighteenth century, to the socially bounded. No doubt the poems themselves are no more artistically conventional than those of the Restoration, but one feels a pressure of social convention upon their content. Love poetry is one of the few genres in which the reader really varies his sense of the work as he is persuaded that the speaker is more or less sincere; one who comes from Restoration verse is not persuaded by that of the early eighteenth century. The pleasures that it offers – and there are some – are minor, real but minor. For some readers, me among them, elegance without sincerity makes for more agreeable poetry than sincerity without elegance (or other marks of cultivated intelligence). Sooner a whole volume of Granville than one piece of artless blurting in pastoral, or any other style. Still, if one goes back to Rochester or Sedley one does not have to make this choice.

The fascination with power, which spiced Restoration poetry, gives way more and more to an eighteenth-century interest in contexts and placement. Forms that exalted individuals, like some love poetry and most highflown panegyric, yield to those that locate individuals within God's dispensation, England's controlling needs, and the rules of society. For some kinds of poem, this is a slight shift of stress; for others, a new life or a sentence to hard labor in the hands of versifying hacks. In the 1690s the Pindaric suffered dilution in favor of more controlled odes, where parts had formal placement; of more generally patriotic poems, where heroes are emphatically social heroes; and of epistles and topographical poems, where the poet's psychological ramblings take cues from another person or a set environment. By no means is this an absolute change nor is any of my second group of forms new. There is, though, a change in popularity, in felt responsiveness to what Englishmen wanted to say and read. Political satire retains its character, though affairs of state dominated men's anxieties less, and the quality of political verse started declining in the 1690s. Social satire, though, did alter. It moved toward the playful and the equivocal, where an unresolved play of values offered different perspectives on the object. In physicotheological poetry, what the speaker sees and hears and thinks takes a place within a metaphysical context. Throughout these various changes, order does not overcome energy, but one might advance the notion – as gently and gingerly as sweeping notions ought to be advanced – that a balance between order and energy becomes more and more part of the content of poems. Order in Restoration poems frequently comes from the power of the writer or the protagonist. After 1690 it comes more frequently than before from the internal dynamics of what the poem describes, in the tradition begun at mid-century by Denham in *Cooper's Hill*.

2 Style

Style, more than anything else about the poetry of our period, has puzzled readers. Few of them have cared to blame themselves, and they have reacted, often enough, with incredulity and contempt; or they have proposed theories to explain why eighteenth-century lovers of Shakespeare put up with such staid metaphors, such stilted diction, with largely standardized speakers who intone generalities, invoke personifications, call birds 'plumy people' (Thomson, *Spring*, l. 165), and dignify the unworthy, as in James Grainger's praise of 'lofty cassia,' a laxative whose 'long pods, full fraught with nectared sweets,/Relieve the bowels from their lagging load' (*The Sugar Cane*, 4:513–17). The theories to deal with this alleged stuffiness, this pomp and circumlocution, are various: cast-iron 'rules,' bourgeois pretentiousness, fawning before classical formulas, too tender a solicitude for the possible slowness or inattention of a well-bred public, or maybe simply the lack of true feeling in a pedestrian, commonsensical, self-satisfied age. Except for the last of these explanations, which is just silly, these all have a kind of truth for marking the sources of poetic failure. One could make a similar list for any other age or idiom, since every age and idiom has its own forms of rules, pretentiousness, formulas, and deference. What such lists cannot do is to show that seeming failures of style, seeming external constraints, may have a firm, complex conceptual base. When that base is understood, and the critic begins to ask the appropriate questions instead of the inherited ones, much disdain evaporates and many theories previously needed can be tossed away.

Positional poetry

I would argue that the conceptual base for the poetry discussed in this study sprang largely from the assumption that poetry should be what I shall call 'positional.' The term is mine; its force, though, comes from a distinction made by the modern linguist Roman Jakobson between 'metaphor' and 'metonymy.' I prefer to save 'metonymy' for its precise literary sense – a figure of speech in which one word replaces another with which it is closely connected – and use 'positional style' or 'Jakobson's metonymy' for something broader: the linguistic placing of an

49

object within a context. The context may be something more comprehensive than the object (table : furniture, house), another member of the same group (table : chair), or something connected to the object by nature or logic (table : Banquet). Jakobson opposes metonymy, in his expanded sense of 'positioning faculty' or 'contextual focus,' to metaphor, which governs relationships of similarity and identity. He postulates that the mental functions typical of his 'metonymy' and 'metaphor' are fundamental to the way we comprehend the world: the essence of individual objects ('metaphor') on the one hand, the contextual classifications for those objects ('metonymy') on the other.

As to literary modes, Jakobson links metaphor with heavily symbolic poetry and metonymy with the ever enlarging and defining perspectives of the realistic novel. To say that in these respects eighteenth-century poetry is closer to the realistic novel than to symbolic poetry is not to accuse it of being prosy. Symbolic poems tend to be primarily self-contained objects, specifying the peculiar nature of their worlds by metaphor, often irrational and multiple. Realistic novels point to the real, shared world, specified through much familiar detail: painted plaster figurines on the mantel, the dull red of a winter sunset, the twitching eyelid, the smell of old socks. These details work by the form of metonymy known as 'synecdoche,' the use of a part for the whole or the whole for a part. Eighteenth-century poetry, like the novel, tends to point to the real world in such favorite genres as satire, didactic verse, and topographical poetry. It also, like the novel, employs synecdoche very freely, for example in satire or didactic verse, and to summon up particular images in poetry of description. The poetic rationale for these 'positional' or 'metonymous' techniques differs from the rationale in novels, but the techniques themselves are similar.

We can apply the logic of Jakobson's 'metonymy' to four obvious subjects: first, the poem itself as a constructed object with words, lines, rhymes, stanzas, genre, and internal patterning, all put together at a given time and for a given purpose; second, the narrative voice that speaks the poem to an audience or in the presence of one; third, the speaker's mind and eye which perceive the things that the poem is about; and fourth, those objects themselves, the represented contents of the poem. One would expect a 'positional poetry' to lay special importance on establishing contexts within which each of these four subjects – poem, speaker, perceiver, and content – can be defined. The poem as constructed object should be related to other poems, the speaker to other members of his society, the perceiver to the perceived objects, and the perceived objects to each other and to larger defining categories.

Of these, the relationship most apparent to modern readers is that between a given late seventeenth- or eighteenth-century poem and other poems, since so many major works of the period assiduously define themselves through genre or allusiveness to earlier poems and poetic traditions. One repeatedly finds versions of the heroic, the pastoral, the traditional ode, sometimes used straight, sometimes ironically, sometimes with the intention of great change in the old meaning of the form involved. Such works announce their poetic citizenship not out of caution or awe for the past but out of a desire for location within the shared, understood esthetic space that poetry, as a social heritage, occupies. In addition, these works draw not only on the procedures of genres like the heroic, the pastoral, and the ode, but also on contexts of value that the genres imply. These accepted patterns, as in the mock-heroic, often end up markedly altered; none the less, the poems need them as agents of definition.

The speaker of the poem anchors it by having his own place, his relation to his audience, defined: in positional poetry we do not discover an ambiguous 'I' confiding his hopes, whimsies, and brand of nostalgia. If the speaker is idiosyncratic, he or she will be a dramatic figure whose personality and character, brought out by a specific situation, have a larger psychological context in terms of which the audience understands his point of view. One thinks of such loud egoists as Rochester's braggart lover Bajazet ('A Very Heroical Epistle') or Dryden's Flecknoe, of Pope's infatuated and captive Eloisa, or, for all that, the spattered, harassed, sick, and sickened 'Pope' of the *Epistle to Dr. Arbuthnot*. When the poem does not assert such a larger context for its speaker, he is likely to be a typical figure, synecdochic for all men or for some conventional kind of person (shepherd, preacher, poet). He, occasionally she, serves as a kind of dramatic chorus or spokesman, often a companion. Eighteenth-century poets, quite unlike modern ones, rarely seek to complicate this speaking figure by giving him (or themselves, through him) a sharply individual voice, an 'authentic' expression of a singular psyche. They shared stylistic ideals and often styles. The poet who strove to distinguish his voice from his fellows' was likely to be advertising his disaffection from them, like Charles Churchill, whose ferocious satires flaunt his honest rage and his contempt for the hirelings in the poetic establishment. But whether the speaker has a clear personality or not, his train of ideas almost never grows private and rarely, except in some odes, grows at all obscure. The flow of his ideas and our responses proceeds in accord with a publicly apprehensible train of associations – by resemblance, contiguity, or causation – so that each element has its position clear within the process of thought and feeling.

In the positional style, then, poems interact with previous poems, and speakers with audiences who appraise and vicariously engage in the speakers' roles. One might expect, by extension, that the perceiver in the poem (usually the same as the speaker) ought to interact with what he or she perceives, and that the objects that the poem describes or sets forth ought to interact with each other. The balance between perceiver and perceived exists in both discursive and descriptive poetry, though in different forms. Discursive poetry begins with concepts and elaborates them with scenes, so that we move from the speaker's mind to what he imagines or sees. Poems like Johnson's *Vanity of Human Wishes* exhibit a great zest for documentation in which the external world confirms the speaker's reflections through emblems and synecdoches: Wolsey, Villiers, Swedish Charles, drivelling Swift, the golden canopy, the glittering plate, the patron and the jail. Descriptive poetry generally works from scene to idea. Nature alone has no profound meaning, but its interplay with the perceiving mind, capable of positional action (inference, analogy), can make its trees, snow, birds into emblems, witnesses of order, or indices of the great context of being in which human life must go on. In both kinds of poetry, discursive or descriptive, we enter a world that demands a very busy syntax. Object jostles or summons object with an internal energy that the speaker often seems hardly to control. Propositions, the 'objects' of discursive poetry, of course crackle with an independent life, especially if they are witty; but natural objects in descriptive poetry need not. In the eighteenth-century, they too assert their places with a great buzz of defining adjectives and present participles, as objects in action, like the speeding atoms in the physics of Hobbes, the circling and falling particles in the cosmos of Newton, the flowing of vibrations (objects turned pure energy) in the perceptual systems of David Hume and David Hartley. Those same perceptual systems, indeed, also describe the mind of poetic speakers and readers as working by association of ideas, which is itself a jostling and summoning process: the mind that perceives the poem works analogously with the objects in the poem it perceives.

Jakobson's theory sets metaphor over against metonymy, and in fact positional poetry in the eighteenth century does subjugate metaphors. Much of their function in enlivening verse is taken over by imagery and description. So is much of their function in governing feeling. Little eighteenth-century verse, for example, lets metaphors move as far toward the purely emotional as Burns's 'my luve's like a red red rose/That's newly sprung in June,' where the terms of the comparison are ambiguous. By far the most common metaphors have structurally analogous tenor and vehicle, like James Merrick's 'Bid a tide of sorrow flow,/And whelm the soul in deepest woe' ('An Ode to Fancy,' ll. 5–6). By mid-century the great bulk of such metaphors appear through personification, as in Francis Fawkes's 'A Vernal Ode': 'Enough has Winter's hand severe/Hurled all his terrors round' (ll. 9–10). When overt and uncommon metaphors do emerge, they tend to work as a sort of zeugma (juxtaposition or linking of unlike objects), where the poet intends to stress differences between tenor and vehicle for the sake of wit; the objects in the tenor and the vehicle are not equated, but compared for the sake of judging them, as when Smart in *The Hilliad* addresses Hill, his butt, as one 'Whose baseless fame by vanity is buoyed,/Like the huge earth, self-centered in the void' (ll. 9–10).

Once again, although poets may introduce descriptions through metaphor, simile, or implied comparison, the strong force of poetic metaphor in creating identity seldom exists. Perhaps an exception should be made for another occasion for unusual metaphors, when the primary reference is not to the poem as a whole but to the nature of the speaker, whether a witty narrator (as in the example from Smart, above) or a speaker in the throes of individual passion. In representing passion, however, metaphor lags behind other figures of speech. Elaborate metaphors – 'metaphysical' conceits, for instance – seemed implausible in the mouths of the overwrought, and dense metaphors, which might have been psychologically plausible, were thought to make the reader pause to decipher what he should be responding to with immediacy of heart. No theory, no practice, could be more contrary to the modern notion that metaphor distinguishes poetic energy. Imagery, so richly used in eighteenth-century poetry, does provide a mark of energy, when taken as a stimulus to cooperation between reader and text; more of this later. The movement of the poem – trains of argument, thought, and feeling – provides another such mark, as the reader engages with the mental, emotional, and perceptual processes behind the speaking voice. Those who demand metaphor instead will usually, not always, come away unsatisfied.

Unsatisfied, perhaps, but not dissatisfied if such readers understand how metonymy, in Jakobson's sense, lies behind the poetic strategy of a Gray, a Thomson, or a Pope. The logic of 'positional' poetry might lead one to expect and, with the blessings of history at their richest, to find poetry like this:

> The curfew tolls the knell of parting day,
> The lowing herd winds slowly o'er the lea,
> The ploughman homeward plods his weary way,
> And leaves the world to darkness and to me. . . .
>
> Beneath those rugged elms, that yew-tree's shade,
> Where heaves the turf in many a mouldering heap,
> Each in his narrow cell forever laid,
> The rude forefathers of the hamlet sleep.
>
> The breezy call of incense-breathing morn,
> The swallow twittering from the straw-built shed,
> The cock's shrill clarion or the echoing horn
> No more shall rouse them from their lowly bed. . . .
>
> Let not Ambition mock their useful toil,
> Their homely joys and destiny obscure;
> Nor Grandeur hear, with a disdainful smile,
> The short and simple annals of the poor.   (ll. 1–4, 13–20, 29–32)

These lines from Gray's *Elegy*, perhaps the most famous and consistently admired poem of the century, have a great deal 'wrong' with them. They certainly lack interesting metaphors, with 'sleep' and 'bed' as substitutes for 'death' and 'grave,' or with personifications ('Ambition') pulling one from specific identities to the abstract. About half the nouns have adjectives attached to them, but some of those seem useless for meaning: at curfew, of course the day is 'parting'; the ploughman's plod conveys weariness without explicit statement; clarions must by nature be shrill. Elms and yew have no mythological or symbolic meaning at work here, and if the yew is unavoidable in a graveyard one can still wonder why elms rather than oaks, beeches, or aspens. Worst of all to some tastes, the moralizing is direct, not oblique, not wound about by philosophic musings, not glimmering through the dark glass of symbols.

One may look at Gray's lines in a different way, noticing the complex positioning of poetic objects as the poetry bobs between the particular and the general, perception and interpretation, given objects and the analogues they suggest but clearly differ from. Personification, as in Grandeur's smile, combines sensory and moral contexts. Objects fit into spatial contexts, too, so that the eye is led from the 'ivy-mantled tower' (in the stanza, unquoted here, before the elm is

mentioned) down to the elm – a tree vertical in basic form but broader and lower
than the tower – to the yew to the mounded turf of the graves. The mixture of
cyclical life and stony permanence in the ivy-mantled tower is appropriate too for
the elm rugged with seasonal leaves, the evergreen yew, and the graveyard turf:
under the living and dying shagginess of persistent life, 'rude forefathers' may well
'sleep.'

Their sleep, of course, is an analogue of sleep at day's end with which the poem
begins, and this explains 'parting' and 'weary.' 'Knell' goes too far: its insistence
on death betrays more about the speaker's mood than about a mere curfew, and its
ominousness (reinforced by the onomatopoeia of 'toll'/'knell') needs the calming
anticlimax of 'parting day.' Its threat is again muffled by the next line,
syntactically parallel, which also starts with a dull, perhaps mournful, but this
time obviously harmless sound, 'lowing,' and which describes a literal, harmless
parting. This process of analogy and modification then appears in the ploughman
of line 3, parting like the herd, but marked by an explicit weariness so as to join him
to, yet divide him – morally as well as physically – from the world-weary speaker.
In passing from the material world (bell, day) to animals to a man seen as human
figure, the speaker has come closer to himself as a human consciousness, capable of
the analogy between the exhausted ploughman, his own state of mind, and the
metaphorically extended exhaustion of the 'sleep[ing]' ploughmen buried in the
graveyard. 'Parting' and 'weary,' the adjectives with which we began, are needed
not to explain the nouns that they modify but to place those nouns (or the objects
to which those nouns refer) in a sequence. The same holds true for 'shrill' before
'clarion.' The clarion contrasts with the softer twittering of the swallows, as the
sounds become progressively less diffuse (the morn's unspecified 'call,' the
continuous twitter, the sudden piercing clarion, the repeated functional sound of
the horn); and their sources progressively more human (the general morn, the
wild swallow nesting and using the straw analogously with the farmer, the
domesticated and useful barnyard cock, the horn-blowing shepherd or cowherd).

Given that the adjectives keep situating the objects in scenic and poetic
relationships, one might expect those that are sensory to appeal principally to
senses that determine relationships. Sight, hearing, and muscle sense
(kinaesthesia) – this last working in empathy with seen movement, like the
ploughman's plod – should predominate over taste, smell, and touch, which deal
more with the object itself than with its position. The three dominant senses
provide 'lowing,' 'rugged,' 'narrow,' 'straw-built,' 'shrill,' and 'echoing,' with only
one adjective, 'incense-breathing,' representing smell and one more, 'breezy,'
touch – and both these suggest spatial movement, the approach of day. 'Breezy'
and 'incense-breathing' also, as it happens, refer to action at a distance, as
adjectives of smell and touch often do not and as those of taste almost never do.
Eighteenth-century positional poetry, except with certain dramatic speakers, likes
to keep perceiver and perceived apart. The speaker scans the world as an observer,
the witness of a prospect separate from him and which he cannot affect. Sight,
hearing, and kinaesthesia suit this posture, since sight and empathic kinaesthesia
(muscular movement in sympathy with someone or something else) always work

at a distance, and hearing typically does. The dominant senses, not so coinciden-
tally, have a public esthetic status in visual arts, auditory arts, and arts of
movement like the dance, whereas gourmet dining (no doubt unfairly),
perfumery, and massages with fur and silk have not yet had Muses, esthetic
treatises, and government subsidies assigned to them. Finally, an appeal to the
dominant senses produces clear and distinct ideas much more often than one to
taste, touch, or smell. What sensory impression is produced by 'sun'? by 'carrot'? I
suspect that for most people 'sun' brings to mind a radiant disc rather than a
sensation of warmth, and 'carrot' a narrow orange cone rather than a slightly
springy hardness, a crunch in the mouth, and thin, rather sweet juice trickling
over the tongue. If I am right, an appeal to the dominant senses will create a scene,
a context within which objects have position, more readily than would an appeal
to senses that are vaguer and more private.

Gray plainly hopes to create scenes and fragments of scenes. To do so, he uses
synecdoche to evoke wholes: a church at twilight or the flurrying of swallows in a
shed strikes the imagination into creative life. Once struck, the imagination
continues to enlarge on the text; the use of obvious synecdoche, the obvious stress
on scenes, encourage a synecdochic, scenic habit of reading. For poetry so given to
personification as mid-century lyrics, that habit needed cultivation. Readers had
to be ready to envision the mocking Grandeur and disdainfully smiling Ambition
of Gray's *Elegy*, and so they were. As Jean Hagstrum says about personifications in
The Sister Arts (1958), 'a reader trained to see pictures in poetry would see one even
when the poet gave him only the slightest visual hint' (p. 267). In terms of this
training, the positional style is not only a manner of writing but also a coaching
into shared expectations, a style that needs and feeds a certain manner of response.
We find that a large proportion of the metaphors in eighteenth-century poetry too
encourage scenic response by making the non-sensory sensory, as in Gray's 'Their
sober wishes never learned to stray' or '[his merits and frailties] alike in trembling
hope repose' (*Elegy*, ll. 74, 127). These do not present objects but rather evoke
kinds of scenes and imaginative behavior, the bases for the positional mode.

The details in Gray's *Elegy* gain positions from the movement of the poem and
from the way they stimulate the reader to imagine contexts for them. Still a third
principle works here, that of the genre itself. In Gray's and other elegies, the
speaker inducts us into his experience through mournful scenes and reflections – or
sometimes tender ones – by which a situation is appraised. His coming toward full
appraisal, here a full acceptance, determines the positional value of the successive
elements of the poem. The genre sets up a pattern that the poem fulfills.

Narratives, poems of reasoning, and panegyrics or satires fulfill patterns too,
different ones, naturally, from elegies. Each of these genres implies a certain subject
to be 'covered': a plot or plots in narrative, a topic in poems of reasoning, a
paragon or a body of vices in panegyric and satire. One might call such types
'encyclopaedic' in their obligation to fill a given conceptual space. Each has
certain traditional ways to fill that space, as is suggested by the rough
correspondence each bears to one of the Aristotelian modes of oratory. Panegyric
and satire resemble 'demonstrative' oratory, speeches of praise or blame; poems of

reasoning, 'deliberative' oratory or speeches about policy; and narrative poetry, 'forensic' oratory, which deals with moral values through case histories. Like the oratorical modes, the poetic have implicit within them a set of rubrics to be dealt with so as to 'cover' the subject; and these heads often prescribe in part the larger poetic order. Narratives, of course, take shape from their plots. Arguments, as has been clear from the poems discussed in the previous chapter, follow conventions of exposition, thrust and counterthrust, rebuttal, and peroration. In panegyric and satire, along with conventions of praise and dispraise (lineage, achievements, destiny and other such topics), one finds patterning through analogy, whether metaphoric emblems of glory (panegyric), historical comparisons (panegyric and satire), social catalogues (satire), or allusory narrative sequences. Non-narrative modes, too, abound in the forms of argument, without necessarily its substance, so that they keep referring one to processes of causation and inference. They make conspicuous use of maxims, for instance, behind which lie implicit or overt trains of logic. The positional style flourishes in these traditional genres.

Descriptive poetry may be equally 'encyclopaedic' in trying to deal with a prospect from a hill, the process of growing hops, or the manifestations of a season. But despite the model of Virgil's *Georgics*, this kind of poetry has no traditional set body of topics and no built-in connections. Even eighteenth-century readers had complaints about the best work of the type, James Thomson's *Seasons* (1726–46), written in the Miltonic style popular for long, serious poems throughout the century. Dr Johnson, protesting against James Thomson's 'clouds of words,' claimed to have been able to read a passage while omitting every other line (*Life*, 11 April 1776). With a bit of tinkering, one can:

> Now when the cheerless empire of the sky
> And fierce Aquarius stain the inverted year,
> Scarce spreads o'er ether the dejected day.
> His struggling rays, in horizontal lines,
> Weak, wan, and broad, now skirt the southern sky
> And, shading all, the prostrate world resign.
> Light, life, and joy the dubious day forsake,
> Deep-tinged and damp; and congregated clouds
> Involve the face of things. Thus Winter falls,
> Through nature shedding influence malign.   (*Winter*, ll. 41–59)

The passage almost makes sense this way, and anyhow, images keep luring one from too much fuss about meaning. As I will suggest, an eighteenth-century reader would have been especially susceptible to being lured in this way, so that Johnson was right to point out the dangers of his luxurious style. Suppose, however, that one compares this piece of poetic hopscotch with what Thomson really wrote:

> Now when the cheerless empire of the sky
> To Capricorn the Centaur-Archer yields,

And fierce Aquarius stains the inverted year,
Hung o'er the farthest verge of heaven, the sun
Scarce spreads o'er ether the dejected day.
Faint are his gleams, and ineffectual shoot
His struggling rays in horizontal lines
Through the thick air; as clothed in cloudy storm,
Weak, wan, and broad, he skirts the southern sky;
And, soon descending, to the long dark night,
Wide-shading all, the prostrate world resigns. (ll. 41–51)

The whole passage deals with the placement of objects, beginning with sky, Capricorn, and 'the Centaur-Archer'; and in fact, the principle of Jakobson's 'metonymy' governs it in terms of perception, of mood (emotional relation to a developing whole), and of procedure through association of ideas. We perceive the scene through visual and kinaesthetic sensory images, which enforce on our minds the play of interactions described. Even the adjectives 'dejected' and 'horizontal' stress their interplay because, as often in eighteenth-century poems, such words have etymological meanings as well as common ones: 'horizontal' relates the rays to the seen horizon, and 'dejected' (Lat. *dejectus*, 'thrown down') gives us a placing action as well as a mood. Thomson keeps varying directions and degrees of energy, so that the cyclical motion of the constellations takes the passive form of yielding (l. 42), then the active form of staining (l. 43), while the sun hangs, struggles, is hidden, and finally resigns. Such a mixture of energies demands a kind of physical participation by the reader, in muscular empathy with the verse. The reader also participates in the associative process by which, for example, we move, through alliteration and distinctions of species, from Capricorn (a beast) to 'the Centaur-Archer' (beast and warrior) to 'fierce Aquarius' whose water 'stains' the new year, 'inverted' suggesting both the calendar change and Aquarius's overturned ewer. As we pass from cycle (the zodiac) to moment (the presence of the faint sun) to cycle (the sun's movement), association of ideas takes us from 'inverted' to hanging over the verge to the casting down of 'dejected' (l. 45), and then, after a weak struggle and skirting action, to another descent (l. 50). The extension of the rays across the horizon (ll. 46–7), and then the sense of the sun's own breadth (ll. 48–9), similarly associate with the ideas of the sun's arc of passage, and the 'wide-shading' and 'prostrate world' at the end of the passage. Thomson is describing an action in the external world and also an action of the perceiving, empathizing mind. These are not identical in pattern – for example, Sagittarius really yields to Capricorn, though the order of the verse has Capricorn preceding Sagittarius (l. 42) – but they are analogous. To the reader who takes his proper position toward *Winter*, there can be no question of plucking out half the lines, so as to leave Thomson's meaning but to ruin his closely considered (and not in the least 'cloudy') texture of experience.

Thomson's descriptive style differs from Gray's in that he uses a typical rather than a dramatic speaker. More of the emotion in the passage, therefore, comes from perceived nature rather than the voice of the reflective perceiver: we are in empathy with Gray's speaker, but with Thomson's scene. For this reason, Thomson makes use of that transfer of feeling to which the nineteenth-century critic Ruskin gave the misleading name of 'pathetic fallacy.' He peoples the winter sky with the zodiac and gives us a sun that skulks along; but, as is typical of eighteenth-century poets, lays less emphasis on the anthropomorphic qualities of objects than on their independent life in terms of movement and will, less on their imagined states of mind than on states that cause emotion in the reader. Thomson's use of the 'pathetic fallacy,' to interweave nature as objective fact with nature as perceived process, does not come from the morbid personal imagination that Ruskin feared. Partly it results from Aristotle's stress on achieving vividness (his word is 'energeia'; *Rhetoric* 3.xi.1–4) in poems; partly from the blurring of traditional lines between spirit and matter which one finds throughout philosophical writing from Hobbes on.

Other characteristics of 'positional' poetry appear in Thomson and Gray both. *The Seasons* joins the georgic or topographical genre, originated by Virgil, with an adaptation of Milton's style. It slavishly imitates neither, but makes its literary parentage known. So does Gray's *Elegy*, filled as it is with echoes from Dante (the curfew of the first line) to Petrarch ('trembling hope' of the next-to-last), as well as their predecessors and successors aplenty. Neither works through striking metaphors or precisely described individual objects, yet they evoke vivid images. Objects in action, positioning themselves in relation to other objects, crowd the poems of Gray and Thomson. The 128 lines of Gray's *Elegy* contain only two passive verbs, where the passive insists on a passivity before the force of destiny: 'Perhaps in this neglected spot is laid/Some heart once pregnant with celestial fire' (ll. 45–6) and 'many a flower is born to blush unseen' (l. 55). Gray makes no use of the copula 'is' or 'are.' In the first 250 lines of *Winter* Thomson uses two passives. One specifically indicates perception ('Long groans are heard' (l. 192)) and the other, the divine power ('Air, Sea, and Earth are hushed at once' (l. 201)). Of his half-dozen copulas in these lines, one is an imperative ('Be these my theme' (l. 3)) and another a statement of perception ('Nor is the night unwished' (l. 52)); two further uses of 'to be' employ it with the force of 'to exist' ('Where are you now? and what is your amount?' (l. 211)). If Gray's quiet musings and Thomson's onrush of winter both similarly reject the passive, with strikingly few exceptions, and display worlds of constant interaction, one has reason to suspect that the positional style may dominate descriptive poetry. The particular grammatical evidence of the style in the use of 'to be' appears less persuasive for verse – like Pope's *Essay on Criticism* – that depends on propositional assertions and hypothesized laws ('A little learning is a dangerous thing'; 'Some neither can for wits nor critics pass,/As heavy mules are neither horse nor ass'). Yet even in a didactic poem contemporary with *The Seasons* and the *Elegy*, such as Akenside's *The Pleasures of Imagination* (1744), copulas and passives are generally avoided. In verse so given to adjectives, this transitive style of predication is especially telling.

Lines, phrases, syntax

Poem, speaker, perceiver and perceived, objects within the poem, the associative mind of the reader – all fit the pattern of the positional style, which in turn employs scene, personification, synecdoches, and the expectations of genre. In accord with this pattern, one would expect such poetry to be syntactically involved, so that each word, each idea has its proper place in the unit of the sentence. Such poetry should also bind line to line with care, and give each poetic unit an exact relationship to those around it. Nothing could be better suited to the two verse forms most common in the eighteenth century, the rhymed couplet (and its stanzaic variants) and Miltonic blank verse. Long stanzas, like Spenser's, waned in favor except in deliberate Spenserian imitations; and eighteenth-century versions even of that Restoration standby, the irregular ode, usually had stanzas made up of couplets and quatrains. Richard West's *Monody on the Death of Queen Caroline* (1737) may serve as an example. The twenty lines of its first stanza, albeit varied in length, turn into six couplets and two quatrains. Each of the twenty is end-stopped, and only one of the couplets (and neither of the quatrains) breaks so that its first line goes with what precedes it, the second with what follows. All the others are closed. Such an ode can make full use of the devices used to manage the couplet. So can those written in the simpler stanza most typical in the eighteenth century, rhyming aabccb, like James Merrick's 'The Benedicite Paraphrased':

> Light, from whose rays all beauty springs;
> Darkness, whose wide-expanded wings
>   Involve the dusky globe;
> Praise Him, who, when the heavens He spread,
> Darkness His thick pavilion made,
>   And light His regal robe.   (st. 13)

Similarly, Miltonic blank verse can stand for almost all the blank verse of the period, with only one prestigious exception, Robert Blair's evangelical monologue on death, *The Grave* (1743). Because so greatly admired a writer as Milton established the serious blank-verse tradition in English non-dramatic poetry, his model offered his successors the procedures they mastered and transformed for their own ends.

One can see how the couplet typically worked by taking some lines from an accomplished but hardly brilliant mid-century poet, James Cawthorn (1719–61), writing on a common subject in 'Of Taste: An Essay' (1756), where, like so many others, he treats architectural fads:

> Of late, 'tis true, quite sick of Rome and Greece,
> We fetch our models from the wise Chinese:
> European artists are too cold and chaste,

59

For Mandarin only is the man of taste,
Whose bolder genius, fondly wild to see
His grove a forest and his pond a sea,
Breaks out – and, whimsically great, designs
Without the shackles or of rules or lines.
Formed on his plans, our farms and seats begin
To match the boasted villas of Pekin.
On every hill a spire-crowned temple swells,
Hung round with serpents and a fringe of bells;
Junks and baloens along our waters sail,
With each a gilded cock-boat at his tail;
Our choice exotics to the breeze exhale
Within th'enclosure of a zigzag rail;
In Tartar huts our cows and horses lie,
Our hogs are fatted in an Indian sty,
On every shelf a joss divinely stares,
Nymphs laid on chintzes sprawl upon our chairs,
While o'er our cabinets Confucius nods
'Midst porcelain elephants and China gods.   (ll. 99–120)

Cawthorn treats each couplet as a unit, sometimes, as in the first two couplets quoted, composed of an antithesis, but more often, as in the rest of the passage, as a single conceptual element: the rhyme words ending each couplet after the first two are verb/noun so that the couplet has syntactic unity. This syntactic unity helps create the movement of the passage, which presents a different grammatical structure line by line and couplet by couplet for the first eight lines, and appropriately billows out of shape when 'bolder genius' 'breaks out' into a five-line sentence ('the man of taste,/Whose . . . rules or lines'). The fifth couplet ('Formed on his plans') resembles the first, and thereafter Cawthorn gives us the same grammatical structures again and again, to mock his catalogue of equivalent oriental beauties.

  Both where the lines mirror each other grammatically and where they do not, every couplet has its exact place in a spatial movement from absurd inflation ('His grove a forest and his pond a sea') where landscape echoes mind ('fondly wild,' 'whimsically great') through a series of diminutions, from farms and seats, to individual hills and waters, to railed-in exotic gardens, to huts and stys, and finally to salons choked with bibelots, with fragile idols, and with sprawling, painted nymphs. Cawthorn's exuberant imagination, which depicts elephants and gods crowded into cabinets and enormous Siamese barges (baloens) cruising on private estates, imitates and caricatures the ambitions of the Mandarin-loving man of taste. Trapped as this exuberance is within rigid, repeating couplet structures, we find the same effect of tension between content and syntax as we find between the masses of exotica and the confined British domesticity of shelves and cabinets that must accommodate them. Through sense and syntax both, the man of taste's 'breaking out' 'without shackles' turns into an act of absurd confinement.

Of course the specifics of Cawthorn's needs and procedures apply only here. The creative handling of the closed couplet, however, the skill in arranging the order of couplets, and the way in which he achieves a harmony of syntax and the demands of his verse form – these traits are usual among capable poets of the eighteenth century. I should add that Cawthorn shares the positional style we have discussed: vivid images without striking metaphors or precisely described individual objects, each object positioned (the whole passage is about inappropriate position), active verbs (only two copulas and one quite deliberate passive), typical speaker, place within generic convention. In tune with this style, chosen patterns of sound (assonance, alliteration, play of vowel sounds) and abstract patterns of syntax (prepositional phrase/noun/verb in one line, noun/verb/prepositional phrase in the next) add to one's sense of precise placement of words. Even the most casual reader, or perhaps I should say especially the most casual reader, is struck by the obvious care with which eighteenth-century poems in couplets are composed; one sometimes comes across modern folderol fitting that care in with an age of minuets, symmetrical periwigs, and tidy rationalism. At best, these are glib parallels. Cawthorn's control tells us, implicitly, that human activity – the activity the poem describes or the activity that *is* the poem – can be understood only by contrast, analogy, and other comparative measures that positioning makes possible.

The couplet itself, in Restoration and eighteenth-century poems, has no meaning: it is only a vehicle, unlike, say, the shaped poems of Herbert and Herrick. It does not imply completeness or finality with regard to its subject matter. One can argue, in fact, that its polish often contrasts ironically with the openness of the subject matter which it makes accessible to us but which it cannot tame. As with most other poetic forms, small and large, in the period, the couplet does not arise from the nature of the subject but from the needs of the speaker to make himself understood in presenting the subject to an audience. (Of course the nature of the subject enters into the speaker's decision about what form to use, but in order to be categorized, not directly expressed.) One of the poetic accomplishments of which writers from Waller to Pope were proudest, and reasonably so, was the development of the couplet as a public medium, flexible, unforced, musical, economical, an understandable means for understanding. Waller and his contemporaries – he himself gets from literary historians more credit than he deserves – developed the closed couplet with internal dynamics, free of the crabbedness that marks Jonson's and Donne's work, and yet kept from lapsing into flaccidity or rocking-horse regularity. Dryden improved it, Pope brought it to its peak.

To join strength and sweetness, these poets cultivated a balance whereby the four strong beats characteristic of an English pentameter line are divided two on each side of the caesura. For example, the passage from Cawthorn shows a good deal of variety in the placement of the caesura, but in most lines two strong beats on each side of it: late, true//Rome, Greece; fetch, models//wise Chinese; European artists//cold, chaste; Mandarin only//man, taste. Parallels and antitheses reinforce the balance of the line, and assure that the strong beats fall on

61

words crucial to the meaning. The archetype of the 'rough' poet, John Oldham, does not exhibit this line pattern; here is the opening of the third of the *Satires upon the Jesuits*:

> Long had the famed impostor found success,
> Long seen his damned fraternity's increase,
> In wealth and power, mischief and guile improved,
> By popes and pope-rid kings upheld and loved.

These lines have five strong beats and a balance of parallels only in line 3. The opening of *Absalom and Achitophel*, written very slightly later, exhibits the pattern to perfection:

> In pious times, ere priestcraft did begin,
> Before polygamy was made a sin;
> When man on many multiplied his kind,
> Ere one to one was cursedly confined;
> When nature prompted, and no law denied
> Promiscuous use of concubine and bride;

Dryden's caesura here works something like the bar in music, which was introduced into English notation as a regular feature in the mid-seventeenth century. He segregates similar rhythmic units without losing the forward impulsion one feels in Oldham. When this line pattern conflicts with specific poetic effects, Dryden or Pope drops it for a line or two, to achieve the majestic force with which *Religio Laici* opens:

> Dim, as the borrowed beams of moon and stars
> To lonely, weary, wandering travellers,
> Is reason to the soul: and as on high
> Those rolling fires discover but the sky,
> Not light us here, so reason's glimmering ray
> Was lent, not to assure our doubtful way,
> But guide us upward to a better day.

The extra stress in the first half of the first line, the suppression of caesura in the second, and the single stress before the caesura in the sixth – these deviate from the pattern, but derive from their contrast with it the emphasis on the crucial 'borrowed' (marked also by alliteration), the imitative straying of the description of the travelers, and the powerful insistence on 'lent.' The end of John Ogilvie's 'A Town Eclogue (1762) demonstrates other kinds of special effects within this mode:

> 'Thou lovely cause of all my woes!' he cried,
> Then sighed, and swore, and wept, and swore, and sighed;
> Groaned, fainted, sunk, then took a last adieu,

And breathed his soul out on the billet doux.

(Poems on Several Subjects, p. 120)

The two middle lines break with the pattern while they keep control by being balanced at mid-line, one by inversion (sighed, swore; swore, sighed), the other by dividing into a set of three verbs followed by a short clause. Again, part of the comedy in them comes from the metric play between the verb-clogged line and a half describing the fop's acts and the regular couplet pattern in the lines couched in his verbal idiom.

In the hands of Pope especially, but many of his contemporaries and successors too, most effects did not involve breaking the line pattern. The elements of the line gained their positions through the poet's reconciliation – not compromise – among three potentially warring pairs of demands: lucidity and flexibility, ease and economy, musicality and flow. Lucidity and flexibility give the elements position in regard to the reader's perception of the subject: the line must clarify the subject for the reader in the proper idiom. For instance, Donne's fourth satire (1597?) has the couplet, 'Ran from thence with such or more haste than one/Who fears more actions doth haste from prison' (ll. 153–4); Pope's version (1733) links 'ran' and 'haste,' explains how the jailed man gets out, distributes the stresses on the important words, and puts the rhyme to work: 'Ran out as fast as one that pays his bail/And dreads more actions hurries from a jail' (ll. 182–3). The idiom here is the civilized colloquialism basic to Pope's verse, capable of majesty, rage, dry irony, imitation of speech – in short, whatever Pope chooses – without destroying the pattern described. Ease and economy, two more demands on the line, define its position as speech to the reader. For social and esthetic reasons, he should not have to endure the stilted or contorted for the sake of meter, nor should he have to waste his time puzzling out meanings or yawning his way through superfluities. Socially, these vices would be thoughtless or boorish in spoken conversation and become more so in written verse; esthetically, affectations, enigmas, and wordiness tend to block that immediacy and continuity of response so prized in Restoration and eighteenth-century poetry. The last two demands, flow and musicality, define the position of each element in relation to the rest of the poem. Under 'flow,' I include such formal characteristics as development of imagery, of argument, of parallels and contrasts, of dramatic scenes, and such means of giving the verse coherence and forward movement. Under 'musicality,' I include sound patterns that are proper to the subject, supporting it by imitation and embellishment, and patterns of sound and rhythm that introduce a pleasing variety within the poem as read aloud. What is required here is like what is valued in setting a song to music, where a melody's beauty and fascination and its fitness for the words (mournful, laborious, turbulent) must be weighed. All three pairs of criteria enter into most poetry, but I dare say that at no time have all been so equally balanced in English poetry and so skillfully given their due as in our period.

Many eighteenth-century critics might have disagreed with me, and argued that the couplet paid too much for the exactness with which it could position each word and line. For them, the couplet, with its four-beat line pattern and its repetitive closure, made the author's control damagingly visible. A modern reader who thinks that it was the typical or dominant form of the age would be surprised by the frequency and vigor with which it was attacked. Some of the critics take their cue from Milton's prefatory note to *Paradise Lost*, in which he says in effect that he does not like the sound of rhyme, that it is a form of bondage, and that the ancients did not use it. Over and over, one finds objections that rhyme is 'jingling' or 'tinkling' or 'chiming,' that it 'fetters' or 'chains' or 'shackles' the author, and that it is Gothic rather than classical; indeed, Samuel Cobb discredits it – in his own obviously postlapsarian couplets – by telling us that Adam did not use it, that in Eden 'No shackling rhyme chained the free poet's mind;/Majestic was his style, and unconfined' (*Poetae Britannici* (1700?), p. 4). A more dire objection was that the French, that nation of fops and slaves, did use it. Brockhill Newburgh's *Essays Poetical* (1769) exhort 'bold British bards' to 'reassume/The free-born rights of Greece and Rome' while leaving 'slavish France in jingling strain' to 'hug the servile chain' (p. 39). Besides these protestors waving the banner of the classics, anti-French or anti-Gothic placards, and liberty caps daubed with the Union Jack, others raised more serious versions of their objections. Basically, three arguments appear: that visible ornament is bad in verse (or in some verse); that rhyme is merely an ornament, of dubious value; and that the couplet hinders long-breathed, expansive, exuberant poetry. The first two were debated openly in the Restoration, especially in relation to the drama, and the third had at least implicit currency then, as witness the rhyming but irregular Pindaric. All three kept their hold in the eighteenth century also, often used to hide expressions of taste behind a rational façade.

The upshot of these ongoing debates was a theory in rough accord with Mary Barber's principle in 'The Prodigy': 'Though rhyme serves the thoughts of great poets to fetter,/It sets off the sense of small poets the better' (*Poems* (1734), p. 22). Originally, as in Thomas Fletcher's preface to his *Poems* (1692), blank verse was for heroes, the proper subject for 'great poets'. 'Methinks,' writes Fletcher, that

> blank verse carries in it somewhat of the majesty of Virgil; when rhymes, even the most happy of them (after tedious pumping for them, and having good expressions balked for want of them), do but emasculate heroic verse, and give it an unnatural softness. In songs, pastorals, and the softer sorts of poetry, rhymes may perhaps be not unelegantly retained, but an hero dressed up in them looks like Hercules with a distaff.

Miltonic verse was to be Hercules' invincible club. In fact, theory and practice did not mesh well. The important epic translations of the Restoration and eighteenth century, Dryden's Virgil (1697), Pope's Homer (1715–26), Nicholas Rowe's Lucan (1718), and Christopher Pitt's Virgil (1740), like Thomas Creech's Lucretius (1682; a work on a grand imaginative scale, though not an epic) and Francis Fawkes's Apollonius Rhodius (1780), were all rhymed. So were Sir Richard Blackmore's epics at the turn of the eighteenth century and William

Wilkie's *Epigoniad* (1757), a Theban epic in 'simple and artless language' for 'an air of antiquity,' according to its author's prefatory comments. The other best known original epics of the period, Richard Glover's *Leonidas* (1737) and James Macpherson's Ossianic poems (1762–73), avoid rhyme and use many Miltonisms; but Glover's attempt at catching Leonidas' Spartan efficiency makes him laconic rather than expansive, and Macpherson imitates the primitive simplicity of the ancient Celts in poetic prose. Two other lofty and energetic modes, the great ode and Juvenalian satire, also rhymed. A few unrhymed odes exist, like James Ralph's 'The Muses' Address to the King' (1728), where blank verse is to offer 'the utmost latitude of numbers and boldness of expression' (p. ii), but the practice never caught on. Juvenalian satirists liked the snap and finality of the couplet and, uniformly as far as I know, followed Dryden's and Pope's examples. The poets who made most use of blank verse were authors of long descriptive poems, where the play of the mind over scenes and reflections needed syntactic equivalents and where all attention was to be on the percept rather than the poem. For these ends, great freedom of phrasing and lessened artifice were demanded.

The style may be seen in the passage from Thomson quoted earlier; or in one from Richard Jago, a poet pretty much on Cawthorn's level, though better known to scholars. Book 2 of his *Edge Hill* (1767) begins:

> The sun, whose eastern ray had scarcely gilt
> The mountain's brow while up the steep ascent
> With early step we climbed, now wide displays
> His radiant orb, and half his daily stage
> Hath nearly measured. From th' illumined vale
> The soaring mists are drained, and o'er the hill
> No more breathes grateful the cool balmy air,
> Cheering our search, and urging on our steps
> Delightful. See, the languid herds forsake
> The burning mead, and creep beneath the shade
> Of spreading tree, or shelt'ring hedge-row tall:
> Or in the mantling pool, rude reservoir
> Of wintry rains and the slow thrifty spring,
> Cool their parched limbs, and lave their panting sides.　　　　(ll. 1–14)

Jago obviously keeps to the positional style, not only in his use of language but also in his visual and kinaesthetic images. He carefully defines the interplay between the landscape, the animals, and the (typical) humans to whom pertain the emotive adjectives ('grateful,' 'delightful') and sympathetic projection ('parched limbs' are not visible but inferred). For example, the positioning of the 'mantling pool,' in terms of the winter and spring that have filled it, reflects a sense of pleasure at the benevolence of the seasonal cycle toward the beasts, as it evokes an alternate temporal cycle to that of misty morning and hot midday. There is less complex use of the positional style in this passage of Jago's than in the earlier passage of

65

Thomson's – less happens, characteristically, in poems by writers of Jago's class than in those by writers of Thomson's – but the men share the same conception of what poetic style should be doing.

Jago's sentences tend to be syntactically complex, full of subordination and phrasal modifiers; this is usual in eighteenth-century blank verse, except for especially exclamatory poems (for instance, Edward Young's *Night Thoughts*). As the strictness of couplet form drops away, sentence structure becomes more necessary for arranging the words. One can catch a reminiscence of the couplet in some of the lines here, as Jago uses assonance or alliteration to bind lines together: gilt/ascent, displays/stage, vale/hill, forsake/shade, -ring hedge-row/rude reservoir, spring/sides. As with couplet verse, lines tend to divide in half, often with a conjunction (lines 2, 4, 6, 8, 10, 11, 13, 14) or a break between clauses or phrases (lines 3, 5, 12, and because of the syntactic looseness of the 'See,' line 9). Those lines, 1 and 7, which do not divide this way, use alliteration (sun/scarcely, breathes/balmy) to mark the halves, as does 9 (-lightful see/languid forsake), and as do a few of the lines syntactically divided (8, 10, 14, and perhaps 5, -ly measured/illumined). Jago's handling of the lines is all of a piece, yet various.

As typically happens in classical and then in Miltonic verse, he also uses what might be called a 'float' of ideas: the order of words differs from that in normal prose so as to present a succession of ideas such as the poet wants. Patterns of line and syntax provide a channel in which the significant terms are borne up for our attention, as at the start of *Paradise Lost*. Man's first disobedience, the apple, death and woe, and salvation through Christ all appear before the imperative 'Sing' which in prose would have begun the sentence. Nothing so tortuously virtuosic comes up in Jago, of course, but the second sentence (ll. 5–9) shows him maneuvering ideas into associative order. The first sentence has been positive in connotation ('gilt,' 'radiant orb'), the third is to be negative, and the second forms a transition in accord with the order of the mind. The first idea is that of the sun ('illumined') overhead, high radiance penetrating the depth of the vale and thus reversing the action of ascent (of men and of sun) in the first sentence. Ascent returns ('soaring') but transiently ('mists') and the emphatic participle 'soaring' turns into a passive 'are drained' as the sun takes on a power absent from the earlier images, restricted to light and movement. Jago repeats the process of ascent ('o'er the hill') and loss ('No more'), reinforced by the rhyme of 'o'er' and 'more,' and by the sense first of death ('No more breathes') then of the death of something valued and responsive ('No more breathes grateful') which he defines logically and emotively ('cool balmy air'). The out-of-place Miltonic adjective 'grateful' and the alliteration of 'breathes' and 'balmy' function in the 'float'; they are not just mannerisms. The air's effect on the will ('search') is emotive ('cheering'), and on action ('steps') it is impulsive ('urging'), while 'delightful' completes the passage by modifying the action (the 'steps' are delightful) emotively. This excursion into agreeable recollection of morning coolness, then, is broken by the imperative 'See' and the realization of the sun's already broached destructiveness, the contrast again reinforced by alliteration (-lightful see/languid forsake) and the slant rhyme of 'urg-' and 'herd.'

Jago tries to achieve, in his own idiom, the variety praised by Gray in Milton, who 'loved to vary his pauses, his measures, and his feet, which gives that enchanting air of freedom and wildness to his versification, unconfined by any rules but those which his own feeling and the nature of his subject demanded' ('Metrum: Observations on English Metre'). By the 1760s, some writers of the couplet were trying for similar effects. They selectively abandoned the exquisite shaping of Pope's school for the looser versification of the late seventeenth century, deliberately so, as Charles Churchill, the best of these writers, suggests in a paean to Dryden in *The Apology* (1761), ll. 366–87. In this new old style of couplet-writing, poets stopped using the caesura like a musical bar line and – as Churchill's *The Times* (1764) shows – they practiced enjambment with great freedom:

> Meanness, now wed to Impudence, no more
> In darkness skulks, and trembles as of yore
> When the light breaks upon her coward eye;
> Boldly she stalks on earth, and to the sky
> Lifts her proud head, nor fears lest time abate
> And turn her husband's love to cankered hate,
> Since Fate, to make them more sincerely one,
> Hath crowned their loves with Montagu their son.
> A son so like his dam, so like his sire,
> With all the mother's craft, the father's fire,
> An image so express in every part,
> So like in all bad qualities of heart
> That, had they fifty children, he alone
> Would stand as heir apparent to the throne.   (ll. 163–76)

If one compares this passage to Cawthorn's and to a piece of inflammatory oratorical prose, one can see how Churchill has relaxed specifically poetic constraints on the position of elements, while he has kept those common to poetry and formal prose. Since he is attacking John Montagu, the Earl of Sandwich, a comparable passage might come from the pseudonymous Junius's attacks on Charles II's great-grandson, the Duke of Grafton:

> You have better proofs of your descent, my Lord, than the register of a marriage or any troublesome inheritance of reputation. There are some hereditary strokes of character by which a family may be as clearly distinguished as by the blackest features of the human face. Charles the First lived and died a hypocrite. Charles the Second was a hypocrite of another sort, and should have died on the same scaffold. At the distance of a century, we see their different characters happily revived and blended in your Grace. Sullen and severe without religion, profligate without gaiety, you live like Charles the Second without being an amiable companion; and for aught I know, may die as his father did, without the reputation of a martyr (30 May 1769).

Churchill's degree of balance and parallel construction is not much greater than Junius's; his rhymes have no real purpose; internal rhymes (hate/fate in ll. 168–9) and alliteration (stalks/sky in l. 166) have the same loose positioning function as in Junius (features/face/First) rather than the tighter function they enjoy in Cawthorn. Although Churchill was a considerable poet, his treatment of the couplet suggests the impending collapse of the positional style brought to its acme by Pope. Thomson's version of the style survived at least till the time of Cowper.

'Ideal presence' and poetic styles

One may accept the description of the positional style so far in this chapter and still be bothered by two of its apparent implications. If poets kept their eyes on the position of objects rather than the objects themselves, is eighteenth-century verse not damned to deal only with generalities and categories, and never with the touch and tang of individual things? Second, does the stress on contexts not mean that the poets ran counter to the intellectual temper of eighteenth-century philosophy and science, where objects themselves were taken as the only external reality? Contexts, the means of classifying objects, were merely necessary systems conceived in the mind. The naturalist Linnaeus (1707–78) looked at the horse and classified it in one way, his rival Buffon (1707–88) looked at it and classified it in another, but both looked at it; was poetry one step more abstracted, hardly looking at horses at all because of a fascination with equinity, quadrupedality, and domestic transportation? I do not think that love of the abstract can suit a poetry so given to personification, where the speaker does his best to give the general a visible, human shape. Nor does it suit a poetry where individual objects or scenes – a blasted heath, a twisted tree, a sward at evening – so plainly are supposed to affect one's emotions, and where they succeeded, according to eighteenth-century critics. The hypothesis of a positional style, then, needs some adjustment, still in keeping with the principle of Jakobson's 'metonymy.' Since we have considered the poems so far as written texts, I suggest that we turn to them as read texts, designed for an audience with certain habits of mind.

I would argue that eighteenth-century readers had especially acute sensory reactions to poetic images when the idiom of the verse invited them to do so. These reactions enabled them to see and hear particular objects with enough vividness to complement the positional effects of the verse. Discursive poets made less use of this special sensitivity, of course, than a Thomson, a Gray, or a Macpherson, and no doubt some readers were readier to exercise imagination than others. Still, throughout the century, critics insisted on the strength of such reactions. For example, the poet Ambrose Philips told the patrons of his periodical *The Free-Thinker* (1719) that when a great poet conveys 'just and lively ideas' (that is, images) to his readers, 'words, in his disposal, are things, and the deception proves so strong that the reader forgets he is perusing a piece of writing' (no. 63). Pope's friend Joseph Spence, Professor of Poetry at Oxford 1728–38, made the same sort of comment in his *Essay on Pope's Odyssey* (1726) when discussing Homer's landscapes: 'They make everything present to us and agreeably deceive us into an imagination that we actually see what we only hear' (p. 66). From comments readers made about specific works, and from the ease of testing this reaction in oneself, we have good reason to believe that these men, and many others who said the same sort of thing, accurately described the response of a very large number of eighteenth-century readers. By 1762 it had been given a name, 'ideal presence,' by Henry Home, Lord Kames, in his *Elements of Criticism*. There Kames talks about the hallucinatory force of language, which can make the reader forget that he or she is holding a book, and instead 'conceive every incident as passing in his presence, precisely as if he were an eyewitness' (7th edn, 1788, 1 : 91–3). Modern readers also visualize in a range from the transient and hazy to the glowingly clear, but surely no modern critic could write as Kames did. It would be arrogant to assume that therefore Kames must have been fond of exaggeration, when the evidence suggests the opposite, that he accurately reflected the way our forebears read poetry in the eighteenth century.

Plainly enough, the theory of 'ideal presence' invites one to supply all sorts of details that words could only present crudely or hint. Even the most elaborative novel, layering modifier on modifier for sentences on end to describe a scene or a simple object – Proust's Marcel evoking his asparagus – can only string together approximations of the object. Receptive readers must complete the image. Much more so with poems, which have less space to squander. Critics who write of ideal presence in poetry, as one would logically expect, make much of the reader's creativity from synecdochic words, creativity along the paths of Jakobson's (in this case, also anyone else's) 'metonymy.' A well-chosen detail or an abstraction sets the imagination at work. The former of these, the use of details to make the mind move to the whole (as in Gray's *Elegy*), is familiar to everyone. 'By the happy choice of some one [particular], or of a few that are the most striking,' writes Hugh Blair in his *Critical Dissertation on the Poems of Ossian* (1763), a strong imagination 'presents the image more complete, shows us more at one glance, than a feeble imagination is able to do by turning its object round and round in a variety of lights' (2nd edn, 1765, p. 89). Minute, laborious description smothers imagination; the metonymous detail spurs it to action. I suggested in discussing Gray that poets cultivated synecdoche to make the reader see the context for details and visualize personifications. My argument here extends these notions: synecdoche, and other invitations to 'ideal presence,' are the poet's only means of completing the poem as an imitative act. The speaker perceives particulars because there are only particulars in the world. He translates them into words in which he can render, to some degree, their behavior and interaction, i.e., their positions. The reader, in empathy with the speaker, must translate the message back into the reality of particulars once again; not, of course, the same particulars that the speaker perceived but their analogues. If one is to hold a representational theory of poetry, as almost everyone in the eighteenth century did, some such procedure as this must underlie poetic endeavor.

In line with this, theorists also insisted that abstractions triggered 'ideal presence.' Nowadays the abstract and the concrete, the general and the particular, seem opposites, although Rudolf Arnheim has argued in *Visual Thinking* (1969) (see especially Chap. 6) that all thought involves visual imagery, some of it in configurations or movements, like abstract art, that have no developed representational content. We have evidence that eighteenth-century readers went further, to translate the general, through imagination, into representational particulars. As Hobbes wrote in his *Leviathan* (1651), 'whereas a proper name bringeth to mind one thing only, universals recall any one of those many' (Chap. 4): the mind individuates. Sir Joshua Reynolds applied precisely this principle to Milton, in his explanation to students that 'a great part of the beauty of the celebrated description of Eve in Milton's *Paradise Lost* consists in using only general, indistinct expressions, each reader making out the detail according to his own particular imagination, his own idea of beauty, grace, expression, dignity, or loveliness' (no. 8, 1778, of his *Discourses on Art*, ed. Wark, 1959, p. 164). At about the same time the critic and poet James Beattie was writing the same thing about Virgil's Dido: from the simple epithet 'most beautiful' and a simile of Diana applied to her, Beattie claims, 'our fancy may form for itself a picture of feminine loveliness and dignity more perfect than ever Cowley or Ovid could exhibit' (*Essays: On Poetry and Music*, 1776; 3rd edn, 1779, p. 92). Both Reynolds and Beattie presumably would have greeted with lifted eyebrows the comment of the modern critic Philip Hobsbaum about the very description of Eve that Reynolds praised: 'the reader will get very little out of this passage unless he has a gift for fiction' (*Theory of Criticism*, 1970, p. 38). Precisely so; and to Reynolds and Beattie, stimulating that gift was part of Milton's poetic genius.

One can see how strong the urge to ideal presence was from a seemingly odd passage in John Ogilvie's preface to 'The Day of Judgment' (*Poems*, 1762), where he claims as a 'remarkable advantage . . . peculiar to divine poetry' that 'the most elevated idea we can form of it will fall infinitely short of reality' (G2^v). His point is that when the reader's eager imagination is defeated by the immensity of the subject, the bottled-up energy of the mind can become part of the poetic effect. For example, Jonathan Richardson explains that we comprehend, visually, Milton's fallen angels by recognizing the tension from knowing that our inner pictures of them are less than the reality. When 'the imagination is raised as much as possible,' he writes, 'let it know still more is unconceived; let the lark sing after he is lost in air' (*Explanatory Notes . . .* [on] '*Paradise Lost*,' 1734, p. 41). The same Miltonic lark sang a few years earlier for Joseph Spence, who says of Satan's fall that it 'has no bounds: it is still continuing lower and lower, and the mind, in endeavouring to conceive it, is lost in its desired infinitude' (*Essays on Pope's Odyssey*, p. 117). A bit later in the century (1765), Dr Johnson criticized Shakespeare's description of Dover Cliff in *King Lear* IV. vi precisely because it made bad use of the pictorial energy of the mind. In his note to this passage in his edition of Shakespeare, Johnson protested that 'the enumeration of the choughs and the crows, the samphire-man and the fishers, counteracts the great effect of the prospect, as it peoples the desert of intermediate vacuity and stops the mind in the rapidity of its descent through emptiness and horror.'

A passage from the second and final version of the first book of Pope's *Dunciad* helps show how 'ideal presence,' with its corollaries of suggestiveness and mental energy, actually works. All the characteristics of 'positional poetry' appear here. Pope sets out relations between objects by showing them in action, with a rush of active verbs, present participles, appeals to relational senses (sight, sound, muscle-sense), and references to placement in time and space. The speaker of the *Dunciad* has little independent personality. The poem's set place in a genre gives Pope his means of modifying traditional contexts of value. His metaphors are more striking than Gray's, Thomson's, Cawthorn's, or Jago's, but not because striking metaphors are valuable in and of themselves: they are exorbitant to fit the grotesque Cibber. Finally, one can see how this impresario of the couplet employs rhythm, rhyme, and association to give each word its precise place in a description of the anti-hero Cibber trying to repair his shattered fortune:

> Swearing and supperless the hero sate,
> Blasphemed his gods, the dice, and damned his fate,
> Then gnawed his pen, then dashed it to the ground,
> Sinking from thought to thought, a vast profound!
> Plunged for his sense, but found no bottom there,
> Yet wrote and floundered on in mere despair.
> Round him much embryo, much abortion lay,
> Much future ode and abdicated play;
> Nonsense precipitate, like running lead,
> That slipped through cracks and zig-zags of the head;
> All that on folly frenzy could beget,
> Fruits of dull heat and sooterkins of wit.
> Next, o'er his books his eyes began to roll
> In pleasing memory of all he stole,
> How here he sipped, how there he plundered snug
> And sucked all over like an industrious bug.   (Book I, ll. 115–30)

In part, this stylistically fascinating passage works by maintaining forward movement while frustrating ideal presence. The forward movement, first, is clear in a sequence of actions and also in a pattern of association of ideas. 'Swearing' leads to its particularization ('blasphemed,' 'damned') and 'supperless,' com-ically, to its logical consequence ('gnawed his pen'). The lack of nourishment (supper or inspiration) in pen-gnawing leads to a 'dash[ing] to the ground,' thus to 'sinking' and 'plunged' and to the abortive chaotic forward movements of 'flounder[ing].' We turn to what lies around Cibber on the floor, having as it were lowered him and extended our radius with 'floundered,' to find the relics of his past attempts, embryonic or aborted, also fallen ('precipitate') or falling ('running lead'). Now the motion of floundering, together with the idea of an embryo and abortion, and that of the hot fluid running through a crack, makes the speaker think of a sexual image (folly begetting on frenzy), so that the lumps of botched literature are 'fruits' and 'sooterkins' (afterbirths). The fruits have been prematurely raised in hothouses ('dull heat'), and sooterkins were thought to be the result of too much sitting near stoves (see *OED*), so that the idea of heat (literal as in molten lead, mental and generative as in frenzy) helps develop and extend images of ruined births ('embryo' for the 'future,' and 'abdicated' 'abortion'). But Cibber's begetting is theft, the hothouses and stoves external, as we see from the play on 'his books' (l. 127), which seems first to refer to what he has written, the pleasingly remembered results of his past folly and frenzy. But the second half of line 128 reveals that 'his' refers to larcenous ownership for a meal, the artistic supper that can buy the real supper the 'hero' lacks. In the last four lines, the kinaesthetic movement grows more precise as creativity shrinks to mere un-principled industry and future hopes retreat to reviving the past through memory. From inspiration to plunder, from floundering to thrusts of the proboscis, from hero to bug – this is the decline of Cibber in the forward movement of the passage.

Pope complicates this forward movement by jumping, unlike Thomson, Gray, Cawthorn, or Jago, to contexts that the actual scene does not immediately imply. Metaphor marks each shift in context, for none exist in lines 115–17 and 127–8, which describe what can be seen, while the rest of the passage (once, ll. 120–2, partly returning to the actual scene) blooms with them. Through this means, Pope encourages and then thwarts ideal presence, making the mind struggle. One begins to see or hear or feel movement (the three senses this passage appeals to), only to have incongruity block the development of the scene. We visualize the first three lines' description but then lose ideal presence as the mind continues from the visual ('dashed it to the ground') to the non-visual ('sinking from thought to thought') in the same downward sweep. Once again, the scattering of fragmentary odes and plays summons an image to the inner eye, only to have visual continuity snapped by the grotesque image of lead dribbling through cranial cracks. A similar passage to the surreal marks the last four lines, as Pope lets us see Cibber sit, his eyes widening, his brow smoothing, his tight mouth loosening, perhaps judiciously pursing, as we read of his sipping and sucking, till we suddenly come to the final image of insect appetite, which makes the reflective human face grow debased and automatic. While our desire to see keeps being stimulated, the nature of what we see keeps changing. As a result, we react to bizarre images more vividly for having been lured into an expectation of ideal presence, and our mental sense of the incongruities in the texture of the imagery makes us more keenly feel the poem's incongruities of content.

Pope's practice and the comments of his associates, like Ambrose Philips and Joseph Spence, tell us that readers felt the 'ideal presence' of poetic images by the 1710s and 1720s. As the century went on, one finds critics discussing it and poets using it more, because psychological criticism and descriptive, 'imaginative' poetry became more popular. Restoration critics and poets mostly address different subjects, though in the mid-1660s, in his preface to *Annus Mirabilis*, Dryden wrote that 'the proper wit of an heroic or historical poem' lay in 'some lively and apt description, dressed in such colors of speech that it sets before your eyes the absent object, as perfectly and more delightfully than nature.' Dryden himself and his almost exact contemporary Charles Cotton – and also Milton, who was of Dryden's father's generation – wrote verse that seems to invite ideal presence; but we simply do not have enough historical evidence to be able to surmise how that verse was read at the time it was published. For the history of poetry, I think one is limited to saying that the Restoration modes typically leaned to the dramatic and the discursive, with wit, vividly illustrative imagery, psychological and argumentative order, and sonorousness among their great virtues; but they did not centrally involve the reader's hearing, feeling, and seeing individual objects. The same modes in the eighteenth century also did not have a central interest in ideal presence, although poets, especially in dramatic verse, became progressively more likely to include stimuli to ideal presence within a discourse or a persona's speech.

A deliberately overblown example may suggest the virtues (and the limits) of the distinctions I am making. James Beattie's 'Essay on Poetry and Music' (1776) contains a parody, in what Beattie calls 'the finical style' of description, of Desdemona's simple comment on her mother's maid Barbara: 'She was in love, and he she loved proved mad/And did forsake her' (*Othello*, IV, iii, 26–8). Or, in the 'finical style':

Even now, sad Memory to my thought recalls
The nymph Dione, who, with pious care,
My much-loved mother, in my vernal years,
Attended: blooming was the maiden's form,
And on her brow Discretion sat, and on
Her rosy cheek a thousand Graces played.
O luckless was the day, when Cupid's dart,
Shot from a gentle swain's alluring eye,
First thrilled with pleasing pangs her throbbing breast!
That gentle swain, ah, gentle now no more
(Horrid to tell!), by sudden frenzy driven,
Ran howling to the wild: blood-tinctured fire
Glared from his haggard eyeballs, and on high
The hand of Horror raised his ragged hair,
And cold sweat bathed his agonizing frame.

(*Essays* (1776), 3rd edn, pp. 248–9)

The tricks of ideal presence tumble over each other in the 'finical' Desdemona's speech, for the purpose of characterization. The hearer would be supposed to feel empathy for someone who images so vividly and so compassionately; shared ideal presence with this Desdemona would complement the empathy. Obviously Beattie's parody of the style indicates that it was popular but optional for such special purposes by the 1770s. Descriptive poetry counted on ideal presence; expository and dramatic poetry employed it for odd jobs.

Poetic language had to permit sensory effects when needed, of course, and to compensate for their absence at other times. At the cost of being reductive, I will isolate three models of poetic language, all current in ambitious poems between

73

1720 and 1780. Two of them evolved only then. The third style, the 'urbane style,' appears throughout the period from the Restoration on. In the 'urbane style,' ideal presence remains subdued or sporadic, as witness most discursive poetry. Speakers make up for the lack of scenery with good conversation, even good oratory. Satire and epistle alike offer rich verbal embroidery, varied, allusive, witty, ornamented with intriguing examples, in short the style of a dramatic monologue uttered by a lively and intelligent speaker as public man. Alongside this central 'urbane style' in the Restoration stood the high style of the Pindaric ode and the simple, colloquial style shared by some occasional verse, some slight lyrics, and some poems with speakers not meant to be confused with the poet. From the high and the colloquial evolve what I will call the 'high, limited' and the 'spontaneous' styles.

As we have seen, eighteenth-century poets deserted the old Cowleyan Pindaric for Miltonics, and later for a kind of ode filled with personification and scenic effects. The style of this blank and rhymed verse mostly fits into the 'high, limited' category. At the other end of the stylistic scale, the simple and colloquial mode continued to be used by writers of occasional verse, but by the middle third of the century had gained new dignity. Its new speaker – in the 'spontaneous' style – is less a man addressing other men, as in the 'urbane' and 'high' styles, than a figure outside ordinary social relationships, such as a bard hymning the past or some ideal, a dramatic character, or a pensive soliloquist. Its language often comes from an oral rather than written tradition, for example, from the contemporary tragic theater or ballads, and so, without violating simplicity, it can indulge in stanzaic forms, sometimes incantatory, and in archaisms. With the 'high, limited' style it shares a restricted lexicon and a relatively narrow range of idiomatic variation. These are imperative for ideal presence. The restrictions make us accommodate ourselves to a set manner of speech that ceases to call attention to itself as language, unlike the witty, ornamental, wide-ranging manner of the 'urbane' style. Once the language disappears as language, and becomes a consistent posture toward the material, the poem becomes, so to speak, transparent and lets us see through words to their referents. The Miltonisms and archaisms, the inversions and incantations, signal us that we are reading poetry, that we are expected to be visionary. Then they fade, as the sense that one is in a cinema fades after one has been acclimatized to the idiom of seeing a film.

The 'urbane' style tells rather than shows. It presents the world positionally, showing us a composite of objects governed by forces and energies, just as the descriptions of a Thomson or the narratives of a Macpherson do; but the objects here are at one remove from reality, since they have already been digested by the speaker's active, civilized mind, and have produced laws and paradigms, type characters, propositions and abstractions. Precisely because laws and paradigms must be put into words, poems written in the urbane style do not aim at transparency of language. One can, of course, be transparent in setting out propositions, as transparent as Euclid or Locke, but for that effect why write a poem? In the Restoration and earlier eighteenth century, poems in this style dazzle with wit, with allusion, with figures of speech, with all the diamonds – their weaker siblings, with all the glass and zircons – that make so-called 'Augustan' poetry famous. Later, as the Popean manner grew threadbare in his imitators' shops, poems in the urbane style preferred the wholesome maxim to the witty one. The ideal of civilized discourse, however, remained.

More specifically, the style conforms to three senses of the word 'urbane' or its Latin root, *urbanus*: courteous, polished, and sophisticated. Because the speaker is a public man, he follows the laws of social courtesy, to be clear, concise, informative, frank within the bounds of taste, entertaining without frivolity or self-advertisement, and attractive as a person. In an age when Englishmen prized the give-and-take of talk as never, perhaps, before or since, poets knew acutely how well they had to discourse if they were to recompense their readers for letting them monopolize the floor. The urbane style is polished because it is urban, socially refined, at once fashionable and meticulous (but without pedantry or fuss). Rural simplicity may be a good subject for the nostalgic or harried gentleman, but not the source of a good style for the verse he writes. Finally, the urbane style is sophisticated in its wit, its taste, its classical allusions, and its subtlety and balance of feelings because speaker and audience are worldly men, educated in schools and salons; hard-headed men, too, whose shrewdness has displaced any wonder at the works of other men. I emphasize 'men' because the style supposes an education and a worldliness quite possible for eighteenth-century women but only if they were willing to adopt male values. The vices of femininity (the dainty, the coy, the catty, and the bitchy) rarely mar Restoration and eighteenth-century verse; those common in men (stuffiness, self-righteousness, glib expansiveness, dull earnestness) often do.

The urbane style makes little of particular objects (and ideal presence) and employs a wide lexicon. Particulars work as illustrations in poems that expound ideas (philosophic verse) or attitudes (e.g., satire), and as illustrations they are quickly and pungently developed and then dropped. One does not expect trains of imagery in such poems. As Walter Harte writes, in satire 'Similes, like meteors of the night,/Just give one flash of momentary light' (*An Essay on Satire* (1730), ll. 61–2). Another use of particulars in this style is as accessories to orient the reader, the way a cluster of trees in the background of a portrait orients a viewer to the fact that the plump gentleman with gun and hound is a squire. To develop the woodsiness of the scene in the poetic version of such a portrait or to invite the reader to visualize an ash grove would be unnecessary and distracting. The lexicon of the urbane style keeps a firm anchor in the colloquial, but allows for such a variety of social exchange that it exploits the resources of English vocabulary as fully as any poetic style in our literature.

In one kind of urbane poem, in fact, the kind of social contact expressed by the breadth of social tone is the real subject; I am thinking of verse taken as the written conduct of social individuals (in friendly epistles, eulogies, certain kinds of love poem), where tone – chatty, winsome, witty, regretful, deferent, and often several or all of these – establishes for the reader what one might call the personality of the relationship between writer and recipient. In other urbane poems, the needs of social discourse can give the poet a partial holiday from even the liberal constraints of courtesy and polite ingenuity, as when the speaker briefly mounts his soapbox or ranges into burlesque, a shared joke of excess. As Geoffrey Tillotson writes in his fine *Augustan Poetic Diction* (1964), 'The vocabulary of all nineteenth-century poetry cowers into a corner when the *Dunciad* walks abroad, seeking whom it may devour' (p. 28). The freedom of social exchange, within the assumed polish, courtesy, and sophistication of both writers and readers in the urbane style, permits a broader lexicon – for quite specific purposes – than one finds even in Pope. The anonymous 'A Tragicomic . . . Poem . . . on the Hyperbole' (1748; by H. Harrison?), for example, goes so far as to parody the language of descriptive verse, like 'the opacuous womb of silent night' (p. 25), so as to level that (non-urbane) diction with its extreme counterpart, a lower-class challenge in slang:

> . . . to grapple with me for
> A shining ridge, nor fear I but to clink
> This clacking cull, and plump his blubbers ere
> The darkee comes. (p. 21)

Like the wit and allusiveness one finds in these 'urbane' poems, the great range of their lexicon has two purposes. It establishes the kind of contact that the author has with his readers, by the assumption that they can enjoy his civilized playfulness, learning, shrewdness, and malice. It also establishes that he and they share a conceptual control of the subject, not that they can do anything about it (they usually cannot) or plumb all its mysteries but that they know how to talk about it, how to place it in terms of the rest of their experience, how to accommodate it intelligently. Otherwise, the poet could not be exact and would not dare be playful.

The language of the urbane style, then, gives the author and reader a position in relation to each other and to their subject. As a corollary, the grander the subject, the more exciting the conversation and the more ground the author and the reader control in their discourse. Like Restoration and eighteenth-century poetry in general, urbane non-occasional verse, such as expository verse, drifts toward the high rather than the low. Mock-heroic, the ceremoniousness of formal couplets, and the oratorical flavor that often scents the speech of those who monopolize the floor – these frequent devices tend to embellish the subject expounded upon. So does hyperbolic discourse, such as Aaron Hill uses in *Free Thoughts upon Faith* (1746) to denounce those who fancy themselves God's elect:

> Out with this avarice of fanatic scrape!
> That, pinching to itself God's nibbled grants,
> Hedged in th'Eternal's common! Greedily
> Forestalled all power of opening mystery's gate
> For its own pick-lock tribe, unkeyed by Heaven.
> Why, if enlightened most, should will most dark
> Bid these few favorite hand-led spies of grace
> Conceal from modest doubts their arts to know? (ll. 52–9)

The compressed violence of Hill's attack creates great energy within his straightforward verse, as the bustle of verbs and very brief hints of ideal presence create energy within the descriptive style. The force of his contempt itself enlarges his poetic subject. I say 'poetic subject' because the objects of his attack do not grow; they are made to breathe within a larger space, which defines their position and becomes the poetic subject. Similarly, in a mock-heroic poem like the *Dunciad*, the petty dunces are the objects of attack, but the poetic subject, from which the poem adopts its grand scale, is the social decay within monuments of epic splendor. Diction and allusion ensure that the objects of attack strut within a grand, defining scheme of implication. From this breadth of language and conception, emotional force flows into the best Restoration and eighteenth-century urbane poems, along with an exuberance of feeling and – to use one of the poets' favorite words – a joy.

Josephine Miles's work in *Eras and Modes in English Poetry* (1957) documents other favorite words which offer a sense of the shape and heft of this poetry. Some of them show the force of the positional style: *high, great, mighty, deep, wide; air, sky, day, night; rise, fall, fly, stand, lie, come, go*. Some of these, and other words too, give the positional style a crucial social force, as one would expect from urbane poetry, which by its nature is socially conceived. We find, for instance: *power, man, head, hand, nature, country, friend, world, heart, virtue, wealth, king, life*. Finally, words of interrelationship emphasize the linkages of man and man, nature and man: *give, take, see, tell, think, know, love* (as both verb and noun); *name, eye, thought*; and words that involve both senses and judgment, like *bright* and *fair*. Three more words, *soul, Heaven*, and *fate*, are sometimes used to suggest a metaphysical context for man and nature. Eighteenth-century poetry of discourse often carries some theological charge, heartfelt or perfunctory. Yet each of these words, like *god* with a small 'g', also accords with the other categories listed: *soul* may be shorthand for 'feeling' or 'deepest intuition,' *Heaven* may be a synonym for 'sky,' and *fate* and *god* reflect a large immanent causal order rather than any actual belief. In any case, they once again represent the drift of this style toward the high. Despite the preeminence of Restoration and eighteenth-century satire over any other in English, these favored words suggest the grand or grandiose, not the vile, the puny, the weak, the low. (In line with a change signaled by the affectionate satire we saw creeping in after 1710, though, tender words of weakness start to appear more often as one moves later in the century: *soft, little, gentle, mild*.) *Vain* is the only really widespread negative word, and that of course can have a biblical ring which implies the grand behind it.

If the urbane style relies on the colloquial as its home base, the high, limited style imitates a colloquy in overtly poetic diction. The term 'poetic diction' applies to all poetry at any time, since the conventions of verse – meter, rhyme, compression, use of figures of speech, repetition, choice of words – differ from those of prose. The poet Gray was right when he wrote to his friend Richard West, in April 1742, that 'the language of the age is never the language of poetry . . . [English] poetry . . . has a language peculiar to itself, to which almost everyone that has written has added something.' Yet the high, limited style went beyond the ordinary kinds of poetic diction, went almost as far as Spenser and Milton had, to achieve a mode of writing that was sonorous, precise, and delimited in suggestiveness. For this mode,

77

poets turned to the classics (mediated most significantly through Milton) and to the language of science. I can suggest reasons for each of these debts more easily than I can disentangle their effects, since both the classics and science encouraged Latinate words and certain mannerisms, even stock phrases.

The classics, first of all, represented a point of contact with the urbane style, where references to a shared culture assured a fellowship between author and reader. Generations of sensitive and cultivated men had communicated with the past and with each other through the medium of the classics, which represented the common speech of poetry. To Latinless students of the twentieth century, barely able to decipher *'nil desperandum'* or *'mutatis mutandis,'* phrases like 'liquid air,' 'the hoary waste, abrupt and deep,' 'vernal suns,' or 'many a bursting stream auriferous plays' seem bizarre. This is not the fault of James Thomson, who wrote them for those who had committed to memory similar phrases in Latin, and had translated them into English under schoolmasters' eyes. The urbane style drew on what was colloquial in speech; the high, limited style on what was colloquial in the poetry one learned and recited in school. Transferred from Virgil to Smart or Akenside, the classical phrases took on an exotic color, admittedly, but the strangeness added its own sense of being special to the dignity inherent in an idiom borrowed from the prestigious classics.

Latin borrowings and resonances, then, gave the 'high, limited' style a dignity, a community of readers, and a base in the speech of the poetry with which all educated men had begun their reading of serious literature, and which cultivated women knew through the fund of translations by the finest poets of the age. That is why the style was 'high.' Its being 'limited' offers the second reason for the use of the classics: to keep poetic language refined from distracting associations. An audience attuned to ideal presence and association of ideas can go off at tangents. These may work to an author's advantage as when archaic language excites 'an effort of imagination' by which 'we place ourselves in the age of the [assumed] author and call up a thousand collateral ideas which give beauties to his work not naturally inherent' (Vicesimus Knox, *Essays Moral and Literary*, no. 47 (1778)). Such efforts of imagination can also be destructive, either by awakening an incongruity in the mind or by stripping an image of its dignity. Classicized English could hardly attract unwanted associations because it was not used outside of poems. As Dr Johnson pointed out in his 'Life of Addison,' nothing in a dead language 'is mean because nothing is familiar' (para. 11). The 'high, limited' style offered an idiom refined from the everyday, what Johnson called the 'familiar,' to approximate the advantages of a dead language – dead in common speech, very much alive and subtle in poetry. One should not make the error of ascribing to pompous gentility or sesquipedalian recklessness the calculated use of even such adjectives as 'uncauponated' (Smart), 'irriguous' (Grainger), or 'flammivomous' (William Thompson). Color words like 'azure,' 'cerulean,' 'ebon,' and 'saffron,' which survived in English verse long after the last eighteenth-century poet was laid in earth, duplicated Latin's largely poetic use of their equivalents, such as *'caeruleus'* (sky-blue) and *'lacteus'* (milky white): in English their meanings are perfectly clear, their associations kept controlled.

Slightly different is another classical formula, of sensory adjective plus group noun, as in 'scaly kind,' 'feathery people,' 'starry regions,' which modern readers – who themselves talk about the 'human race' – find prissy or stuffy. At times it is, at times merely habitual poetizing, but most often eighteenth-century writers use these periphrases for two purposes. They imitate Virgil, whose fish, birds, and sky are, among other things, *'gens umida,' 'agmen aligerum,'* and *'siderea sedes.'* The long list of parallels culled from Virgil and other Latin poets by John Arthos – in *The Language of Natural Description in Eighteenth-Century Poetry* (1949) – shows how good was the company in which eighteenth-century Englishmen placed themselves. More centrally, this technique offered another means of control. It let the poet narrow the focus of connotation to a single, metonymous, sensory trait of fish, birds, or sky. Such non-metaphoric substitutions do not, cannot tell us anything about the object – we must know that fish are finny to understand the periphrases in the first place – but they can evoke the object to the imagination, fleetingly, and thereby give the speaker and the reader a position at once Virgilian and observant in relation to fish, birds, or sky. These periphrases, used with the tact most poets exercised, suit the high, limited style quite perfectly. Moreover, such periphrases satisfy the rules of Jakobson's 'metonymy' by placing objects within an order: 'feathery people' implies that there are non-feathery people in the scale of relations. Here, then, are the elements of the 'positional style': speaker and reader are related to the classics, speaker and reader are related to the objects they perceive (with the act of perception amplified through some degree of ideal presence), and the perceived objects are related to a larger classificatory order of 'kind' or 'people' or 'regions.' The formula of sensory adjective plus group noun, far from being a mindless 'neoclassical' parroting in eighteenth-century verse, fits the intelligently conceived ideals of that verse to perfection.

One can see the style at work in John Dyer's comparison of half-buried antique sculptures to a lounging whale and fish, in *The Ruins of Rome* (1740):

> Deep lies in dust the Theban obelisk,
> Immense along the waste, minuter art
> (Glyconian forms or Phidian, subtly fair)
> O'erwhelming as the immense Leviathan
> The finny brood, when near Ierne's shore
> Outstretched, unwieldy, his island length appears
> Above the foamy flood.   (ll. 26–32)

The image recalls *Paradise Lost (PL)* 1:201–8, where Milton describes a pilot anchoring a skiff in Leviathan's 'scaly rind,' thinking him an island: the skiff's foundering and fall in Milton, whose simile refers to Satan, obviously fit Dyer's needs here. Dyer's deliberately clumsy line 31 recalls Milton's line 202, 'Created hugest that swim,' where the apt awkwardness of sound met with praise in Thomas Newton's edition of *Paradise Lost* (1749), just as similar sound effects for Leviathan in *PL* 7:412–15 are praised, with comparisons to Virgil, in William Benson's *Letters concerning Poetical Translations* (1739; p. 43). The formulas 'finny brood' and 'foamy flood' likewise come from classical Latin via Milton (e.g., 'finny drove' in *Comus* 1. 115 and 'foaming deep' in *PL* 10 :301). Dyer finally uses a Miltonic float of ideas, the technique earlier discussed in our sample passage from Jago's *Edge Hill*, in which the distortions of normal prose order present us with a succession of ideas such as the classical poet or Milton or Dyer or Jago thinks desirable.

Not Dyer's originality but his skill, like Milton's, should occupy the critic. 'Finny brood' (l. 30) moves us immediately from dust to sea, and gives us the idea of delicate, rayed objects, like the subtle, proportioned beauty of the Glyconian or Phidian art, and unlike the unproportioned ('immense' = Latin *in + mensus*, 'un-measured') bulk of Leviathan. 'Finny' alliterates with 'forms'/'Phidian'/'fair' in line 28, to reinforce the parallel. 'Foamy flood' continues the alliterative linking and gives visual definition to the scene of water breaking against the whale's flanks as against the Irish shore (another island, the parallel with which magnifies Leviathan, and given its Greek name Ierne to fit the Hellenic context). The white splash and fall of water, I should add, brings one back to dust again in Dyer's next sentence, in which 'Globose and huge,/Gray-mouldering temples swell.' Though sea and dust seem far apart, except that both are waste, Dyer's imagery creates deliberate paradox, in that Rome is both alive and dead, like Leviathan the island : the rest of the poem recreates Roman culture and history, fecund in memories and lessons, and for this Dyer intersperses imagery of water throughout. Before the lines cited he has glanced at 'yellow Tiber' (l. 12), a mixture of water and dirt that the dust and sea of these lines adapts. In order to continue the imagery without being blatant about its symbolic use, Dyer employs the sharp pictures permitted by ideal presence, for which the formulas 'finny brood' and 'foamy flood' serve him well. I will pass over, as perhaps adventitious, the fitness of sounding like Virgil, the great poetic prophet of Roman empire, in composing *The Ruins of Rome*; the real point is the precision Dyer gets from the high, limited style and its classical or Miltonic devices.

The high, limited style, in topographical poetry, also allies itself with scientific language, first, because both try to describe nature contextually. Science complements positional poetry of any sort by binding the perceived world to causal laws and taxonomic patterns, turning sensations into design. It reconciles the capabilities of objects with their actual behavior. This is the stuff of positional poetry; one has only to think of Pope's *Moral Essays*, which trace the effects of a disposition or 'ruling passion,' Thomson's *Seasons*, which detail the effects of climate, or Gray's *Elegy*, which ponders the effects of rural life. Descriptive poets' allegiance to the objective world meant their accepting scientific accounts of disposition and cause, part of the admirable complexity that made sky, beasts, and landscape such eloquent witnesses to God's wisdom and Nature's kind dispen-sation. Many descriptive poems, besides, were read for the information they pleasingly conveyed: for instance, Robert Anderson praises James Grainger's *Sugar Cane* for 'extending the bounds of natural history while he seems only to address the imagination' (*British Poets* (1795), 10 : 894).

Such an affinity of ends between poet and scientist made affinities of language likely. From both we get Latinate formations and shared methods of creating phrases, such as compound epithets and adjectival forms to indicate nature or disposition (forms ending in -y, -ive, and -ous). Such epithets are close in function to present participles. Part of the charm of the present participle for descriptive verse, where it so often occurs as part of the high, limited style, is that it can specify either an action ('minuter art . . . o'erwhelming' in the example from Dyer above) or a quality ('the spirit-stirring form of Caesar,' 'all-enchanting Greece,' 'good Evander, wealth-despising king,' ll. 102–3, 237, 330 from the same poem). In short, it reconciles disposition or capability with actual behavior, or, rather, keeps the observer's eye on objects poised between potential and actual energy. One has only to glance at *The Transactions of the Royal Society* – I am using the 1809 abridgement – for the same year as Dyer's poem, 1740, to find 'reflecting telescope,' 'neighbouring inhabitants,' and in a description very close in diction to one in topographical poetry, 'the east side cliffy, the west more reclining' (8 : 400, 410, 406). Not only shared interests but also a shared conception of the natural world prompted shared diction, then; and of course the prestige of science as experimental truth complemented that of the classics as recorded beauty, and the Latin neutrality of scientific names that of the Virgilian ring to that same lexicon. Scientific language helped the style be high and limited.

The 'spontaneous' style is hardest to define, except in terms of drama and ballad (or sung poem). It banishes all but the simplest figures of speech in favor of what Arthur Murphy, in the *Gray's Inn Journal*, called 'figures of the sentiment,' which 'consist of such breaks and transitions in discourse as the mind is known to make when under the compulsion of warring passions' (no. 94, 1754). In the Restoration and earlier eighteenth century, one often finds the comic version of the style, as in some of Rochester's imitations of conversation and Swift's 'Mrs Harris's Petition' (written 1700):

> Then the bell rung and I went down to put my Lady to bed,
> And, God knows, I thought my money was as safe as my maidenhead
> So, when I came up again, I found my pocket feel very light,
> But when I searched and missed my purse, Lord! I thought I should have sunk
>   outright.   (ll. 10–13)

More serious versions appear in love poetry, like elegies and imitations of Ovid's *Heroides*, those letters from the lovelorn; one thinks of Pope's *Eloisa to Abelard*.

A younger Eloisa, the heroine of Rousseau's *La Nouvelle Héloïse*, is the presumed recipient of a late eighteenth-century poem of this sort, Thomas Mercer's *The Sentimental Sailor, or St. Preux to Eloisa* (1772), which sets forth some stylistic rules for the kind. Such poems, Mercer observes in his introduction, require 'the genuine language of nature.' Since 'description is apt to stifle sentiment, and sentiment to obscure description,' the poet must subordinate what is seen to what is felt, working on the principle that under the 'powerful illusion' of love 'the mind creates to itself another universe, filled with objects and surrounded with images that exist not but in imagination' (pp. xii, xv). When St Preux's passion does not make him ignore scenic beauty or find it vapid, it forces him to translate the actual world into a series of stimuli, counterbalances, and analogues for emotion. Ideal presence is excited by the clear language and strong feeling, but its purpose is that of empathy, a projective faculty of the imagination rather different in its effects from ideal presence. The reader ceases to be a companion to the speaker, as in poems in the urbane and high, limited styles, and becomes instead his judge and adjunct. This sort of poem in the 'spontaneous style' – it is not the only sort – accommodates more idiosyncrasies of the speaker and fewer of the reader, as the shared vision of urbane men or of strolling gazers at the same prospect gives way to a kind of voyeurism, the reader's watching the speaker's tears, trembling, tender caresses, or fatal swoon. Pathetic parts of narrative poems, in which an old hermit, say, turns out to be the hero or heroine's father – David Mallet's *Amyntor and Theodora* (1747) and John Tait's *The Cave of Morar* (1774) use this very plot – revel in the spontaneous style.

The spontaneous style had other uses besides pathos. Whimsy remained one from the Restoration through the eighteenth century, for in whimsy and other self-conscious moods the author makes himself a dramatic character, glimpsed doing something uncalculated, perhaps the uncalculated activity of being caught at calculating. The spontaneous style in this kind of passage often sprouts as a weed of diffidence in the midst of a poem basically in the urbane style. More closely related to the high, limited style is the spontaneous style in poetry of serious musing, such as 'graveyard' poetry, where we are to follow the turns of a dramatic but didactic speaker's mind. Robert Blair's *The Grave* (1743) demonstrates the abrupt, exclamatory version of the style:

> See yonder hallowed fane! the pious work
> Of names once famed, now dubious or forgot
> And buried 'midst the wreck of things which were:
> There lie interred the more illustrious dead.
> The wind is up: Hark! how it howls! Methinks
> Till now I never heard a sound so dreary:
> Doors creak and windows clap and night's foul bird
> Rooked in the spire screams loud . . . .   (ll. 28–35)

Though Blair uses no questions in this passage, he frequently bursts out with them: 'Where are the jesters now? the men of health/Complexionally pleasant? Where the droll?' (ll. 115–16). Such questions and exclamations in Blair and still more in Edward Young's *Night Thoughts* (1742–6), the most popular poem of this general sort, try to link the emotive world of the speaker with the will of the reader who is commanded to answer (or look at, listen to, consider, realize) this or that. Socially and linguistically, one is also called on to sympathize with the value judgments implied by interjections. In short, what seems merely to be a device to indicate urgency on the speaker's part, as he stares at mortality, converts us into participants in his emotional state by drawing on our usual responses to forms of the command.

82

Not much is made of ideal presence in whimsical, self-conscious verse, but poets like Blair and Young do require it and achieve it through the spontaneous style. So do still another group of authors who use this style, the writers of serious ballads, bardic, and 'primitive' poems. The simplicity of the style fits eighteenth-century ideas of folk poems and some, not all, works by primitive bards. In these records of past civilizations, almost always elegiac or heroic, the eighteenth-century author disappears as he never does in the urbane or high, limited styles. We confront the event directly, seeing it through ideal presence, feeling it through empathy. To make the author disappear, such poems employ folk meters, as in the traditional ballad stanza, or rise into the impersonal ecstasy of music, as in some odes, or sink to prose, as in the Ossianic poems of Macpherson, where the author pretends to be no more than an imperfect translator. Alas for the poets who wrote with high hopes in this mode: posterity has seen that one generation's simplicity is affectation and silliness to the next, even from the pen of the poet laureate:

> Havoc, havoc raged around,
> Many a carcass strewed the ground;
> Ravens drank the purple flood,
> Raven plumes were dyed in blood;
> Frighted crowds from place to place,
>   Eager, hurrying, breathless, pale,
> Spread the news of their disgrace,
>   Trembling as they told the tale.
>   (William Whitehead, 'The Battle of Argoed Llwyfain' (1784) (ll. 41–8)

But heartfelt and oracular poetry, poetry from the folk, and other spontaneous modes were to have great success after 1780, and were to import a subjectivity and idiosyncrasy that was to wreck the bases for the positional style. When the reader declined from colleague to eavesdropper, and the outside world was swallowed in personal experience, the kinds of poetry we have been discussing had to defer to others outside the scope of this history.

3 The uses of the past

The Graeco-Roman past

To believe that one can bundle up the poetry of our period in the term 'classicism' is to place one's faith in a rope of ashes. It merely dirties and makes slippery what it is supposed to bind. No one, however, would deny what the previous chapter has just asserted, that the classics profoundly influenced Restoration and eighteenth-century poets. The education of these men and women would alone have led them to draw as they did on the Greek and Latin past. A sampling of 187 male poets who wrote between 1660 and 1780, and on whose formal education the *Dictionary of National Biography* comments, shows that a remarkable number went to university: about 80 per cent for the period from 1660 to 1750, about 65 per cent for the period from 1750 to 1780. Only ten men, just over 5 per cent of the total, seem to have had no formal schooling (six of them, about 11 per cent, writers of the last thirty years). Another group – four who were tutored, nineteen who stopped with public or grammar school, thirteen who studied law or medicine – were presumably (like the university students) drilled day after day and year after year in Latin and Greek, for Latin and Greek made up the great bulk of the school curriculum for eight years, and if one went to university, more than eight. No student who saw that his country's educational system made paramount the reading, memorizing, writing, and often speaking of classical languages could forget what he, in his public role as poet, owed to the past as a living root of culture.

A comparably well-known group of sixteen female poets could not learn Latin and Greek in school, so that their classical attainments bear further witness to the extraordinary prestige of those languages and culture. Anna Aikin Barbauld learned them from her father; Elizabeth Tollet wrote Latin verse; Constantia Grierson edited Latin classics and also knew Greek and Hebrew; Lady Mary Wortley Montagu taught herself Latin; Mary Mollineux knew Latin well, Greek less well. Unlike the men, they did not, perhaps, memorize and recite great swatches of Ovid, Horace, and Virgil, or do set translations of Latin verse into English, English into Latin. Their capacity for creating quick echoes and transpositions of classical texts was perhaps less. But like the men, these learned ladies did gain familiarity with the texts and with the forms – the ode, the satire, the epic, the epistle – in which they appeared. From translation, the standard way of learning to use classical languages, women and men also learned to weigh poetic words for sound, placement, and connotation as well as meaning. Tutors and schoolmasters, along with schoolbooks, lighted classical poetry with detailed literary criticism. Such a classical master, for instance, showed the eighteenth-century boy Coleridge 'that poetry . . . had a logic of its own as severe as that of science; and more difficult, because more subtle, more complex, and dependent on more and more fugitive causes,' and made him consider the precision of poetic language (*Biographia Literaria*, Ch. 1). Young men and women also grew to know another great culture, and to appraise their own comparatively, from teachers and from the generous footnotes in widespread editions of the classics in the original (like the Delphin series) and in English translations (Pope's Homer, Philip Francis's Horace, Christopher Pitt's Virgil).

A habitual reader of verse would have felt how pervasive and many-sided the classical legacy was. English poems echoed, imitated, parodied, and tried to catch the resonances of classical ones, most obviously in declared imitations. In the Restoration and eighteenth century, the body of verse more imitated than any other was Horace's *Odes*, overshadowing his *Epistles* and very much overshadowing his *Satires*. The dominance of the *Odes* may seem odd to those who bow to the last century's (still current) critical wisdom, which claimed that the lyric languished in the 'Age of Reason'; but odder still, then, would be a list of other poets most often overtly imitated. I surmise that such a list would contain, in this rough order, Martial, Anacreon, and Virgil; Tibullus, Claudian, and Ovid; Catullus, Propertius, and Juvenal; and Ausonius and Seneca. No doubt my list bends toward men who wrote shorter poems, like Martial, which are easier to imitate closely, especially in one's spare moments, than, say, several hundred packed lines of Juvenal. The list also ignores the sort of powerful oblique influence exerted by the tone and techniques of the satiric Horace, the Virgil of the *Georgics*, and epic poets. Nevertheless, it does reveal a strong interest in the lyric (Anacreon, Tibullus, Catullus, and Propertius as well as Horace) and in post-Augustan Latin poetry (Martial, Claudian, Juvenal, Ausonius, Seneca).

It also reveals the bias of the period toward Latin over Greek works, except for Anacreon's, though this bias diminished around mid-century. The pastoral model of Theocritus, for instance, exercised oblique influence on those who wanted more nature, less art in pastoral; but the direct model for Theocritans was the Spenser of *The Shepheardes Calendar*, despite praise for Theocritus by Dryden and Pope, partial translations by the two most prestigious Restoration translators, Dryden and Creech, and acknowledgment in an edition of Virgil by Joseph Warton (1753) that Theocritus was 'the great storehouse of pastoral description; . . . every succeeding painter of rural beauty (except Thomson in his *Seasons*) hath copied his images from him, without ever looking abroad upon the face of nature.' They did not look upon Theocritus' face either, as they did upon Virgil's, but copied intermediaries' versions of his originals. Conceptual patterns, then, and modes of response come from both Greek and Latin sources; actual poems used as models, lines quoted, and tricks of style imitated are likely to be Latin.

Restoration and eighteenth-century verse often does embed lines translated or adapted from Latin in it. As John Smith wrote in the preface to his *Poems on Several Occasions* (1713), he has borrowed from the 'ancients' 'such fragments as . . . serve for a kind of inlay to the work, and afford a graceful variety. And indeed, it sometimes so falls out that the scions we graft upon our own crab-stock imbibe a poignancy from thence that quickens the juices and improves the fruit.' Often these grafts are simply inserted into the stem of the original, as in James Hammond's *Love Elegies* (written 1732; pub. 1743), which repeatedly take cuttings from Tibullus. By their nature, burlesques borrow allusions too, though for irony: when Delia makes a shuttlecock in Anthony Whistler's poem of that name (1736), she pierces a cork which 'returned a doleful sound,/As if it pity begged and felt the wound,' thus parodying Laocoön's javelin (*Aeneid* 2:50–3) which makes the Trojan Horse groan, both Dryden's and Pitt's translations say, as if wounded. Here the mildly amusing incongruity remains simply that. The specific reference adds little to the already clear mock-heroic tone, and the allusion has no further force. Besides simple and ironic grafts, some deepen a compliment or insult by adding an extra tang to the poetic fruit. Pope, in his *Epistle to Burlington* (1735), gives himself more stature when his summary advice on gardening imitates Horace's summary advice about poetry. 'He gains all points' (or votes), writes Horace in the *Ars poetica* ll. 343–4, who can mix profit and pleasure, delighting and teaching the reader at the same time; and Pope (ll. 55–6): 'He gains all points, who pleasingly confounds,/Surprises, varies, and conceals the bounds.' Pope also imports from Horace a moral tone for his advice about gardening. His mutuality between art and nature (itself a central topic in the *Ars poetica*) quite clearly becomes, through the allusion, pleasurable and profitable for the person of taste.

Pope here draws on his source for specific context as Hammond and Whistler do not. A more complex example of allusion, along lines that Pope himself developed in his so-called 'Epistle to Augustus' (his imitation of *Epistles* 2 : 1), appears in the Third Book of Thomson's *Liberty* (1735), borrowed from Horace, *Odes* 4 : 4.57–60. Horace wrote, in Philip Francis's translation (1742), of Roman strength in the Punic Wars:

> That race, long tossed upon the Tuscan waves,
>   Are like an oak upon the woody top
> Of shaded Algidus, bestrowed with leaves,
>   Which, as keen axes its green honors lop,
> Through wounds, through losses, no decay can feel,
> Collecting strength and spirit from the steel.

The purpose of Horace's praise in this ode, characteristically written at Augustus' request, is to give the empire a proud lineage from the first Trojan exiles to Hannibal's foes to the present. Republican virtues glorify Augustan reign. Thomson's history of Rome in *Liberty*, however, takes that reign as an evil end to a tradition of freedom, a creation of 'slaves that licked the scourging hand' (l. 360).

To use Horace but reject his smooth political pandering, Thomson presents the decline of the republic by transferring Horace's simile of the sea ('long tossed upon the Tuscan waves') to one of a becalmed vessel:

This firm republic, that against the blast
Of opposition rose, that (like an oak
Nursed on ferocious Algidum, whose boughs
Still stronger shoot beneath the rigid axe)
By loss, by slaughter, from the steel itself
E'en force and spirit drew; smit with the calm,
The dead serene of prosperous fortune, pined.   (ll. 361–7)

Although the passage makes perfect sense if one misses the allusion, it gains ironic depth as an answer to Horace if one is alert to the echo.

Thomson's bowing to Horace the poet so as to rebuke the citizen Horace, his reinterpretation of Horace's order of history so as to invoke the Roman example for Britain, his probable use of scholars' notes (in the Delphin Horace or in the editions by Dacier and Sanadon) to tell him that Horace's ode was requisitioned by Augustus – all these make Thomson's allusion a paradigm of complex use of the classics. How common a paradigm it was, I leave to the judgment of that reader who recalls as much Latin verse as every eighteenth-century schoolboy had to memorize. Despite the admirable craftsmanship of many of Thomson's fellow poets, however, I doubt that it was a common paradigm. I am inclined to believe that for most people the great quantities of Latin devoured in school lingered in the memory like the picked carcass of a holiday goose: the shape was there, and scraps of the meat, but with most of the nourishment already assimilated and the taste a recollection. Poets who insisted on central complex allusions advertised them in footnotes or title. Otherwise, the allusion was unlikely to be central and was not often complex.

Some modern critics, I recognize, interpret poems not only through specific allusions but also through standard scholarly glosses to these allusions. To do so implies that poets expected readers to have such annotations in their heads or hands. The latter is hardly possible except for declared imitations. The former presumes that facts learned about poems in school were thereafter cemented to the texts in people's minds. We cannot capture what long-past schoolmasters told their generations of scribbling students, but we do know that the most important schoolmaster of the seventeenth century, Richard Busby of Westminster School, used texts without explanatory notes. If poets had no assurance that common schoolbooks had given their audiences necessary facts for catching allusions, I suspect that they did not make elaborate allusiveness an important practice. The poetry, after all, was mostly written for public consumption, not for self-expression or a coterie. One is best off assuming that allusions were to texts, not notes, and to plain rather than esoteric themes and ideas in the texts.

Some evidence for my skepticism comes from the poets' use of classical names in satires. Edward Young's second satire (1725) in his *Love of Fame*, for instance, mocks a 'Codrus.' There was more than one Codrus, but Young presumably takes the name from Juvenal's first and third satires. Young also indicts characters with Italianate or allegorical names, and some English contemporaries represented by an initial letter and a dash. This sort of mixture, common in satire, gives a sense of a diversity of targets and a tradition of abuses to be lashed, a sense of universality. Young did not ask more from it. In his Codrus, a wealthy book-collector whose costly editions glow in crimson bindings, he playfully inverts Juvenal's, whose name had become proverbial – e.g., in Erasmus's *Adagia* – as that of a penniless poet with a few Greek pamphlets in an old chest. The allusion serves no particular poetic end. Even Pope makes little active use of it in his three Codruses, coming closest in the second book of the *Dunciad* (1728), where the resemblance of his Codrus (l. 136) and Juvenal's points and makes typical a satire on the 'broken bookseller and abusive scribbler,' so Pope calls him, John Dunton. Much earlier, in his first satire ('To the Author of a Poem Entitled *Successio*,' written 1702?), he had attacked Elkanah Settle with the same reminiscence of Juvenal. Here, though, Settle's poverty is at most implied and the only characteristic he shares with Juvenal's Codrus is that of having written bad heroics (Codrus's tragedy *The Theseid*, Settle's poem *Eusebia Triumphans* on the Hanoverian succession). Even looser is the allusion to Codrus in the *Epistle to Dr. Arbuthnot* (ll. 85–9), where he simply stands for any bad, vain tragedian. We can see how little the specific Juvenalian context – still assuming Juvenal's 'Codrus' is meant – counts for Pope. In *Arbuthnot*, Codrus 'stand[s] unshook amidst a bursting world,' the theater bursting with laughter at his inept tragedy. Pope here plays not on a line of Juvenal's but one of Horace's, in the noble ode (3 : 3) where the man of virtue remains confident despite mobs, a tyrant, and the ruin of the world (ll. 1–8). Some of these four 'Codruses' come closer than others to being active allusions, but they contribute a flavor rather than evoke a rich Juvenalian context. Even Pope's play in *Arbuthnot* on the beginning of one of Horace's most famous odes – which *is* a significant allusion – draws on the plain sense of the lines, not on anything *recherché* or due to a Dutch scholiast. And, not trusting to his readers' remembered Latin, Pope footnotes the Horatian lines he borrows.

Declared imitations gave poets more leeway to be subtle about allusion. As with allusions to individual lines and phrases, one finds a wide variety of imitations. Swift's half-dozen treatments of Horace written between 1712 and 1720 will suggest some of the range beyond the mere Englishing of a text by inserting modern names and references (itself a popular form). Two are tributes to Swift's friends Archbishop King and the Earl of Oxford. Both follow Horace's original quite closely, yet with differences, because the lonely patriot King opposes the court, unlike the consul Lollius to whom Horace wrote the ode (4 : 9) Swift adapts; Oxford too Swift saw as a lonely patriot, imprisoned for making peace, unlike the soldiers Horace praises in the adapted ode (3 : 2). Swift emphasizes Archbishop King's solitude by adapting only parts of the ode (ll. 24–38 and 45–52 in Horace). He omits a long lineage of poetic heroes, a recital of public services, and even the approving 'I' of Horace the public bard. In order to intensify the image of King environed by enemies whom he alone awes and repels, Swift also introduces personified vices, 'Pale Avarice and lurking Fraud,' as allegorical foes. For the Earl of Oxford, Swift omits Horace's martial beginning and converts to irony Horace's famous 'Dulce et decorum est pro patria mori': Oxford may well die for his country, not in war but for having achieved the Peace of Utrecht. Certain Horatian particulars are also adapted. For instance, since Oxford had been impeached by the House of Commons he had led, Swift turns Horace's crime of betraying the divine mysteries of Ceres into the crime of betraying a friend.

A different and freer kind of adaptation occurs in the comical poems Swift made from Horace's *Epistles* 1 : 7 and *Satires* 2 : 6. In both he treats his own contacts with the Earl of Oxford, then still Lord Treasurer Harley, by expanding the originals with satiric detail and contemporary allusions. In both poems, too, he employs the familiar style of epistle and Horatian satire to express pointedly personal statements, unlike the impersonality and lofty sententiousness of the odes adapted to praise Archbishop King and the Earl of Oxford. Horace's epistle tells how the gregarious town-crier Vulteius is made an independent farmer (a *rusticus*) by the amused indulgence of the wealthy and powerful Lucius Philippus; his new duties and dependence on fortune drive Vulteius to beg to be restored to his old job. This tale, which occupies the second half of Horace's poem (ll. 46–98), documents the poet's desire for freedom and a modest life (ll. 1–45). Swift eliminates the character of Horace entirely, to efface himself by a direct comparison with Vulteius: the bustling Roman town-crier becomes a shy but vigorous English political pamphleteer, the independent farm becomes the deanery of St Patrick's Cathedral, and agricultural perils (bad harvest, sick animals) turn into the systematic deceit of tenants, tithers, and steward. More to the satiric point, whereas Vulteius easily and cheaply gets the Sabine farm he has been led to crave, Swift does not get what he wants, a canonry at Windsor, but instead a splendid, expensive Irish exile, a dubious recompence for valuable services. In fact Swift and his friends settled for St Patrick's after months of struggling and politicking – that, of course, is *not* in the poem, but lies behind its irony. In the other Horatian imitation for Harley, Swift expands and adds satiric details to a wish for rural life. He apologizes for his apparent rejection of Harley by making London more obnoxious and the Crown's demands on him more peremptory than anything in Horace's Rome..Compelled to London by duty, he is pestered in the city and promoted by public opinion to an influentiality that causes him to be fawned on and courted:

> I get a whisper and withdraw,
> When twenty fools I never saw
> Come with petitions fairly penned,
> Desiring I would stand their friend.
> This, humbly offers me his case;
> That, begs my interest for a place;
> A hundred other men's affairs
> Like bees are humming in my ears.
> 'Tomorrow my appeal comes on –

Without your help the cause is gone.'
'The Duke expects my Lord and you
About some great affair at two.'   (ll. 43 – 54)

Harley's own political weakness at the time the poem was presumably begun – he had fallen and the Queen had died by the time it was finished – made this treatment of Horace, addressed to this recipient, tactfully comforting.

In addition to these two amusing expansions of Horace and the two more strictly translated panegyrics, Swift's Horatian canon holds two ironic inversions, printed with the Latin originals so that readers could see what he had done. One of these poems arises from an agreement for legislative logrolling between the Tory Earl of Nottingham, nicknamed 'Dismal,' and Harley's Whig opponents. In Swift's 'Toland's Invitation to Dismal, to Dine with the Calves-Head Club,' Nottingham's new allies, typified by the religious radical John Toland, invite him to join them in a blasphemous tavern dinner celebrating the murder of King Charles I. Swift writes this invitation to personal and political debauchery after the model of Horace's *Epistles* 1 : 5, in which the poet invites a friend to his home for a tranquil, patriotic evening of dinner and friendly talk. With some devastating exceptions, the adaptation is quite close, the irony all the more biting. Similarly Swift uses Horace's *Odes* 2 : 1, in praise of Asinius Pollio's history of the Roman civil wars, to attack Richard Steele's pamphlet history of the Revolution of 1689 and its constitutional results. At a time of wobbly public stability, Horace asks Pollio to stop writing tragedies and to turn his energies to deepening men's knowledge of conflicts. Swift's poem, written when England's state is also wobbly, shows Steele the pamphleteer trying to inform men about civil war only to incite them to still more fighting. Pollio the tragedian who writes history becomes Steele who gives up 'farce' and 'wicked verse' to vent his spleen and political nonsense. Horace's Pollio, noble comforter of the oppressed, becomes a Steele who comforts 'buxom lasses' in his closet; Pollio's military triumphs in Dalmatia shrink to Steele's electoral victory as MP for Stockbridge; the clarion trumpets that salute Pollio's generalship turn into Steele's loud, shrill voice; the great leaders, stained with honest dirt (*'non indecoro pulvere'*), who crowd about Pollio dwindle to the low mob, 'a blackguard rout,' who love Steele's demagogy. Here, alone in his Horatian imitations, Swift departs from Horace's tone. The loftiness of the Roman ode drops to a slangy familiarity that forbids Steele to fancy himself another Pollio, public benefactor and deep delver into the 'authentic records' and 'just causes' that he advertises on the title-page of his pamphlet, *The Crisis*. Horace ends his ode humbly, confessing himself fit for Venus' counsel, not the grandeur of Pollio. Swift seizes on this to urge, with contemptuous bonhommie, that he and Steele retire to a tavern cellar to 'immortalize our Dollys and Jennys,' not the affairs of a nation.

None of these six poems of Swift's makes much capital of the originals being Horatian or classical. Any well-known model with the same sentiments would do, from Roman or any other culture. Though the Horatian originals represent norms of value, at least poetic value, only the satires on Nottingham and Steele, where Swift prints the originals along with his adaptations, demand much knowledge of the Latin text, though all require one to know that there is such a text. In these matters, Swift's Horatian poems fit with much Restoration and eighteenth-century practice. They are also quite typical in their posture toward the originals. We have no idolatry but a considered and flexible employment of the past in the interests of the present. Swift's range of use marks him, however, as an early eighteenth-century rather than Restoration poet. Rochester's 'An Allusion to Horace' (written 1675–6), an attack on Dryden that adapts Horace's *Satires* 1 : 10 more or less as Swift's attacks on Nottingham and Steele adapt their Horatian originals, is one of very few Restoration imitations that change the original rather than simply modernize it. By the first decade of the new century, poets had begun to exploit imitations further, so that in William Walsh, for example, we find Horace's *Odes* 3 : 3 adapted for William III (1705) as Swift adapts odes for Oxford and King, and Virgil's Fourth Eclogue (the 'Messianic' Eclogue) bent for acid satire of the often-used prophetic mode (1703). In Congreve's hands Horace's *Odes* 2 : 14, a frank and rather melancholy *carpe diem* poem, becomes a bitter declaration of the futility of life. Rowe's saucy imitation of *Odes* 2 : 4 could be enjoyed in comparison with not only the original but also other English adaptations, like the sentimental one by Thomas Yalden ('To His Friend, Captain Chamberlain'). As poets exposed new creative possibilities, the mode of the imitation became part of every versifier's stock, and remained so till mid-century or later.

Certain classical poems were so often imitated, loosely or not, as almost to be genres in themselves. For instance, Horace's *Ars poetica* produced a whole series of 'Arts,' such as John Gwynn's(?) or Robert Morris's(?) *The Art of Architecture* (1742), William King's *The Art of Cookery* (1708), and so on through 'Arts' of *Life* (James Miller, 1739), *Living in London* (1768), *Modern Poetry* (also by Miller, with the main title of *Harlequin-Horace*, 1731, 1735), *Politics* (James Bramston, 1729), *Preaching* (Robert Dodsley, 1738), and *Stock-Jobbing* (1746). These 'Arts' should be kept separate from another group of poems, those written between about 1680 and 1720 that try to extend Horace's method of giving precepts about poetry, with the specific stimulus of Boileau's own Horatian imitation, *L'Art poétique* (1674; Eng. tr. 1683); Pope's *Essay on Criticism* is the best and best-known of the group. The 'Art' poems mostly come later, in the 1720s to 1740s, and draw directly on Horace's text. *Stock-Jobbing* and *Living in London*, the latest of these, draw least on Horace. They are rambling how-to-do-it poems, with the advice loosely strung together. *Architecture* and *Life*, the next latest, come closer to Horace's manner in giving their counsel, about building and morality respectively, to beginners who must be shown the commonplaces in a sage, amiable way. Like many imitations, they are made to vary in their distance from the Latin, sometimes rendering Horace closely, sometimes inverting him, sometimes straying. Both call only for an intermittent memory of the original. Miller's *Harlequin-Horace* represents a different mode, the ironic parody of the Horatian content. Here the speaker advises 'modern connoisseurs' to be preposterous, heterogeneous, and aggressively novel: 'Thus ne'er regard connection, time, or place,/For sweet variety has every grace.' Since the reader needs a continuous, exact knowledge of the original to enjoy Miller's cheerful conversion of familiar precepts into absurdities, the Latin text is printed at the foot of the page. The absurdities, of course, are so obvious that the poem defends the ideals of the original. Like Swift when he puts folly in the mouths of the speakers in his satires on Nottingham and Steele, Miller intends no challenge to Horace.

If not a challenge then at least a revision of Horace's method appears in one of the most creative adaptations of the *Ars poetica*, James Bramston's *Art of Politics*. As one can tell from the Horatian text at the bottom of the pages, Bramston adapts his original freely, modernizing, translating, expanding, deleting, inverting, and warping. For example, adapting Horace's advice that one can coin words if need be, provided they have Greek roots and are used sparingly, Bramston encourages his politicians to employ jargon and neologisms, to 'Coin words; in coining ne'er mind common sense,/Provided the original be French' (p. 7). More subversively, he reminds his reader of the difference between Horace's time and his:

> Kings and comedians all are mortal found,
> Caesar and Pinkethman are under ground.
> What's not destroyed by Time's devouring hand?
> Where's Troy, and where's the maypole in the Strand?
> Peas, cabbages, and turnips once grew where
> Now stands New Bond Street, and a newer square.
> Such piles of buildings now rise up and down,
> London itself seems going out of town. (pp. 7–8)

The proper names of Horace's contemporary, Caesar, and Bramston's, the late low comedian Pinkethman, make suspiciously grotesque the quite Horatian sentiment about the leveling of all men in death. Sententiousness about 'Time's devouring hand' drops into non-Horatian mock-heroic by the coupling of legendary Troy with the vulgar maypole, which had been removed a decade or so before the poem. Moreover, the society that can offer only a maypole to match a Troy does not, like Horace's Rome, reclaim marsh for farmland (one of the public works mentioned in the corresponding passage of the *Ars poetica*). Instead modern England destroys farms for fashionable streets, for transitory buildings and urban sprawl. Bramston maintains Horace's point, that everything is transient, but, by using Rome as a norm, changes the implications of that point for the 'art' (politics) he is writing about. Horace's Caesars (ll. 63–9) battle transiency, Bramston's politicians promote it.

The choice of the *Ars poetica* has tactical advantages for Bramston which it does not for the other 'Art' poems. First, the comparison implicit in this imitation makes politics into a calculated, rhetorical art, politicking instead of wise governing. Thus Horace's legitimate comparison of poems to paintings, some better if seen close and some if seen from a distance (ll. 361–2), turns into Bramston's rhetorical maxim, 'Not unlike paintings, principles appear,/Some best at distance, some when we are near' (p. 36). Second, Horace's and Bramston's, like any how-to-do-it poems, catch at the reader's self-interest. Admirable for the artist who wants to improve his craft, self-interest is less innocent in the politician. The Horatian poet finds his in true knowledge, the fount of good writing; Socrates' thoughts and a sense of patriotic duty and familial love will guide one to the proper words (ll. 309–13). Bramston substitutes a political philosopher for Socrates and political counters for words: Machiavelli and 'ready money.' The politician then can 'Give to his country what's his country's due,/But first help brothers, sons, and cousins too' (p. 31). These twin accusations, politicking and self-interest, may merely be expressions of Bramston's distaste for political life. Such distaste, however, was often affected by those in opposition to the Prime Minister, Sir Robert Walpole, whom the poem satirizes obliquely three or four times. Therefore, the third advantage in the *Ars poetica* for Bramston the Opposition poet is in the Roman analogy it affords him, for the Opposition made a stock in trade of historical comparisons with Roman virtue and corruption. As Horatian sententiousness turns into farce because the modern age can offer only a Pinkethman for a Caesar, a maypole for Troy, a pilloried Defoe when 'rotten eggs besmeared his yellow face' for Thespis (p. 27), so the Roman analogy indicts Walpole's England.

We have not yet touched another sort of imitation, the attempt to write a new poem like that which a classical author might have written if he had spoken eighteenth-century English. Translators and modernizers tried to do this, of course, sometimes very well; but to write a new poem in the manner of a major classical poet and at his level of quality demanded the talents of a Dryden, a Pope, a Thomson, a Collins, a Gray. Dryden and Pope did not try. Thomson stutteringly touches the level of his model, Virgil's *Georgics*, in parts of the *Seasons*. Collins's *Ode to Evening* is worthy Horace in one of his moods, not the most dynamic, philosophical, genial, or magniloquent. The greatest success came to Gray in his two superb Pindaric odes (1757), 'The Progress of Poesy' and 'The Bard,' poems barely overpraised in their own time (by those who could comprehend them) and grossly undervalued in ours. As we have seen, Restoration Pindarics followed the model set by Cowley. His celebratory enthusiasm, by the early eighteenth century, was abandoned to dutiful cobblers of commendations, and his irregular stanzas became cheapened by overuse. Congreve urged, and got, a revaluation of Pindar's own regular, strophic, and coherent practice, so that the difference narrowed between the two eighteenth-century models for the 'greater' ode, Pindar and Horace. Even when poets rejected the exact stanzas of Horace and the elaborate strophes of Pindar in favor of Cowleyan freedom, as John Dyer, for instance, did in one version of his lovely 'Grongar Hill' (1726), rhyme schemes were simpler and the poetic movement more lucid. By the next generation, in the 1740s, we find the most distinguished odes, those of Collins and Akenside, keeping still better to the strophic pattern, though in content they are farther from Pindar's celebratory patriotism than were their Cowleyan ancestors. Once this diversity of approaches to the ode had wiped away Cowleyan assumptions, however, poets could, as Gray did, try to recreate the Pindaric original.

Gray employs Pindar's strophic form, repetition of a base unit comprising three parts, two complex and metrically identical stanzas followed by a third complex stanza of different structure. Pindar's allusiveness elicits Gray's, which extends to poetic models. By his own statements, Homer, Phrynicus, Virgil, Petrarch, the

Bible, and Cowley contributed phrases to 'The Progress of Poesy,' and from the mid-eighteenth century up until the present day, scholars have discovered a great many more parallels, conscious or unconscious, within that poem. To similarly wide cullings and echoings from classical and English sources 'The Bard' adds a declared debt to Welsh prosody. Of course Pindar himself is among the poets on whom Gray draws. For example, in the *First Pythian Ode*, Pindar wrote (as translated, 1749, by Gilbert West):

> The bird's fierce monarch drops his vengeful ire;
> Perched on the sceptre of th' Olympian king,
> The thrilling darts of harmony he feels
> And indolently hangs his rapid wing
> While gentle sleep his closing eyelid seals
> And o'er his heaving limbs in loose array
> To every balmy gale the ruffling feathers play.   (ll. 14–20)

'The Progress of Poesy' incorporates Gray's briefer, better translation:

> Perching on the sceptered hand
> Of Jove, thy magic lulls the feathered king
> With ruffled plumes and flagging wing:
> Quenched in dark clouds of slumber lie
> The terror of his beak and lightnings of his eye.   (ll. 20–4)

As these lines show, Gray tries to imitate Greek rhythms in English. In other parts of the poems, he also reproduces the salient features of Pindar's expression, the torrential lines, the abrupt movements, the bold images, the obscurity (for which Gray's contemporaries scolded him), and the 'wonderful short phrases,' as Francis Bacon called them, 'that strike the unsuspecting mind as with a sacred rod' (*De Dignitate et Augmentis Scientiarum* 8 : 1).

Gray's poems make Pindar contemporary by recreating his art. They also, simultaneously, make one aware of his pastness, along with Homer, Virgil, and legendary lyre-strumming Welshmen. This double historical sense carries over to theme, for the structure of Gray's odes comes from the interaction of liberty, the triumph of the free spirit, with historical entailment. Poesy progresses from enslaved to free lands, which, themselves enslaved in turn, see it then pass from them. The Welsh bard's prophecy damns the royal line of his land's English oppressor to a succession of aborted lives and loss of power, repeating and revenging through history the murder of the bards at one historical moment, till the Tudors redeem both Wales and poetry. Such a theme is perfect for the Pindaric ode. The poetic form, at once modern and inherited, at once arranged by the artist and (because of the strict repetitions) inevitable, is in harmony with the theme.

In both these great odes, the cyclical stanzaic pattern regulates the order of events. 'The Bard,' for example, sets the scene with three stanzas in which ruin is invoked on the oppressor, King Edward I, and in which there rises a vision of the bards the king has had murdered. Then, in the middle, metrically identical three stanzas, the bards' ghosts spell out the recurrent disasters to afflict Edward's line, with murders and unlamented deaths in a varied but analogous series: the poetic army of chanting Welsh ghosts and the single falls of English kings in these stanzas complement the royal army of English Edward and the single fated Welsh bard of the first three. The last metrically identical set of three stanzas presents the resolution, in which the ghosts of the past melt away, to be replaced by a vision of the future Tudors, and an evocation of poetry renewed by Spenser and Shakespeare, then Milton and his successors. Similar variety and cyclic analogy, in imagery, forms of motion, and units of time (night/day, winter/summer, historical succession), inform the cyclical stanzas of 'The Progress of Poesy.' This is wonderfully Pindaric, but with a difference. Pindar celebrated physical victories on given occasions for which the past provided analogues. His rejoicing over the recurrent games (Nemean, Pythian, Olympian, Isthmian) suggests the theme of renewal through time. In updating him, Gray has given this theme a depth that also marks the difference between Greek culture, where the poet is the laureate of the youth of the state, and that of eighteenth-century England, where history and politics mean something much harder to assimilate for the poet, a private citizen. Gray's victories are spiritual, embodied in given events and understood in their implications through historical analogues. The analogues, though, differ from each other, so that renewal, always incomplete, implies historical alienation too. This is precisely the status of Gray's odes in relation to Pindar's. Neither antiquarian nor arrogant about capturing the 'soul' of a dead poet, they recreate Pindar's art in a new way just as their content gives voice to a cyclical, yet always differing pattern of history.

The discussion so far has suggested three eighteenth-century attitudes toward classical allusion and imitation. The classical work may be a neutral model, useful because familiar and therefore available for reworking and parody. The classical work may be a norm as art and as a bearer of values: Restoration and eighteenth-century poets then can draw on it for its prestige alone or, as often happens in satire, for a contrast between its artistic and/or cultural values and those of a modern work or society. The third and rarest treatment of a classical model is to accept its artistic value but to challenge or reject its statement. I have singled out Thomson's treatment of Horace's ode about the strength of the Roman Republic and Swift's of his ode to Lollius as examples of this third kind of treatment. Another, more familiar to students of eighteenth-century literature, is to be found in Johnson's *Vanity of Human Wishes* (1749), where an imitation of Juvenal's Tenth Satire replaces majestic pagan savagery with an equally majestic, but compassionate Christianity. Like Swift's and Thomson's poems, *The Vanity of Human Wishes* dates from the first half of the eighteenth century; so do virtually all the poems of this third sort, which accept the art of a classical work but reject its statement. The brunt of the challenge was borne less often by paganism, as in Johnson, than by imperial politics, a rotted weapon in the minds of those who lived under the dispensation of the balanced British Constitution. Such politics, as I have indicated, seemed especially odious in the time of Walpole. The flaws of paganism intrigued few, scattered classical imitators, and then more in ethical than in religious terms, if those can be separated. None of these three kinds of treatment has much to do, of course, with the run-of-the-mill bad poet, who simply kept grinding out his student exercises into adult life, in what was contemptuously called – from at least the mid-seventeenth century on – 'servile imitation' of a specific poet or poem. For the uncreative, imitation offered great savings of thought and work. It offered the creative great profits in complexity and delicacy of meaning, whether the classical model was treated as neutral, normative, or culturally flawed.

The most creative imitations, of course, were those of Pope himself. He rarely used neutral models, as he did in his 'Imitation of Martial' (1717), a friend's birthday greeting. Normative models of a general sort, however, used for their prestige or for a cultural contrast unflattering to modern England, appear in the *Pastorals*, *Windsor Forest*, *Eloisa to Abelard*, the *Dunciad*, and various epistles; one cannot be surprised that a poet of such inclinations might use specific classical models for the same purposes, as Pope used poems by Horace in the 1730s. Except for the scandalous (and anonymous) *Sober Advice from Horace*, a fair enough adaptation of *Satires* 1 : 2, Pope's Horatian imitations try to portray him as a disinterested, temperate, rural patriot. He takes on, as most imitators do not, the rich though edited personality of the Horatian speaker, the public Horace himself. In the imitations, he spreads magnificently before us the full range of Horatian tones as expressions of this personality. (His 'Horatian' poems that are not direct imitations, such as the *Epistle to Dr Arbuthnot* (1735) and the two *Epilogues to the Satires* (1738), differ. They infuse their generic models with a righteous anger and epigrammatic vengefulness that owes more to Juvenal, Persius, and Martial than Horace.)

Paradoxically, the logic of this impersonation of one great poet by another drives them apart as well as joins them. Disinterestedness, temperance, country values, patriotism – these were the values flaunted by the Opposition to Walpole, Pope among them. To flaunt them in the 1730s colored the imitations politically in a manner foreign to Horace, and sometimes sharply critical of him. Horace, seen through the eyes of the Opposition, was not only a great poet and wise man but also the tyrant Augustus's toady, the pensioned and flattered bard of the imperial Establishment. Through the 1730s, Pope made progressively more of his independence, a fidelity to Horatian values beyond Horace's own appraisal of them. His last Horatian imitations and his last finished poems of a Horatian type came in 1738, and his last fragment of the type in 1740, before he abandoned the persona for that of the exuberant and scornful Apocalypt who orates the final version of the *Dunciad* (1743).

During the five years when he wrote Horatian imitations, Pope kept to one group of tactics. He translated the text brilliantly, very rarely omitting a passage of the original but characteristically expanding and developing it through examples and imagery. For instance, in *Epistles* 1 : 1, Horace addresses an imagined 'tireless merchant' who runs 'to the farthest Indies, fleeing poverty over the sea, over rocks, over fire'; Pope's imitation is longer, more concrete, more epigrammatic:

To either India see the merchant fly,
Scared at the spectre of pale Poverty!
See him, with pains of body, pangs of soul,
Burn through the Tropic, freeze beneath the Pole!   (ll. 69–72)

He modernizes, of course, using his contemporaries' names (or alluding to them) even when Horace remains general, and often wittily adapting Horace's specifics. When Horace (*Epistles* 1 : 1) has the cry for money first, virtue later, echo from the top to the bottom of Janus street (where Roman bankers practiced), Pope theologizes the same cry into 'the saving doctrine, preached to all,/From low St. James's up to high St. Paul' (ll. 81–2). The pun on 'saving,' the play on 'Janus' and 'James's' (wordplay, but also a suggestion of God made pagan), the transference of the physical top and bottom of the Roman street into the theological 'high' and 'low' of English churches, and the bringing of the moneychangers into the temples of London – these are all captured in a couplet. As one would expect, Pope fills his versions with politics as Horace had not. Horace's advice that a good conscience be a protective wall of brass serves Pope as a means of alluding to two labels, 'screen' and 'brass,' that always referred to Sir Robert Walpole (l. 95). The King is mentioned with scorn (ll. 105–6) and distrust (ll. 115–20). The old retired gladiator with whom Horace begins (ll. 3–5) offers Pope a chance to snipe at the old retired actor Colley Cibber, King George's Poet Laureate, and also at the King's military policy of peace for England but readiness to fight for his German electorate (ll. 6–10). Behind these open allusions flies a swarm of hints in other passages.

The poet whose youthful eye fell as quizzically upon Homer as upon Hampton Court in *The Rape of the Lock* did not, when older and more serious, treat Horace with piety. In Pope's version of *Satires* 2 : 1, his 'Caesar,' George II, 'scarce can bear' the 'lays' of his Poet Laureate Cibber while in the corresponding Latin passage (ll. 18–20) Augustus Caesar pays attention at suitable times to Horace: the change implies that George has no taste for poetry and no Laureate to have a taste for, but it also implies that in flattery (the subject of the preceding eight lines of Horace's poem) Horace was his Caesar's Cibber. Later in the same poem, Pope appropriates for himself Horace's lines about the bold, virtuous Roman republican satirist Lucilius, and he casts scorn – as pensioned Horace does not – on hireling poets (ll. 105ff.). Horace's epistle to Caesar's confidant Maecenas (1 : 1) becomes Pope's to the King's and Walpole's chief opponent, Bolingbroke.

Still more pointed is Pope's ironic imitation of Horace's encomium for Augustus, *Epistles* 2 : 1. Scholars who thought that the 'Augustan' poet Pope must have honored Augustus Caesar (a fair assumption, if one puts one's trust in labels) have habitually treated this poem as one of contrast, the splendor of Augustan Rome and its enlightened patronage (Horace's subject) as against the pettiness and philistinism of Georgian England. If inversion had been Pope's tactic, ironic encomia of minor authors would have properly replaced Horace's history of Latin poetry; but in fact Pope follows Horace rather closely in this part of the poem. The satire is elsewhere. Pope parodies flattery of a monarch, with Horace's own flattery

97

of his Caesar as Pope's satiric butt. The praise that sits so grotesquely on the narrow shoulders of George II copies praise almost equally unfitting for Augustus, a successful tyrant and subverter of poetry instead of, like George, a fumbling manipulator through Walpole and fawning Cibberians. The paradoxically bad taste of imperial Rome, which Horace would cure through patronage and legislation, turns into English bad taste encouraged through the Horatian means of royal patronage and legislation – the specific reference is to the licensing of the Theatre Royal in 1737, the year of Pope's poem. Writer and ruler must be kept separate for Pope, not, as Horace would have them, made patron and employee. The nobility of art, like disinterestedness, country values, temperance, and patriotism, was a Horatian value; Pope, in his poetic imitations, supports these values by refusing to imitate Horace's actions.

Classical verse did not supply the only material for allusion and imitation. From the Restoration to 1780, poets drew on English verse too, but much more simply. Imitations of specific poems rarely treated anything written before 1660, and after 1660 almost only by way of parody. We have, for example, John Wilkes's celebrated – for constitutional, not esthetic reasons – obscene parodies of Pope, the 'Essay on Woman' and companion poems (1762?). Parodies of Gray, sometimes malicious and sometimes more playful, were still more popular than those of Pope. The suicide of his bard ('He spoke, and headlong from the mountain's height/Deep in the roaring tide he plunged to endless night') supplied anti-Revolutionary sentiments to the author of *The Bostonian Prophet* (177a): 'He spoke, and darting from the mountain's height/Snug in the arms of squaw disported all the night.' Parodists of the *Elegy*, like John Duncombe, even manage at times to mingle wistfulness with comedy; others, in the manner of *The Bostonian Prophet*, use Gray's text neutrally to attack something or somebody else, at times disclaiming any animus against the *Elegy* itself, a poem 'superior to all praise,' as the 'Advertisement' to *An Elegy Written in Covent-Garden* (1765) says. These parodies, unlike classical imitations of the earlier eighteenth century, have no significant place in the history of poetry. Allusions to English poems do, especially in the work of poets after Pope's generation: Gray, Collins, the Wartons, Akenside, Mason, Macpherson. These men consciously went back to sixteenth- and earlier seventeenth-century verse to quarry lines and images. One cannot read their poems well without responding to the strangeness and patina they tried to achieve by borrowings. None the less, these borrowings remain more a matter of style and genre than of specific reference. They add to the feel of the poem, not its content, and they are consequently less interesting uses of the past than are classical borrowings, of which we have seen the rich potential.

Old and new genres

The most common use of the past was for a resemblance less precise than imitation, that is, for establishing genre. Restoration and eighteenth-century verse epistles tend to sound like Horace's or at least to draw on the same poetic devices which he did; pastorals often sound like Virgil's or try to. To some extent, the resemblances were deliberate, as poets dignified or legitimated or amplified their own work by giving it the ring of someone else's, someone else formidably established. Their guides were their own sensibilities, of course, but also critics, whether the schoolmasters of their boyhood or the theoreticians of the day. Most critical activity from the Restoration to about 1720 or 1730 centered on the various genres and their 'rules,' rules drawn from examining and reasoning about the works of the best poets. These rules, critics thought, would help assert the dignity of poetry and criticism as disciplines, not mere collections of fancy and whim. After the example of investigators like Newton and Boyle, they hoped to study empirical phenomena – the great literature of the past – as systems of law. As cosmopolitans, too, they longed to give English criticism the light, perhaps the sweetness, borrowed and blended from the flowers of ancient and modern (Italian, French) continental criticism. To a great extent, they succeeded; we, as well as poets of their own time, are their debtors. No one should believe, however, that these critics and their 'rules' had any serious effect on the history of poetry. Poets took from them what looked useful for the job at hand and left the rest. If that had not been true, poetic change would have stalled, whereas in fact it went on at about the same rate and the same degree of smoothness and jouncing as before and after. Of the generic resemblances between the classics and poems of the Restoration and eighteenth-century many more were natural than deliberate: they resulted from the later poets' using the stylish idiom of the day. When that idiom changed, as idioms always do, the idea of genre changed too.

Because for the first time in English literature criticism flourished along with poetry, it provides an index of altering taste. I suggested that from the Restoration to about 1730, most critics practiced formalist, preceptive criticism. They tried to work toward a set of principles for each genre from the epic and the greater lyric down to the epigram, the epitaph, and the song. They examined models, mostly classical, in those terms, and built on the observations of other formalists, like Aristotle, Horace, Quintilian, the elder Scaliger (1484–1558), the poet Vida (1490–1566), and – with more reservations – French critics of the later seventeenth century like Rapin (1621–87) and Le Bossu (1631–80). Obviously the subject is exhaustible; it became exhausted; critics turned their attention elsewhere, and in particular to an investigation of why certain techniques within the established genres worked. By the time of Locke's and his followers' probing explorations of psychology in the last decade of the seventeenth and the earlier part of the eighteenth centuries, numbers of critics had begun asking in detail why, for example, audiences took delight in plays about disaster or poems about simpleton shepherds. By the middle of the eighteenth century, when every important philosopher was engaged in studying psychological response, this line of enquiry had grown enormously. Critical discourse veered from the study of classical models to the study of those elements in works of art which would produce desired psychological effects: a mixture of unity and variety, novelty, delicacy of sentiment, and other stimuli for esthetic pleasures.

Thus criticism paralleled changes in poetry. Ambitious Restoration poetry, like

Dryden's, kept an eye on classical models, and the earlier eighteenth-century poets through the time of Pope explored in great detail the possibilities of classical imitation. By the time of Pope's death in 1744, those possibilities had largely been exhausted. Just as early psychological critics worked within the framework of formal criticism, asking why the genres affected people as they did, so within the framework of poetry based on classical models writers began to write poetry that exploited imaginative stimuli like, for example, ideal presence. More descriptive poems appeared, more poems that treated nature as a stimulus rather than a backdrop, more poems in which the association of ideas was carried along on a stream of sensory images. Just as in criticism, where discussion of emotional effects absorbed the discussion of genres that had previously created the framework for critical discourse, so in poetry the genres progressively became means to achieve certain emotional ends rather than the constitutive elements of poetry itself. Classical models had a new importance and a less privileged position, so that there was a change in the debt of poetry to the past.

Empathy and ideal presence, more and more popular emotional effects as the eighteenth century wore on, renew a compact between poet and reader. They call for the reader to join the speaker in looking and/or feeling, so as to demand a certain social kinship. Other mid-to-later-eighteenth-century poems have a reduced range of tone for the sake of intensity, and still others have author-speakers who announce their own involvement with the poetic process, thereby appealing for an improvisatory kinship with the person going through the process of reading. I say 'renew a compact' because the classical genres made such a compact by engaging writer and reader in a shared discipline, a shared cultural form. Any genre, of course, does this to some extent. When a poet writes a sonnet, when a reader reads one, both commit themselves to a bandwidth of expectations. Sonnets tend to be personal, often meditative statements about deeply felt issues. Not sonnets but limericks tell about the young lady with bizarre genitalia; not sonnets but stanzas or blank verse serve Spenserian or Tennysonian knights for their joust; not sonnets but couplets, epigrams, stanzas once again build a pillory for the dull, the foolish, the vicious. Fun, fights, and flaying do not belong to what was called in the seventeenth and eighteenth centuries the 'decorum' of the sonnet, the material and treatment for which the sonnet is fit; but religion, love, tributes of honor, and psychological brooding do suit the decorum of the sonnet. With the classical genres, the most dignified precedents and the weight of scholarship set the decorum, the basic assumptions that did not have to be spoken aloud, the basic idiom that defined the force and rightness of a poem's elements within a socially understood context. The decorum of a poem by Dryden or Gay or Collins created the conditions of its performance, so to speak. Nowadays only in performance does the decorum of fixed genres seem very fully to exist. A lover of vocal music has a clear notion of how Mozart should be sung, or Fauré, or Puccini; the balletomane expects leaps and lifts to be done properly, and he knows what 'properly' implies. Performers and audience have a compact. Such a compact may be irrelevant to poetry meant to be a private reverie on which one eavesdrops. But Restoration and eighteenth-century poems do not cloister their virtues: they are created to be performed in the larynx as well as the mind and imagination, and they insist on a compact of performance. When the fixed classical genres waned, a more intimate compact took its place, with the writer coaxing and compelling the reader by the use of empathy, ideal presence, intensity of tone, and other such means. Precisely because the waning was so gradual, so intermittent, the growingly important kinds of the mid-to-later eighteenth century could profit from old bonds between poet and reader, renewing them and revising them for new interests.

This framework offers a logical scenario, largely if not wholly confirmed by historical fact. One might expect the new, more emotionally charged poetry not to reject the past but to turn to it in a different way. However much the classical 'rules' shrank in prescriptive value, the actual sound of past poems should have kept echoing in those of the present. Latin classics, which continued to be strictly and worshipfully read in schools, might lose their absolute preeminence, but would hardly vanish. Later poets would likely draw on a wider variety of models useful for the effects they wanted to achieve, the more so as British pride swelled with the nation's growth in economic strength and cultural weight (especially in science and philosophy), as certain kinds of exoticism (the Gothic, the oriental) swung into fashion, and as a sense of history spread.

In this scenario poets might well decide that Spenser and Milton could serve descriptive poetry along with Virgil's *Georgics*, and the current drama could help the dramatic poetry along with Ovid's *Heroides*. Narrative might look once again to Spenser and the sources of his episodic narrative in Ariosto and Tasso, as well as to classical narratives and current fiction. Older native forms, like the ballad, could offer a pathos and simplicity, often with reminiscences of national heroism which furthered the reader's sense of community with the writer. Since ideal presence depended on imagery, since empathy depended on sincerity of feeling, poets might seek out 'primitive' poetry where less polish of language and manners covered the passions and the responsiveness to the natural world. (Some folk poetry, like ballads, would have the same virtues.) Models of this sort would have appealed to those who agreed with John Brown, in his *Dissertation on The Rise, Union, and Power . . . of Poetry and Music* (1763), where he 'proves' the antiquity of Macpherson's Ossianic poems by their abundant sincerity and vision.

> the grand simplicity of imagery and diction, the strong draughts of rude
> manners and uncultivated scenes of nature, which abound in all these
> poems, pictures which no civilized modern could ever imbibe in all their
> strength nor consequently could ever throw out (p. 159).

The figurative and passionate Hebraic style of parts of the Old Testament also fit this bill. In short, whereas the old genres had adapted a narrow range of classical sources for a wide range of effects, a new pragmatic and emotional poetry might adapt a wide range of sources for clusters of specific effects, all aimed at a psychological poetry that would preserve a compact between reader and writer.

I said earlier that this logical scenario largely but not wholly tallies with the facts. Any parts of it that use causal terms ought to be discounted as pure speculation, as is generally true when histories of ideas try to deal in causes. Let me emphasize, too, that there was no rapid shift of modes, as is perhaps implied by some modern accounts of the period. As in every discipline except those that a new scientific model (Newton's system, the discovery of DNA) or a new technology can revolutionize, poetic processes of change – eighteenth-century changes very much included – are gradual. No one suddenly abandoned 'neoclassicism' or 'Augustan humanism'; no one tiptoed rapturously into the bracing bay of 'preromanticism' or 'sensibility.' Such scorn as the so-called Augustans had for earlier poetry had largely to do with language and versification, which were thought liable to be uncontrolled and crude. There was no quarrel with Elizabethan energy, lyrical impulse, or ideas. Naivete in style or subject (e.g., fanciful Arthurian allegories) met with the same sort of indulgent wistfulness as it would if anyone thought of modeling his own poetry upon it today. Earl Wasserman, in *Elizabethan Poetry in the Eighteenth Century* (1947), has shown that 'a rather large body of Renaissance literature was very much alive in the eighteenth century, and the Augustans not only read . . . it, but often found in it the substance for their own literary products' (p. 35; see pp. 35–48). As to ballads, one cannot forget that 'artful Addison' of the 'coldly correct' verse (the epithets come from young Joseph Warton's *The Enthusiast*, 1744) lent his authoritative eloquence in three *Spectators* of 1711 (nos 70, 74, 85) to the praise of 'Chevy Chase' and 'Two Children in the Wood,' the former being 'the favourite ballad of the common people of England' and the latter 'one of the darling songs of the common people.' Such ballads, he writes, 'cannot fail to please all such readers as are not unqualified for the entertainment by their affectation or ignorance' (no. 70), and adds that Dorset and Dryden, like 'several of the most refined writers of our present age,' 'took a particular pleasure in the reading of them' (no. 85). One of these may have been the urbane Matthew Prior, who borrowed the story of another ballad, 'The Nut-Brown Maid,' for his 'Henry and Emma,' an account of true love and trial which was cited with affection and respect throughout the century. In short, the idols and models of later eighteenth-century (and nineteenth-century) poets were not hidden, stubbornly rooted plants that classicists labored to expel with the pitchfork of rules. They were read, approved, admired, and sometimes imitated despite their old-fashioned language and prosody.

One should go still further: as Dryden was, in Dr Johnson's phrase, 'the father of English criticism,' so he, his contemporaries, and the generation after them were the inventors of 'English literature.' They kept the past, with its sense of pastness, alive. As I have said, they were unfortunately less ready than we to put aside contemporary standards in judging earlier poets' idioms; but even today, of course, when everyone is taught to read historically, we still hear educated laymen snicker and yawn at the conventions of the *opera seria*, the paintings of Greuze, and the poetry of Thomson. In the century of Thomson, Greuze, and the *opera seria*, when no one was taught the principle of reading historically, people's ardor of response to the out-of-date eloquence of Chaucer, Spenser, and Shakespeare suggests admirable openness.

As in no other age, the greatest men of letters – Pope and Johnson – bent to annotating and collating editions. For the first time, the standards proper for the Greek and Latin classics one read in school were applied to English texts. Readers learned that a medieval Englishman, Chaucer, might be thought by the refined John Dryden to be a better writer than the Augustan Ovid, Spenser's pastorals to vie with Virgil's. Pope, that allegedly rabid 'neoclassicist,' planned to write a discourse on the rise and progress of English poetry and, whether in connection with that or not, talked to his friend Joseph Spence about Gower, *Piers Plowman* (of which Pope owned an edition of 1550), Skelton, Sackville, Robert Heath, William Habington, Walter Map, and other 'ignotos' (Spence's term; *Observations* . . ., ed. Osborn, 1966, entries 410–20). In a letter of 26 September 1723 he advised Judith Cowper to imitate Provençal poets and Chaucer. The point is not whether Pope was enraptured by these authors, or the minor sixteenth- and seventeenth-century playwrights, or the 'metaphysical' poets on whom he commented to Spence. (He had judiciously mixed feelings.) It is that he and his contemporaries thought them worth systematic reading, with the measure of respect that such study implied. Any seeming abruptness in surface effects, one style sweeping in over another, exists upon a continuous roadbed.

Another reason to treat my scenario of change cautiously is that the normative force of the fixed classical genres is uncertain. The familiar verse epistle, for example, has a Horatian smack to its amiable colloquialism, but is that because of Horace? Perhaps Romans and Englishmen simply shared common sense about how one addresses a friend. The range of genres for both ancients and moderns was so broad and so open to variation – we have seen what happened to the Cowleyan Pindaric – that the degree of pressure exerted by the classics is hard to fix. Then again, despite critics' talk of fixed genres, Restoration and earlier eighteenth-century poets by no means kept to them. Prior's two long poems, *Alma* and *Solomon* (published 1718) one of them a mock-didactic and the other a kind of disquisition on *Ecclesiastes*, have no real classical precedents. Neither does the great bulk of Swift's poetry or much political poetry from the Restoration on. Although most ambitious verse before 1720 or 1730 followed (or parodied) the fixed genres, the great preponderance of other verse either had no significant classical precedents or had ones probably irrelevant as influences.

Although my scenario correctly predicts that poets would keep using classical forms, it does not predict an odd pedantry by which old non-classical genres would be revived with some of the same zeal that had marked earlier revivals of the modes of Horace, Virgil, and Martial. The sonnet, which I mentioned earlier, is a good example. When Shakespeare's and Milton's imitative Italo-French sonnets dropped from use at the Restoration, many poets kept writing closely-worked lyrics in stanzas, which they labeled 'sonnets.' Their definition of 'sonnet,' as a glance at the OED confirms, was as old as the one that involves fourteen lines and a small, orthodox set of rhyme schemes; and their mode represented a continuous tradition that lost the name 'sonnet' only when eighteenth-century literary antiquarians elbowed it aside. (Modern critics who imply that fourteen-liners like Shakespeare's or Milton's are the only legitimate 'sonnets' are avatars of the Le

Bossus and Rapins who laid down adamantine rules for the genres in Louis XIV's France.) The sonnet, in the narrow sense of the word, emerged in the spate of Miltonic imitations. Those of Thomas Edwards in the 1740s borrow from Milton nearly everything but his genius, which was not out to loan, just as earlier satires had got themselves up in toga and tunic.

As might be expected, the development of the form to 1780 closely resembled the earlier development of classical forms. Experiments with the sonnet led to a great variety of rhyme schemes, e.g., in Hugh Downman, even to a number of unrhymed sonnets, like the unrhymed odes of James Ralph and William Collins. The newer sonnets adapted themselves to the idiom of the time: they made less than Milton had of the divisions into quatrains and sestet and of the climactic ending, so as to concentrate on a single statement, often spoken to a person or animal or personified abstraction like Evening. One can see these changes by comparing John Bampfylde's 'The Return,' published in 1778 when the poet was twenty-four, with its recently published (1775) inspiration, Gray's 'Sonnet on the Death of Mr. Richard West' (written in 1742, when Gray was twenty-five). Gray erects a logical structure. The first stanza is dominated by the lament of how vain is the joy of nature, the second by the solitary sorrow of the speaker, the third by the breadth of joy in morning, and the couplet by barrenness: 'I fruitless mourn to him that cannot hear,/And weep the more because I weep in vain.' Each stanza, too, is balanced, with 'In vain . . . in vain' in lines 1 and 3, color imagery in lines 2 and 4; 'these ears . . . repine,/ . . . these eyes require' in lines 5 and 6; and so on. Stanzaic breaks, balance, and argument alike disappear in Bampfylde's more fluid treatment of the material:

> As, when to one who long hath watched the morn
>   Advancing, slow forewarns the approach of day
>   (What time the young and flowery-kirtled May
> Decks the green hedge and dewy grass unshorn
> With cowslips pale and many a whitening thorn),
>   And now the sun comes forth with level ray,
>   Gilding the high-wood top and mountain grey,
> And, as he climbs, the meadows 'gins adorn;
> The rivers glisten to the dancing beam,
>   The awakened birds begin their amorous strain,
> And hill and vale with joy and fragrance teem.
>   Such is the sight of thee, thy wished return
>   To eyes like mine, that long have waked to mourn,
> That long have watched for light and wept in vain.

As one can see, later eighteenth-century sonnets were miniature later eighteenth-century odes. The process of change from Milton's sonnets to Bampfylde's parallels that from a classical form to its later eighteenth-century version.

There were, however, two further differences between the old genres and the new, both having to do with a narrowing of poetry. The new genres were antiquarian, in that they drew on neither current learning, like the school-taught classics, nor current writing, like Cowley (for Dryden) or Gray (for the author of *The Bostonian Prophet*). Strangely, yet understandably, they gave less sense of their cultures of origin, medieval and Renaissance, than the classical genres had. Pope weighed his culture and Horace's in each other's terms, but later eighteenth-century poets never weighed Spenser's or Milton's. For them, history vaporized into nostalgia for stalwart simplicity, for freedom from the mundane and the refined, for heaths peopled with the creatures whom modern men knew to be figures of superstition, for wonder, bravery, spontaneity – in short, for the costume drama of history. To Pope, classical Rome was close enough (like, say, contemporary France) that he could deal with it as an equal. The ages of British chivalry, Gothic superstition, and the noble savagery of Norsemen, however, could only be regarded as ages lost forever (and perhaps a good thing too!), except as they offered a retrospective release for the imagination. In order to achieve their innocence and simplicity, eighteenth-century poets had to use cunning and selfconsciousness quite unnecessary for the Horatian Pope.

This paradox carries over to poetic diction. Most of the poems that owed primary allegiance to classical models required what I have called the 'urbane' style and therefore do not try to reproduce the special linguistic effects, if any, of those models. Even in translations of epic, where the style grows high, as in Dryden's rendering of the first book of the *Iliad* (1700), the voice is contemporary:

> He prayed, and Phoebus hearing, urged his flight,
> With fury kindled, from Olympus' height;
> His quiver o'er his ample shoulders threw;
> His bow twanged and his arrows rattled as they flew.
> Black as a stormy night he ranged around
> The tents and compassed the devoted ground.   (ll. 67–72)

Most of the poems that had a divided allegiance between the classics and Milton or Spenser, however, required what I have called the 'high, limited' style and therefore needed a special language to channel connotations. This language had a fine poetic resonance to it, but implied no cultural comparisons: its closeness to the originals made a kind of appeal to the reader quite different from the appeal made by those originals when they were written. In fact, the whole thrust of the psychological criticism that justified such diction was to relate a language to the conceiving imagination rather than to the prior needs of the poem, to one person sitting in his study instead of to the conventions of a socially established form.

The second difference between old and new genres is that the new were fewer. The classical past bequeathed to Restoration and early eighteenth-century poets a great variety of modes with a great range of tones. No distinction between 'poetry' and 'verse' (worse yet, 'poesy' and 'verse') scared them into solemnity or made them condescend toward such old forms as the instructional poem or the chatty epistle. In the hierarchy of genres, these too had their respected place, below the grave and lofty narrative (epic) and lyric (the Great Ode) of Homer and Pindar. A

105

pragmatic and emotional poetic theory redefined the same hierarchy, justifying the genres at the top by their power to excite the imagination and passions. In turn, this procedure elevated lesser lyrics (e.g., the sonnet) and lowered the instructional poem (e.g., poems prescribing rules for poetry) so as to disturb the traditional hierarchy. The descriptive poem was the first beneficiary, for it could embed narratives and imaginative appeals within its associative structure; then came various 'personal' or 'spontaneous' expressions of melancholy or quiet joy in shorter lyrics. Genres that treated experience differently began to drop from the respected canon, to be denied the status of poetry. By 1780 people's notions of what subjects and what styles were fit for poetry were far narrower than in 1680. The sole criterion of emotional intensity – latent in the criticism of the seventeenth century and still by no means thorough in that of the 1770s – made predictable the substitution of a polar system, 'poetry' and 'verse,' for the gradations that were part of the classical legacy. (This damage has never been fully repaired for readers or poets; but to pursue that goes outside the bounds of this book.) Pope was almost as various as Dryden in the kinds of poem at which he tried his hand; none of their eighteenth-century successors came close. Moreover, within their most serious original poems, Dryden and Pope are often funny, Thomson rarely, poets born in the eighteenth century virtually never: new definitions of genre straitened what was permissible in poems as well as what was permissible as poetry.

National and 'primitive' traditions

The turn to a national tradition, first as well as and then to some extent instead of a cosmopolitan one, began with the imitation of that great classicist, Milton. He was the most revered non-dramatic English poet throughout the eighteenth century, and the most recent figure of what was felt to be the past. In fact, he was two years younger than Waller (b. 1606), and not much older than Butler (b. 1612), Denham (b. 1615), and Cowley (b. 1618), the four men who became early models for the Restoration mode. During the Restoration and early eighteenth century, their reputations, even Butler's, shrank somewhat as other poets took up where they left off; Milton's kept growing as he remained without direct disciples and, of course, without equal in the epic. Without disciples but congenial: one should not forget that Milton's greatest poems came after the Restoration and that they are Restoration works in more than the accident of date. *Paradise Lost* both dwells on and questions the idea of heroism, alludes to the classics to enrich its texture and to support its own (Christian) culture against the Greek and Roman, and claims to assert the rule of reason through what is in fact a chronicle of power and arbitrary will. Learned debates fill it. Its narrator has keen intelligence and abiding values, and its protagonist (if Satan deserves that title) has delusions of grandeur. All these characteristics mark *Hudibras*, published before Milton's poem, and *Absalom and Achitophel*, which draws on it. Buoyed by the Restoration, *Paradise Lost* needed only some critical obeisances and a popular taste for magnificence to exalt it as the English response to Homer and Virgil. Critics did write copiously and enthusiasti-

106

cally about Milton, *Paradise Lost* was published – staggeringly – over a hundred times in the eighteenth century, and, as Raymond D. Havens says, 'Milton occupied a place, not only in English literature but in the thought and life of Englishmen of all classes, which no poet has held since' (*The Influence of Milton on English Poetry* (1922), p. 71). No poet, of course, held or could have held such a place earlier.

Through the first quarter of the eighteenth century, Havens finds 155 pieces in blank verse, about two-thirds of which smack of Milton's style (p. 120). The only ones that attracted much notice were John Philips's *Splendid Shilling* (1701) and *Cyder* (1708), one a burlesque and the other a Georgic; but the style was kept alive, biding its time till the acclaim for Thomson's *Winter*, the first of the *Seasons*, brought it into sudden vogue. One should remember that in choosing the loftiest of English styles for squeezing apples and watching hares scrabble at the frozen ground, Philips and Thomson followed a classical example, that of Virgil in his *Georgics*. As Joseph Warton was to write in 1753, dedicating a translation of Virgil's *Works*, 'there is a profusion of the most daring metaphors and most glowing figures, there is a majesty and magnificence of diction throughout the *Georgics*, that . . . is scarcely equalled by Homer himself' (1 : iv–v). If the style of the *Aeneid* suited the *Georgics*, that of *Paradise Lost* could very well suit *The Seasons*, and the more so because of Thomson's penchant for sublime, sweeping effects. *The Seasons*, like *Paradise Lost*, is also a divine poem, about a postlapsarian world ruled by a benevolent but inscrutable God; Thomson's Miltonism is in this sense almost allusive. For stylistic reasons detailed in the previous chapter, finally, Milton's ornate style with its limited, exotic lexicon was just what descriptive poetry needed. Thomson demonstrated the rightness of Miltonic verse for the epic of the English land as well as for that of an earlier, more nearly perfect and comprehensible Paradise, and he drew a great flock of poets after him. None was so good as he, but some were quite good indeed. They followed the Miltonic style developed by Thomson, a native style (or a style made native), without having to draw, as Thomson did, on native and classical traditions both. So naturalized did his style become that after Thomson one cannot identify burlesques of Milton's epic style specifically (as opposed to a standard eighteenth-century grand blank verse). He had ceased being distinctive enough, firmly enough lodged in the past, to be parodied.

Milton's minor poems were not parodied either, maybe because the original texts were not well enough known verbatim. Poets did base odes and monodies on them (imitations that certainly were parodied), like the dutiful William Mason, whose early verse includes 'Il Bellicoso' and 'Il Pacifico' in the manner of the 'companion poems' and *Musaeus: A Monody* after 'Lycidas'; he later wrote Miltonic sonnets. These Miltonic forms had been kept alive by a small number of poets, like Thomas Parnell and John Dyer, till the late 1730s and the 1740s. Then one finds a profusion of monodies, hymns, odes, and rural octosyllabics on their models. Such poems tended to be about moods and to invoke some personified abstraction (often with a court of other personified abstractions) whose genealogy and effects the poet surveys, like Milton's cheerful and serious men. The monody, or dirge, is a special form of this general sort: the mood is that of mourning, rustic or pastoral scenes prevail, and the address centers on a person rather than an abstraction, though abstractions and mythological figures (the Muses, the Graces) may well be summoned. Serious lyric poetry of the forty years between Pope's death (1744) and Johnson's (1784) found these Miltonic forms most sympathetic. Their conventions allowed the visionary and descriptive elements of the 'new' poetry full play; they used mythology to transmute the homely and the personal into universal patterns; and they permitted poems to be beautifully wrought without suffering a damaging loss of spontaneity. The same poets also tried to give their verse the Miltonic cachet by actual borrowings or slight adaptations as when Thomas Warton took 'To the tanned haycock in the mead' ('Ode on the Approach of Summer,' (1. 142)) directly from 'L'Allegro,' line 90. I suspect the line is not meant to be recognized as an allusion (unlike, say, the allusion to *Paradise Lost* 1 : 26 in *An Essay on Man* 1 : 16) but felt as a welcome presence with a faint charge of *déjà-vu*.

Milton seems to have drawn his elders in the wake of his own popularity. Thus in a 'Life of Mr. John Philips' prefaced to his *Works* (4th edn. 1728), George Sewell writes that Philips studied Milton

> with application, and traced him in all his successful translation from the ancients. There was not an allusion in his *Paradise Lost* drawn from the thoughts or expressions of Homer or Virgil which he could not immediately refer to; and by that he perceived what a peculiar life and grace their sentiments added to English poetry, how much their images raised its spirit, and what weight and beauty their words, when translated, gave to its language. Nor was he less curious in observing the force and energy of his mother-tongue but, by the example of his darling Milton, searched backwards into the works of our old English poets, to furnish himself with proper, sounding, and significant expressions, and prove the due extent and compass of the language. For this purpose, he carefully read over Chaucer and Spenser, and afterwards, in his writings, did not scruple to revive any words or phrases which he thought deserved it (p. 7).

Philips treated the classical past and the English past in the same way, as he thought Milton had. Milton helped make his eye cosmopolitan, through the allusive techniques of 'classicism'; I suspect Philips was not the only poet so trained. Once more, Philips's training, and probably that of others, had to do with the English poets' language ('proper, sounding, and significant expression') rather than with the 'thoughts,' 'sentiments,' and 'images' mentioned for the ancients. Language was the main barrier. When the older English poets stopped sounding quaint, or alternatively when quaintness and patina became prized, the way was fully open for eighteenth-century poets to use them.

The use of Spenser was complicated by his stanza. Although *The Faerie Queene* remained the most familiar Elizabethan poem throughout the period, and (by the testimony of the poets themselves) among the greatest sources of poetic inspiration,

Spenser's long, interwoven stanza offended the ideal of refined colloquialism as much as his deliberately antique language. Except for free verse, which must follow the form of thought, and Shakespearean blank verse, which usually does, the couplet of Dryden and Pope is one of the least coercive measures in English prosody. It accommodates the rhythms of casual speech, exclamation, oratory, and narrative, and it does not require epithets and expletives to pad it. The Spenserian stanza is one of the most coercive, and its intricate repeated rhymes struck many in the eighteenth century as both ostentatious and tedious. Poets experimented with simplifying it, as Prior did – in *An Ode ... to the Queen* (1706) – into two quatrains and a couplet, like a decapitated Shakespearean sonnet, or they treated the genuine Spenserian nine lines as couplets by closing the sense after every two lines (or, at one place in the stanza, three lines). Others took the diffuseness, ingenuousness, and archaism of his manner as a fine medium for affectionate burlesque. Shenstone's 'The Schoolmistress' (1737–48) and Thomson's *Castle of Indolence* (1748) are best known but one should add Richard Owen Cambridge's dexterous 'Archimage' (ca. 1742), William Julius Mickle's half-comical *Sir Martyn* (1767; first named *The Concubine*), and, earlier, Gilbert West's somewhat indignant satire on the Grand Tour, *On the Abuse of Travelling* (1739). All, like Pope still earlier in his brief 'The Alley' (written by 1709), took advantage of what Mickle called 'the ludicrous of which the antique phraseology and manner of Spenser are so happily and peculiarly susceptible' ('Advertisement' to *Sir Martyn*). Cambridge, for example, presents a wig-dresser in 'Archimage' as a Spenserian villain:

> These [hairy scalps] would he with a deadlie engine fell
> Harrow and claw, his foul heart to aggrate,
> And wreak his malice, strange it is to tell,
> On object senseless and inanimate
> As though it were his living foeman's pate.
> Als would he rub a magic ointment eft
> O'er heads of luckless knights, such was his hate,
> Which of their curlèd tresses them bereft,
> That nought but naked scorne and baldness vile was left.　　　　　(st. 9)

Still others reserved the Spenserian stanza for the genre of visionary allegory, especially allegorical processions, to be adorned with the rich descriptions that abounded in *The Faerie Queene*. Hugh Downman's *The Land of the Muses* (1768) uses it this way. But for the Spenserian stanza to emerge into less specialized poems, someone had to employ it successfully in such a poem. As Thomson's *Winter* (and Philips's *Cyder* before it) had shown the potentialities of the Miltonic style, James Beattie's *The Minstrel* (1771–4) dropped archaisms and partial imitation to show the modern potentialities of Spenser's. Those who followed Beattie fall for the most part outside the chronological limits of this history; for our purposes, the relation of poetry to the past, Beattie's importance is that he made the Spenserian style essentially independent of Spenser. The styles of the past, now translated and

109

transformed, became the styles of the present, and thereby both more and less attractive to poets.

A different pattern developed from the first Elizabethan poem to win eighteenth-century imitators. Spenser's *Shepheardes Calendar*, as we have seen, inflamed the debate over pastoral which began with Ambrose Philips, Tickell, and Pope (1713), with later contributions by Thomas Purney (1717), Gay (*The Shepherd's Week*, 1714), and perhaps Swift ('Pastoral Dialogue,' 1729). As one would expect from early eighteenth-century poets, Philips and Purney both refer the reader to classical as well as English models—Purney's first volume is entitled *Pastorals after the Simple Manner of Theocritus* – though both choose a kind of Spenserian style. Neither was good enough to encourage imitators, especially when one risked the mockery of Pope and his friends. (Purney actually may have been emboldened because he never knew there was a risk. He was thick-headed enough to miss the irony in Pope's wicked praise of Philips in *Guardian* no. 40.) The style petered out. Cuddie and Hobbinol cropped up largely in comic songs, while the Chlorises and Damons of Pope's Virgilian countryside had a longer serious life (as well as one in comic songs). Eventually both began to disappear, as the traditional pastoral disintegrated. The myths of the Golden Age and rural retirement moved into Horatian or topographical poems; the elegy into more Miltonic pastoral or into grave laments, some reminiscent of 'Lycidas'; love complaints into monologues or ballads; and so forth. This sort of cannibalising represents another way in which eighteenth-century poets made use of the past. The old fixed genres supplied topics and emotional effects for the new criticism to redistribute, thus emptying the old genres of their special functions. When no up-to-date pastoral style offered itself to mid-eighteenth-century poets, they could discard the traditional genre because its effects were available in more modish poetic kinds and because its form – once regarded as the core of the genre – had been reinterpreted by the new criticism as a mere pragmatic device for achieving certain effects, a device that writers could put aside for more efficient, more novel, or more stylish ones. My description overintellectualizes and simplifies the process, but is essentially valid.

During the years when poets were seeing what they could draw from *The Faerie Queene*, there was new interest in going still further back culturally, to the style of the Bible, of primitive songs, and of medieval verse. An interest in the Bible as a poetic rather than cultural source was hardly new. Rewriting the Psalms was a venerable English activity from the sixteenth century on. A survey of the works of a hundred eighteenth-century poets – those in Anderson's *British Poets*, on the grounds that they might be expected to be the most influential, together with another dozen taken at random – reveals twenty who wrote paraphrases of one or more lyrical sections of the Bible, almost all of them Psalms (with Job and Isaiah next in popularity, but far behind). Specific impetus came from the use of metrical psalms as hymns in the English church, starting with the reign of Edward VI. By the eighteenth century, the dreary doggerel of the old Hopkins-Sternhold version had mostly given way to a version by Brady and Tate (1696), but the quality of the widely accepted metrical psalters of any kind made other poets think they could do better. They tried in large numbers, sometimes for reasons of private devotion, sometimes for public, often sectarian use. Unlike the classical, Miltonic, and Spenserian imitations we have considered, these rarely tried to match the style of their original. Instead, they branched into elaborate variations on the simple texts. Poets could hardly have done anything else in paraphrases that were to fit into singable stanzas. As hymns, these metrical psalms tended to be simple in statement, fervent rather than profound in their piety, wordily assertive in their praise. They were, in short, good singing but bad poetry. The exceptions nearly all occur in paraphrases not cast in stanzaic form.

Rewriting of the Psalms resembles imitation more than translation because of the freedom poets felt in deviating from the text. Christopher Smart admittedly goes farther in expanding and christianizing the Old Testament than the bulk of eighteenth-century psalmists, but that is a matter of degree rather than of kind. Sometimes his changes seem to rebuke the pre-Christian darkness of the allegedly Davidic text, almost as *The Vanity of Human Wishes* rebukes Juvenal. *Psalms* 11:6, 'Upon the ungodly he shall rain snares, fire and brimstone, storm and tempest: this shall be their portion to drink' (*Book of Common Prayer* psalter), becomes:

> Yet tempest, fire and snares,
>   And brimstone of the lake,
> Which vengeance still prepares,
>   And wrath and terror make,
> He shall from penitents avert,
> Through Christ his infinite desert.

Similarly, though David's 'righteous' man in *Psalms* 58:10 'shall rejoice' at divine vengeance and 'wash his footsteps in the blood of the ungodly,' Smart's 'shall exult' in God's 'powerful mercy' which brings to the shore of salvation the 'tortured souls,' the 'wracks and ruins' of the previously impious.

The biblical texts stayed familiar from being read through once a month at morning and evening prayer; changes in them probably had the sort of allusory strength and force of cultural self-assertion that one finds in some of the century's classical adaptations. Like those adaptations, the revised psalms bring inherited texts up to date, whether in Smart's giving Christian England the New Law for the Old or Isaac Watts's importing the tone of early eighteenth-century social verse into a descant on the single word 'maidens' in *Psalms* 148:

> Virgins, who roll your artful eyes
> And shoot delicious danger thence
> (Swift the lovely lightning flies
> And melts our reason down to sense),
>   Boast not of those withering charms
>   That must yield their youthful grace
> To age and wrinkles, earth and worms.

The nice turns on 'withering' (transitive or intransitive in force?) and 'grace' (since the poem is about God's gifts), and the visual parallel between 'wrinkles'

111

and 'worms' announce a wit that David never knew in the service of a piety that he knew deeply.

This sort of use of the Old Testament differs radically from its use as a primitive text, similar in many ways to Homer's epics, Norse and Celtic sagas, laments, and chants, and the strikingly simple, figurative verse of other peoples far removed from eighteenth-century England in time, place, and degree of refinement. As one can imagine from what has been said about other poetic developments, this kind of biblical study hit its stride in the middle of the eighteenth century but by no means began then. In 1713 Richard Steele, hardly an original thinker, explained in *Guardian* no. 86 that 'to express violent motions which are fleeting and transitory . . . requires great spirit in thought and energy in style, which we find more of in the eastern poetry than in either the Greek or Roman'; his example of eastern poetry is the book of *Job*, where the imagery is not only bold but also so psychologically evocative that 'the sacred poet makes all the beauties to flow from an inward principle in the creature he describes.' Steele's notions in the popular press resemble those of Joseph Trapp, whose Latin lectures on poetry at Oxford (1711–19; Eng. tr. as *Lectures on Poetry*, 1742) mention biblical hymns and psalms in asserting that the lyric is 'of all kinds of poetry, the most poetical, . . . the boldest of all other kinds, full of raptures . . . . It is well known, the eastern eloquence abounded . . . with metaphors and bold hyperboles . . . , as is sufficiently evident from the sacred writings' (pp. 203–4). Upon a crest of such critics' treating the Old Testament as in large part a book written by men, inspired but part of a specific foreign culture with its own turns of mind and phrase, came the most important eighteenth-century study of its style, Robert Lowth's *De Sacra Poesi Hebraeorum* (1753).

One of Trapp's successors as Professor of Poetry at Oxford, Lowth brought together in the book his lectures given during the 1740s. No doubt aided by his sense of the end-stopped and balanced couplet, the style of Pope, Lowth perceived that Hebrew poetry also fell into two- or three-line groups, each line of about the same length and balanced with the others in its group for meaning. Like Aaron Hill, in the preface to his Pindaric 'The Creation' (1720), Lowth stressed the simplicity of Hebrew poetry; like Steele and Trapp, its bold, figurative, sententious style; like these men and William Smith, a translator of Longinus' *On the Sublime* (1739), its sublimity of diction, thought, and feeling. These characteristics, of course, had been those praised in the Pindaric ode, the advocates of which would have agreed with Lowth's declaration (supported from classical precedent) that 'the first and most important source of poetic speech is powerful emotion' (2nd edn, 1763, p. 46; the Latin is *'vehemens mentis affectus'*). To a body of rhetorical ideals already accepted, then, Lowth added an analysis of how the sacred poets had written to achieve those ideals. His perceptive exploration of the Hebraic past joined those classical rhetorics, with their Homeric, Virgilian, Pindaric, and Horatian examples, with which educated men were at least passingly familiar. No one would claim that a Latin treatise, however perceptive, was likely to make the poets' best-seller list, but Lowth's rapidly influenced more widely read criticism. It drew attention to the Bible as a poetic model and helped confirm, by sacred example, secular notions about poetry and the passions. It also made the Hebraic style, like Miltonic and Spenserian styles, a practical option for poets trying to achieve the emotional effects of the higher genres.

Two extraordinary poetic works may have taken direct inspiration from Lowth. One is the Ossianic collection (1760–3) by James Macpherson, the other, Smart's incomplete experiment entitled *Jubilate Agno (Rejoice in the Lamb)*. Smart worked on this medley of blessings, exhortations, personal references, and musings from 1759 to 1763, during his confinement for madness, but left it fragmentary. It was published only in 1939. Since all but the first two extant lines begin with 'Let' or 'For,' he seems to have had a liturgical poem in mind, through which someone and/or something (usually a biblical person and an animal) is bidden to rejoice and an answering voice provides the reason, typically oblique. Thus, 'Let Hushim rejoice with the kingfisher, who is of royal beauty, though plebeian size./For in my nature I quested for beauty, but God, God hath sent me to sea for pearls.' Though we do not have the antiphon for each line to prove any plan throughout and though much of what does exist wanders from any perceivable fixed plan, the *Jubilate Agno* clearly involves the amplification of such typically biblical moods as bidding (in exhortation or in prayer), celebration, and submissive meditation. Smart expresses them through stylistic devices that the Bible shares with much eighteenth-century verse, like the maxim, the ceremonious declaration, and the word used in its root sense.

Jubilate Agno might be the jottings of an eclectically and eccentrically learned, Bible-reading, eighteenth-century poet, no more. But since Smart had read Lowth, whose work he had praised in the mid-1750s and whom he at least later knew personally, scholars have supposed that *De Sacra Poesi Hebraeorum* focused the poetic energies of this private, universal liturgy. Lowth discusses and Smart employs antiphonal structure, parallels of meaning and phraseology in successive lines, and most of all, perhaps, evocative metaphors rather than those that lead to ideal presence. As the adoring singer of the Song of Songs compares his love's hair to a flock of goats and her breasts to roes, so Smart imagines that 'the nets come down from the eyes of the Lord to fish up men to their salvation' and he rejoices 'like a worm in the rain in him that cherishes and from him that tramples.' Smart's figures are far less cognitively vague than Solomon's, but for better or for worse they still are closer to the 'bold' eastern metaphors cited by Lowth than to the sort discussed in the previous chapter as part of a positional style.

During the same years when Smart sat in Potter's asylum, polishing a line or two of *Jubilate Agno* each day, James Macpherson was startling the literary world with what he claimed were translations of primitive Gaelic poetry, of epic dimensions. While Smart drew pity and condescension, Macpherson enjoyed a poet's honors and, having weathered a hurricane of charges that he was a forger and impostor, lived rich and renowned. Since the first quarter of the nineteenth century or so, Smart's reputation has risen, Macpherson's fallen, and now the Ossianic poems are read only by antiquarians, and then with numbed contempt, while Smart soars on modern esteem for the rapture, autobiographical insight, and scattering of magnificent lines in the *Jubilate Agno* and his masterpiece, *A Song to*

113

David. A pretty irony, but not a happy one. Macpherson is worth study and respect, even if he did pretend to be translating what he in fact concocted himself. Ignorance as well as personal taste create, for example, the perplexity of André Fermigier, writing in *Le Monde* (21 February 1974) on the occasion of an exhibition of Ossianic paintings:

> I went so far as to page through Ossian: dismal, totally devoid of talent, twenty pages will bore you to death. . . . It is hard to see why so many men of the first rank . . . were excited by such stuff. Why that sudden passion for rainstorms, filthy weather, the sadistic climate of a hellish country? Were the summers in Europe around 1770 especially hot? (p. 13).

Summers, no; but imaginations, yes. As Macpherson's eighteenth-century admirers wrote again and again, and as the painters whose work M. Fermigier viewed also testified, the Ossianic poems make an extreme and constant demand on one's capacity to create an imaginary scene, to respond to ideal presence. As that capacity shrank, so did the poems' reputation.

Ideal presence is crucial in part because the poems are supposed to be the products of the blind poet Ossian's memory, and therefore come to life in his mind through ideal presence. We read by an act of sympathy with the speaker, which produces the mixture of elegy and excitement in the poems, as well as their shifts in perspective, shadings of response, and easy passage from visual to evocative metaphors. Ideal presence is also crucial because, in stitching together and filling out and rearranging his actual scraps of ballad and legend to create the Ossianic poems, Macpherson had to pose as the humble servant of a great Gaelic text. Inasmuch as verse translations must tamper with meaning, he pretended to a literal prose translation which denied him verbal ornament. He found himself writing a peculiarly bare poetry of description, and had to depend on ideal presence to give it life. Instead of the Miltonic, Thomsonian 'high, limited' sublime, well suited to ideal presence, Macpherson resorted to the more spontaneous biblical sublime, perhaps familiar to him from studies in divinity during the 1750s and from the work of Lowth. Here he found the right ring for the verse of a warlike, primitive tribe, expressed in images, direct language, and conceptual simplicity. The parallels of meaning and phraseology, the evocative metaphors, and the choice of images from the likely experience of a primitive people – all are clear in these 'translations':

> The hero moved on before his host, like a cloud before a ridge of green fire, when it pours on the sky of night, and mariners foresee a storm. On Cona's rising heath they stood: the white-bosomed maids beheld them above like a grove; they foresaw the death of the youth, and looked towards the sea with fear. The white wave deceived them for distant sails; the tear is on their cheek. The sun rose on the sea, and we beheld a distant fleet. Like the mist of the ocean they came, and poured their youth upon the coast.   (*Carthon*, para. 16)

114

Macpherson's debts to the past did not stop with his Gaelic originals and the Bible. Like other eighteenth-century poetry, his resonates with Milton, Virgil, Homer (whom Macpherson really translated in 1773), and the generation of descriptive poets before him. Since every man speaks the language of his time, echoes of Thomson and his contemporaries are not surprising; those of the older epics are less tokens of Macpherson's insecurity about his talents than unassertive assertions of the dignity of a British epic and British heroes. Another assertion of the same sort comes in the ethic of the poems. As Smart made the Psalms fit for Christian England, redeeming the Old Testament with the doctrine of the New, so Macpherson replaced the savage egotists of Homer with more tender, more social, maybe more Virgilian heroes, except that they lack Aeneas' spur of piety, and act instead from bounty of spirit. Through the mediation of the old bard Ossian, himself a warrior before becoming a poet, the exploits of great men turn into assertions of corporate values, so as to deepen the mixture of nostalgia and awe with which eighteenth-century Britons read. North Britons especially. Macpherson was a Scot, a citizen of a land at which Englishmen sneered for its backwardness, and he was also a Jacobite: praise for the glimpsed, lost glories of a primitive, romantic past had a special worth for him and his nation. He may well have felt that the resonance of a scriptural style fitted the import of his myth, with its analogues to biblical suffering, battle, elegy, and redemption. Whatever his intentions, the style worked to make readers look back to a past profound with spiritual rigors, like the biblical past, and apprehensible only through an act of the sympathetic imagination. As with these historical scenes, so with language: readers had to use sympathetic imagination to recapture a depth of spiritual vision, a glow of poetic beauty, at which Macpherson's 'translation,' however skilled, could only hint.

Ossian's songs, of course, did not initiate poets into Asiatic flavors akin to a biblical style or into the poetry of peoples from whom Britons descended. William Collins wrote his *Persian Eclogues* (1742) in – as he put it in his preface – a 'rich and figurative' style suitable to that people; and the two 'Runic Odes' attributed dubiously to the elder Thomas Warton (d. 1745) in his *Poems* (1748) evoke the bravery of the Goths. In fact, one should remember that Warton's odes are near translations of Latin originals reprinted and praised by Sir William Temple in the last decade of the seventeenth century as having 'a vein truly poetical and in its kind Pindaric' (*Works*, 1720, 1: 216), that the elder Samuel Wesley commented on the Eddas and Taliessen in 1700 (*An Epistle to a Friend concerning Poetry*), and that Alexander Pope discussed with John Gay writing 'American pastorals, or rather pastorals adapted to the manners of several of the ruder nations as well as the Americans' (Joseph Spence, *Anecdotes*, ed. Osborn, 1966, no. 339). But Temple, Wesley, Pope, the elder Warton, and Collins were all dead before these kinds swung into vogue. Ossian prompted Michael Bruce's (or John Logan's?) 'Eclogue in the Manner of Ossian' (pub. 1770) and probably Gray's translations of Norse odes in 1761, 'The Fatal Sisters' and 'The Descent of Odin' (pub. 1768), to which Bruce's two 'Danish Odes' may be indebted. Thomas Penrose, Hugh Downman, and William Bagshaw Stevens followed suit. As to those poems where the speaker's culture is primitive, a social equivalent to pastness, one finds Stevens's 'Indian Odes' (1775), Henry Brooke's 'Conrade: A Fragment' (1778), and John Scott's mixed bag of 'Oriental Eclogues,' one Arabian, one East Indian, one Chinese (1782). The impetus behind them, as Temple had said of the Runic odes eighty years earlier, resembled that of the Restoration Pindaric, though for Pindaric expansiveness the new poems substituted a style more lurid, more abrupt, and more incantatory.

So popular were these Ossianic modes that they show up in that compendium of the most popular styles of the late 1760s, the poems of Thomas Chatterton (1752–70). Along with the elegies, mock-elegies, religious and physicotheological poems, mock-heroics, and songs of 1769–70, one finds 'Ethelgar,' 'Gorthmund,' and four other poems with similar titles, all 'translations' from the Saxon, no doubt as English answers to Macpherson's triumphant Celts. They are clotted with Teutonic proper names and enjoy, like Macpherson's poems, antiquarian notes here and there. 'Narva and Mored' and 'The Death of Nicou' represent the primitive exotic of African eclogues. But of course Chatterton's most famous, though unwitting, flattery of Macpherson was in imitating him (during 1768–69) as a forger. Using a collection of old words chosen from dictionaries and glossaries, a few medieval customs, and a great many antique and pseudo-antique spellings, Chatterton simply made up 'old' poems which he assigned to fictitious medieval authors, chiefly a fifteenth-century cleric Thomas Rowley. 'Englysh Metamorphosis,' for instance, begins:

> Whanne Scythyannes, salvage as the wolves theie chacde,
> Payncted in horrowe formes bie nature dyghte,
> Heckled yn beastskyns, slepte uponne the waste,
> And wyth the morneynge rouzed the wolfe to fyghte,
> Swefte as descendeynge lemes of roddie lyghte
> Plonged to the hulstred bedde of laveynge seas,
> Gerd the blacke mountayn okes yn drybblets twighte,
> And ranne yn thought along the azure mees,
> Whose eyne dyd feerie sheene, like blue-hayred defs,
> That dreerie hange upon Dover's emblaunched clefs.

Though Chatterton may well have been a 'marvellous boy,' in Coleridge's phrase, he was no marvel as a forger. The crust of age he glued to his poems made some silliness and banality less visible, and allowed some very nice effects in sound and metre through extending his lexicon. By and large, I suspect, he damaged the poems by slowing down the reading pace erratically. His often rather mechanical activity (unlike Macpherson's) is a bit like sandpapering a modern operatic gramophone record so as to enrapture devotees of the 'Golden Age.' The Rowley poems come from eighteenth-century Spenserian imitations, freighted with more odd words and Olde Englysshe spellings: 'The Battle of Hastings,' for instance, uses the stanza of Prior's 'Colin's Mistakes. Written in Imitation of Spenser's Style'

(1721), and 'Englysh Metamorphosis' uses a variant of the same. Chatterton's debt to the past was to the eighteenth-century past.

If one shrinks the Ossianic narrative to a shorter, finer-boned, tamer form, one gets the narrative ballad. (I say 'narrative ballad' because the popular ballad, like Gay's 'Of all the girls that e'er were seen/There's none so fine as Nelly,' and the ballad of commentary, huzzahing or damning something seriously or ironically, was a continuing tradition – especially in political verse – that bears no relation to a new fervor for medieval verse.) Macpherson and Chatterton, like Spenserians and perhaps Miltonians, effectually achieve their style by first simplifying language of its usual eighteenth-century poetic ornaments and then saturating it with 'figures of sentiment,' ornaments of their own; the ballad's 'spontaneous style' remains relatively simple, like Mickle's 'Hengist and Mey' (1770):

> Where in the dale a moss-grown cross
>   O'ershades an aged thorn,
> Sir Elmer's and young Hengist's corse
>   Were by the spearmen borne.
>
> And there, all clad in robes of white,
>   With many a sigh and tear,
> The village maids to Hengist's grave
>   Did Mey's fair body bear.   (ll. 169–76)

This does not improve the verse, but it does work toward three interrelated goals. It prepares one to accept the simplification, the purification, of narrative and feeling as a means of evoking basic, direct response. In this way the ballad does what the pastoral had done, but without restriction to shepherds: a hypothesized past culture, alleged in the case of Mickle's ballad to be Arthurian, takes the place of the pastoral's hypothesized state of life tending sheep. The ballad style, with its refusal of the analytic, also compels the reader to accept the contents uncritically, as given, just as the characters in the ballads accept the sudden turns of fate. A distance, even a sense of strangeness, about the clear and yet alien world laid before the reader, makes him willing to suspend disbelief to an unusual degree. Finally, the ballad's simplicity makes a direct appeal to a nostalgia for simplicity itself, for a world of romance and codes of behavior (chivalry, pure love, strict dictates of honor), so that even that which is inexplicable can be assimilated into larger patterns of understanding and given a just solution. Since directness of response, empathic belief in a text, and nostalgia for a simpler and better world were among the aims typical of later eighteenth-century poetry, the narrative ballad enjoyed a good measure of success toward the very end of our period. Writers pursued these aims even when they involved rejecting authentic ballads, as in Mrs J. Hampden Pye's reworking – in *Poems by a Lady* (1771) – of 'Childe Waters' as 'Earl Walter: a Ballad.' The new version is purified of references to illicit love and its results, simplified of repetitions, and made more fully pathetic.

From the special standpoint of this chapter the rise of the narrative ballad has its own significance. Poets who imitated the classics followed where great masters guided them. Sometimes they asserted an equality with Horace and Pindar but even that assertion made a claim that the old and new masters spoke the same artistic language, bent themselves to the same craft. The use of fixed genres proved that by setting forth the conditions of that craft. Much the same attitude prevailed among imitators of Milton and Spenser, though here no one dared challenge either poet at his own most intricate game: there are imitations of pastorals, the monody, sonnets, not the epic. Poets began to run the danger of too much reverence, significantly enough at a time when critics of the third great 'Renaissance' figure, Shakespeare, were starting to lapse into 'bardolatry.' This antiquarian awe among readers obviously affected the audience for Macpherson and Chatterton, if not those two poets themselves, and comes most strikingly to the fore in the vogue for the ballad. Here we have not the creation of a great craftsman but an utterance from what the next century would call the 'folk,' not a work of art but a work of artlessness. Dryden and Pope had embraced the monuments of classical culture; the writer of ballads embraced an anonymous sensibility, so that the egalitarian sharing of emotion pushed aside the elitist sharing of a craft. The slow change from one kind of attitude toward the other, a change by no means complete by 1780, marks a telling shift in the uses and perceived meaning of the past.

4   Later eighteenth-century poetry 1720–80

The preceding three chapters have shown, I think, that the Restoration and eighteenth century saw an extraordinary inventiveness and self-aware exploration of poetic modes. Changes came so fast that one can easily see why much outdated (though still current) literary history has persisted in finding seismic fissures here and there throughout the period: hence 'the Age of' and 'ism' descriptions. For the everyday reader of verse at the time, these changes looked less dramatic. They appear more strikingly in ambitious poems than in the miscellaneous verse with which the poets' creative exuberance filled their various collections of *Poems on Several Occasions* or the appropriate pages of periodicals like the *Gentleman's Magazine* (after 1731) and the *Annual Register* (after 1758). Nicholas Amhurst could be speaking for dozens of his contemporaries when he advertizes his *Poems on Several Occasions* (1720) as 'composed of poems, sacred and profane, original, para-phrased, imitated, and translated; tales, epigrams, epistles, love verses, elegies upon departed friends, and satires upon living enemies. It begins with the creation of the world and ends with the discovery of that ingenious utensil, a bottle-screw' (2nd edn, 1723, p. iv). Just as the eclectic, conservative programming of present-day symphony orchestras and recording companies prevents sharp changes in the texture of musical experience nowadays – at least for the listener to classical music – so the eclectic freedom of eighteenth-century poets gave readers far more continuity than disjunctions. The process of change was, if anything, smoother than my account so far has suggested.

No doubt the cushioning of change allowed poets to experiment all the more without fear of losing contact with their public. The public, in fact, enlarged during the period, to judge from the number of books of verse that publishers found it worthwhile to risk. Near the end of the eighteenth century, massive poetic collections edited by Dr Johnson (1779–81) and Dr Robert Anderson (1792–5) brought together systematically – as literally hundreds of poetic miscellanies had been doing unsystematically – the evidence of Englishmen's appetite for writing and reading verse. Poets' sense of a widening audience may have encouraged them to be less learned and less savage. (One may compare the raw court poetry of the Restoration with even the bawdry of a century later: how tame, next to Rochester, Etherege, and Dorset, are the mildly salacious *Forty Select Poems* (1753) attributed

119

to Thomas Hamilton, Earl of Haddington, or the cheerful phallic punning of 'Adam Strong' in his volume of satiric odes, *The Electrical Eel* (1777)!) A desire to appeal to the more popular readership earned by poetry in the eighteenth century may also have edged writers toward greater concern with immediate, non-reflective emotional techniques such as have been discussed in the two previous chapters. As usual, one ought to go no further than 'may have' when speculating on historical causes, both for lack of evidence and for lack of knowing quite how the available evidence should be applied. I feel surer about the changes themselves, less learning and satiric savagery, more use of rhetoric for emotion unmediated by thought, as the century moved on.

At the beginning of the first chapter, I tried to define what seems to me most distinctive about Restoration poetry in terms of a theme, that of power. No single theme replaced it; rather, the focus of poetry shifted from a central *theme* – power – to a central operating *principle*, that of interaction, corporateness, treatment of all themes in terms of social, intellectual, or moral composites. Some genres, like satire, fitted in with both the theme of power and the principle of corporateness. Others, like panegyric, did not, and gave way to the corporate genre of the patriotic poem or the epistle, as in Pope, who ennobles noblemen by making them his moral peers. Still others, like the didactic or preceptive poem, began to flourish only as the principle of corporateness flourished. In the early to mid-eighteenth century, the corporate genres dominate ambitious poetry, the positional style (which centres on interaction) enjoys its most sustained development, and the relationship between past and present poetry is at its most complex. Again, no single principle replaced that of corporateness and no theme, like that of power, took over the focus of poetry in the mid- to later eighteenth century. What was most distinctive about the verse of these years was, I think, a *posture*, an *attitude*. That controlling attitude was one of sympathy, a call for fellow-feeling. Odes and elegies gained favor, while satire began to lose its teeth from a diet of too much sugar. Ideal presence, where reader and speaker see the world together, and narrative demands for empathy spread throughout the verse of the period. Poets treat the past less specifically in regard either to it or to their own culture, and turn instead to a mingling of external history as imagined (brave savages, dark Celtic combats, superstitions and feudal ties) and personal history as imagined or remembered.

If the diagrammatic statement I have just made holds up as well as one can expect of diagrams, it should offer some guidance about the terrain this book traverses. To it I should add one more observation, that the Restoration emphasis on the poet as spectator continues all the way to 1780. In the scientific model established by Newton, Boyle, Hooke, biologists, physiologists, and chemists, the observer necessarily stands outside his irrational object (stars, gases, cells, particles); and in the psychological models used by Hobbes, Locke, Hume, Hutcheson, Hartley, and their fellow philosophers, the observer also stands outside his irrational object, the mind, which has its own inner Galilean or Newtonian mechanics. So in poetry. Throughout the period, despite some pious or vain-glorious claims about the moral effect of poetry, speakers typically cannot affect the

120

external realities they perceive. Growingly in the period, speakers cannot even organize these realities, at least not with the intellect. Searching and spontaneity take on increased value. Association of ideas and other non-rational but psychologically plausible means of organization replace the abstract or rhetorical patterning of some of the Restoration poems discussed in Chapter 1. Furthermore, poems increasingly appeal to non-rational faculties in the reader, so that they tend to explore passions and sensory impressions but almost never explore ideas. These poems by and large reinforce, not challenge prior beliefs, and however much their authors assert didactic ends, one can suspect that they deal with ideas at all to strike responsive emotional chords rather than to teach.

In so extremely diverse a period as the one from 1720 to 1780, generalizations are open to even more caveats than usual. I believe that mine at least stand up well against the major poems of Thomson, Pope, Johnson, Gray, Collins, Goldsmith, and Macpherson. Each speaker faces a universe about which he can do little, and which typically is privative or painful. One may think, for example, of the sense of limitation, precariousness, and dark fate in Pope's Horatian poems and the *Dunciad, London* and *The Vanity of Human Wishes*, Gray's *Elegy* and parts of his odes, parts of *The Seasons*, Goldsmith's *The Traveller* and *The Deserted Village*, and the Ossianic poems. Even when this universe is morally mixed or divinely comedic, it is overwhelming, as in *The Seasons*, Thomson's *Poem to Newton, An Essay on Man*, and Gray's Pindaric odes. Pope's four moral epistles and some of Collins's poems, which do not quite fit this pattern, share with other major works of the period a separation between the speaker and his subject. That is, except for some of Pope's Horatian imitations and some odes, all these major works are prospect or survey poems, with a speaker alongside of whom the reader stands and looks out on a varied scene, listening and associatively following the speaker's comments. Sometimes the scene is actual, sometimes imagined, sometimes (*The Deserted Village* or the Ossianic poems) remembered. Neither speaker nor reader affects it except in emotional coloring. Though all these poems are commonplace in ideas, they all dwell on intriguing images, subtleties of tone, and, often, discrepancies between imagined ideals and presented reality. These discrepancies evoke discomfort, pathos, nostalgia, and/or situational irony, effects that mark the speaker's impotence. The virtues the poems celebrate tend to be those of counterbalancing strength, making the best of the situation. Whether these depend on an external object (faith, affection) or not (stoicism, righteousness), they are often won through proper understanding. Humans cannot do much to alter the world outside them, but by joining epistemology and ethics can alter the world within.

As I have said, certain genres grow, others wane, and almost all change with the emphases of the period. Four in particular suit this complex of attitudes well: the elegy, the topographical poem, the comprehensive satire, and the ode. (The didactic poem has affinities with the topographical poem and the comprehensive satire.) Elegies are typically about an impervious universe to which one must adjust with the help of affection and, often, faith. The prospect mode, which contributes both the topographical poem and the comprehensive satire, also treats the poet as spectator of either physical nature or – despairingly – social nature. Odes, finally, exalt the imagination and the passions, and produce allegorical figures with ideal presence (unlike Restoration Pindarics) so as to join the ethical (noble, lofty conceptions) and the epistemological (sensory validation through an imaginative act). All the major poems mentioned in the last paragraph inhabit one of these four genres or exist nearby one or more of them.

Forms of satire

The most social kind of poetry, in audience if not in origin, is satire, and satire on poetry itself brings to public view the public's expectations about an artist's role. Apart from lampoons and general accusations of dullness, most such satire in the Restoration and earlier eighteenth century is essentially progressive: it mocks outmoded forms, servile imitation, and hackneyed language. Thus Dryden has his dunce Flecknoe recommend the preciousness of the earlier 'metaphysicals' to Shadwell: anagrams, acrostics, picture poems (ll. 203–8), all old verbal tricks against which Addison was to inveigh for a week of *Spectators* (nos. 58–63). Mary Barber's or Swift's 'Apollo's Edict' (1721) cries out against imitators of Denham's most famous couplet:

> Nor let my votaries show their skill
> In aping lines from *Cooper's Hill*;
> For know, I cannot bear to hear
> The mimicry of *deep, yet clear*.   (ll. 46–9)

This Apollo also denounces poetic cant, like the anonymous author of 'Parnassus to Be Sold' (1735), in which a countryman who inquires realistically about a poet's land is answered with stock poetic phrases about gentle zephyrs and stormless climes. It is against cant that Pope writes about 'expected rhymes' in *An Essay on Criticism*: 'Where'er you find *the cooling western breeze,*/In the next line it *whispers through the trees*' (ll. 351–2). It is against slavish imitation that Matthew Green cautions the reader of *The Spleen* (1737) that he has not used theft or a recipe of rules – 'poetic buckets for dry wells' (l. 16) – to compose his 'motley piece.' These writers and a number of others like them reminded readers that poetry is not a mechanical art, in which success comes from docility and copying (where success did come in writing Latin verse for school), and not a trifling art, in which word play can replace the play of ideas. By the mid-seventeenth century, when late 'metaphysical' and university verse were popular, and when French and English critics were articulating 'rules,' one needed such reminders. (I should add that even the most prescriptive critics insisted that 'rules' were not enough, as readers of their own time may have forgotten.) Satiric poets also warned against vapid poetizing, against writers' abandoning the common concerns of their fellow men in favor of airy fancies. The ideal of a Dryden, a Pope, a Swift, was of the poet as citizen.

During the mid- and later eighteenth century, many kept to this ideal, but others challenged it for a more individual kind of poetry. Much satire then becomes conservative, in defense of Dryden's old principles instead of the Wartons' new ones. By the 1730s, flatulently inflated bards start appearing in satires like Joseph Mitchell's 'The Cudgel' and 'Peter,' proclaiming that 'in oddness lies my muse's whole delight!' (*Poems* (1732), 1 : 396). Mitchell still teases old-fashioned methods: 'Peter' uses an outdated mode, typology, to tie Czar Peter the Great, who died in 1725, to the 'wolf-boy' Peter, found in the same year living wild in George I's Hanoverian electorate. Rapidly, though, the newfangled took over from the trite. Mitchell's successors found their butt in the ode and other florid, passionate, or sublime kinds. Robert Lloyd's and George Colman's *Two Odes* spoof Gray and William Mason. The *Satires* (1760) of 'Porcupinus Pelagius' include 'The Porcupinade,' a blank verse, rambling, stream-of-consciousness parody of the sublime poem. Andrew Erskine's *Town Eclogues* (1773) 'expose the false taste for florid description which prevails so universally in modern poetry' ('Advertisement'); the first of these eclogues offers a dialogue between two hangmen, in which Jack exclaims to John, 'Your words reanimate my drooping frame,/And my soul kindles in the bursting flame' (p. 3). Among the amusing and complete parodies is Soame Jenyns's 'Burlesque Ode,' which strings together inconsequential stanzas of rant and description (e.g., of 'morning, robed in saffron-coloured gown,/Her head with pink and pea-green ribbons dressed,' who 'climbs the celestial staircase' while lustful old ocean longs to have her in his bed again and 'roars amain/To hasten back the lovely fugitive'). It has lavish apostrophes to the sun and moon and seasons, and a final:

> Hail Liberty, fair goddess of this isle!
> Deign on my verses and on me to smile;
> Like them unfettered by the bonds of sense,
>   Permit us to enjoy life's transient dream,
> To live and write without the least pretense
>   To method, order, meaning, plan, or scheme;
> And shield us safe beneath thy guardian wings,
> From law, religion, ministers, and kings. (st. 13)

Jenyns's conservative esthetics and politics create appropriate silliness here; most genuine odes were in fact apolitical, though as noted in Chapter 2, English devotion to liberty did affect arguments about poetic constraints like rhyme.

To someone who has been wading through a swamp of late eighteenth-century 'inspired' verse – someone, say, like a historian of the poetry of the period – the most devastating conservative attack is *Bagley: A Descriptive Poem with the Annotations of Scriblerus Secundus* (1777), probably by Alexander Crowcher Schomberg (1756–92). *Bagley* displays the bad points of modern poetry not by caricature but by deliberate imitation so as to produce their epitome. The abuses of men like John Ogilvie, John Langhorne, and William Mason find their way into the Scriblerian footnotes (in the manner of Fielding's play *The Tragedy of*

Tragedies), to justify the stylistic mannerisms and verbal clichés caught in *Bagley*. Often Schomberg signals direct, acknowledged imitation or indebtedness for a description, a pathetic love tale, an invocation to Britannia at the end. The notes also mock the ingenious apologists for such poetry, who explain, for instance, that one may 'condemn "murky gloom of obscure [night]" as mere expletives in the verse, used for the sake of variety in the words instead of "dark darkness of dark night"; but the [reader of taste] will perceive that the repetition of the same object sets it stronger in his view' (pp. 56–7). Why not inconsistent and obscure metaphors, since 'common sense has nothing to do with true poetry,' and obscurity has been called sublime by Edmund Burke (pp. 10, 13, 62)? Unfortunately, *Bagley* and its companion *Ode on the Present State of English Poetry* (1779) do not bear quoting: Schomberg is so accurate that the lines are no funnier, at least in short extracts, than a very bad poem by one of the mocked poets would be. He exaggerates, for instance, the broken line to indicate passionate speech, like 'I ne'er will leave thee. No! I'll rather—I'll—' (*Ode*, l. 69), but the dramatic verse he imitates abounds so with pauses and cries that his exaggeration seems slight. Schomberg's calculatedly false grandeur, personification, mixed and meaningless (but colorful) imagery, and adulation for 'the grand characteristics of modern poetry' (*Ode*, p. 8) instead of the restraint of 'the frigid ancients' – the cumulative impact of all these is lethal.

Schomberg's and the others' immediate target is verse they find silly and affected. For the first time in the period a widespread serious style is blamed in this way rather than simply bad variants of an acceptable style (as in Pope's prose satire *Peri Bathous* (1727)) or individuals' novelties (Ambrose Philips's pastorals or his poems for children, the latter scathingly parodied by Henry Carey in 'Namby-Pamby' (1725)). The problem, then, is social. Modishness endorses the fancy inanity of *Bagley*'s victims or the plain inanities in the 'Sonnets, odes, acrostics, madrigals' lamented by Richard Tickell's 'The Wreath of Fashion' (1778), sentimental verse made up of 'A motley heap of metaphoric sighs– /Laborious griefs, and studied ecstasies—' (ll. 135–6). For some plaintiffs, the target is not merely silly verse but a social corruption of poetry and poets. Charles Churchill, who believed in defending his own satire with a stout offense, repeatedly charges during the early 1760s that other poets have retreated into insipidity at the behest, overt or not, of the government. Publius, for instance, in *The Author* (1763) 'blasphemes' the power 'of sacred numbers' by advising Churchill not to meddle with 'states and statesmen,' but to 'frequent the haunts of humble swains,' 'indulging the poetic whim/In quaint-wrought ode or sonnet pertly trim' like Gray and Mason (ll. 117–28). The same year finds Churchill attacking Mason and George Lyttelton in *The Prophecy of Famine*, disclaiming 'prattling streams o'er flower-empurpled meads' in favor of Nature in a different sense; Churchill will not be like David Mallet, from whose example

> simple bards, by simple prudence taught,
> To this wise town by simple patrons brought,
> In simple manner utter simple lays,

And take, with simple pensions, simple praise.   (ll. 135–8)

Independence (1764) devotes itself to this subject.

Churchill's charges gain some color if one reflects that every poet who made much of a name between 1660 and the year of Churchill's birth, 1731, wrote significant verse satire or political poetry, generally both; but that in the half-century after 1731, almost no new poet of note, except Churchill himself, did so. Johnson stopped after his first published English poem, *London* (1738), if one considers *The Vanity of Human Wishes* – unlike Juvenal's original – to be essentially elegiac; Gray's 'On Lord Holland's Seat' (written 1768) is savage political satire, but only twenty-four lines long; Christopher Anstey's prickling rather than pungent *The New Bath Guide* (1766) may be the most notable exception to the rule. Especially after Walpole's overthrow in 1742, poets who devoted their efforts to satire or politics tended to be third-rate – Robert Lloyd, Evan Lloyd, Paul Whitehead, Edward Thompson, Macnamara Morgan – while better or more prestigious authors ignored both or practiced verse satire only occasionally (Smollett, Smart) or lightly (Garrick, Goldsmith). Such detachment becomes more surprising when set against the way poets scurried for their quills and foolscap during the reign of Charles II and the Walpole years; the 1760s and early 1770s, the years of battling over a much-hated royal favorite, the Earl of Bute, and his foe, the radical demagogue John Wilkes, gave a heyday to political cartoonists but not to poets. Changes in poetic style seem to have entailed changes in the social role of the poet. Churchill roared in the void, and roared the more, perhaps, from fright at hearing his own lone voice: he is the most defensive, explanatory, self-justifying, autobiographical of the Restoration and eighteenth-century satirists.

The watershed between these two conceptions of the poet comes in the same fifteen or twenty years during which new genres began mingling more strongly with the old, the later 1720s through the earlier 1740s. Pope marked these years with three kinds of poems about human change and fixity. In one group, the bulk of the Horatian poems, he more and more angrily indicted Walpole's government, a new and gluttonous monster, by using himself, the disinterested man of integrity, as the fixed point. Churchill's autobiographical gesturings come from this political mode of Pope's, even to enlarging (in his attacks on descriptive poets) on Pope's boast in *An Epistle to Dr. Arbuthnot* (1735) that 'not in Fancy's maze he wandered long,/But stooped to truth and moralized his song' (ll. 340–1). In another group or pair, the two versions of the *Dunciad* (1728, 1742–3), Pope narrates an epic of growing historical chaos, ending in the petty apocalypse of slumber. Here the trivial and transient achieve the permanence of absolute dominion, so absolute that the proof and cost of their triumph must be their own annihilation along with the rest of the ruined world. The third group, about which I will say more later, mediates between the sharply focused, personal mode of the angrier Horatian poems (exploring the implications of the joint reign of George II and Walpole vs. those of being Alexander Pope) and the broad, impersonal mode of the *Dunciad* (exploring the implications of mindless cultural chaos within a culture that can give and receive definition through the inherited form of the epic). This third group includes some of the Horatian poems, but much more important, the four moral essays and *An Essay on Man*. *An Essay on Man* (1733) provides the metaphysical context for the essays (1731–5), just as Pope's integrity and epic ideals provide ethical and cultural contexts for the other two groups. The *Essay* places the variable, fortune-tossed world we know against the fixed order of Providence; the moral essays place the seeming arbitrariness of social behavior against a fixed pattern of psychological causation. Each of these groups is profoundly historical, and in each Pope looks at history – the history he was living through – from a different conceptual position.

The previous chapter discussed Pope's direct adaptations from Horace, but not two other poems in the Horatian mode, *An Epistle to Dr. Arbuthnot* and the two-part *Epilogue to the Satires*. Freed from the obligations and advantages of a Latin text to imitate, Pope develops in these poems (1735, 1738) the image of integrity first set forth in his earliest Horatian imitation, *Satires* 2 : 1 (1733). He thus justifies his position, that of satirist, toward his subject. In Horace's *Satires* 2 : 1, the Roman weighs social duty against the dangers to him of malice or revenge; Pope adds to this the danger of corruption from being, like Horace, a court pensioner. Now, in *Arbuthnot*, he reworks these themes. Three figures represent the demands of official society, each himself artistically meaner than the one before, each politically more powerful and more sinister: the dead Addison ('Atticus,' ll. 193–214), the composite wealthy patron Bufo (ll. 231–48), and Queen Caroline's active confidant Lord Hervey ('Sporus,' ll. 305–33). Over against this trio stands Pope, their opposite in his disinterested independence (he is first glimpsed at home in his country retreat) and his depth of affection for his friend Arbuthnot and his parents. As a famous poet, he is also the analogue of Atticus, Bufo, and Sporus, begged for the oblique patronage of his help in mending bad verse and plays, and accused of writing satire from cruelty or spite. Analogue and contrast, with these three and with the swarm of poetasters, offer Pope the means of explicating his own identity, his own position. This comprehensive view of him – sick, flustered, reclusive, loyal, libeled, outraged, contemptuous, earnest, loving – permits us to make one further analogy, from which he delicately refrains, an analogy with the healer Dr Arbuthnot. Pope's lancet presses only into distempered spots.

The double *Epilogue* deals with the way in which fear, law, and custom dull such lancets. By writing the *Epilogue* as two dialogues with a friend who urges him to stop his overbold satire – another reworking of Horace's *Satires* 2 : 1 –Pope implies his own isolation, disingenuously so (since the whole intellectual community had herded into the anti-Walpole stockades) but somehow poignantly. One year earlier the Licensing Act had gagged the stage, as Pope reminds us in 'Dialogue I'; as he reminds us in the first line of 'Dialogue II,' the Solicitor to the Treasury screened all new publications for libel. To fear and law, Pope adds custom, which insists that one be civil, as Horace was with 'his sly, polite, insinuating style' ('Dialogue I,' l. 19), or even as Pope's fellow Opposition satirists are, so that his 'Friend' can protest that 'none but you by name the guilty lash' ('Dialogue II,' l. 10). Nowhere in Pope's verse is he more impassioned than here, when he cries out, perhaps, sincerely, against the social laming of poetry and enacts his rejection of Horace the court poet by ending each 'Dialogue' with a breathtaking Juvenalian tirade. Ironically, in style he comes close to the plain flow of emotive rhetoric which the new poets of the 1740s (Joseph Warton, Collins, Akenside, Gray) were to cherish and for which they were to turn from Pope's tradition. In the 1760s the rough, ringing declamations of Churchill – another of Pope's slighters – descend from the *Epilogue* in style as well as in concerns. The anti-Popeans are here, at least, the master's children.

If Pope's Horatian poems demand that the poet act as a citizen, the two versions of the *Dunciad* demand that citizens, Pope's readers, take poetry seriously as a bearer of central cultural values. Pope may have begun his great satire about 1719 or 1720, when the events of the poem are supposed to take place; he published it in 1728, with an elaborate and partly burlesque body of annotation added in 1729; he added a final Book in 1742; and brought out a revised version of the entire poem in 1743, seven months almost to the day before his death. In the preface 'by' Pope's and his friends' invented pedant, Martinus Scriblerus, he sets out the action and rationale of the *Dunciad* accurately: the action is the introduction of 'the lowest diversions of the rabble' at Bartholomew Fair into 'the court and town; or in other words . . . the removal of the imperial seat of Dullness . . . to the polite world, as [the action] of the *Aeneid* is the removal of the empire of Troy to Latium.' His rationale for mock-heroic, predictably, is its poetic justice, a reward for the dull writers' 'self-opinion' that makes them 'seem to themselves vastly greater than' they are. Dryden's treatment of Shadwell springs to mind; it also sprang to Pope's, for the epic burlesque, the Grub Street setting, the coronation of a dunce, and the prophetic flights owe a great deal to *MacFlecknoe*. What may be more important is that the central images of the *Dunciad* do too: materiality, excrement (i.e., material 'creation'), falling and sinking, darkness, instability, the stage (hollow appearances), and plagiarism are among motifs that Pope adapted.

To these Pope added pedantry, which appears only marginally in *MacFlecknoe* as prescriptive imitation. Here Pope deserts Dryden and draws on the satire that he and other members of the Scriblerus Club (Swift, Gay, Arbuthnot, Parnell, and the Earl of Oxford) had made their sport in 1714–18, and that he and Swift revived during Swift's visits to England in 1726 and 1727. For the *Dunciad*, the prose satire *Peri Bathous, or the Art of Sinking in Poetry* (March 1728, two months before the *Dunciad*) is the most suggestive Scriblerian production, with its attack on bad poets and critics through mock-praise, its patterns of imagery, and its metaphor of sinking. Common to both *MacFlecknoe* and *Peri Bathous* is the use of the mock-form (epic, essay in literary criticism) as a catchall for varied satire, unlike such mock-heroics as Garth's *The Dispensary* and Pope's own *The Rape of the Lock* (see Chapter 1 above). The *Dunciad* follows them in this, at least to a great extent. On its epic base, it builds an astonishingly heterogenous edifice in which farce and grandeur, grotesque filth and grotesque beauty, epigram and detailed action, minute scandal and prophetic sweep become office mates.

Apart from the pungency and brilliance of Pope's verse, the *Dunciad* destroys its cast of dunces by rendering them faceless, far less than living people, and less even than caricatures. *MacFlecknoe* and *Absalom and Achitophel* dwell on the individuality, however distasteful or bizarre it may be, of each of their satiric butts. In the *Dunciad*, though, background and foreground blend, so that figures have little more than positional roles, like bees in a swarm or rotten eggs pelting a pilloried forger (*D* 3 : 25–6). One distinguishes them only if one wants to chart their trajectories. Dunces, bees, and eggs also lack will, propelled into association as they are by instinct or mechanical force. So Pope catalogues them striving against each other at times, clustering at others, with an order he the poet chooses, not they:

> Heywood, Centlivre, glories of their race!
> Lo, Horneck's fierce, and Roome's funereal face!
> Lo, sneering Goode, half malice and half whim,
> A fiend in glee, ridiculously grim.
> Jacob, the scourge of grammar, mark with awe,
> Nor less revere him, blunderbuss of law.
> Lo, Bond and Foxton, every nameless name,
> All crowd, who foremost shall be damned to Fame?   (3 : 145–52)

The dunces' ambitions and contests become absurd because no personal will directs them; here Pope uses sinking and scatology (e.g., the urinating contest, 2 : 153–82) to act as images of materiality as well as to besmirch his victims. Like atoms and machines, bees and hurled eggs, the dunces have an energy of their at once discrete and corporate beings. This energy vibrates splendidly in the poem, along with the energy of mind that Pope supplies. His poem, through Pope's conscious choice, directs both these energies – the dunces' physical activity and Pope's artistic activity – to create a magnificent cultural bulwark against social decay. The dunces, who lack individual identity and therefore choice, simply buzz themselves to sleep at the ends of Books 2 and 3, and thus annihilate personal action.

So sharp is the *Dunciad's* attack on will and identity that a dunce acts like a puppet, manipulated and incoherent. He is also, though, a producer in society, be it of plays, verse, edicts, urine (in social competition), or dictionaries. This double role, individual and cultural, makes the dunce destructive: he both inhabits and manufactures cultural junk. He seems to be performing someone else's unwitting, witless slapstick, Bartholomew Fair sideshows, spectacles engineered with cheap illusion, and farces; but part of the performance is to spawn more slapstick, sideshows, spectacles, and farce. The producer embodies and begets his own tuppenny product. And in the England of the *Dunciad*, this product sells well, typified by incoherent, manipulated stage pieces that come into 'the court and the town,' into 'the polite world' as if they were art. Just as the dunces are mechanical simulacra of people, so these stage pieces reject the natural, which is the proper basis for art, in favor of devices for functions extrinsic to art, such as puffing up an author, making money, or amusing the mob. Pope clarifies these analogies in the *Dunciad Variorum* (1729) by extending them to still another mechanical, derivative, disjointed, ostentatious cultural product: pedantry. The metaphor of the popular stage informs the text of the poem, and that of pedantic learning informs the annotations.

For the 1728 *Dunciad* Pope hit on an enemy, Lewis Theobald, who was both playwright and critic; the poem makes him Tibbald the farce-writer and pedant. As such, he subverts art and its source, nature: farce and pedantry make art and nature into mere starting-points for excursions into the fanciful, the vain, and the eye-catching. Farce and pedantry, those analogues that seem so opposite, also discard the need for taste, and create their own worlds to escape from it: the world centered on books (Book I) and the world centered on stage effects (Book III):

> Hell rises, Heaven descends, and dance on Earth,
> Gods, imps, and monsters, rage and mirth,
> A fire, a jig, a battle, and a ball,
> Till one wide conflagration swallows all. (ll. 233–6)

Book II, sandwiched in between books and stage effects, presents the grotesque epic strivings of the duncens, a hybrid spectacle that draws on learning and public exhibitions both. This third world also denies taste, and Pope makes it gross in the narrow sense of 'bad taste.' Each of the three books in 1728 redefines the past (past literature in Book I, epic values in Book II, English history in the hack playwright Settle's prophetic vision that takes up all of Book III) in terms of these duncens' worlds. Merging with the metaphor of the popular stage are images of creation, as the duncens dimly bring to momentary life their self-protective counterfeits of the real world. The more they evoke the real world, the more they expose their poverty of being.

Pope no doubt hit on the plan of the *Dunciad* of 1728 as a means to flog his enemies. In the process of giving his revenge a vehicle, he created a superb short satire (just over a thousand lines long) about taste. He also left open the possibility of transforming the poem into a satire on modern culture, the society that exalts duncery. By the end of Walpole's era, after the gall of the Horatian poems had thickened in the *Epilogue to the Satires*, Pope was ready for the transformation. He tossed the insignificant Theobald aside for Colley Cibber, a playwright much in the repertory, a governmentally licensed theater manager with control over the rest of that repertory, and – most important – Poet Laureate to George II. As a man who helped rule and corrupt public entertainment and who flattered England's corrupt rulers in verse of despicable quality, Cibber beautifully symbolizes the London of the revised *Dunciad*, as the 'piddling Tibbald' (*Ep. Arb.*, l. 164) typified the faceless duncens of the first version.

Another change points to the heightened seriousness of the new *Dunciad*: in 1728 the apocalyptic vision of anarchy and universal darkness simply forms the end of the prophecy spoken by Settle's ghost for the 'rapture' of the chief dunce; but by 1743, it has become the poet's own vision, including not only 'physic,' 'metaphysic.' and 'mystery,' but also 'religion,' 'morality,' 'human spark' and 'glimpse divine.' At the end of the prophecy in 1728, the ghost passes through the ivory gate allotted by Virgil to false visions. Fifteen years later, the vision is true, for

129

the new *Dunciad* closes with anarchy's curtain dropped, so that 'universal darkness buries' – in 1728, only 'covers' – 'all.' The apocalyptic passage has been transplanted from the end of Book III to that of the new Book IV, a pageant of dullness in the arts, the sciences, and education, where the 'uncreating word' has made the light die and the world revert to primal chaos.

The *Dunciad* of 1743 extends to teachers and pupils, travelers and antiquaries, naturalists and philosophers, throughout the realms of the understanding. Pope carefully adjusts this new material to the old. Each new group embodies fancy, vanity, or both, the traits that the first three books of the poem associate with dullness. The *Dunciad* thereby coheres and its items of recorded behavior point to a single meaning; in the England that the poem describes, the wholeness of nature breaks into fragments at the hands of educators, scientists, and metaphysicians, while spiritual meaning fades from the material objects that the dunces pore over and adore. Thus the educators of Book IV 'ply the memory [and] load the brain,/Bind rebel wit, and double chain on chain' (ll. 157–8) to keep students 'in the pale of words till death' (l. 160) and separate them from mind and meaning. Youths on the Grand Tour shed their classical learning for whores and *hors d'oeuvres* (ll. 311–22), and antiquaries fascinated with possessing objects mingle the false with the true, or dig in certifiably modern excrement for allegedly ancient medals gulped down by one thief to keep them safe from others (ll. 347–94).

Not only do these activities sit well in the universe of Tibbald and Settle, they also form parts of a large poetic design. For example, the apocalyptic sleep at the end of Book IV, preceded by Settle's ecstatic vision at the end of Book III, has already been foretold by the sleep at the end of Book II preceded by the Cibberian triumph at the end of Book I. As Book II (the games) extends Book I (the introduction of the King Dunce) in terms of space, and Book III (Settle's vision) extends Book II in terms of time, so Book IV represents the cultural extension of the broad historical pageant in Book III. As Book II makes objective what was personal or individual in Book I, so Book IV makes objective what was a personal prophetic vision in Book III. Books I–III exhibit a subverted, unnatural, anthropocentric art, and Book IV extends these corruptions to history and nature. Books I–III mock farce and spectacle on the stage, and Book IV documents a whole series of transformations, false appearances, and exaggerated feelings. The footnotes to Books I–III, added by Pope for the *Dunciad Variorum* of 1729, stake out the motif of pedantry, as does the character of Tibbald, so that the great indictment of abused learning in Book IV opens out like an umbrella of which we have all along been gripping the handle. Despite the decade and a half that separate the second *Dunciad* from the first, the poem holds together magnificently.

Book IV by itself holds together too. Pope seems to follow an obvious logical or associative order, not inevitable in sequence but plausible and interlinked. He begins with education in school and university, then its extension in the youths' Grand Tour. The youths supposedly travel to acquire a full sense of the riches of other places and other times, so Pope next turns to the most material version of this (fit for the appetitive youths) in the antiquaries' greed for old, exotic coins. From these collectors of relics he passes to collectors of natural objects ('A nest, a toad, a fungus, or a flower' (l. 400)) and then to natural scientists; they in turn lead him to their extension in students of the supernatural made natural, metaphysicians who 'thrust some mechanic cause' into the place proper to the hand of God (l. 475). When the freethinker Silenus ends his speech, wizardry takes over (l. 517) with cheap imitations of the divine power of creation and transformation: dunces change identity, nature boils down into the 'specious miracles' of elaborate cookery, Queen Dullness ennobles her protégés, and all England becomes 'one mighty dunciad' in leaden slumber. With all the world the same, analogy comes to its *reductio ad absurdum* and the associative logic of the narrative has nowhere it can go.

If one looks more closely, one can see that Pope uses the associative order that gives his poem system, and the analogical patterning that equates vastly differing kinds of dullness, to evolve a brilliant concessive argument. That is, he begins with young students whipped into memorizing words; what they lack, therefore, is judgment; and so in his next group he grants the students added judgment, and shows us the pedant locked in his college. Free the pedant for travel and we watch the youth lolling in the fleshpots; let us grant the youth an interest in the classic lands he traverses, and Pope ushers in the greedy, credulous antiquarians; let us turn them away from dead relics to living nature, and the result is the fatuous naturalists; let us beam in on them the power of thought to inform their natural studies, and the beam darkens in the mind of the 'gloomy clerk' (l. 459) who 'reasons downward till [he] doubts of God' (l. 472). From sheer memory to pure reason, dullness asserts itself though every grace be granted it.

With reason, the *Dunciad* became the most influential satire of its century. It prompted a host of (less apocalyptic) poems with titles ending in '-iad' or edited by a Scriblerus, the neatest example being Richard Owen Cambridge's *The Scribleriad* (1751), a refined but dull mock-heroic. It also gave impetus to satires on two topics: from the first *Dunciad*, that of taste, and from the second, that of the corruption of the times. In Chapter 2 I discussed a sample of James Cawthorn's 'Of Taste' and in Chapter 3 some imitations of Horace's *Ars poetica* which dwell, at times satirically, on the same subject. Their modes differ from the *Dunciad*'s though less from Pope's epistles. Taste was a burning issue in eighteenth-century England because a great influx of commercial money coincided with a long-standing social urge toward gentility and the connoisseurship of the fine and decorative arts (including speech, dress, dining and behavior) that marks one as genteel. The 'rules' guided real or hopeful ladies and gentlemen to understand an idiom within which they could make discriminations by employing a cultivated taste. Often the prestige of rural retirement led them to the country, to build or to plant, so that gardening, large domestic architecture, and interior decoration (furnishings, table settings, bibelots) achieved a luxurious beauty unmatched in England before or since. Gardens, buildings, and furnishings also, however, became subject to fads and exaggerations on which poets liked to swoop. Most of the verse about taste, like most of the verse about fashions in poetry, tended to be conservative by mid-century: the criterion of the natural, which led satirists to blackball the old – formal gardens, for example – in the first part of the century, led them later

131

to sneer at the new – the Gothic, the Chinese, and other crinkum-crankum modes that became all the rage in gardening.

However liberal or conservative the satire, it resembled the *Dunciad* in attacking either (or both) pedantry and caprice (the *Dunciad's* 'farce'). Those who plod along with rules or fashion, unthinkingly making their homes and/or gardens document someone else's taste (or lack of it), are pedants. For them, old and new alike are rote, and their aim is not beauty but a display of knowledge, the gentleman's *savoir faire* warped into his mimic's *savoir lire*. Those who toss all principles aside for whimsy end up with the incoherent fancy of farce. 'What is beautiful that is not new?' asks James Bramston's eponymous Man of Taste (1733), and so commits himself to the credo that mere 'expense and alteration show a taste' (p. 11). This is, once again, the *Dunciad's* theme of mechanical transformation. Like the *Dunciad* too, these poems often smell the odor of social decay – or say they do – in aberrations of taste. Writers had a perhaps ill-defined but certainly sharp sense of the sociology of taste in the eighteenth century. From Mandeville's great *Fable of the Bees* (1714–32), they knew everything about conspicuous consumption except a snappy alliterative term for it; and a variety of works kept bringing to every literate Englishman's attention how a nation's economics, politics, and state of culture fit together. Taste, it was argued, affected a large class, the most influential in the country: the moneyed men who had become England's inheritors and her artists' potential patrons.

As a result, eighteenth-century satire as a whole shows the same blending of satire on taste and satire on the times which one finds in the new *Dunciad*. Sometimes, politics too got caught in the poets' net. Basically, in the Restoration and early eighteenth century, social and political satire were distinct. One implied the other only in so far as a jaundiced view of court manners and morals indicated a jaundiced view of the King's priorities. As parliamentary authority grew under Walpole, beginning in the 1720s and 1730s, and matters that had been settled by custom began to fall under the rule of written law, there was an increasing sense that government was one fount of the country's ills. The rapid economic growth that made taste a touchy issue was encouraged by the government, which moralists saw as aiding the growth of decadent luxury. Wealth enriched the age with a great variety of projects and inventions, a new bounty of technology; 'patriots' – as the anti-Walpole group called themselves – groaned that technology encouraged a shallow, pragmatic morality or perhaps amorality, for which Walpole's own private and governmental conduct were thought to set the unhappy example. Aberrant taste served here as a symbol of a public concern with the superficial and showy, the false use of riches. From this kind of social implication, there flowed general satires on the 'times' or the 'town,' lamenting such real or imagined sores as the exaltation of the moneyed and money-making, the decay of spiritual virtues through indifference and cynical ecclesiastical and artistic patronage, and a concern with the transient, the superficial, and the immediate instead of ordered and comprehended wholes.

Some of the poems in this group announce their sweep in their titles: John Loyd's *A Satire on the Times* (1730), *A Trip to Vauxhall or A General Satire on the Times* (anon., 1737), Francis Manning's (?) 'An Essay on the Vicious Bent and Taste of the Times' (ca. 1742; pub.1752), *The Times! An Epistle to Flavian* (anon., 1759), Charles Churchill's *The Times* (1764), and *A Sketch of the Times* (anon., 1780). Not all these poems, much less all poems of this type, indict a government nor – obviously, from their dates – do they all attack any one government or any set bill of offenses. Some, like Manning's, Thomas Newcomb's interminable *The Manners of the Age* (1733), and the anonymous *An Apology for the Times* (1778) actually favor the powers that were. None the less, these satires by and large resemble Juvenal's dark verdicts on imperial decadence, with suggestions of disorder that give them an angry, elegiac gloom well beyond anything to be found in any satire (except perhaps Marvell's, in particular his *Last Instructions*), Juvenalian or not, between 1660 and 1720.

Such satires could not keep to the gentility and delicacy popular in the early eighteenth century, but tended to retreat to such models as Oldham's *Satires on the Jesuits*, rough and ferocious, which were cited (for example) in the anonymous *The World Unmasked* (1738) and by Thomas Gilbert in his satires of the 1730s (printed in *Poems on Several Occasions* (1747)). In this and earlier chapters, we have seen that Pope and his most distinguished follower, Churchill, adopted the Juvenalian tone, Churchill doing so by deliberately going back to Restoration forms of the couplet. To go with this angry style, satirists chose to attack vices thought unnatural and sordid but also perversely refined, like homosexuality, as in Gilbert's 'A View of the Town' (1735), Smollett's *Advice* (1746), and Churchill's *The Times*. Ostensibly, such vices marked London as the new luxury-pocked, declining (or festering) Rome; more to our point, they allowed satirists to appear boldly outspoken and outraged, while they titillated coffee-house and salon readers, thus satisfying the public's eagerness for emotionally exciting verse. Again, let me suggest that Churchill and Macpherson, who had some similarities in temperament and person, had more in common as poets than either, it may be, would have enjoyed admitting.

Poets who did differ from Churchill and the 'times' satirists were likely to be well-to-do amateurs living outside London: William Shenstone, Richard Graves, Richard Owen Cambridge, Christopher Anstey. All these men wrote attractive social and occasional verse, and the kind of satire that will never accuse its author of gall or ill-breeding. From Pope, they took not energy, not even polish so much as politeness, that quality of tone by which poet and audience agree to converse as urbane, refined, unaffected men – very much what one does not find in Churchill or Macpherson. Shenstone, Graves, and Cambridge remain poets whose work the casual reader might stop for rather than seek out (or shun). This holds for even the single poem by any of them still anthologized, Shenstone's well-done but to my taste jocosely mawkish evocation of a rural schoolhouse, 'The Schoolmistress.' Anstey wrote one satire of real verve, *The New Bath Guide* (1766); it was, rightly, an immediate hit, as suggested by a sudden crop of parodies, like *Tunbridge Epistles* (1767) and *Poetical Epistles to the Author of the New Bath Guide* (1767). In fact, Anstey himself tried vainly to recapture his success in other poems of the same sort (also, equally vainly, of different sorts). *The New Bath Guide* presents a group of letters

133

from the Blunderhead family, taking the waters in Bath and writing to family or friends in a variety of verse forms but particularly anapaestic couplets:

'Twas a glorious sight to behold the fair sex
All wading with gentlemen up to their necks,
And view them so prettily tumble and sprawl
In a great smoking kettle as big as our hall:
And today many persons of rank and condition
Were boiled by command of an able physician.   (Letter VI)

This is the sort of sophisticated naivete, one eye wide and the other winking, on which eighteenth-century periodical essayists thrived: it is precisely the tone for the innocuous follies of the modish.

Anstey strays no nearer vice than in his satire on religious enthusiasm – that of the moment was Methodism – which leads Prudence Blunderhead to succumb to her lover Roger ('an apparition' who comes angelically, 'Saying, "By Divine Commission/I must fill you full of love"'). Prudence's account (Letter XIV) gets rather spicy:

I began to fall a-kicking,
        Panted, struggled, strove in vain;
When the Spirit whipped so quick in,
        I was cured of all my pain.

Still, Anstey remains amused, in contrast, for example, to his fellow satirist of the same year Evan Lloyd, who also linked Methodism and lust. For Lloyd, Methodism involved 'foul corruption' and 'diabolic fruit.' His young lady is obviously a practiced slut, who,

        cloyed with carnal bliss,
Longing to taste how spirits kiss,
Bids chapels for her Saints arise,
Which are but bagnios in disguise
Where she may suck her T——'s breath,
Expiring in seraphic death.   (*The Methodist*, pp. 15, 16, 37)

Lloyd was a disciple of Churchill's, and magnified evils; Anstey tries, if not to mock the Prudences of the world out of Methodism, at least to tease us into the right sort of good-humored contempt for its hypocrisy.

Anstey and Churchill brought individual voices to later eighteenth-century satire, but neither had the genius or the temperament to restore it to its heights of the early to mid-1740s. This is a pity, because both men wrote just after the lean years for satire between Walpole's overthrow and the rise of the Earl of Bute. During those years, no one wrote satire of weight but Thomson (*The Castle of Indolence*) and Johnson (*The Vanity of Human Wishes*), neither of whom used his poem as a vehicle for the traditional satiric ends of scorn, ridicule, or arraignment. Those who did tended to imitate the *Dunciad*, if they were ambitious enough: Cambridge's *Scribleriad*, Smart's *Hilliad*, and the 'Pasquinade' of Macnamara Morgan (perhaps William Kenrick; the title-page attributes the poem to 'Porcupinus Pelagius'). Churchill, then Anstey, had the chance for a new beginning, more especially Churchill, who was a professional man of letters rather than a country gentleman devoted to being the most skillful of amateurs.

Churchill did, as I have said, try to develop his own voice, partly by reversing the mock-heroic and taking from Pope less a style than a role, that of the poet as alienated hero, such as Pope cultivated in the later Horatian poems. This is the Pope who, in the second dialogue in the *Epilogue to the Satires*, says that malefactors 'Safe from the bar, the pulpit, and the throne' are yet 'touched and shamed' by his 'ridicule alone.' Traditional mock-heroic willingly inflates the presumptuous; in Pope's late Horatian poems and in Churchill, society itself has solemnly granted the inflation. The speaker, instead of sliding into ironic agreement, dramatizes his own act of defying the values that society's act implies. Churchill's use of this role lets him keep a firm link with earlier satire but does not condemn him to repeating a style of thought and language brilliantly exploited by a far greater poet. By defining a mainstream of eighteenth-century satire in this way, and extending it with examples from his own pen, he might possibly have developed new forms and able followers. This historical position was not his (or anyone else's), partly because he died so young (at thirty-three, in 1764), partly because he wrote too quickly and furiously to elaborate any new, distinctive satiric mode. From March 1761 through September 1764, he published fourteen longer poems (about 14,000 lines in all) and had two more well under way. Such journalist's speed helped him seem to glow with spontaneous anger and to tint the speaker with the real colors of Churchill's personality. The liveliness of surface repays one for the wordy, over-vehement style that the same speed caused. Without the leisure to reflect and tinker, though, Churchill himself learned much less about writing than 14,000 published lines might be expected to teach. He died without distinguished followers; satire did no better in the decade and a half after his death than in the decade and a half after Pope's.

Teaching, perceiving, feeling

Satire is a traditional genre; the next body of verse I will discuss, moral poetry or 'happiness' poetry, includes texts from several genres or types. Verse of this sort tries to explore, rather than expose, human frailty. Unlike the late satire of Pope or Churchill's attacks, this sort of verse reaches for a social consensus – the very consensus that no longer existed, if one was to believe the satires 'on the times,' and that a good deal of genteel satire ignores in favor of colloquy among a small, select group. As usual, no one should try to draw sharp black lines between two adjacent bodies of verse: an (admittedly marginal) example of moral poetry is Edward Young's *The Love of Fame*, which in conventional generic terms is a satire as much

135

as Pope's *Epistle to Dr. Arbuthnot*. Young's poem (or group of poems), however, centers on one ethical universal, as does each of Pope's moral epistles and his *Essay on Man*, as do Johnson's *The Vanity of Human Wishes*, Goldsmith's *The Traveller* and perhaps *The Deserted Village*, and Gray's *Elegy*. The continuum I suggest from Young to Gray has its own conceptual integrity; if one objects that *The Love of Fame* is also very close to *Arbuthnot*, in most ways closer than it is to Gray's *Elegy*, I would not disagree, but would argue that the grouping I propose reminds one of connections and lines of development that usually vanish in the crannies between the familiar genres. In particular, it throws into relief the crucial eighteenth-century ideal of happiness. Most of the satires we have been discussing mention that ideal only peripherally; most of the poems we shall discuss in this section make it central.

In theory, all seven satires in Young's *Love of Fame* (1725–28) branch, as Young says in his Preface, from the same root, a need for public esteem. Each satire has a dedicatee who has achieved esteem without striving for it, and each mocks those who strive for it and make themselves miserable or bizarre. By rewarding with laughter those whose chief goal is esteem, Young thwarts them directly; since he lessens the motive force for folly, he can use mild satire to counter it, without naming names, in the manner of the delicate, judicious Horace whom his Preface praises. The *Love of Fame*, unlike its contemporary the *Dunciad* (1728), has an overt base in human psychology, and thus the capacity to go beneath behavior to its causes, about which the speaker can comment philosophically. Young tries to do this in the last of the seven satires, where he points out that the love of fame may be a 'generous ardor . . . burning brightest in the noblest mind,' and is 'of blots and beauties an alternate source,' depending on how closely bound it is to virtue. So much for the potentialities of Young's poem: in practice, he takes the chance for mildness as an invitation to tiptoe, and the claim of philosophic unity as license to sprawl. The satires consist of assorted verse paragraphs crocheted together; they have – but barely – enough wit and shrewdness to make them worth reading, but not enough to let them survive reading with care.

Results, predictably, were different when Pope tried his hand at similar poems, the four *Epistles to Several Persons*. Each, like each of Young's, had a noble or honored dedicatee: *To Cobham* (1734), *To a Lady* (Pope's friend, unnamed in the poem, Martha Blount; 1735), *To Bathurst* (1733), and *To Burlington* (1731). The first of these, with the subtitle 'Of the Knowledge and Characters of Men,' sets up the general principle that behavior presents us with bewildering variety, and hypothesizes that one can make sense of it only by aligning each person's actions around a single central disposition (what Pope calls a 'ruling passion'). *To a Lady* then tests this hypothesis by applying it to a complex subset, the characters of women. They seem – in the words of the Argument to the poem – 'yet more inconsistent and incomprehensible than those of men.' None the less, what looks like a nebula of personality really reflects light from two suns, the love of pleasure and the love of power.

The symbol for still undefined pleasure and power is money. In the last two epistles, Pope explores the zeal to acquire it in society (*To Bathurst*) and to spend it for those monuments – great houses and their landscapes – that treat nature itself as a symbol of personal magnificence (*To Burlington*). The women's maneuvers in salon, dressing-room, and bedchamber (Epistle II) foreshadow the men's in the larger worlds of city and countryside (Epistles III and IV). Put in a different way, the first two poems show how an understanding of individual psychology leads to ethical understanding; the second two, how the workings of that psychology produce ethical action. Because action is God's province as well as man's, the second pair of poems tell us that if one does not choose balance, does not sublimate for social ends the blind, dogged compulsions of his personality, Providence or Nature will enforce balance upon him or his possessions. The miser's heir turns profligate, the gardener's dense trees become lumber for his airy son's broomsticks, the self-absorbed magnate feeds a generation of laborers with the money he spends on conspicuous lavishness and will feed the next generation with the 'deep harvests' that, after his death, will 'bury all his pride has planned' (*Burl.*, l. 175).

Providence, balance, the relation between understanding and ethical action, the limits of power, the elusiveness of pleasure, the compulsions of personality, the multiple reconciliations between the greedy, gaudy self and other men – these themes dominate the *Epistles* as well as Pope's didactic *tour de force*, *An Essay on Man* (1733–4), which gives the epistles their large philosophic frame. At one time the *Essay* and epistles were to be parts of a huge moral work, including an epic, *Brutus*, and some of the material absorbed by the *Dunciad*, as well as more epistles of the sort we are discussing. Just as the doctrine of the ruling passion claims that a single trait most fully reveals itself in a great variety of forms of behavior, so Pope planned a variety of poetic forms to display one body of doctrine.

Within the individual epistles, he also illustrates his theme with a variety of means, borrowed from the techniques of English verse satire and Horace's epistles: imagined scenes, pointed analogies, aphorisms, characters, fluency and flexibility of tone, and impersonation of other speakers. The need to encompass the broadest range of experience, whether intellectual, poetic, or argumentative, affects many eighteenth-century works; but here, more specifically, it springs from Pope's realization that long moral verse epistles hold together only as epistles that one gets in the post hold together, because one cares about the mind of the writer, its breadth, intensity, and focus. Intriguing arguments do better in prose. Brilliant portraits and sage aphorisms tempt readers to dip, once they know where, rather than go steadily from start to finish. I suspect that eighteenth-century readers in particular, fond as they were of purple passages, oft-heard wisdom, and set exempla, loved to dip. Only the directed force of the speaker's quick, lively, associative mind could keep a moral epistle from curdling into some 'elegant extracts' (to steal a title from a popular eighteenth-century anthology) and a thin, discardable whey of lines in-between.

Of course, as in his essays on criticism and on man, Pope could manage this intellectual version of the prospect poem splendidly. (And of course, most of his followers could not.) The first two epistles, for instance, keep the reader going by moving from confusing externals toward a depth of understanding. In *To Cobham*, Pope uses half-answered questions to discomfit us and pique us toward the kind of solution he offers. He begins the companion poem to *Cobham*, the epistle *To a Lady*, in almost the same way, now with paradoxical images instead of questions. Sappho stands in diamonds and dirty smock, greasy by day and fragrant by night (ll. 24–8), for us to gaze at but not to comprehend, thus again discomfiting us till we turn to the speaker for understanding. In *To Cobham*, logical formulations – the questions – get logical answers, the theory of the ruling passion; in *To a Lady*, imaginative formulations – paradoxical images – get imaginative answers, a series of incisive, sometimes pathetic portraits of women who remain paradoxes but now paradoxes that can be at least intuitively understood. I am thinking of Atossa (ll. 115–50), Cloe (ll. 157–80), and the aging beauties (ll. 219–48) who 'haunt the places where their honour died':

> See how the world its veterans rewards!
> A youth of frolics, an old age of cards,
> Fair to no purpose, artful to no end,
> Young without lovers, old without a friend,
> A fop their passion, but their prize a sot,
> Alive, ridiculous, and dead, forgot!   (ll. 243–8)

The end of *To a Lady* brings the reader to an emotional as well as (or under the guise of?) an intellectual understanding of what enigmatic behavior has meant. In poetic and epistemological method, the poem has both complemented and documented *To Cobham*.

   To Bathurst, written after *To Burlington* but placed before it in the collected *Epistles*, does not tally with it so nicely as *To Cobham* does with *To a Lady*. Still, Pope connects them somewhat as he connects the first pair. *To Bathurst* puts forth an argument as *To Cobham* does; *To Burlington* centers on an imaginative scene, a day at Timon's villa, which serves a function like that of the long portraits of Atossa and Cloe in *To a Lady*. Pope turns to an abstract rhythmic structure to give Timon full weight, so that the six sections of the poem have a rough ratio of 2:5 (in fact groups of 22 and 48; 28 and 70; 12 and 28 lines): the large central group includes a set of small portraits and the long one of Timon, and its force is increased by its vividness in comparison to the first group (a general introduction and an address to Burlington on building and landscaping), which is prefatory to it, and its serving as a fable for the moral of the last group (a reflection on Timon's unwitting, providential nurture of the land and a paean to the chosen, active nurture of the land by wise nobles, particularly Burlington). 'Pope's' day at Timon's villa is a sustained scene of interaction between man and nature, host and guest, servants and served; nothing at all like it appears in *To Cobham* or *To a Lady*, which focus on individuals, but *To Bathurst* does provide such scenes, though not quite at such length. One finds dramatic versions of social interaction in the section on the grotesque cumbrousness of barter (ll. 35–64), old Cotta's penury (ll. 179–98), Buckingham's fate (ll. 298–318), Sir Balaam's rise and fall (ll. 339–402), and more abstractly, the benevolence of the Man of Ross (ll. 249–80). Pope also advertises his theme of interaction by lending *To Bathurst* a flavor of real give-and-take through much use of questions and answers (here, far more than in *To Cobham*, answers as well as questions), and the suggestion of friendly disputants' dialogue.

Pope's variety of techniques to keep his poems whole and his readers reading ought to have schooled later poets. The bulk of them, though, took the ethical epistle only as a means to be witty or earnestly grave in verse (wittier in the earlier part of the period, graver later). In reading their work, one realizes not how much more clever and forceful Pope was, not how much finer a craftsman – though that too – but how much more nimble and comprehensive his mind, how much keener his imagination, how much deeper his sense of the precariousness of formulas preached or lived by. Even the most Popean epistles, like Cawthorn's 'The Regulation of the Passions' and 'The Vanity of Human Enjoyments' (1749), Horace Walpole's 'To Thomas Ashton' (1748; written 1740), John Brown's 'On Honor' (1743), or Benjamin Stillingfleet's 'On Conversation' (1737), do not try to catch Pope's vivacity of surface, his sensory involvement with the process of exploring his subject, and his grasp of strategy. They imitate him where he is plainly imitable, his colloquialism, his amused urbanity, his fundamental seriousness, his couplets (although Sneyd Davies wrote some ethical epistles in blank verse), and his concern with happiness as a social as well as an individual – I should say *the* social, *the* individual – goal. Robert Nugent spoke for a consensus in 1739:

> Through the wild maze of life's still varying plan,
> Bliss is alone th'important task of man.
> All else is trifling, whether grave or gay,
> A Newton's labors or an infant's play. *(Odes and Epistles*, p. 57)

Eighteenth-century ethical epistles kept this principle in mind. The poems' colloquial but urgent tone implies readers who care about the practical, and who want verse to earn its claims on their time by being useful. They required and got something rarely crass and still more rarely fanciful, addressed to every man's chief secular end.

Especially after mid-century, helpful poets took up the subject directly, informing readers that happiness comes from keeping busy, that 'what in rest we seek, in toil we find' and learn to 'Teach every curse the happiness it brings,/And reap the vintage midst the wild of things' (Henry Mackenzie, *The Pursuits of Happiness* (1771), pp. 3–4); or that – if one already has 'Health, Peace, and Friendship, Competence and Love' – happiness comes in sex, a 'Vast sea of ecstasy that drowns the mind!' (p. 15) and in other instinctual loves (John Bland, *Genuine Happiness* (1767)). Mackenzie and Bland agree that a deliberate search for happiness *per se* will fail. Most poets, expectedly, vote for achieving happiness through virtue, like Giles Jacob in 'Human Happiness' (1721), John Duncan in *An Essay on Happiness* (1762), and the anonymous author of *Pursuit after Happiness* (1777), who dramatizes his theme by giving up on the usual couplets and Miltonics for Shakespearean monologue in the manner of Blair's *The Grave*:

Wretch that I am! where shall I fly? – in vain,
Deluding Godhead! dost thou offer me
Again the mantling bowl – ha – come not near,
Lest sullen ire dash from thy tempting hand
Th'intoxicating draught! farewell to thee!   (ll. 46–50)

Several of the writers agree that one should scorn the baubles of this world (but keep clear too of Epicureanism and Stoicism), and some – fewer perhaps than might be expected – announce that 'real felicity' (on which Martin de la Garde has an *Essay* (1760?)) must be found in divine love. Duncan says this, as does George Meen, whose dream vision, *Happiness: A Poetical Essay* (1766), displays men of all stations discontented, the villager for poverty, the monarch for fear, the bourgeois for the shakiness of his financial and social aspirations, and so on through the debauchee, the miser, the recluse, and others, like the men visited by Johnson's Rasselas (1759).

Mackenzie is much the best of these writers, but none is worth more than civil attention. The group of poems is of interest in that it shows the kinship between the ethical epistles of writers like Pope and the elegiac prospect poems of Johnson, Blair, Goldsmith, and Gray, as the speaker standing apart and contemplating his ordering perception of the environment is less or more moved by the poignancy of isolation. Although Meen's dream vision and the Shakespearean monologue in *Pursuit after Happiness* do not offer the quick, astute 'I' of Pope's epistles, each tries to give all the particulars of the poem coherence within a single psyche. The simplest way to attempt this is to use first-person narration; as *The Vanity of Human Wishes* proves, however, success depends on no devices but an intuited unity in the quality of perception. Johnson's reheated Juvenal turns out to be very Johnsonian, very unlike Juvenal. The extraordinary compression of sentiment and detailed patterning (parallel, antithesis, alliteration, etc.) speak a mind that has thought matters through. From the tone of solemn pathos, foreign to the sardonic Juvenal, the reader infers the speaker's charity and objectivity (no gloating or melodrama here), which make one accept both the statements of the poem and its merciful conclusion. While Juvenal, in his tenth satire, revels in anecdote and caricature, Johnson probes minds and draws general observations; while Juvenal limits himself to obvious wishes – riches (ll. 23–53), power (ll. 54–113), eloquence (ll. 114–32), glory (ll. 133–87), long life (ll. 188–288), and beauty (ll. 289–345) – Johnson impresses us by contrast as a man with a far more comprehensive, intricate sense of human hopes, vanity, and interactions. The quality of perception takes on its unity in part because comparing Latin and English texts sharpens our eyes to the single voice behind Johnson's poem, and in part, of course, because Johnson has given us the raw materials from which such a single perceiving and ordering mind can be intuited.

The Vanity of Human Wishes, unlike its source, mourns the inevitable failure of earthly hope, about which man can do nothing but pray for serenity and transfiguring grace, leaving 'to heaven the measure and the choice' (l. 352). It also commemorates the aloneness of man, in its refusal to put into English the social chitchat with which Juvenal's ordinary citizens express their community before the fallen great (ll. 67–72, 81–8) and most of his other indications of mundane fellowship. Even Juvenalian historical specifics often drop away in Johnson so that individual human figures have nothing but the evocative, glimpsed emblems of their positions: 'The golden canopy, the glittering plate,/The regal palace, the luxurious board' (ll. 114–15). They are isolated from every reality of their lives except the void where hope had been. Through this kind of implied pathos, the poem frees itself from mere moral irony to ascend to the elegiac.

Most other poets achieve similar effects more easily, if not more powerfully, by making the speaker himself the isolated figure, as in Goldsmith's *The Traveller* and Gray's *Elegy* and *Ode on a Distant Prospect of Eton College*. Each of these takes advantage of the narrator's own growth as Johnson, exploiting Juvenal's magisterial voice, could not: the process of thought and argument, so well dramatized in Pope, becomes in Goldsmith and Gray a process of discovery. For example, Goldsmith's traveler, 'Impelled, with steps unceasing, to pursue/Some fleeting good that mocks me with the view' (ll. 25–6), surveys the merely sensual bliss of Italy, the tough but coarse Swiss, the refined but over-social French, the sensibly solid but venal Dutch, and England, fiercely righteous but combative and too much in need of the dangerous restraints of law. Like Book IV of the *Dunciad*, *The Traveller* uses a concessive structure, in which the repairing of one evil creates vulnerability to the next. Individual freedom in Britain leads to the tyranny of the privileged, which leads in turn to exile painfully close to the traveler's own plight. He must look within, to 'That bliss which only centers in the mind' (l. 424), and surrender a search for happiness at least as frustrating as that recounted in *The Vanity of Human Wishes*.

Johnson's and Goldsmith's poems enlighten by keeping the reader from being trapped in pleasing delusion (about secular possibilities, about national values), and they do offer hope in a deliverance from solitude, Johnson's responsive heaven and Goldsmith's brother's charitable hearth (*Trav.*, ll.7–22). The same issues occupy Gray. His image of peaceful and happy community is not a brother but a younger self at Eton, 'A stranger yet to pain' (l. 14), or the simple villagers with whom the meditative process of the elegy brings him to identify. Etonians remain in childish delusion, like Johnson's strivers and Goldsmith's nationals; the reflective speaker and his reader live in a colder world because of their experience and thought, as does the youth in the *Elegy*, looking at the graves of those who were too busy and too bounded to meditate. Each of the three poets has a visionary prospect, visionary inasmuch as Johnson can hardly have scanned from China to Peru, or Goldsmith have been able to enjoy the Grand Tour by eye, even if athletically perched amid 'Alpine solitudes' above 'An hundred realms' (ll. 31, 34). Gray begins the *Ode* and the *Elegy* with what he can see physically, and then defines that by what he can see in his mind. Baleful and deformed, the figures of the passions and 'The painful family of Death' (l. 83) quiver in ambush around the playing school boys. Over the country churchyard graves linger the imaginings of life past, of lives that might have been, and again of allegorical enemies (Ambition, Grandeur, chill Penury) who abridged the villagers' prospects or the respect due them. Finally, each of the four visionary speakers lacks the power to do much for himself as the result of his knowledge. Johnson's turns to Someone Else; Goldsmith's understands that 'Our own felicity we make or find' (l. 432) but not how we actually make or find it; Gray's elegist can only accept a world he cannot change; and the old boy of Eton announces that since suffering cannot be avoided he wishes that knowledge could be. As is so usual in eighteenth-century poetry, the firmly controlled verse form, the finality of the statements, and the comprehensiveness of the survey all refer to the broad but limited area the speaker can know, and not to causes and solutions. Craftsmanship here reflects humility.

The end of *The Traveller* proves that the poem is no mere survey but an alien's search among scenes of companionship, familial and social: he has 'strayed' to 'seek a good' as a longing outsider (ll. 425–6). Gray's speakers search in the same way. Beginning with cool formality in st. 1, the Etonian speaker warms to an association of ideas from an actual tactile sensation ('I feel the gales that from ye blow/A momentary bliss bestow') with memories of youth in st. 2. He recoils to formality in his Latinate address to Father Thames in st. 3, only to find himself passing once again from the distant and external to the psychological, a loss of the present self to bask for a moment in the reflected past of sts 4 and 5. He recoils a second time, and now sees the boys' innocent competition (the boys are playing, not studying or talking) become more deadly. The visionary competition is between incipient men (like him in his present state as real man, recollected boy) and their skulking destroyers – personal (st. 7), social (st. 8), and physical (st. 9) – listed in the order that a growing person typically encounters them. The last stanza declares the speaker's unity with the boys as fellow humans and his separation from them in degree of experience, so as to resolve the two points of view in the *Ode* and to define the position of the self.

Near the end of the *Elegy*, too, Gray resolves the poem by presenting the speaker at once set apart from and like the unlettered villagers. Secluded from greatness and vice by their station, as the Etonians are by their childhood, the rustics long for neither extreme. We discover that the speaker's defense of them is in fact a defense against his own longings, which divide him from the community; the *Elegy* seems originally to have ended with a stanza, one of four unpublished but written to follow line 72, in which he openly recognizes his inner battle:

> No more with reason and thyself at strife
> Give anxious cares and endless wishes room,
> But through the cool sequestered vale of life
> Pursue the silent tenor of thy doom.

Gray preferred a less cool, sequestered conclusion, and has his speaker imagine men who will recall and commemorate him as he has the villagers. These are the 'kindred spirit' and 'hoary-headed swain' of ll. 96–7, and perhaps the writer of the epitaph, tender to the point of sentimentality (ll. 117–28). The success of the poem as a whole, beyond its superb, quotable lines, depends, I think, on one's seeing how the analogy between speaker and countrypeople develops so as to make sense of the rather blatant emotion the speaker shows in imagining the swain's and the gravestone's words about him. By accepting a humble form of eulogy in communal memory and epitaph, he proves that he believes what he has been saying through the poem. By accepting it with such a mixture of proud self-depreciation ('wayward fancies,' 'drooping, woeful wan,' 'crazed with care or crossed in hopeless love' (ll. 106–8)) and self-aggrandizing pathos ('He gave to Misery all he had, a tear' (l. 123)), so different from what has gone before, he proves how keenly he has felt that his moral generalizations applied to himself as well as to others and how painful has been his awareness of his frustrated powers and his isolation from the community.

I have been using 'elegiac' to refer to a sorrowful tone, a lament for the vanity of human wishes and the melancholy of isolation and lost happiness. By no means are all eighteenth-century elegies 'elegiac' in this sense. Five very mildly attractive elegies written by William Whitehead from Rome in 1756, the year before he became poet laureate, lament nothing but simply offer quatrains of precepts. John Scott wrote four elegies in 1767 about the four seasons, Thomson put in quatrains without Thomsonian sight or sentiment. Love elegies, the most popular group being James Hammond's (1743; written 1732), abounded. Here nested all the inbred fledglings of pastoral, the Damons and Sylvias amid throstles, sweetbriars, and mossy oaks, telling the world about their love, sickness, health, riches and poverty, better times and worse, till death or infidelity parts them, or tedium parts us. Generally, elegies share formal characteristics: they are relatively simple, non-satiric, short-to-medium poems written in quatrains without emotional extravag-ance. They moralize but avoid long, dryly didactic passages. Their language remains dignified, with personification and static description preferred over more intellectually conceived images and shifting, developing events. Effects that Spenser achieves, of allegorical pageantry moving with the movement of his stanzas, recur in miniature in the elegy's quatrains. Many of them, of course, are about death or misfortune, but whatever the subject, the tone tends to be meditative. Although no major elegies but Gray's were written in the eighteenth century, poets found the mode appealing for their more placid serious verse after the mid-1730s. Ladies in particular met the ideals of propriety in a form so given to elegance, high-mindedness, and decorous sensibility.

Gray's *Elegy* has some kinship with a far more lurid kind of poem, the religious meditation on tombs, of which Blair's *The Grave* (1743) is the best example. Designed as a *memento mori* in verse, this sort of graveyard poetry lingers on mouldering corpses, 'The high-fed worm' surfeiting itself on an erstwhile beauty's 'damask cheek' (*The Grave*, ll. 246–7), 'yon black and funeral yew,/That bathes the charnel-house with dew' (Thomas Parnell, 'A Night-Piece on Death' (1722), ll. 53–4), as well as other appropriate flora and fauna (leathern-winged bats, humming beetles, lizards), and – as in the elegy – pageants of allegorical figures, or, in the manner of Charles Emily's 'Death' (ca. 1758), diseases:

> Marasmus, knotty gout, and the dead life
>   Of nerveless palsy; there on purpose fell

Dark brooding, whets his interdicted knife
  Grim suicide, the damned fiend of hell,
There too is the stunned apoplexy pight,
  The bloated child of gorged intemperance foul;
Self-wasting melancholy, black as night
  Lowering, and foaming fierce with hideous howl
The dog hydrophoby, and near allied
Scared madness, with her moon-struck eyeballs staring wide.

(ll. 173–82)

(Blair's Shakespearean blank verse, Parnell's tetrameter couplets, and Emily's mixture of Shakespearean sonnets and Spenserian alexandrines, not to mention elegists' quatrains and still others' Miltonics, prove that graveyard poetry was no more limited in form than elegies were in subject matter.) Obviously Gray's *Elegy* drew on – and swelled – the vogue for this sort of poetry, but without succumbing to the melodrama that was intended to frighten readers out of pride and into piety, or even yielding to the piety itself. The *Elegy*, except marginally at the very end, is not a religious poem, nor are eighteenth-century religious poems often poems of personal discovery like the *Elegy*.

Plenty of melodrama and piety mark the most popular of the graveyard poems, though, Edward Young's *Night Thoughts* (1742–5). Baron Ochs, from the Hofmannsthal-Strauss opera *Der Rosenkavalier*, assures Sophie that in his embrace no night will seem too long. In Young's embrace, every night does, and there are nine of them. Many fine lines and some fine flights of imagination founder in the intellectual disorder and creative unevenness of the poem. (Indeed, Young's verse suggests that the most serious flaws in eighteenth-century poetry are likely to lie precisely where the generality of critics have been least inclined to look for them: in too little craftsmanship and logic, in too much sublime ambition and free-flapping imagination, or – to put this another way – in flaws typical of those poems that overawe readers' critical faculties.) Whatever one's judgment of *Night Thoughts*, readers for the next hundred or hundred-fifty years felt answering throbs in their bosoms as Young's speaker tried to chasten the loose-living Lorenzo, mourned the deaths of Narcissa, Philander, and Lucia, expostulated on the providential order of the world, and brought to his colloquialized Miltonic verse the crispness and aphoristic skill that distinguish, for all their faults, the seven satires of *The Love of Fame*: 'All men think all men mortal, but themselves' (Night 1), 'Thou thinkst it folly to be wise too soon' (Night 2), 'Good lost weighs more in grief than gained in joy' (Night 3), '[They] spike up their inch of reason on the point/Of philosophic wit' (Night 4), 'Some mourn in proof that something they could love' (Night 5), 'Like damaged clocks, whose hand and bell dissent,/Folly sings six while nature points at twelve' (Night 5), 'Disappointment lurks in every prize,/As bees in flowers, and stings us with success' (Night 6), 'Renounce St. Evremond and read St. Paul' (Night 7), 'A man of pleasure is a man of pains' (Night 8), and – perhaps with a scornful pun – 'The miser earths his treasure, and the thief,/Watching the mole, half-beggars him ere morn' (Night 9). For a rapid reader with an eye for good phrases and a taste for sermons, *Night Thoughts* still has its rewards. Read with care or without prior sympathy, it does not.

Night Thoughts asks to be read fast, like other poems of mid-century or later. Successful Restoration and earlier eighteenth-century poems typically call for close scrutiny of allusions, ironies, and shades of tone. Later ones typically call for a sweep of the eye across broader tonal effects and washes of color, as in Young, Macpherson, Churchill, or – for all his presumed 'Augustanism' – Goldsmith. One can see this change clearly in the class of poems to which numbers of moral or 'happiness' poems belong and to which most of the others are akin: the didactic. The years from the 1730s to the late 1750s were bumper for didactic verse. One can start the list with *Night Thoughts* and *An Essay on Man*, the imitations of Horace's *Ars poetica* which have already been discussed, and fables along the line of Gay's (1727, 1738 – but these latter were written in the early 1730s, since Gay died in 1732). Then, even if one does not count some religious-descriptive poems like Smart's four on the Supreme Being (1750–4) and William Thompson's *Sickness* (1746), one still has, for example, Henry Brooke's *Universal Beauty* (1735), William Somervile's *The Chase* (1735), Samuel Boyse's *Deity* (1739), Somervile's *Field Sports* (1742), Mark Akenside's *The Pleasures of Imagination* (1744), John Armstrong's *The Art of Preserving Health* (1744), Robert Dodsley's *Agriculture* (1753), and John Dyer's *The Fleece* (1757). My list includes only better-known poets; it could be considerably extended.

However heterogeneous the subjects of such poems, one or another of three possible models (not at all wholly exclusive of one another) seems to serve each of them from Brooke through Dyer. These three are the sermon, Horace's *Ars poetica*, and Virgil's *Georgics*. Sermons are continuous moral arguments, with documentation from authorities and exemplary tales. Pope's four *Epistles to Several Persons* use this model; so does *An Essay on Man*. Horace offers a string of useful precepts, appealing to principles inherent in his subject and to taste. The previous chapter has shown how useful this model was. Virgil, the third model, let his practical advice grow from vivid descriptions. More important, he could hardly have intended his advice to be put to actual use, since he did not write for an audience of herdsmen. Therefore he makes his subject alluring and entertaining, while sermons try to make theirs significant and the Horatian poem assumes that its subject is already alluring and significant.

In accord with the hypothesis that people read poetry more rapidly and impressionistically as the century wore on, Virgilian didactic verse tended to replace Horatian. Didactic verse on the model of the sermon seems to hold steady. Moral and religious subjects kept their emotional urgency, that is, but for other matters poets adopted a style with less precise, more generally suggestive diction (that of descriptive verse calling for ideal presence). In mid- and later eighteenth-century didactic poetry, the reader's sense that he was learning and participating became more important than the actual examination of the precepts put forth. The process took over from the educative results. As the critic John Aikin wrote in his *Letters . . . on . . . English Poetry* (1804), the Virgilian mode 'gratifies the perpetual thirst for novelty' rather, perhaps, than a genuine desire to know (Letter

XI). The nature of the connections between facts changes, once 'novelty' becomes a value, since readers may well not know the bases for the information they receive. A train of logic guides Horatian and sermon-like poems, in spots where taste and faith do not, but the Virgilian poem relies on catching the imagination with mingled description, incantatory nouns, and the credibility of an expert speaker, like the one of Dyer's *The Fleece*:

> Of grasses are unnumbered kinds, and all
> (Save where foul waters linger on the turf)
> Salubrious. Early mark, when tepid gleams
> Oft mingle with the pearls of summer showers
> And swell too hastily the tender plains:
> Then snatch away thy sheep; beware the rot;
> And with detersive bay-salts rub their mouths,
> Or urge them on a barren bank to feed
> In hunger's kind distress on tedded hay,
> Or to the marish guide their easy steps
> If near thy tufted crofts the broad sea spreads.   (1:251–61)

Readers do not follow this advice, but simply suppose that shepherds do. Dyer has established an idea of solicitude and water imagery (foul waters/summer showers/*bay* salts/marish/sea) far more important than his specific remedy for rot. Emphases are reversed from Pope's remedy against esthetic rot and Prior's against moral rot: *An Essay on Criticism* and *Solomon* are read quite differently from *The Fleece*. For Dyer's audience, detersive bay-salts differ remarkably little from the names and path of the Argonauts (2:225–301) or the list of 'Cheyney and baize and serge and alepine,/Tammy and crape' (3:480–1).

Virgilian didactic poems had three great subjects, God, Britain, and God's order in the frames of Britons. *The Fleece* celebrates the isles whence comes the wool trade, and calls on nations to rejoice at 'the sway/Ordained for common happiness': Britannia is to 'pour/The fruits of plenty' 'Wide o'er/The globe terraqueous' (4:654–7). Akenside's *The Pleasures of Imagination* ends by referring man's powers to God's desire to be imitated ('He meant, He made us to behold and love/What he beholds and loves'), which explains His order within man. Outside man, of course, divine order was reflected in that of nature. The contexture of man and that of nature so meshed that as Moses Browne says, quoting Fontenelle in the preface to his 'An Essay on the Universe,' 'at the same time [that physical ideas] convince and satisfy the reason, they present to the imagination a prospect which looks as if it was made on purpose to please it' (*Poems on Various Subjects* (1739), p. 288). One version or another of the so-called 'argument from design,' using the kinds of natural, scientific order and economy to 'prove' the immanence of God, was ubiquitous.

Not surprisingly, some poets took it further than others. For Samuel Bowden, natural and human order reflected each other in detail, as he explains in 'The Earth: A Philosophic Poem' (1735):

146

As earth man's structure emulates, we find
Some latent emblems of the Plastic Mind [i.e., the invigorating *anima mundi*]:
See every part analogous in frame,
The human spirit and terraqueous flame. (*Poetical Essays*, 2:91)

For the Huguenot refugee J. T. Desaguliers, FRS, in *The Newtonian System of the World, the Best Model of Government* (1728), George II's England, with liberty and monarchic authority in balance, reflected the divine system discovered by Newton, where the individual inertial movement of heavenly bodies (liberty) is integrated into the dance of the planets by solar gravitational attraction. Bowden and Desaguliers go to extremes, but their contemporaries gloried in more tempered claims of similar sorts. Practiced by eighteenth-century Britons, Virgilian didactic poetry could and sometimes did combine two Virgils, the descriptive teacher of the *Georgics*, whose patriotism is largely implied, and the prophet of national destiny who wrote the *Aeneid*.

Thomson's uneven but awesome masterpiece, *The Seasons* (1726–46), is not a didactic poem, in that its scenes precede and dominate over its advice. Dyer's *The Fleece*, for example, begins with a topic unified in idea: 'The care of sheep, the labours of the loom,/And arts of trade, I sing.' *The Seasons*, in contrast, invokes 'gentle Spring,' 'veiled in a shower/Of shadowing roses,' so that its moral reflections grow from the literal reflections of changing light off the great variety of nature. Whether or not one cares to stretch the label 'didactic poem' to cover Thomson's, though, *The Seasons* gave enormous impetus to the Virgilian didactic poem in England. In part that is because, as I have suggested, the Virgilian didactic comes close to being an essentially descriptive genre, despite its rhetoric of precepts. The external world does not serve principally as an emblem or example, the way it does in *Cooper's Hill* or John Ogilvie's *Providence. An Allegorical Poem* (1764), but rather as a running theme and source.

Still more important is that the subject and methods of *The Seasons* join so many Virgilian didactic practices. Thomson writes about God, Britain, and God's order as perceived by his own Briton's eye and mind. He produces a text that the reader is meant to peruse rapidly, meant to comprehend through ideal presence and through the broad tonal effects and associations of the deliberately non-conversational, Miltonic diction. From the content of *The Seasons*, as from that of the Virgilian poems we have been discussing, the reader derives a sense of learning and participating in discovery. Such information as he gets has much less value item by item than as a means of emotional persuasion that he is making progress in grasping clues to the working of a great whole. This whole, the subject of the poem, interrelates man (his capacity to know, feel, and survive), Britain (man's theater and God's), and divine order within nature. As a work of art, as a means of exploring a subject, and as an instrument of organization, then, *The Seasons* might well have had a strong influence on Dyer and the rest, an influence guaranteed by its enormous, well-deserved popular success.

Thomson's, I have said, is a poem devoted to process, to the reader's sense and the speaker's experience of learning and participating. The texture of *The Seasons*, of course, is associative: almost all the longer poems of the Restoration and eighteenth-century proceed from one line to the next by association of ideas. One can hardly overestimate the importance of moment-by-moment mental processes in the line-to-line, topic-to-topic process of verse throughout this period. In Thomson, however, fewer of these processes are argumentative or narrative than in, say, Pope or in didactic poems. The speaker moves toward truth through the senses. Even when Thomson passes into narrative – the best-known examples are the tale of Damon and Musidora (*Summer*, ll. 1269–1370) and the shepherd 'disastered' by a blizzard 'in his own loose-revolving fields' (*Winter*, ll. 276–321) – sensory perceptions and their emotional effects take precedence over other elements of fiction. As in no earlier poet, the senses become agents of discovery. They operate, of course, the way we normally use them: Thomson is not so much interested that eyes and ears record an influx of light and vibrations as that our brains record clusters of pre-rational meaning, emotion-and-memory-tinted objects in a state of continuous change. These are the base of the poetic idiom, which easily moves down to pure sensation (in particular, of light), up to the larger patterns of order that emotion and memory both create and help us to understand, and horizontally, so to speak, to objects projected upon the screen of the mind with a permanence that nothing has in nature.

Like the other great visionary poem of its time, the *Dunciad, The Seasons* concerns itself with the interplay between order and disorder. Pope exploits the difference between the formal epic, control of the poem as an artifact, and a chaotic society, lack of control of the outside world and thus, paradoxically, both reduction and disintegration. Thomson's epic of the inquiring and intelligent eye partly inverts that. He seems to yield control of the poem as an artifact, and follow only association of ideas. He also chooses a style that promotes ideal presence and restricts connotation, as Pope's does not. The form of *The Seasons* duplicates the form of external nature, with its seeming arbitrariness, its cyclical patterning, its alternation between the sublime (the uncontrollable, the grand, the terrifying) and the beautiful (the controllable, the sweet, the placid), and its possibility of being grasped as an intuited whole. The poem works along the lines that Henry Brooke suggests when describing the cosmos in *Universal Beauty* (1735) as 'Most regular when seemingly most perplexed,/As though perfection on disorder hung' (2 : 265–6).

Let me repeat that the orderliness of a Restoration or eighteenth-century poem does not authorize one to infer that the world the poem depicts is orderly or can be made orderly. The poet's choice of arbitrary order often testifies to his belief in the unruliness of his subject. Thomson avoids arbitrary order, but sees the movement of thought – seeking out pattern and inferences, looking for a natural basis for values – as having an analogue in the world itself. A mind in the process of ordering finds answerable order in the regularity of the heavens and the seasons, the working of scientific laws, and the rewards that duly accrue to the social passions like love, benevolence, refinement, and industriousness. At first glance, one is kept by the limits of human knowledge from seeing these patterns. The outside world appears fragmentary and sudden, as *The Seasons* faithfully presents it. Deeper than rational knowledge, however, lie intuition and feeling, by which these fragments can be fused, and by which man weakly but truly imitates God's creative presence:

> Inspiring God! who, boundless spirit all
> And unremitting energy, pervades,
> Adjusts, sustains, and agitates the whole.
> He ceaseless works alone, and yet alone
> Seems not to work; with such perfection framed
> Is this complex, stupendous scheme of things.
> But though concealed, to every purer eye
> The informing Author in his works appears.   (*Spring*, ll. 853–60)

Thomson's mixture of sublimity, natural description, and physicotheology also welcomed digressions and self-consciousness as logical parts of the poem's emphasis on the mind. Virgil's *Georgics* had been digressive, and non-descriptive poets of Thomson's time had been glad to use fables, parenthetical asides, brief passages of praise or blame for some public figure, versified precepts (in Thomson, scientific facts), or the like, to make their points. Digressions, then, fit as comfortably into the current poetic idiom as they do into a poem that moves by association of ideas and therefore introduces subjects that may not pertain strictly to the subject at hand but that occur to the speaker by the way. Self-consciousness – the speaker's alertness to his own involvement in the act of contemplation, thus making himself part of the nature being observed as well as its observer – reinforces the poem's emphasis on man as a participant in the order of nature, loving, suffering, and enduring like other creatures.

The poet of course reflects from nature to himself, as was traditional. Milton does this, for example, when he laments his blindness and rejoices in his spiritual light after describing the physical light of God flooding through nature (*Paradise Lost* 3 : 1–55). Thomson's epistemology demands that he do still more. In *The Seasons* the actions of body and mind and natural phenomena pass smoothly one into another. Thomson asks, for instance, to have 'Nature's volume broad displayed' to him so that he can create poetry from it in *Summer*. He then uses the sequence of breadth of Nature, the movement of his own body, and the movement of his mind (the latter two expressed through natural analogies) to set up an association of ideas with the rising, clarifying, nature-displaying sun:

> Some easy passage [of Nature], raptured, to translate,
> My sole delight; as through the falling glooms
> Pensive I stray, or with the rising dawn
> On fancy's eagle-wing excursive soar.
>   Now, flaming up the heavens, the potent sun
> Melts into limpid air the high-raised clouds
> And morning fogs that hovered round the hills

149

In particolored bands; till wide unveiled
The face of nature shines . . . .   (ll. 195–203)

Thomson's awareness of himself as both an intellectual being and a natural phenomenon like others no doubt has roots in theories of perception, current then, which stressed the senses as mechanisms following the laws of the physics of motion. Mind lies within the order of nature. The double awareness – introspective and naturalistic – also reflects a typical division between knowledge (mind) and power (external act): the speakers of *The Vanity of Human Wishes, The Traveller* and *The Deserted Village*, and Gray's *Elegy* also can know (understanding) and know they know (introspection), but one thing they know is that their knowledge can not keep them from the vanity, solitude, or death common to wise men and foolish alike. These kinds of knowledge are central to *The Seasons*. Thomson, less elegiac, more engaged in discovery and rapture, studies to know himself much less absorbedly than Johnson, Goldsmith, or Gray, but the knowledge is the same.

As *The Vanity of Human Wishes* ends by counselling prayer, and Gray's *Elegy* by invoking divine justice, so *The Seasons* turns at its conclusion to a hymn. Thomson's encyclopaedic mode has been the slow, progressive equivalent of revelation. A hymn also, though not so formally, concludes *The Excursion* (1728), a descriptive poem full of sublime effects (tempests, 'visionary forms,' volcanos) by Thomson's friend David Mallet. But that sort of conclusion did not prevail in less muscular descriptive verse, especially as time passed and natural description pleased more for its own sake. By mid-century, God in descriptive poetry tends to be an appurtenance of the sublime or the graveyard. A sweet poem of country landscape, like John Dyer's 'Grongar Hill' (1726), moralizes the prospect as verse of rural retirement so often had, but does not see it pervaded with divinity. Poems that focus on specific, local description rather than range widely (Thomson) or create emblems of moral and political circumstances (Denham, Pope's *Windsor Forest*) usually stop before launching into hymn or physicotheology.

At times poets, after Denham's and Pope's example, offer the secular equivalent of divine faith, British patriotism. Jago's *Edge Hill* (1767), for instance, devotes itself, as its first line states, to 'Britannia's rural charms and tranquil scenes,' and their glorification. For such poems no discrepancy exists, as readers of nineteenth-century nature poetry might idly assume, between praise of the country and praise of trade. John Dalton's 'Descriptive Poem [on] . . . the Mines near Whitehaven' (1755) can exalt both the Lake District and 'Creative Commerce.' Its preface suggests that 'rich improvements of a wild and un-cultivated soil,' perceived by someone returning after long absence, carry 'an air of enchantment and romance' (p. iii) – technology, making the desert bloom in whatever way, suited the poetry of admiration and wonder exactly as God did, by creating order, design, blueprints of intelligence. The poet's mind and generous spirit respond with joy to generous spirit and mind in the perceived, ambient world, so that Dalton feels the emotional and ethical welcome of a homecoming at Whitehaven although the landscape is not that of his boyhood there. To many, this prevalent attitude in the eighteenth century may be naive jingoism; perhaps, as with so many such gaps between us and the past, the loss here is ours. In any case, the ethical reflections rising from – and alongside – patriotic pride (or alarm) could mediate the relationship of poet and prospect when Heaven did not, and sometimes when Heaven did, for a great deal of descriptive verse less philosophical than Thomson's. The closeness between the descriptive and the didactic lasted, in this form, well past 1780.

What about the influence of other, less theological traits of *The Seasons*: the stress on the discovery of an intuitional order, on man as observer and participant, on the senses and ideal presence? A rush of topographical poems in the second quarter of the century was prompted by Thomson (some, too, by the popularity of Dyer's 'Grongar Hill'). In general, these followed him in the most obvious ways, such as his blank verse, his mixture of close and more abstract descriptions (invitations to ideal presence), his stating his intuitions of order, and his associative digressiveness. Most later poets, however, were less faithful to the way in which *The Seasons* expresses and acts out Thomson's view of man as an eager explorer and a fellow creature in a world where everything keeps changing roles. In poetry that was not primarily didactic and argumentative, Thomson's landscape of the understanding changed to respond to the tastes that made the later eighteenth century a great age of the novel, landscape painting, and garden architecture. That is, writers began to dwell on verse narrative, pictures of natural scenery, and identifiable locations that could stimulate affection or nostalgia from an individualized speaker. The result was to simplify Thomson's vision.

Alternatively, didactic and argumentative poets selected other elements. In John Gilbert Cooper's *The Power of Harmony* (1745), analogies between nature, esthetic perception, and moral knowledge openly underlie the whole work; but Cooper or Mark Akenside has a thesis to maintain, not, like Thomson, a comprehension to develop though seeing, imagining, thinking, and feeling. For Cooper or Akenside, the process of reading does not parallel the process of understanding the world that the poem depicts, because what these poets record has internal pressure from argument (and documentation) to argument. Thomson has only external pressure to include whatever a given season includes. He has no consecutive argument, no historical or biographical plot, no abstract or rhetorical commitments to mar his openness to the workings of his mind, imagination, and senses. None of his predecessors or successors in English, as far as I know, managed to combine great dignity with such sense of the immediate, the improvisational.

I have been discussing *The Seasons* as a poem of exploration, but cumulatively it can be seen as a hymn of adoration to God and His partially comprehensible works. The two characteristics of contemplation and praise mark the most often used, and most successfully used ambitious form of the mid-to-later eighteenth century, the ode. I say 'most successfully' because other modes depend still more on contemplation and praise, but did not stimulate much good poetry. One example is the blank-verse poem of praise for one or more of God's attributes. (This form, incidentally, provides another instance of apparently didactic genres being used for emotional rather than intellectual ends: argument here is the tool of panegyric, not persuasion.) The annual Seatonian Prize, given from 1750 on for the best poem expounding 'one or other of the perfections or attributes [can there theologically be a difference?] of the Supreme Being,' helped swell the number of these. Headed by Christopher Smart, the pious and the needy burnt midnight oil by the gallon in vying for the prize, but (if I may steal a pun from Dorothy Parker) nothing first-rate ever came out of this fecund rate. Critics other than I have made high claims for another genre of praise, the hymn. It had a distinguished career in the eighteenth century, to the extent that hymns can be distinguished by more than sincerity, simplicity, and fervor. Isaac Watts, Charles Wesley, and Augustus Toplady are best known here. Their written texts, of course, are only one part of a communal, musical, recreated experience that, like the experience of theatrical poetry, lies outside the bounds of this history. On the printed page, these hymns can be neither profound nor complex because complex, profound verse makes awkward, muddled congregational singing.

Close to the hymn in content is still a third popular genre of praise, the paraphrased psalm, which has been discussed briefly in the previous chapter. Psalm 104 ('Bless the Lord, O my soul') is germane here, however, because it presents (or assumes) David's version of the argument from design: 'The glory of the Lord shall endure for ever: the Lord shall rejoice in his works' (104 : 31). This Thomsonian theme delighted receptive poets. Thomas Blacklock, Thomas Fitzgerald, Walter Harte, Aaron Hill, Catherine Jemmat, Christopher Smart, William Stevenson, Joseph Thurston, and Elizabeth Tollet were among others to paraphrase Psalm 104 between about 1720 and 1780. By and large they expanded enthusiastically on the thirty-five verses of the original, like William Stevenson, whose adaptation, 'Hymn to the Deity,' takes up fifteen full pages of his *Original Poems on Several Subjects* (1765). In the manner of topographical poets, as one might expect, these paraphrasers were pleased to include the system of commerce within the system of nature. Blacklock's 'An Hymn to the Supreme Being,' for instance, begins with the Bible's 'There go the ships' (l. 26) to decipher the Lord in cosmopolitan patriotism:

> Tall navies here their doubtful way explore,
> And every product waft from every shore;
> Hence meager want expelled, and sanguine strife,
> For the mild charms of cultivated life;
> Hence social union spreads from soul to soul,
> And India joins in friendship with the pole.   (ll. 125–30)

Blacklock's sentiments do him honor; the level of his verse suggests that the historian of ideas may find his work (and his fellows') more interesting than will the reader of poetry. One must return to the ode for finer artistic results.

The ode was the vehicle by which the Young Turks of the 1740s claimed to reinstate imagination on the throne from which, they thought, Pope and his followers had kept it. The descendants of the irregular Pindaric were to rouse the imagination to sublimity, while the calmer and slighter regular ode (a class that petered off into the song) stroked it into sensations of beauty, melancholy, and tenderness. Such at least was the theory, which contained practice as well as theory usually does, like a militiaman's uniform cut to a standard size and issued to a 300 lb. swaybacked recruit. Suffice it to note that a late eighteenth-century anthology organizes its odes, six volumes' worth, into no fewer than ten classes. These classes themselves are diverse enough to outrage the critic who believes, for better or for worse, that eighteenth-century poets felt bound by generic rules. Most, but not all, these odes are in stanzas, often the quatrains found in the elegy (perhaps more a double-layered couplet than an independent stanzaic form) for quiet or tender subjects. Poets sometimes lengthened this tetrameter quatrain into a sestet with a heroic couplet at its end. Irregular, Pindaric stanzas suited odes to music, for example, in imitation of Dryden's practice; Smart, John Brown, Thomas Warton, and others followed him. The same irregular ecstasies also suited the subjects of patriotism and poetry. For subjects between the high and the tranquil or tender, a favorite stanza was the sestet rhyming aabccb, the a and c lines being tetrameter, the b lines being one foot longer or shorter. Mark Akenside uses this stanza, for instance, in 'Against Suspicion':

> Then many a demon will she raise
> To vex your sleep, to haunt your ways;
>   While gleams of lost delight
> Raise the dark tempest of the brain,
> As lightning shines across the main
>   Through whirlwinds and through night.   (st. 3)

These generalizations, like my earlier awarding the ode the two tones of contemplation and praise, only suggest the most popular forms and uses of what became the catch-all for the eighteenth-century lyricist who did not choose a fixed mode such as the sonnet. If it had been fashionable between the decline of the Cowleyan Pindaric and the 1740s, we undoubtedly would have rhymed, stanzaic versions of, for example, Thomson's glowing *To the Memory of Sir Isaac Newton* (1727; in blank verse) and Gay's well-intentioned 'An Epistle to Her Grace Henrietta, Duchess of Marlborough' (1722; in heroic couplets).

The rehabilitation of the ode was announced by Joseph Warton in 1746, as the conduit for poetic imagination and invention, which he opposed to moralizing in verse. Nothing was novel about Warton's hierarchy, absolutely conventional and universally accepted, at least in so far as any theory is universally accepted. His protest against didactic verse echoes Thomson's twenty years earlier against 'unaffecting fancies, little glittering prettinesses, [and] mixed turns of wit and expression,' which he claimed had usurped the place of 'great and serious subjects' (Preface to *Winter*, second edition). Warton's description of the ode, too, is old; it simplifies Young's in his preface to his own ode, 'Ocean' 1728 : and Young's notions are banal.

If one wants to treat Warton's brief declaration as an important announcement, one must mention three facts that might have made it so. First, the fall of Walpole and the broadening of the ministry, together with the dissipating of factions

153

concerned with Jacobites at home and devious foreigners abroad, gave England a respite from politics. Intellectuals, once the fad for militancy was over, relaxed into the aspirations of their own fancies rather than the fancied good of England. Second, the death of Pope removed far and away the most magnetic exemplar and advocate of stooping to truth and moralizing one's song. At the same time, the general praise by Pope and other 'Patriots' for British tradition and the virtues of classical republics – as against Hanoverian venality and court rule – refreshed the ideals of those cultures, and made it easier for new poets to model themselves on Milton and Spenser and on the Greeks. Pope's increasing personal references and rhetoric of personal emotion also helped support a poetic movement that was to call his preferred modes into question. Third and most important, Thomson and the landscapists (some of them didactic poets themselves) gave the new writers of odes means to glorify the imagination: the engaged speaker, ideal presence, interpenetration of description and moral maxims, and personifications (or, as eighteenth-century writers would have said, allegory). In employing these four Thomsonian techniques, the new odes adapted the ready-made poetic style of their time, so that much of the lyric poetry of the mid-eighteenth century is brightened by the corona of *The Seasons*. William Collins's odes (1746) bear the explicit labels 'descriptive' and 'allegoric' and his friend Warton's, published a fortnight earlier, might well do the same, as the second stanza of 'To Superstition' indicates:

> Thy clanking chains, thy crimson steel,
> Thy venomed darts and barbarous wheel,
> Malignant fiend, bear from this isle away,
> Nor dare in Error's fetters find
> One active, freeborn, British mind,
> That strongly strives to spring indignant from thy sway.   (ll. 7–12)

Collins's unintellectual but exquisite odes are the finest that the 1740s produced, and they are very fine indeed. Slavish to no predecessor, they none the less are aromatic with the phrases and idioms of those in new favor, Greek and English. One of their purposes, in fact, is to assert the proper realm of poetry as being the imagination and passions – the argument being put forth bluntly by Joseph Warton – and Collins's invocations (through echoes) of great imaginative, passionate poets give this assertion authority. He at once celebrates the past masters and places himself in their line by a show of humility before the achievements of Otway ('To Pity,'), Aeschylus, Sophocles, and Shakespeare ('To Fear'), Spenser and Milton ('On the Poetical Character'), and, in a memorial ode, Thomson. Since six of the odes furthermore deal with passion mediated by the arts, particularly poetry, Collins makes Warton's argument by practice rather than discourse. So closely does he bind poetry and passions that critics whose expectations have been colored by early nineteenth-century poetry have assumed that he was the unsure precursor of self-absorbed 'Romantics.' Collins may have been unsure, as a young man well might be, but I doubt that he was self-absorbed, since as far as I know, poets of the period wrote about their own poetical process only whimsically. There is every reason to take Collins's 'I' as a dramatic projection and to take his themes as part of a demonstrative program.

The order of Collins's volume supports me here. He begins with four odes about poetry and, openly or tacitly, about 'his' (i.e., the speaker's) place in poetic tradition, especially British tradition. Next he moves to four odes of patriotic sublimity, in which the poet is public spokesman. Finally, four odes conclude the book, offering peace in nature ('To Evening') and in society ('To Peace'), and celebrating the twin worlds of human action ('The Manners') and feeling ('The Passions') as they emerge in imitative comedy and musical lyric. Looked at this way, Collins's odes are linked in a typically eighteenth-century argument by the dialectic of analogy and contrast: a consideration of pity makes one ask about its complement, fear; of fear and its wildness, about its complement, simplicity; of the clear and simple as poetic subject, about its complement, the inspired and vatic. Through such a dialectic of analogy, Collins explores the role of poetry in the Britain of the 1740s.

He reinforces one's sense of this dialectic by using association of ideas to have one poem melt into the next. For example, at the end of the first ode, 'To Pity,' the speaker retires to a temple of tragedy to 'waste the mournful lamp of night' over the tragedy that he himself plans to write. In the darkness, having earlier 'melt[ed] away' in 'dreams of passion,' the speaker naturally can be imagined to begin seeing the 'shadowy shapes' and 'unreal scenes' with which the second ode, 'To Fear,' opens. The movement of 'To Fear' in turn may seem anticlimactic by itself, for the poem grows progressively quieter, leading toward the speaker's plea to be able to feel with Shakespeare's intensity; but one has less sense of anticlimax if one reads it before the third ode, 'To Simplicity,' which starts by invoking Shakespeare's great predecessor Sophocles and his language of nature and freedom. Simplicity, in Collins's sense, contrasts with fear, but 'To Simplicity' extends the realm of discourse marked out by 'To Fear.' It also suggests a quality of feeling that 'To Pity' evokes. The bold 'Ode on the Poetical Character,' which comes fourth, ought then to suggest a quality of feeling evoked by 'To Fear' and to develop from 'To Simplicity.' One cannot be surprised to find that the penultimate stanza of 'To Simplicity' brings forth the blessings of taste and genius 'To some divine excess' needed for 'some mighty task' (ll. 43–44, 50). This soul-raising inspiration forms the subject of the 'Ode on the Poetical Character,' where the sublime and supernatural, last present in 'To Fear,' now recur, so as to complete, as well as close, the first group of four odes.

Collins's method of association, contrast, analogy and modification, and achieving unity ('covering' the subject) through maximum variety but without plot or overt argument – this method reminds one of Thomson's and the topographical poets'. Expectedly, then, he also follows them in connecting external nature and the visionary and individual passions with British patriotism. In each of the first four odes, the last stanza begs that the speaker, a British poet ('To Pity,' l. 42) identified with such other British poets as Otway, Spenser, Shakespeare, and Milton, be granted his predecessors' gifts. In the fourth ode, 'On the Poetical Character,' the plea is denied: after Milton's death, Heaven and Fancy have curtained Eden and visionary scenes 'from every future view.' This panegyric device now lets Collins pass to further panegyric, a British elegy in praise of the fallen, heroic dead ('Written in . . . 1746'), which opens the second group of four odes. These ascend in vigor though the contrasting 'To Mercy' and 'To Liberty,' to conclude with another elegy, 'To a Lady on the Death of Colonel Ross.' Collins sees him celebrated by 'The warlike dead of every age' (l. 25), a martial group of precursors who remind one of the poetic troop in the first four odes. While they warm 'Again for Britain's wrongs,' the other subject of this ode, the mourning lady, cannot be soothed by sublime history. Instead, 'social grief' must be her comfort, as cottagers and shepherds weep at 'the sad repeated tale.' Each of the four odes of the second group reasserts central elements of the first four odes, extending and altering the realm of discourse by the pattern of analogy and modification that I have stressed. Here 'To a Lady' ends the second group as 'On the Poetical Character' ends the first: a triumphant lineage is reaffirmed while at the same time a single figure (the speaker, the lady) remains cut off from visionary joy and fulfillment, able to contemplate the past but not to join its pantheon.

With the first two odes of the third and final group, Collins reworks this double theme of farewell and continuity. 'To Evening' depicts the cooling and calming of the day and – toward the end of the poem – the seasons, so as to show farewell as part of a cycle within a greater cycle of time. What 'To Evening' does for nature, 'To Peace' does for patriotic history. The 'holier reign' of Peace in Britain is to end 'the rude tyrannic sway' of 'War, by vultures drawn from far' in his iron chariot; yet, married to 'warlike Honour,' she promises a state of noble readiness. 'To Evening' and 'To Peace' look back to the preceding odes in another way. In keeping with the personal point of view in the first group of odes, 'To Evening' has an individual speaker to 'hail/[Evening's] genial loved return' and look out on the falling of her 'gradual dusky veil' (ll. 20, 40); 'To Peace,' however, like the patriotic odes, remains comparatively impersonal. The last two odes in the volume then place all the rest in the broadest perspective of human action and passion. 'The Manners' bids farewell to the speculative life of academia and welcomes the continuing empirical world of human action in society. Comedy, the literary mode it praises, is the most mundane, prosiest, most simply representational kind of art. Throughout the volume Collins has varied his stanzas (though not without some repetition), even abandoning rhyme in 'To Evening,' and now, in 'The Manners,' he abandons stanzas entirely in favor of a typically unelevated form, the tetrameter couplet. 'The Passions,' by contrast, ends the volume on the high note that Collins and his friends urged for mid-century poetry. Written in the most ecstatically lyrical mode, the ode for music, 'The Passions' uses verse to imitate the passions represented:

> Thy numbers, Jealousy, to nought were fixed,
>   Sad proof of thy distressful state,
> Of differing themes the veering song was mixed,
>   And now it courted Love, now raving called on Hate.

With eyes upraised, as one inspired,
Pale Melancholy sat retired,
And from her wild sequestered seat,
In notes by distance made more sweet,
Poured through the mellow horn her pensive soul.
    And dashing soft from rocks around,
    Bubbling runnels joined the sound;
Through glades and glooms the mingled measure stole,
    Or o'er some haunted stream with fond delay,
      Round an holy calm diffusing,
      Love of peace and lonely musing,
In hollow murmurs died away.   (ll. 53–68)

Action and passion, external and internal, the local made universal and the universal given local concreteness – this final pair, 'The Manners' and 'The Passions,' summarizes and properly ends Collins's *Odes*.

In the odes published together in 1746 and in later ones, such as the memorial ode for Thomson and 'On the Popular Superstitions of the Highlands of Scotland,' Collins – like other eighteenth-century poets – centers on the recurrent, not the 'general' or 'universal.' At times, like all writers, he and they generalize; often they employ ideal presence to bring individual objects or scenes to mind; but their focus is on the intersection of the momentary event and the larger law. (Such a focus fits well with the 'positional style.') Collins, in his subject matter and his imitations of earlier poets, presents us with patterns of historical repetition, held together by analogy. So does Gray, some ten years later, in both his two great Pindaric odes, 'The Progress of Poesy' and 'The Bard.' The principle of variation built into the ode by its Greek division (strophe, antistrophe, epode), or even by the stanzaic form given to English versions of monostrophic odes (in the manner of Sappho, Anacreon, Catullus, and Horace), made it apt for such patterning. Admittedly, shorter, more trivial odes to robin redbreasts, spring, and young ladies on their birthdays lack it, since they aspire to no more than a little charm and a little moral. But ambition required a different level of coherence. No eighteenth-century ode I know better embodies these ideals than Christopher Smart's 'A Song to David' (1763). Highly patterned, focused on David as both man (individual) and type (manifestation of recurrence), the 'Song' also employs the six-line aabccb stanza so often used for Horatian odes in the eighteenth century. (Smart himself was engaged in translating Horace in the years directly following the publication of the 'Song.') Although Smart did not label the poem with its genre, there seems no question as to which genre he likely had in mind. No other so well suited the twin aims of contemplation and praise, a praise rising from all nature, which had elicited Thomson's blank-verse 'Hymn' in 1730 but for which the idiom of the 1760s required rhyme, stanzas, and rapt incantation.

So great was the fad for lyric bursts that Smart's advertisement for the poem claims that his 'judicious friends and enemies' frowned on the 'Song' for 'the exact regularity and method with which it is conducted.' This may be a former madman's boast of sanity, disguised as the relaying of others' criticism, but the criticism is plausible: the advertisement to Richard Graves's 'The Love of Order' (1773), for example, begs (sardonically?) 'that the reader of taste may not be prepossessed against an attempt, in this age, to recommend regularity and uniformity.' All the method Smart could muster did not save his poem from being taken as a lingering proof that all was still not quite well in his head, and in fact even his partisans nowadays have been unable to explain what some of the poem means. Sections like that on the seven pillars (sts 30–7) also smack of occult or recondite learning, which eighteenth-century readers would have thought pedantic in a hymn. At times, too, Smart's stanza locks him into crude rhythms, archaisms ('wilk' for 'whelk' in st. 42), padding or contorted phrases, and even journeyman's phrases like 'briny broad' for 'sea' (st. 20). Smart's regularity, however, does give the poem coherence and, especially in the last half, a magnificent dynamic force.

It also enables him to use the eighteenth-century zeal for comprehensiveness – for the intellectual (usually also the perceptual) prospect – to summon up all the elements of man ideally typified by David, and of God's created world for a chorus of adoration. In Thomson, the fullness of the world, perceived bit by bit, slowly warms the speaker's inferring mind to a recognition of the divine; in Smart, the fullness of the world gathers simultaneously, though of course, since poems proceed in time rather than appear all at once, the speaker must acknowledge the gathering *seriatim*. The difference between the two poems appears in their different principles of order. Thomson's blank verse has the changes of pace and tone that can accommodate discovery, but Smart's tight stanzas do not permit, and do not need, such local freedom. Instead, the architecture of the poem as a whole reminds us that everything is known from the start and merely needs logical or rhetorical arrangement.

The logical arrangement of the 'Song' follows from David's roles. As King and 'Best man' (st. 5), he imitates God as far as a human can; as psalmist, he praises God. The Davidic poet, his mirror, imitates David as far as a poet can; and also sings his praises. Being a poet, a voice, he cannot imitate David's sublime life, but he can David's sublime song. He borrows copiously from Psalm 104 and weaves other biblical images and injunctions through his stanzas, as David did through the Psalms. Most of Smart's imitation of David properly reflects the psalmist's spiritual rather than simply formal acts: like David, Smart praises God and calls upon nature for adoration and gratitude to their Creator. The 'Song' begins, then, with a praise of David, moves to imitation of David (in praise of God), and ends with a conflation of the two. In accord with a symbolic system for which one can imagine various explanations, Smart builds the poem in threes and fives. An introduction of three stanzas precedes two more groups, each of thirteen stanzas (twice five plus three), on David as man and David as poet (sts 4–16, 17–29). Five more groups complete the poem, the first and fourth of them consisting of eight stanzas each (five plus three), the second and third of them consisting of thirteen stanzas each (twice five plus three), and the last group consisting of fifteen stanzas (five times three). In these five groups, Smart begins by turning to the divine architecture, pillars of wisdom that establish the phenomenal world of creation (sts 30–7), and then to the manifestation of that divinity in man through the law (sts 38–50).

As David has reached toward God by his moral integrity and his use of God's creation in his hymns, so God reaches down toward David, from the constitutive pillars of wisdom to the peculiarly human law. The point of contact, so to speak, is dramatized when the 'pillars' section merges with the 'law' section, and Smart gives us three stanzas (sts 38–40) on David as 'scholar of the Lord,' the Incarnation, and God's showing Himself to Moses. At the end of the 'law' section, another pair of stanzas (sts 49–50) adds to the general commandments for all men two further adjurations for David, that he speak the truth about God and that he praise Him. These stanzas serve to introduce a magnificent paean in which the poet, himself a type of David, invokes all nature in adoration of God (sts 51–71); in sustaining this lyrical doxology, Smart signals the break between the thirteen-stanza and eight-stanza groups only by returning to the figure of David (st. 64) and by beginning every stanza in the second group with the words 'For Adoration.' The final group, broken into three-stanza units, celebrates Davidic spiritual sweetness, strength, beauty, preciousness, and glory, each transcending its physical analogues, and permitting the poem to close on still another sort of transcendence, David's disappearance in favor of Christ, the Man of whom he is the type.

Smart's 'Song' did not rouse much admiration from eighteenth-century readers. At once overrational and overmystical for them, at times crabbed and obscure, it seemed like the work of a man whose mind was somewhat askew (as Smart's was). A hundred and twenty years earlier, when the systematic mystics of the seventeenth century engaged in hermetic rhapsodies, or a mere generation later, when Swedenborg was all the rage in some circles, perhaps Smart would have thought himself in better company. Perhaps not: his encyclopaedic form obviously owes a great deal to the school of Thomson, and his stanzas proceed by association of ideas, analogy and contrast, in the orthodox manner of his own time:

Of fowl – e'en every beak and wing
Which cheer the winter, hail the spring,
   That live in peace or prey;
They that make music, or that mock,
The quail, the brave domestic cock,
   The raven, swan, and jay.   (st. 23)

Smart achieves comprehensiveness by shifting the contexts of analogy and contrast: the last three lines present, in linked series, music/mockery, ridicule (the mocking)/cowardice (quail), wild/domestic, bird of awakening/bird of doom, black (raven)/white (swan), royal (swan)/common (jay). Even in so abstractly ordered a poem as this, one finds a texture made up of apparent disorder,

159

arbitrariness fitted together by association. The categories, the synecdoches ('every beak and wing'), and the devotion of the whole poem to constant action all form part of the positional style. And the choice of the ode as the genre is very much of its period. One is pleasantly surprised to find verse of the quality of the 'Song' at any time, but the poem itself could have been conceived and written as it was only when it was. Like other fine poems of the mid-to-later eighteenth century, it shows the flexibility and potential energy of the poetic tradition within which it was written.

5   Conclusion

The practice of literature, like that of language itself, follows a course of erratic, unrevolutionary change. This change is also aggregate, not uniform, over a gradually altering canon in which each work has its own blend of old and new, ephemeral and long-lived, personal and communal. 'Periods' are only scholars' inventions, mental versions of surveyor's lines to help one name and know the terrain. This volume has begun with 1660, but as Joseph Frank discovered in studying Commonwealth verse, 'the evolution of English verse in the seventeenth century was a continuum. ... It is ... true that Dryden obviously writes differently from Drayton. Yet the transition from Drayton to Dryden is so gradual and intermittent, as well as chronologically so irregular, that one cannot point to a time at which "Restoration" poetry began – except as a historical rather than a literary designation' (*Hobbled Pegasus* (1968), p. 17). Throughout the eighteenth century too, the course of English poetry was a continuum. That does not mean that poetry was insulated from events. Restoration verse reflected the bells and throngs for the return of Charles, the founding of the Royal Society, the vogue for things French that swept in with the new King's court, and the revelry in popular entertainment let loose from the Commonwealth pillory. To a much lesser degree, the poetry of the 1770s and 1780s was sensitive to the colonial rebellion, a refractory paraliament, and a riotous citizenry. This lack of insulation, in fact, ensures the continuum. Precisely because the ongoing pressure of so many externals – political, social, cultural, economic, and linguistic – never stops affecting poetry, there can almost never be revolutionary change of a sort to make a 'period' natural rather than arbitrary. And since a literary 'period' does not correspond to anything fixed and rounded off in reality, it can look neat only if imperious historians, by fiat, make the crooked straight and the rough places plain. A more accurate map, I think, requires one first to describe and interpret aggregate changes through whatever block of years he has chosen to discuss. Second, more warily, he must select and examine those works that best harness – and even visibly redirect – the inertial energy of an accepted style.

One way of looking at poetic change from 1660 to 1780 is to consider a shift in preference of genres. The models favored from 1660 to 1720 all predated the Restoration or had appeared by the early 1660s: Cowley's irregular odes (1656 and later), courtly verse in panegyric and short lyrical forms (typified by Waller's, 1645 and later), Denham's *Cooper's Hill* (1642 and 1655 before the final version of 1668), John Cleveland's fierce satires (1647 and later), and Butler's *Hudibras* (first appearing in late 1662). Perhaps one might add Cotton's *Scarronides* (1664) as an adjunct to *Hudibras*. From these works and, naturally, from those of Virgil, Horace, and Martial, one can trace the great bulk of verse, save for the most hortatory and topical. The only important intermediary for the classics, I believe, was Boileau. His Horatian satires and epistles influenced Rochester, his Horatian preceptive verse stimulated some poets of the 1680s and the early eighteenth century, and his mock-heroic, *Le Lutrin*, affected *The Dispensary* and *The Rape of the Lock*, and conceivably *MacFlecknoe*.

From the 1660s into the 1690s, poets characteristically explored these modes in terms of praise and blame. Narrative and persuasion for their own sakes, rather than for praise or blame, tended to appear only in love poems before 1680, and till the mid-to-late 1690s, only in love and preceptive poems. Rochester, Butler, Marvell, and Oldham all fit this pattern; Dryden does, except for his religious poems of the 1680s; Charles Cotton is the only poet of any importance who does not. Even verse of love and retirement, as we have seen, often devoted itself to praise and blame or, in a more self-centered form of the same thing, pleasure and pain, especially in the verse of the adventurous and up-to-date court wits. Because of these emphases, Restoration poetry is likely to be single-minded, with clear normative patterns. Later, in a period more given to narrative for its own sake, readers did not demand such clear patterns. One then finds the affectionate satire of the early eighteenth century and the ambiguities of value in much of Gay's poetry before 1720, in much of Pope's (*The Rape of the Lock, Eloisa to Abelard*, 'Elegy to the Memory of an Unfortunate Lady'), and in a host of tales and fables which do have morals but in which the process of telling receives more stress than the lesson to be learned. By 1720, verse of praise and blame, which continued to flourish, was now supplemented by these narratives and a new, broader range of preceptive verse.

I have suggested in the Introduction and in Chapter 4 that one may treat this aggregate change in poetic modes as part of a shift from a focus on the theme of power to a focus on the principle of interrelatedness. This is a tenuous generalization. Poets kept on treating the theme of power, as in *The Rape of the Lock*, for example; and of course earlier satire and panegyric give their heroes and victims a place within at least implied social norms. Still, I believe it helpful to see one body of verse, that of the Restoration, as centrally concerned with people's exploiting (or being exploited by) elements of their surroundings, and a later body of verse as centrally concerned with presenting interdependent, cooperative systems of order. Early eighteenth-century panegyric increasingly stresses social virtues and the glories of England. Nature poetry increasingly stresses God's dispensation and man's discovery, through science, of His design. Allusions to other poems – signs of taking the world of poetry as interdependent – grow more complex. In the 1720s, for the first time since Milton, the principle of interrelationships led to the creation of great imagined worlds, those of Pope's

Dunciad and Thomson's *Seasons*. Both poems, especially as they were elaborated through the 1740s, insist on the wholeness of nature, perceived though it may be in fragments. Pope's and Thomson's political verse of the 1730s also requires the principle of interdependence, invoking the laws of history – not merely particular examples – to evaluate the egoistic and despotic rule that the Opposition saw in George II and Walpole. And, as I argued in Chapter 2, both Pope and Thomson refined a 'positional style' in their verse.

Despite the aggregate changes from 1660 to the 1740s, many emphases remained constant. Among these is a use of psychological patterns, whether for association of ideas as a means of poetic organization, for the supposed rapture of a Pindaric bard or the tortuous process of self-congratulation that one gets from Rochester's Bajazet (1675?) and James Bramston's Man of Taste (1733), or for maintaining the appearance of sincerity in love poetry and raging satire. Along with psychological patterning comes an expectation of a speaking voice behind the poem. Often the voice is that of a spectator (as in the prospect poem) and often that of a victim (the suffering lover); typically the speaker, unless he is a boastful persona (architect of the point of view in mock-heroic poems), cannot do more than organize and comment on what he sees. Since association of ideas and the process of inquiry – by which one does organize what he sees – both depend on analogy, analogy is at the core of poetic order in this period. Metaphoric langauge, kept strictly analogical in its comparisons and contrasts, tended to be used only for ornament in the ubiquitous 'positional style,' whereas positional analogy informs the entire structure of such characteristic poems as Gray's *Elegy*. Comparison and contrast between the end of the day and the end of life, the living and the dead, the speaker and the villagers, the humble and the grand, make up the content of the *Elegy*, just as other comparisons and contrasts make up the content of *Absalom and Achitophel* and *Eloisa to Abelard*. The more that poems employed association of ideas instead of abstract patterns of organization, and the more that they tried to present interdependent, cooperative systems of order, the more thoroughly they relied upon analogy.

In keeping with these four emphases – on psychological patterns, on the use of the speaking voice, on the treatment of the speaker as spectator, victim, and/or dramatic projection, and on analogy – the personal epistle (like Pope's Horatian poems) and the topographical survey (like *The Seasons*) became increasingly favored modes. The creation of the self as a dramatic character is not new in Pope, who had Horace and Dryden as obvious models, nor is it specific to him, writing as he did just before Fielding's triumph with the same technique in the novel. Similarly, Thomson's inquiring 'I' has precedents in Virgil and Denham, and a novelistic counterpart in the composite, process-oriented novels of Richardson. One does not want to attribute too much individual influence to Thomson and Pope themselves. It is enough to say that at least until 1780 variants keep recurring on a manner they typified: the highlighting of the self, the 'politics of nostalgia' (as the historian Isaac Kramnick calls it) that they professed in the 1730s, and their visionary, sometimes prophetic style. In terms of poetic tradition, later poets cleave to practices founded on Pope and Thomson; but as I have pointed out in

Chapter 4, these later poets adapted, rather than accepted, what they received. The self becomes, for instance, reverently aspiring (Collins), noisily defiant of social orthodoxy (Churchill; the novelistic parallel here, explicitly mentioned by Churchill, is Sterne), or absorbed in elegiac, vicarious contemplations ('Ossian'). The 'politics of nostalgia' appears in a new guise, the choice of English (and other) 'primitive' models; and also, thematically, in the elegiac strain that makes the Penseroso speaker so much more prevalent than the Allegro in the later eighteenth century. The visionary style turns into the style of the ode, which became the lyric form most flaunted for imaginative freedom after the mid-1740s. More than in Pope or Thomson, visions in the ode were of personified abstractions or were rapidly suggested through brief, clear invitations to 'ideal presence,' as discussed above in Chapter 2.

A stress on the self within poetic modes that dwelt on interdependency and that fostered analogy – one can logically see how this pattern might cohere in poetry that centered on fellow feeling, sympathy, empathy. In general, although by no means exclusively, Restoration and early-to-mid eighteenth-century poetry of any ambition used pathos, when needed, for persuasion. Later one growingly finds feeling for its own sake, as in ballads whose plots were rewritten for weepy endings, touching interludes in survey poems (following Thomson, whose interludes do have a persuasive or cognitive purpose), and in the spreading mode of the 'humane' poem, of which John Langhorne's *The Country Justice* (1774–7) is an excellent example. These are the poetic versions of the 'sentimentality' so voguish in the mid-to-later part of the century, with moralizing and generous pity aplenty; it was to continue, with some changes in technique, for many decades after 1780. Just as various social forms, like the epistle, the preceptive poem, and the survey, came more into play when – according to my rough chart – the principle of interdependence began to interest poets more than the theme of power, so the personal lyric, the affecting narrative, and the dramatic monologue came more into play when the attitude of fellow feeling began to interest poets more than any principle or theme. One senses the aggregate change as one senses the slow change of the mix of trees in forested land as one moves from a cooler to a warmer climatic zone.

There is no discontinuity within the period from 1660 to 1780, any more than there is from 1600 to 1680 or 1750 to 1850. As at nearly every time since the end of the sixteenth century, moreover, British poetry easily bore comparison with that of any European nation. If there is something special about eighteenth-century poetry – something other, that is, than the historical distinctiveness common to the modes and styles of any time in poetry, language, home decoration, clothing, music, and habits of thought – perhaps it is a heightened understanding of techniques and a sharpened awareness of the past. These matters are reflected in the discussions of Chapters 2 and 3. There I have suggested at length the importance of the past to cosmopolitan poets whose 'positional style' included the placing of poems within living traditions, classical or more modern. I have also touched on the understanding of technique and its growth along with serious, systematic literary criticism during the Restoration. Before 1780, exploration of artistic effects had attained such subtlety and incisiveness that two hundred years later, in 1969, the psychologist James Hogg could remark, 'the mass of writing on taste in the eighteenth century is particularly stimulating and relevant to many of the problems with which psychologists are now concerned' (*Psychology and the Visual Arts*, p. 18). Theories of the sublime, of the pastoral, of poetic diction, and other such elements of poetry, all largely or wholly psychological in their emphasis, rolled from eighteenth-century presses. The result was to expand markedly the poets' knowledge of their tools and their potential goals, a knowledge that had previously been imparted only by traditional books of rhetoric.

If one asks how the quality of poetry was affected by widespread awareness of the past, the answers are mixed: weak poets retreated into servile imitation and better ones employed allusion, resonance, imitation, and borrowed diction with the varying degrees of tact and complexity discussed in Chapter 3. As to the development of psychological criticism, its effects on poetry are much harder to pin down. The influence of criticism on poetry can rarely be disentangled from the influence of poetry on criticism, and of climates of opinion on both. I must confess myself enough a believer in the intellect to have confidence that the more poets know about their craft, the better. Some others have argued that 'rules' drawn from the past and from critics fettered Restoration and eighteenth-century poets; or that these poets sank under the unequal, implied competition between them and their great predecessors; or that too much data about how to affect readers made these poets able and eager to do no more than crank up machines for thrills, tears, and lively raptures. As with the effect of the past on poetry, so here: these theses may help explain why bad eighteenth-century poets were bad in the ways that they were. The theses become useless when one comes to able poets, let alone good and great ones. We have seen the rapidity with which change took place despite critics and rules, the fervor with which poets remodeled what they received from the past, and the artistic complexity that rebukes any notion of writers' simply exploiting a handy new rhetoric. I suspect that every culture offers its poets advantages denied to poets in other cultures; that these offered advantages frequently are used so facilely as in fact to damage poetry; and that Restoration and eighteenth-century poets in this regard followed the same pattern as did the distinguished and indistinguishable at any time, Edmund Spenser (1552?–99) and Chidiock Tichborne (1558?–86) or Alfred, Lord Tennyson (1809–92) and Wathen Mark Wilks Call (1817–90). In this as in other things history erects no boundary posts between periods, and the historian does best to appraise each idiom on its own terms, with as much information, as much sensitivity, and as much sympathy as his nature and the state of scholarly knowledge allow.

Appendix 1: Chronology

This Chronological Table lists and comments on principal poems published each year, lists poetic collections by many minor poets (often with summary comments on such a poet's corpus of verse), and suggests for each five-year period the important historical events, largely in political history, of that period. Poems printed well after the time that they first were significant – Traherne's, for example, that did not appear in print till this century, or political verse long-delayed in the printing – and poems treated in general entries for minor poets are listed in years other than years of publication. The Table does not pretend to original bibliographical research, but relies on the *Short-Title Catalogues* of Pollard and Redgrave and of Wing, on David Foxon's invaluable *English Verse 1701–1750*, on standard editions of poets' works, and on other perhaps less faithful sources. I have used an asterisk to indicate works mentioned in the chronology but discussed at greater length in the text; the Index should be consulted for the page references.

1660–4 This period of readjustment saw the restoration of the monarchy; the reestablishment of an Anglicanism that – after exclusions and the closing of ranks – turned out to be broader-based than before the Civil Wars; and the founding of the Royal Society (chartered 1662), which lent great social prestige to empiricism and the exploration of the natural world. There was a crystallizing and prompting of new definitions – of state, church, authority, and also of poetry.

1660

John Cleveland, *Cleveland Revived*. Between 1647 and 1700 appeared some twenty-five editions of poems attributed to Cleveland, most of them not his; 1660, two years after the poet's death, marked the second appearance of the posthumous *Cleveland Revived*. The attributed canon grew to 147, and despite the efforts of editors in 1677 (in *Clievelandi Vindiciae*) to rectify the attributions, the *Works* (1687) continued to present a large body of disputable verse as his during the eighteenth century. For the history of Restoration and eighteenth-century verse, then, Cleveland's mode is more important than his actual personal achievements. That mode was of tough, contemptuous, angry satire, without that smoothness of verse which came to be admired, but with a vividness of imagery and extravagance echoed in Butler and Oldham, and sometimes ('A Ramble in St. James's Park') in Rochester. These qualities are perhaps best illustrated by 'The Rebel Scot.'

John Dryden, *Astraea Redux*. A richly figured celebration of Charles's restoration, filled with classical and scriptural allusions, this poem was Dryden's first success in the grand panegyric mode. It testifies to his skill in binding heroic couplets, themselves polished, into larger units more flexible than the groupings of quatrains he used a year earlier for his *Heroic Stanzas to the Glorious Memory of Cromwell*.

Sir Robert Howard, *Poems*. Skillful and rather aloof love poems and lyrics in Waller's mode, in which imagery tends to be illustrative rather than continuous and integral (as opposed to the practice of some earlier seventeenth-century poets) and in which syntactical devices (antithesis, zeugma) work to clarify rather than complicate the conceptual level of the poem (as opposed to the practice of some later poets, like Pope). There are panegyrics to Charles II and to General Monck, who engineered the Restoration.

Robert Wild, *Iter Boreale*. The most popular poetic welcome for Charles II, the poem relates, in crude pentameter couplets, the historical events leading to the King's return. As a dissenting minister who was also a royalist, Wild chose the Presbyterian General Monck for his hero. He mingles panegyric with satiric invective and exuberant detail, to create a poem that lacks esthetic complexity but that admirably conveys a sense of directed energy and jubilation.

1661

John Dryden, *To His Sacred Majesty, a Panegyric on His Coronation*. In heroic couplets.
Edmund Waller, *On St. James's Park, as Lately Improved by His Majesty*. This panegyric, in heroic couplets, moves from the King's works in perfecting nature to his powers as public benefactor; a variant on the topographical patriotic mode of *Cooper's Hill* and 'To His Honoured Kinsman' (see pp. 11–14 above).

1662

Samuel Butler, *Hudibras*.*The title page of the First Part is dated 1663, but the volume was published in late 1662; the Second Part, dated 1664, appeared in late 1663. Butler made changes and added annotations in 1674. *Hudibras. The Third and Last Part*, finally, appeared in 1678, two years before Butler's death. There were several editions of each part at the time of first appearance, and an enormous influence on subsequent satire, documented bibliographically (in part) in E. A. Richards, *Hudibras in the Burlesque Tradition* (1937) and R. P. Bond, *English Burlesque Poetry, 1700–1750* (1932).

1663

Abraham Cowley, *Verses Written on Several Occasions*. The irregular odes and eulogistic verse, some of high quality, in this volume added to the prestige of a poet most of whose major work slightly predated the Restoration – his first collection appeared in 1656 – so that he was the dominant poetic figure by 1660. He retained that position for the next two decades, even after his death (1667), despite the rival claims of Denham (chiefly on the basis of *Cooper's Hill* alone) and Waller.

1664

Charles Cotton, *Scarronides*. Cotton's imitation of Paul Scarron's poem *Virgile Travesti* (1648) in the style of *Hudibras* popularized for seventeenth-century England the French fashion of burlesquing the classics – Virgil, Ovid, Homer. Nine editions before 1700 suggest its importance as a text; it also served as a stimulus far more ribald and boisterous than any French model. Despite the guying of the classics by making the gods talk like porters and cinder-wenches and using a narrator like Butler's, *Scarronides* and similar burlesques did not share in the cynicism of *Hudibras*. They represented a kind of saturnalian fun rather than satiric re- or devaluation; they experimented cheerfully with the classics, as school-friends.

Edmund Waller, *Poems &c.* The first post-Restoration collection of Waller's verse, which provided poets with dominant models of courtly lyric and panegyric verse until well into the eighteenth century.

1665–9 Plague (1665), the Great Fire (1666), war with Holland (1665–7), and the internal struggles that led to the dismissal of the Lord Chancellor, the Earl of Clarendon, marked these years. National and parliamentary support for the King began to ebb; so did his private exchequer, which led him to bargain secretly with Louis XIV of France. The royal court was widely perceived as wasteful and immoral.

1665

Edward, Lord Herbert of Cherbury, *Occasional Verses*. The only published collection by this poet (1583–1648); one edition, though some of the lyrics are fine.

Andrew Marvell, *The Character of Holland*. This reedition in some ways typifies the social use of Restoration political verse. Presumably written by Marvell in 1653, when the English took a large number of Dutch ships, this sneering satire (rather in the manner of Cleveland) was revived for the Dutch War in 1665, but truncated at line 100 (of 152) and given an updated eight-line conclusion of poetic quality low enough to make one doubt that Marvell had any hand in it. In 1672, when another Dutch War was under way, the poem again reappeared.

1666

Edmund Waller, *Instructions to a Painter*. Waller's narrative panegyric of English victory over the Dutch, loosely couched as a set of instructions to a painter of heroic canvases, begot a brief but numerically impressive flood of imitations. (See M. T. Osborne, *Advice-to-a-Painter Poems* (1949), for a list of these.) Many of the imitations were satiric, not only because topical panegyric in the Restoration typically was turned upside-down by someone but also because advice to a painter obviously requires striking visual detail, such as can serve a satirist's grotesque or malign effects. In 1666–7 alone came *The Second Advice to a Painter*, presenting a fuller, corrected, hostile version of the battle with the Dutch, and *Third, Fourth*, and *Fifth Advices*.

1667

John Dryden, *Annus Mirabilis: The Year of Wonders, 1666*. A long (1216 lines) royalist historical poem about the Dutch War and the Great Fire, this was Dryden's last sustained effort in epic quatrains, the metre of Davenant's *Gondibert* (1651). In reponse to fears that fire and plague were divine punishments, Dryden exalts England's King, navy, Royal Society, merchants, and future glory, typically enough creating poetic splendor with an especially lavish and broad-ranging body of imagery that makes one ignore the political expediency behind the poem. He does not, however, remain in full control, slipping into occasional gaudiness or proving unable to sustain a theme as the mature Dryden was triumphantly to do.

[Andrew Marvell], *Last Instructions to a Painter*.* Written in 1667 but not published till 1689, unlike the 'Advices' calendared under 1666 above, this is the only poem in the sequence whose attribution to Marvell has been unquestioned; it is the best of them, with a greater range of tone than any seventeenth-century satire, *Absalom and Achitophel* aside. Its brilliance of detail, however, does not quite mask its lack of structure. Marvell wrote over a dozen political satires from the mid-1660s to the mid-1670s, though attributions remain still uncertain.

John Milton, *Paradise Lost*. The ten-book version.

Katherine Philips, *Poems*. A pirated edition in the year of Philips's death, 1664, followed by others in 1667, 1669, 1678, and 1710, prove the appeal of 'the matchless Orinda,' as she was called; authors of commendatory verses to the volume of 1667 include the Earls of Orrery and Roscommon, Abraham Cowley,

169

and the ubiquitous elegist Thomas Flatman. Her verse has the feeling of sincerity and it floats on graceful cadences, but the content and expression are banal: these meditative lyrics, retirement poems, and verse of friendship have little to distinguish them apart from their having been written by the first Englishwoman not of noble blood to be celebrated for her writing.

1668

Abraham Cowley, *Works*. This posthumous edition – Cowley died in 1667 – was the first of a dozen by 1700; it enhanced the very high esteem for Cowley's Pindaric odes* and his love verses in *The Mistress* (1647) and later. It also reprinted his biblical epic *Davideis* (1656), unfinished like the other much-read Commonwealth epic, *Gondibert*.

Sir John Denham, *Poems and Translations*. The volume contains the third version of *Cooper's Hill**, the first two having appeared in 1642 and, with sharp revision, in 1655. The rest of Denham's later poetry is translation, including a version in couplets of Cicero's *Cato Major* (published too late in 1668 for inclusion in this collection). Grave but not prosy is the fine elegy in tetrameters 'On Mr. Abraham Cowley's Death'; and neither grave nor prosy, a tough, cynical poem in thirty-four triplets, 'Friendship and Single Life against Love and Marriage,' which has a nice smattering of Restoration savagery.

1670–4 The consequences of another Dutch War (1672–4) were to make the Commons' relations with the King more strained, as Parliament broadened their criticism of national policy and entertained bills with radical constitutional implications for royal prerogative and succession to the throne. Charles in turn fought back with repeated prorogations and exercises of personal authority, as in his Declaration of Indulgence to Catholics and Dissenters. Political contempt and fractiousness had its parallel in the more and more corrosive verse of the court wits.

1671

John Milton, *Paradise Regained, Samson Agonistes*.

Oxford Drollery. This volume may stand for the great number of *Drollery*s published during the Restoration, year after year, including *Dregs of Drollery* (1660), *Merry Drollery* (1661 and thereafter), *Westminster Drollery* (1671), *Windsor Drollery* (1671), *Covent Garden Drollery* (1672), *Holborn Drollery* (1673), *London Drollery* (1673), and even *Grammatical Drollery* (1682). These were collections of light verse, especially songs, theatre pieces (prologues and epilogues), love poems, and occasionally satires. Despite the title, not all the poems tried to be amusing; for example, *Covent Garden Drollery* includes 'Upon His Dead Mistress, Represented in a Dream.' Contributors – willing? by piracy? – included Dryden, Dorset, and Behn.

1673

Sir William Davenant, *Works*. This posthumous collection, five years after Davenant's death, largely comprises work written before 1660, the chief poem being the very lengthy heroic *Gondibert* (1651). Some of his earlier verse now appeared for the first time, along with some poems of similar sorts – panegyrics, epistles, occasional verse, lyrics – written after the Restoration. Although Davenant was most admired for his heroics, I think he should have been for his shorter lyrics, like 'The Philosopher and the Lover, to a Mistress Dying,' of which the lover speaks the first quatrain:

> Your beauty, ripe and calm and fresh
>> As Eastern summers are,
> Must now, forsaking time and flesh,
>> Add light to some small star.

Matthew Stevenson, *Poems*. A miscellany of purely personal and occasional poems, on country parsons, 'the boy that brought up the bottles of bad wine,' a dog called Fudle, and so forth, the volume is usually lively, sometimes clever, now and then graceful. In reading such books, one is reminded that Restoration and early eighteenth-century verse accommodated personal experience as gladly as nineteenth- and twentieth-century verse, but accommodated it, mostly, in light social verse rather than in recollective and meditative forms.

1674

Thomas Flatman, *Poems and Songs*. This is the earliest edition, which Flatman kept revising and augmenting. Flatman is best known for his lugubrious elegiac Pindarics, but he also wrote pastorals, amusing songs, classical and biblical paraphrases, and occasional verses of middling quality.
Edward Howard, *Poems and Essays*. Jibing at Howard, mainly for the badness of his heroic poem *The British Princes* (1669), was such good sport for the court wits that one is not surprised to find his verse at once like theirs (in its lasciviousness, cynicism, and wit) and unlike theirs (in its aloofness and acceptance of rural retirement). His spare, dry voice lends itself well to irony, as at the end of 'Love Defined': 'The fair and honest ask no more/Than what's illegal in a whore.'
John Milton, *Paradise Lost*. The twelve-book version.

1675–9 Growing anti-French feeling and suspicion of Charles was exploited by the inventors of the Popish Plot in the summer of 1678; rumors of treachery and violence, current throughout the 1670s, focused here; and eager politicians seized on the chance to ride to power on the chariot of demagogy. Various Exclusion Bills, debarring the Catholic James, Duke of York, from the royal succession, were passed. Blood was shed.

1675

Charles Cotton, *Burlesque upon Burlesque, or The Scoffer Scoffed*. Cotton puts Lucian's *Dialogues of the Gods*, written to scoff at myths, into Hudibrastics so as to create a stylistic burlesque of Lucian's narrative burlesque.

Richard Leigh, *Poems upon Several Occasions and to Several Persons*. Reflective poems, panegyrics, and lyrics of moderate interest in a style smacking of the tamer 'metaphysicals' in both ingenuity and an ungainliness surprising after Waller – these make the volume somehow anachronistic, and remind one, in connection with the smart new style of Dryden and the court wits, that the old school survived among men like Leigh, who practiced medicine quietly in the country.

Thomas Traherne. Traherne's only important religious publication, his *Christian Ethics*, appeared this year, the year after his death; almost none of his poetry was published till the twentieth century. The lengthy *Thanksgivings* and about a hundred English poems (some in two versions) testify to his ecstatic piety.*

1676

Sir John Suckling, *Works*. It is probably no accident that a post-Restoration collection of this most amoral of the Cavalier poets (1609–42) should appear in the 1670s – there may have been an earlier one too, in 1672 – when Rochester, Sedley, Dorset, Etherege, and other court wits had their heyday. One might note that no editions of Herrick or Lovelace appeared between 1660 and 1700; Carew's *Poems* were reprinted in 1670 and 1671; but overall the influence of the Caroline cavaliers on their successors may have been slimmer than might be expected.

1678

Henry Vaughan, *Thalia Rediviva*. The one edition of the only volume Vaughan published after 1660 – his others date from 1646–55 – collects English and Latin original poems, both secular and religious, and translations from the late 1640s on. The volume also contains some Latin poems by Vaughan's twin, Thomas (died 1666). By and large the poems are not among Vaughan's best, the most distinguished among them, I should say, being 'The World' (II), beginning, 'Can any tell me what it is?'

1679

[James Carkesse], *Lucida Intervalla*. While Carkesse was confined for madness, he wrote these poems about his ill treatment (some of which is probably factual, some imaginary). They bear the marks of his mental disorder in the obscurity and private symbolism of his verse.

'Ephelia' (Joan Philips?), *Female Poems on Several Occasions*. The volume contains love poems to shepherds, especially 'Strephon' (a code name for 'J. G.'); some acrostics, despite the scorn in which such trick verses supposedly were held; and numbers of poems by courtiers like Rochester and Scroope rather than by 'Ephelia' at all. Some of the 'J. G.'/Strephon poems are presented so as to form a group, which is a bit uncommon in the Restoration.

[John Sheffield, Earl of Mulgrave, and John Dryden], *An Essay upon Satire*. The circulation of this poem in manuscript during 1679 – it was not published till 1697 – may have been the cause for the brutal ambush on Dryden in mid-December. An undistinguished satire on the court wits rather than the preceptive poem its title would suggest, the *Essay* reads more like a product of Mulgrave's pen than one of Dryden's.

John Oldham, *A Satire against Virtue*. This Pindaric ode is 'supposed to be spoken by a court hector' declaiming boldly against 'dull morality.' Oldham also uses the self-damning persona in 'Garnet's Ghost,' the first of the *Satires against the Jesuits*, which appeared in 1679 in a pirated edition; the next year, 1680, he used one – this time nonchalant instead of ferocious like Garnet and the hector – in his libertine drinking song *The Careless Good Fellow*. Oldham's personae of this sort, unlike Rochester's, have little psychological complexity to make his poems complex or give them structure. Still, the proclamations of egoism burst forth with splendid energy and vividness.

Samuel Slater, *Poems in Two Parts*. The two parts are playlets in doggerel pentameter couplets, the first a discourse on the Creation, Fall, and Redemption (according to Slater, after 'learned Mr. Milton's cast and fancy,' but in 'a more plain and familiar style' than *Paradise Lost*) and the second a dialogue about faith.

1680–4 Clever parliamentary maneuvers by the King and the dying of popular furor over the Popish Plot led to Charles's regaining control, to the trials of the leading promoters of uproar over the Plot, and to a change in the market for spies and informers, who now ferreted out Whigs (so the Opposition had come to be called) instead of Papists. As a result of the alleged Rye House Plot (1683), the Whig cause was temporarily destroyed, and the last year and a half of Charles's reign brought him a measure of supremacy that he had not enjoyed for twenty years.

1680

Thomas Otway, *The Poet's Complaint of His Muse, or A Satire against Libels*. A strangely bipartite, lengthy (711 lines) ode, first bemoaning the poet's poverty and then defending the Duke of York (the future James II) against libels. One can invent connections between the two halves, including that of an astonishingly cynical and blatant call for patronage, but probably Otway glued the political poem to the personal poem he had already begun. Laments about a poet's poverty, sometimes with envious glances at those more prosperous but less meritorious, were frequent enough: T. W.'s *Poeta de Tristibus* (1682) and Oldham's 'Spenser's Ghost' (1683) are two examples close to the time of *The Poet's Complaint*.

John Wilmot, Earl of Rochester, *Poems on Several Occasions*. A series of editions appeared this year, shortly after the Earl's death, purporting to have been published in Antwerp and to comprise Rochester's poems. In fact, 'Antwerp' was London, in all likelihood, and many of the poems in the volume were by other court figures, among them Sir Carr Scroope, Sedley, Dorset, Lady Rochester, Thomas Durfey, Etherege, Behn, Oldham, and Alexander Radcliffe, as far as the best modern scholarship can sort out the attributions. The title-page attribution to Rochester of course was a device to make the volume sell, based on a reputation for lewdness, love, and wit, all of which this volume has in plenty. Few of the poems had ever been published, though many had circulated in manuscript, so the buyer got novelty as well as print. An enormous body of poems of the 1660s and 1670s, of course, never saw print, or did see it well after the time when the poems were written.

Wentworth Dillon, Earl of Roscommon, *Horace's Art of Poetry Made English*. A standard, perhaps the standard Restoration translation of this central text.

1681

Charles Cotton, *The Wonders of the Peak*. A rambling topographical poem in the country-house mode of Marvell's *Upon Appleton House*, except that instead of praising house and estate directly, Cotton gives the house and lands of Chatsworth a foil in the 'deformed' country around it, 'Nature's pudenda.' Chatsworth is of an order, opulence, and refinement quite opposite to the chaotic, barren, wild, and countrified area and people Cotton has been describing; it is a 'paradise, which seated stands/In midst of deserts and of barren sands.' Obviously the sublimity and the awed communion with nature which one finds in Thomson and his followers has no place here, nor does the wholly emblematic nature that *Cooper's Hill* and *Windsor Forest* depict.

John Dryden, *Absalom and Achitophel*.* Short epic, both panegyric and satiric, in defense of Charles II. With this poem, Dryden marked the near-suspension of his playwriting and began publishing his major satiric, argumentative, and lyric verse, the great bulk of which, except for translations, came in the 1680s.

John Oldham, *Satires upon the Jesuits*.* These five poems, the first of them a 'Prologue,' were written 1678–81 at the time of the Popish Plot, but unlike any other Popish-Plot verse except Dryden's, kept being read, with many editions to the end of the century and into the next, either separately or with Oldham's other verse. Oldham drew on classical and modern Latin models in his

denunciations, three of them using self-convicting personae to provide catalogues of evils done and intended by the ruthless, fanatical, predatory Jesuits. In
fact Oldham deserves better than to be remembered by the single-mindedness of
these satires. Some of his translations and adaptations written between the
Satires and his death in 1683 show an impressive command of colloquial rhythms
and dignified declaration as well as of his familiar declamatory style.

1682

Matthew Coppinger, *Poems, Songs, and Love Verses*. This banal collection includes
translations and even acrostics and anagrams with the promised songs and love
verses.

Thomas Creech, tr., Lucretius, *De natura rerum*. An exceptionally important
poem in the Restoration because of both its materialism and its union of natural
description and science, *De rerum natura* (as the three words are now arranged)
found an ideal translator in Creech, whose version met with enthusiasm and
remained the standard translation throughout the seventeenth and eighteenth
centuries. Excellent annotations were added in the early eighteenth century.

John Dryden. In this most extraordinary year for Dryden, he saw published his
devastating satire *The Medal*,* his better-tempered but equally devastating
MacFlecknoe* (written 1676?; authorized publication, 1684, a superb
lampoon; the first of his two poems of religious controversy, *Religio Laici*; and his
collaboration with Nahum Tate, *The Second Part of Absalom and Achitophel*. This
last poem, a wraith of the first *Absalom*, is probably largely by Tate, to whom
Dryden accommodated his style except in one long section of attack mostly on
those who had attacked him for *Absalom*, the writers Samuel Pordage, Elkanah
Settle, and Shadwell. *The Medal* and *MacFlecknoe* are of course among the great
achievements of English satire; and *Religio Laici*, in support of the Anglican
'middle way' rather than the Deists' zeal for rationalism or the Catholics' doting
on tradition, so eloquently varies the poet's speaking voice that the argument
has the ring of thoughtful personal conviction.

John Sheffield, Earl of Mulgrave, *An Essay upon Poetry*. Mulgrave discusses, in the
manner of Horace's *Ars poetica*, the genres and their rules.

N. O., tr., Boileau, *Le Lutrin*. This is the earliest and in some ways the best English
translation of Boileau's high burlesque poem (1674). It lacks cantos 5 and 6,
added by Boileau in 1683, which appear in John Ozell's standard version
(1708). John Crowne also tried his hand at *Le Lutrin* in his *Daeneids* (1692).

Alexander Radcliffe, *The Ramble: an Anti-Heroic Poem, Together with Some Terrestrial
Hymns and Carnal Ejaculations*. Captain Radcliffe was a hanger-on with the court
wits, and this account of drinking and whoring, written in a tone both vulgar
and burlesque, echoes their wished-for insouciance. Most of Radcliffe's poems,
including *Ovid Travesty: a Burlesque upon Ovid's Epistles* (1680), share this tone
and the sporadically amusing doggerel style of *The Ramble*.

1683

John Chalkhill, *Thealma and Clearchus*. The first printing of this early seventeenth-century rhymed pastoral romance.

[John Mason], *Spiritual Songs, or Songs of Praise to Almighty God*. Thirty-three songs in praise of God in stanzas and a lengthy paraphrase of the Song of Songs as a dialogue between Christ and the Church.

George Meriton, *A Yorkshire Dialogue*. This, and a similar dialogue of 1673, are the earliest pieces of modern English dialect verse. The speakers are country folk and the style – in couplets – is simple and earthy.

Thomas Shipman, *Carolina, or Loyal Poems*. The volume collects Shipman's work dating back to the 1650s, most of the poems of thirty to forty lines in couplets or stanzas, addressed to someone in polished colloquial diction. The proportion of Shipman's amorous poems increases in the 1670s, as one might expect from this nicely typical Restoration poet.

Sir William Soame and John Dryden trs., Boileau, *The Art of Poetry*. Largely Soame's work with Dryden's polishing, this translation of *L'Art poétique* (1674) anglicized the French verse essay on the genres and their rules: Waller and Spenser (ll. 17–18), for example, replace Boileau's Malherbe and Racan.

1684

Thomas Creech, tr., Horace, *The Odes, Satires, and Epistles*. Although this Horace enjoyed numbers of editions well into the next century, it was much less highly regarded than the Lucretius or than Creech's translation of the *Idylliums* of Theocritus, which also appeared in 1684 and remained standard for eighty years.

P[atrick] K[er], *Flosculum Poeticum*. The religious verse here has some epigrammatic sharpness but is mainly interesting because of the use of paradox and Hudibrastics for serious purposes; similarly, Ker's political verse uses anagrams seriously. The volume also contains love epistles and ballads on various occasions.

Walter Pope, *The Old Man's Wish*. This genial poem of retirement had great success when set to music, so great as to encourage two versions of *The Old Woman's Wish*, one pious and one impious.

Wentworth Dillon, Earl of Roscommon, *An Essay on Translated Verse*. This rhymed poem giving Horatian advice on how to translate incorporates an imitation of Milton in a section on writing blank verse.

1685–9 Charles II died in February, 1685, and his inept, arrogant successor, James, was driven from power in the Bloodless Revolution of 1688–9. The turmoil including Monmouth's Rebellion and the Bloody Assizes of 1685, continuing violence in Ireland, and the constitutional depredations of James made the Revolution Settlement and the assumption of William and Mary widely accepted.

Perhaps the most important events of these years, however, were not political: the publication in 1687 and late 1689 respectively of Newton's *Principia* and Locke's *Essay Concerning Human Understanding*, which for many decades provided dominant intellectual models that went well beyond merely scientific and philosophical thought.

1685

John Dryden, *Threnodia Augustalis*. A 'funeral-pindaric' ode for Charles II.

Thomas Otway, *Windsor Castle*. A long (578 lines) elegiac poem for Charles II in couplets but with an interwoven refrain. The castle is emblematic of Charles's continuity with the English monarchy and of his might and sumptuousness; and the art in the castle allows Otway to move to a lofty ending through instructions to a painter in an allegorical scene.

Samuel Wesley (the elder), *Maggots, or Poems on Several Subjects*. This amusing collection specializes in mocking the heroic on subjects like mice, lice, hogs, a cow's tail, and a pair of breeches; there is an argument for precedence between a herring and a whale. Wesley waggishly but genuinely annotates all his allusions and references.

John Whitehall, *Miscellaneous Poems*. These are mostly Pindarics marked by a great deal of biblical imagery, most of it the simple comparison of modern and scriptural persons which is prevalent in Restoration verse (rather than any typological specificity) and which became more so toward the turn of the century.

1686

Anne Killigrew, *Poems*. Noteworthy for nothing but Dryden's great ode 'To the Pious Memory of . . . Anne Killigrew'.*

1687

Philip Ayres, *Lyric Poems*. The collection includes, uncharacteristically, sonnets as well as other lyrics; and also uncharacteristically displays translations from a wide range of Italian and classical Greek poets, as well as Latin ones. Ayres's variety perhaps contributed more to the culture of his times, in making unfamiliar texts available, than did the poetic merit of anything he wrote.

John Cutts, *Poetical Exercises*. Lyrics of the Strephon – Dorinda sort, an epistle praising Boileau, a self-defense as a soldier-satirist, and miscellaneous poems in Waller's manner.

John Dryden, *The Hind and the Panther*. This lengthy dialogue, drawing on the conventions of the beast fable, treats of faith and churches in their religious and political roles. Dryden had become a Catholic like James II, so that this poem rejects the thrust of many arguments in *Religio Laici*, though not its insistence on toleration and on reasoned understanding as ancillary (and only ancillary) to faith in revealed truth. To keep the poem interesting and appealing to his overwhelmingly Anglican audience, Dryden mingles dramatic dialogue, satire, inspired eloquence, personal statement, and fables within the central dialogue of beasts.

John Dryden, *A Song for St. Cecilia's Day*. The earlier and shorter of Dryden's odes to music, celebrating its imitation of cosmic harmony and its power to move human passions. The celebration of St Cecilia's Day, 22 November, was annually honored by a song or ode, at least from the early 1680s, so that Dryden's poems are part of a much-practiced subgenre.

John Rawlet, *Poetic Miscellanies*. Simple religious and moral poems, with emblematic treatment of nature; versifications of Seneca's epistles.

Spenser Redivivus, Containing the First Book of the Faerie Queene . . . Delivered in Heroic Numbers. This interesting document of taste has an essay on epic that precedes the modernized, rewritten text.

1688

Jane Barker, *Poetical Recreations*. Barker's usually rather tame poems of rural retirement are followed by a miscellany of university poems, of which the most interesting is T.L.'s 'A Satire in Answer to the Satire against Man' – he praises reason, condemns Rochester and Hobbes, and attacks the odd trio of Dryden, Shadwell, and Settle. Barker too attacks immoral modern poets, not by name, in 'To My Friends against Poetry'; these attacks may be evidence of changing times.

John Dryden, *Britannia Rediviva*. In celebrating the birth of James II's son, who was in fact to become the Old Pretender, Dryden recognizes the dangers to the crown, and writes an exalted rather than exultant poem, with exceptionally powerful panegyric use of classical and religious imagery. The same, to a large extent, is true of the ode 'On the Marriage of . . . Mrs. Anastasia Stafford,' written in December 1687 or early 1688 but published only in 1813, and then in what probably is truncated form. Here reverently used motifs of martyrdom and resurrection recall the political persecution of the two intermarrying families.

1689

[Charles Goodall], *Poems and Translations*. Goodall died, aged eighteen, in 1689 after having attended Eton. His typical collection by a man associated with a public school or university sounds a series of classical themes – love, friendship, honor, pastoral retirement – in classical genres; he translates or paraphrases the classics; and he has joking poems about school figures, in this case about the nose of one John Pigg.

Robert Gould, *Poems*. As Gould's elegy to Oldham suggests, he endorses and writes Juvenalian satire on Juvenalian enemies, like women (Juvenal's Sixth Satire is the great repository of anti-feminism), the mob and its idols (like actors; see pp. 30–1 above), and political sycophants (like Dryden, in 'The Laureate'). Elegies, songs, love poems, and Pindarics share the volume with these satires and satiric epistles.

Poems on Affairs of State. Under this name or that of *State Poems*, edition after updated edition of this important miscellany poured out till the end of Queen Anne's reign and the Jacobite Rebellion of 1715. This first edition and its immediate successors effectively supported the new regime of William by mocking the old with largely satiric verse; current satire did not start proliferating in *Poems on Affairs of State* till the next decade, when the lapsing of press licensing laws allowed new verse to supplement the body of poems accumulated in print or manuscript under Charles II and James II.

1690–4 William militarily quelled popular discontent in Scotland and Ireland, and prosecuted naval and then both naval and land war against the French on the continent. At home he increased judicial independence and religious tolerance, two sore issues under James II. His drab court made some long for his predecessors' gaiety, but fitted well with a moral sobriety that pervaded England in the 1690s and early eighteenth century. There was general hostility, especially after Mary's death in 1694, toward his bevy of Dutch, rather than English, advisors, with whom he was rumored to have homosexual liaisons. The final end to press licensing in 1694 – censorship before publication – encouraged satirists to make free with such subjects.

1691

Thomas Heyrick, *Miscellany Poems*. Heyrick emblematizes and moralizes nature so that objects are given metonymous positions within a moral order, for example in his extravagant four-part Pindaric 'The Submarine Voyage,' which presents an underwater survey of the world with moralization and scenic description. He also discusses ideas of the physical universe in line with a prevalent theme in Restoration poetry, skepticism about human reason ('The Skeptic, against Mechanism').

John Wilmot, Earl of Rochester, *Poems &c. on Several Occasions*. An expurgated selection by the publisher Jacob Tonson, containing a number of poems not in the 'Antwerp' editions of 1680.

1692

John Dryden, *Eleonora*. Dryden writes that he used Donne's *Anniversaries* as a model for this panegyric on the Countess of Abingdon as a pattern of personal and social virtues. (The most recent edition of Donne's *Poems* was the seventh, of

179

1669, which was to be reprinted in 1719, thus suggesting a continuing if somewhat waning audience for elaborately 'metaphysical' verse.)

Thomas Fletcher, *Poems on Several Occasions*. Besides religious verse and translations, the volume includes odes, one of which is an ode for St Cecilia's Day, 1686, the year before Dryden's, and another of which is a Pindaric without rhyme.

[William Walsh], *Letters and Poems, Amorous and Gallant*. An interesting preface on amorous poetry is followed by dull amorous poems and pretty good epigrams – among the former is a sonnet, unusual in the 1690s. When Walsh tries to be amusing, as in 'The Despairing Lover,' or satirical, as in his later, ironic Tory version of Virgil's 'Messianic' Fourth Eclogue, 'The Golden Age Restored' (1703), he succeeds in a mild way.

1693

John Dennis, *Miscellanies in Verse and Prose*. Though Dennis was a considerable critic, he was a mediocre poet, as proved by his panegyrics, classical translations and paraphrases, and Aesopian fables in this volume. He prefaces the volume with a discourse on burlesque poetry.

John Dryden *et al.*, trs, Juvenal and Persius, *Satires*. Dryden contributed the encyclopaedic preface ('Discourse on the Original and Progress of Satire'), translations of five satires by Juvenal, and all the Persius (one of the six with the help of a son, presumably either Charles or John Jr, each of whom translated one satire of Juvenal's for the collection). Other translators of Juvenal here included Nahum Tate, William Congreve, and Thomas Creech, along with several minor poets. This version remained standard through the eighteenth century.

Benjamin Hawkshaw, *Poems upon Several Occasions*. These Pindarics and love poems, poems of rural retirement, and translations by an eighteen- or nineteen-year-old Cambridge student indicate in the titles of the poems alone a continuity of conception between a volume published by someone born in the 1670s and those published a half century earlier: 'Discontent,' 'The Consolation,' 'The Consummation,' 'On a Fly That Was Drowned in a Lady's Mouth.'

1694

[William Dingley], *Poems on Several Occasions*. Translations, epistles, and religious and moral poems of low competence.

Charles Hopkins, *Epistolary Poems on Several Occasions*. Poems to friends and translations of amorous tales from Ovid's *Metamorphoses* and of Tibullan elegies.

[Matthew Prior], 'A Satire on the Poets.' This poem, probably written in 1687, was published in a collection of 1694; Prior's 'A Satire on the Modern Translators,' probably written in 1685, was published in a collection of 1697; both were disowned by him, most likely because of their personal reflections on the Earl of Mulgrave. Both poems also make personal attacks on Dryden and others: they are a good sample of volleys in the continuing paper war that marks the period, within a society sufficiently closed to give piquancy to lampoons. 'Modern Translators' takes the unusual position that translating is itself bad because of the damage done the classical originals; 'Poets' voices the usual plaints about the poverty of writers.

1695–9 The time was one of acute factionalism, including the literary factions of moralists and (or versus) wits. By 1697 the Peace of Ryswick had quieted matters abroad, and the foundation of the Bank of England and the revamping of the East India Company helped England emerge as a great financial power. Jacobite plots in 1696 were thwarted. The King's desire to maintain a strong army for continental war, however, was looked upon with suspicion by his domestic opponents and with distaste by war-weary, insular Englishmen.

1695

Sir Richard Blackmore, *Prince Arthur*. Heavy borrowings from *Paradise Lost* and – in structure (as Blackmore says) – from the *Aeneid* mark this epic: the vision of posterity, which for Aeneas culminates in Augustus, here does so in William III; and Christian Arthur's marriage to the Christian convert Octa, daughter of a pagan king, repeats with Britons and Saxons the Virgilian marriage between Trojan Aeneas and the Latian Lavinia. Though Blackmore prefaced his epic *King Arthur* (1697) with the claim that *Prince Arthur* met with great 'favour and approbation,' his poetic pretensions in fact met with derision. One can see why, when his verse sometimes groveled like this:

The Briton stooped, and lifted from the field
A ponderous stone which both his hands did wield,
So vast that two in our degenerate days,
Though men of strength, the like can scarcely raise.

By no means all Blackmore's verse is *this* contemptible, and his energy led him to write a series of ambitious poems. After *King Arthur* (about victory over the French), he produced two full-scale epics, *Eliza* (1705) and *Alfred* (1723).

1696

Nicholas Brady and Nahum Tate, *A New Version of the Psalms of David*. Metrical versions of the Psalms, which gradually replaced the sixteenth-century doggerel of Hopkins and Sternhold; a useful bibliographic guide to such material is J. Holland's *The Psalmists of Britain* (1843).
[John Oldmixon], *Poems on Several Occasions*. Of more interest than these

translations and love verses are the repeated claims for 'naivete of thought' and sincerity in Oldmixon's amorous poetry.

John Tutchin, *A Pindaric Ode in the Praise of Folly and Knavery*. Dullness, folly, knavery, and nonsense are praised as the only ways to prosper nowadays. The ode mixes irony with straight denunciation in a manner familiar from Oldham and, to some degree, Rochester, two poets whose examples Tutchin had followed in his *Poems on Several Occasions* (1685).

1697

Daniel Baker, *Poems upon Several Occasions*. Love verses, panegyric, translations, Pindarics. In line with much Virgilian commentary, Baker christianizes Virgil's 'Messianic' Fourth Eclogue, remarking coolly that 'Virgil was not so happy as to understand his own verses.' A comparison of Baker's verse with Shipman's (*Carolina*, 1683) will suggest how typical poets treated the same basic body of imagery ever more simply as the Restoration progressed.

William Cleland, *A Collection of Several Poems and Verses*. Besides odes and songs, the volume contains long Hudibrastic poems on Scots affairs of the 1670s and 1680s.

John Dryden, *Alexander's Feast, or The Power of Music*, This second of Dryden's two odes for St Cecilia's Day is unparalleled in its onomatopoeic and rhythmic effects as an ode for music. The passions that music evokes are celebrated in narrative stanzas devoted each to an emotion associated with one of the ancient Greek musical modes.

John Dryden, tr., Virgil, *Works*. A 'Discourse on Epic Poetry' precedes Dryden's translation, the first after 1660 and standard until 1740 for the *Aeneid* and 1753 for the other works, after which it shared its place of honor with the Pitt-Warton translation.

1699

Thomas Brown, *A Collection of Miscellany Poems*. Tom Brown and Edward (Ned) Ward were perhaps the two most prolific hack writers of the Restoration, and Brown kept producing verse till his death in 1704. Aside from translations, mostly of Horace and Martial, he wrote odes, satires, and epigrams, with much occasional verse. The satires aim at usual targets: other writers, women, quacks, the French.

Samuel Garth, *The Dispensary*.* An admirable and influential mock-heroic about feuding doctors.

Wit and Mirth; or Pills to Purge Melancholy. The first publication, edited by Henry Playford, of the most popular and – by the time of Durfey's six-volume edition of 1719–20, with more than 1100 pieces – the fullest song collection in the period.

1700–4 The question of succession was set by the Act of Settlement (1701), which put further limitations on the crown and fixed the succession in the House of Hanover after the deaths of William (which occurred in 1702) and Anne; James II died in 1701. The war declared against the French in 1702 was to last till 1710; from it emerged a new hero, the Earl (later the Duke) of Marlborough, who at Blenheim (1704) achieved the greatest English victory since the fifteenth century.

1700

Sir Richard Blackmore, *A Satire upon Wit*. Blackmore attacks the 'merry sickness of the head' which makes wits, whom he accuses (e.g., Dryden) by name, mock at true learning and religion. In his satire *Chremes*, written at about the same time, he generalizes the same thematic materials in giving an ironic recipe for success.

Samuel Cobb, *Poetae Britannici*. Cobb's history of English poetry to his own time belongs to a subgenre begun for English in the late Restoration. He also attacks rhyme (which he, however, employs) and emphasizes simplicity of style and beauty of content: 'True wit requires no ornaments of skill:/A beauty naked is a beauty still.' These attitudes are conventional too; in them one can see an ideal of stylistic transparency and freedom that prepared the way for the development of visual and sublime effects in early to mid-eighteenth-century verse.

Daniel Defoe, *The Pacificator*. Defoe presents a combat between Wit and Sense, giving a pseudo-military description in heroic couplets of the literary battles of the century's end (Blackmore, Jeremy Collier, Dennis, Dryden, and others).

John Dryden, *Fables Ancient and Modern*. This miscellany presents largely narratives translated, often brilliantly, by Dryden from Chaucer, Ovid, Boccaccio, and Homer. Original poems include 'To My Honoured Kinsman, John Driden of Chesterton'.*

John Hopkins, *Amasia, or The Works of the Muses*. Mostly love poetry, some of which, like 'On a Fly That Flew into a Lady's Eye and There Lay Buried in a Tear,' builds on 'metaphysical' conceits.

John Pomfret, *The Choice*.* An extremely popular poem of rural retirement. Pomfret's other poems include Pindarics 'Upon the Divine Attributes,' 'A Prospect of Death,' and 'On the General Conflagration and Ensuing Judgment'; moral and conventionally amorous verse; and a skeptical poem, *Reason* (1700), arguing 'Let none then here his certain knowledge boast;/'Tis all but probability at most – here too he was thoroughly of his time.

Matthew Prior, *Carmen Seculare for the Year 1700*. Several poets wrote carmina secularia, a Horatian idea carried out by some on Horace's formal model (for instance, Dryden's 'Secular Masque,' performed at the end of Vanbrugh's adaptation of Fletcher's *The Pilgrim*, played in November 1700) and some of other models: Prior's is a panegyric ode to the triumphs, past and anticipated, on William III. Prior does attempt a patriotic solemnity like that of Horace, though, while Dryden inverts Horace to produce a disillusioned retrospect of a vain, violent age.

John Tutchin, *The Foreigners*. A rough satire on William III's court favorites, using the same biblical fiction as *Absalom and Achitophel*.

Samuel Wesley (the elder), *An Epistle to a Friend Concerning Poetry*. The preface includes a denunciation of lewd, fatalistic plays; the poem has advice on particularity, wit, style, method, meter, genre, and even has critical commentary on Chaucer, Spenser, the Eddas, and Taliessen.

1701

Daniel Defoe, *The True-Born Englishman*. Over 1200 lines in pentameter couplets rebuke the xenophobia of William III's enemies, particularly as expressed in Tutchin's *The Foreigners* of the previous year. Defoe mixes demonstration, panegyric, satire, the self-condemning persona, and other devices common to poetry and prose (for his verse rarely benefits much from devices particular to poetry alone) to prove that England has prospered as a melting pot, and that – as the poem asserts at its end – 'Fame of families is all a cheat,/'Tis personal virtue only makes us great.' A popular and controversial poem.

John Philips, *The Splendid Shilling*. An excellent burlesque of Milton on the miseries of being a debtor, the poem first appeared in two verse collections in 1701 before separate publication in 1705. Philips in no way attacks Milton but plays, like his contemporary Garth in *The Dispensary* (1699), on incongruity of style and subject. Here the mock-heroic is justified psychologically by the intense importance that the poverty-stricken speaker assigns his state. His excess, however, is not really the object of satire: the inflated style is a means to geniality. A useful finding list for Miltonic imitations is in R. D. Havens, *The Influence of Milton on English Poetry* (1922).

George Stepney, *Poems*. Undistinguished panegyrics and translations.

1702

Edward Bysshe, *The Art of English Poetry*. This collection of 'rules for making English verses' and of verse excerpts (from Butler, Cowley, Dryden, and many others) on subjects from 'absence' to 'zones,' all followed by a rhyming dictionary, was the most popular instructive florilegium of the period – it went through seven more editions in the next thirty-five years. Such volumes, paralleling Latin florilegia like the contemporaneous *Synopsis communium locorum* (1700; fourth edition, 1727), testify to a respect for English alongside classical poetry, and to a great eagerness to write and recall it.

Mary Southworth Mollineux, *Fruits of Retirement*. The posthumous fruits – Mollineux died in 1695 – are prayers and gently exhortatory religious poems.

Thomas Yalden, *Aesop at Court, or State Fables*. The beast fables are patriotic and in praise of the King but also anti-Whig and anti-ministerial. Of some interest among Yalden's other verse are his 'Hymn to the Morning, in Praise of Light' and 'Hymn to Darkness,' because they carry on the seventeenth-century tradition of panegyric based on debate subjects ('Which is better, day or night?') which one finds in poets like Milton, Cowley, and Norris; and his 'Human Life. Supposed to be Spoken by an Epicure,' an ode to pleasure by a self-incriminating persona. Yalden exhibited middling talents in an 'Ode for St. Cecilia's Day' in 1693, and in numbers of translations.

1703

Mary Chudleigh, *Poems on Several Occasions*. Chudleigh uses Pindarics freely for various purposes, including 'The Song of the Three Children Paraphrased,' with a good bit of scientific reference; she also wrote psalmic paraphrase and satire.

Daniel Defoe, *A Hymn to the Pillory*. Defoe published this ode while he stood in the pillory. In Pindaric stanzas almost entirely rhyming in couplets, the poem satirizes miscarriages of justice, much more through argument than through devices associated with the Pindaric.

Edward Ward, *The Writings*. Ned Ward's writings continued throughout his career as a prolific hack writer from about 1690 to about 1730. A collection of his work appeared 1703–9, with further collections later. He produced a good bit of Tory political verse and social satire involving tours of various parts of London or other prospects (*A Journey to Hell*, 1700), and even a *Don Quixote* in his usual earthy Hudibrastics (1711–12). The episodic and processional, loose modes of poetic organization suited him best, and his prolixity makes one doubt that he revised much.

1704

[William Shippen], *Faction Displayed*. This Drydenian satire attacks the Whig leaders through the fiction of Catiline's conspiracy, as creatures of boundless greed; it elicited several sequels and responses.

The Trial of Skill, or A New Session of the Poets. The session of the poets or advice to Apollo, in which candidates for the bays present their claims, was an exceptionally popular mode, with the prestige of Suckling (*A Session of the Poets*, 1646) and Rochester ('A Session of the Poets' in the 'Antwerp' Rochester of 1680, though most likely not his). Shortly before *The Trial of Skill*, other such poems by Matthew Coppinger, Daniel Kenrick, and Thomas Phillips (?) were published. In this lively version, written in anapaestic quatrains, twenty-four poets come to Apollo's bar before Garth wins the bays.

William Wycherley, *Miscellany Poems*. A much better playwright than poet, even with the advice of the young Alexander Pope, Wycherley wrote amorous and argumentative verse, sometimes Hobbesian ('Upon the Boldness of Cowardice') and cynical ('On Orpheus' Descent to Hell'), sometimes satirical ('A Panegyric on Dullness,' 'A Consolation to Cuckolds,' 'The Bill of Fare'), but often surprisingly conventional for the author of *The Country Wife* and *The Plain Dealer*.

1705–9 Marlborough's prosecution of the war led to further victories at Ramillies (1706) and Oudenarde (1708), but the zest for war kept slackening in England. Union with Scotland, marked by turbulence, took place (1707); the first real law of copyright was enacted in 1709.

1705

Joseph Addison, *The Campaign*. Addison's was the most famous poetic celebration of Marlborough's victories. His ceremonious couplets catch the proper tone, and patriotic Englishmen thrilled to his Marlborough, the avenging angel:

> Calm and serene he drives the furious blast,
> And, pleased the Almighty's orders to perform,
> Rides in the whirlwind and directs the storm.

Other such celebrations include Blackmore's *Advice to the Poets* (1706) and *Instructions to Vander Bank* (1709), both in the advice-to-a-painter tradition; Prior's ode in simplified Spenserian stanzas *Humbly Inscribed to the Queen, on the Glorious Success of Her Majesty's Arms* (1706); and John Philips's *Blenheim* (1705), a heroic narrative like *The Campaign*.

Joseph Addison, *A Letter from Italy to . . . Lord Halifax*. Written in Italy in 1701, this poem in couplets makes common contrasts between past imperial glory and present sunken state, and between the favors of art and nature on the one hand and political tyranny on the other. This standard view of Italy appears in Addison set against paeans to British liberty, as in a great many poems thereafter.

Bernard Mandeville, *The Grumbling Hive, or Knaves Turned Honest*. This fable of the bees who surrender prosperity when they give up luxury for virtue launched one of the most brilliant, profound, and funny works of the century, *The Fable of the Bees* (1714–29). Presumably Mandeville's earlier verse adaptations of fables from La Fontaine (1703) gave him impetus for the Aesopian form of this poem.

1706

William Congreve, *A Pindaric Ode on the Victorious Progress of Her Majesty's Arms*. Congreve's verse is largely panegyric (like this 'regular' Pindaric), amorous, classical translation or paraphrase, and theater pieces; its quality is mediocre.

Sarah Fyge Egerton, *Poems on Several Occasions*.* Emphatic feminism marks this volume, especially 'The Liberty' and 'The Emulation.' There are the love poems typical, as Egerton says, of 'a woman's pen,' but there are also poems of praise and blame, a survey poem, and others defending ideas of Robert Boyle's and John Norris of Bemerton's.

Elijah Fenton, *Cerealia*. Because this tribute to English ale is in Miltonics, it was long attributed to John Philips; it reflects the cheerful patriotism of the period when England basked in the sun of the Sun King's fall at Blenheim.

William Harison, *Woodstock Park*. This topographical poem in heroic couplets is of interest because of its praise, at this date, of Chaucer, whose 'lively images' are paintings in verse and whose 'majesty' requires simple language ('His language only can his thoughts express,/As honest Clytus scorns the Persian dress').

Isaac Watts, *Horae Lyricae*. Watts was the most popular of the Restoration and eighteenth-century poets whose work is no longer read. A dissenting minister, he wrote in verse almost only devotional pieces, about which Dr Johnson has the properly pungent words: 'His devotional poetry is, like that of others, unsatisfactory. . . . It is sufficient for Watts to have done better than others what no man has done well.' *Horae Lyricae* has original poems and adaptations 'sacred to' – in Watts's division – 'devotion and piety,' 'honour, virtue, and friendship,' and 'the memory of the dead.' There were repeated editions – the enlarged one of 1709 has a preface of critical interest on the religious lyric – as there were of Watts's *Hymns and Spiritual Songs* (1707) and his *Divine Songs . . . for the Use of Children* (1715). In 1719 he attempted, like so many others, a metrical version of *The Psalms of David Imitated*.

1707

Sir Charles Sedley, *The Poetical Works*. This collection by the old court wit, who had died in 1701, includes miscellaneous poems by others along with Sedley's own pleasant, craftsmanly, sometimes elegant, now and then poignant songs and lyrics.

1708

Ebenezer Cook, *The Sot-Weed Factor*. Description in tetrameter doggerel of some customs, terms, and entertainments of colonial Maryland, as well as of the narrator's being cheated there.

[Edward Holdsworth], *Muscipula*. Along with the English poetry being written, a considerable body of Latin poetry developed in England, some of it school verse but much of it not; and besides the work of well-known poets like Johnson and Gray stands that of men obscure today, like Vincent Bourne, whose *Poemata* enjoyed five editions (1734–64) and considerable acclaim. *Muscipula*, a mock-heroic in Latin about the invention of the mousetrap, was the most popular single Latin poem, republished often in the original and translated in print by no fewer than eleven people within the first twenty years after it appeared.

187

Holdsworth's poem thus became, along with Addison's Latin poems of 1696 about the battle between the cranes and the pygmies ('Pygmaiogeranomachia') and the bowling green ('Sphaeristerium'), a source for what I have called the 'affectionate mock-heroic' in the early eighteenth century.

William King, *The Art of Cookery*. An entertaining, loose imitation of the *Ars poetica*, prompted by Dr Martin Lister's learned, annotated edition of Apicius on Roman cuisine; the poem is preceded and followed by prose epistles to Lister in the Scriblerian manner, mocking his pedantic labors. King, a versatile and clever miscellaneous writer, published numbers of other poems about food ('The Furmetary,' 'Apple Pie,' 'The Art of Making Puddings,' 'A Panegyric on Beer') and numbers that adapt classical texts, sometimes for burlesque ('The Art of Love,' 'Rufinus, or The Favourite,' 'Orpheus and Eurydice').

John Philips, *Cyder*. Philips returned to Miltonics for this georgic about cider-making, with great success as measured by numbers of editions, separately and in collections, throughout the century.

1709

Alexander Pope, *Pastorals*. These four pastorals, one for each season, appeared in a miscellany collection; Pope's first published verse, they started his first controversy by representing a Virgilian alternative to the six rusticized pastorals of Ambrose Philips printed in the same volume, and separately published in 1710. When Pope reprinted these poems in 1717 he added a short 'Discourse on Pastoral Poetry.'

Matthew Prior, *Poems on Several Occasions*. Among the poems Prior included in this first authorized collection of his verse was 'Henry and Emma', a love story of a baron's daughter and a disguised lord, based on the ballad 'The Nut-Brown Maid' (the text of which Prior printed with his poem); this became one of his most loved pieces. Also alluded to often throughout the century were three slightly rowdy tales after the fashion of La Fontaine's *Contes*, 'Hans Carvel' (first printed 1701), 'The Ladle' (first printed 1704), and 'Paulo Purganti and His Wife.'

Jonathan Swift, *Baucis and Philemon*. Swift rewrote an Ovidian tale as a dazzlingly ingenious satire on dull materialism, with what may be a side glance at christianized typological readings of Ovid.

Anne Finch, Countess of Winchilsea, 'The Spleen.' Lady Winchilsea's Pindaric on 'the English malady' of nervous depression, probably written well before 1709, is the best Cowleyan Pindaric after Cowley's own and Dryden's. Not sublime or ecstatic, 'The Spleen' uses the swift metrical changes and slow tonal changes of the Pindaric, together with its seriousness, to fine effect; and it also has some excellent lines, like those describing the hand that will not 'in fading silks compose/Faintly the inimitable rose' or 'the jonquil [that] o'ercomes the feeble brain:/We faint beneath the aromatic pain.'

1710–14 A new Tory ministry made peace abroad and at home fought within itself – Robert Harley, later Earl of Oxford, and Henry St John, later Viscount Bolingbroke, were the rivals – till the death of Queen Anne in the summer of 1714. George I then became king, and a period of Whig dominance began, an alliance between the crown and large mercantile interests.

1710

John Dunton, *Athenianism, or The New Projects. Athenianism*, a medley collection of – by its own claim – 'six hundred distinct treatises in prose and verse' – suggests Dunton's prolific pen, even if he did not write all the light verse, songs, satires, and panegyrics here. In 1710 he still had two decades of writing ahead of him.

Jonathan Swift, 'A Description of a City Shower.' A splendid crescendo of description in heroic couplets (rather than Swift's usual Hudibrastics) of a downpour increasing till

> Sweepings from butchers' stalls, dung, guts, and blood,
> Drowned puppies, stinking sprats, all drenched in mud,
> Dead cats and turnip tops come tumbling down the flood.

Some critics' attempts to read apocalyptic significance into the poem are over-ingenious. As a descriptive poem of urban life it follows Swift's briefer, lesser 'A Description of the Morning' (1709), also first published in the *Tatler*, and it should be regarded as in the same genre.

1711

Alexander Pope, *An Essay on Criticism.** This masterfully presented synthesis of much early eighteenth-century critical theory, in three parts, is made to cohere by the equilibrating energy of Pope's mind.

Jonathan Swift, *Miscellanies in Prose and Verse*. The verse includes the first, or first authorized publication of some of Swift's best and most characteristic verse, like the two attacks on Vanbrugh ('Vanbrugh's House' and 'The History of Vanbrugh's House,' dated by Swift 1703 and 1708); the wonderfully rambling 'The Humble Petition of Frances Harris' (1700?); the savage attack on John, Lord Cutts, 'The Description of a Salamander' (1705); and the satire on ex-Lord Treasurer Godolphin, 'The Virtues of Sid Hamet the Magician's Rod.'

1712

Sir Richard Blackmore, *Creation*. Seven books in couplets 'to demonstrate the existence of a Divine Eternal Mind' through the physicotheological argument from design.

William Diaper, *Nereides, or Sea Eclogues*. These marine pastoral dialogues have debts to Theocritus and Virgil, but have Tritons instead of shepherds to offer the usual quota of love and moralizing. Better is *Dryades* (1713), a topographical poem of the patriotic, descriptive, sententious sort, but with a good bit of natural history and leisure for the active eye. Diaper's other poems include an adaptation of a Horatian epistle and translations from Claude Quillet and from the Greek poet Oppian (*The Halieutics*, on the nature of fishes).

John Ozell, *et al.*, trs., Boileau, *Works*. The standard translation of the great French model for satires, epistles, preceptive verse, and mock-heroic.

Alexander Pope, *Messiah*. A christianized adaptation of Virgil's 'Messianic' Fourth Eclogue, using passages from Isaiah.

1713

John Gay, *Rural Sports*. Gay's first important poem, this georgic underwent marked revision in 1720 but kept to the same matter of hunting and fishing. These sports at times appear to be innocent, at times cruel, and at times emblematic of the betrayal and rapacity of the urban world.

Thomas Parnell, *An Essay on the Different Styles of Poetry*. Despite its title, this poem does not detail the genres but gives a ride on the Pegasus of wit past the lands of defective verse to those of proper rhetoric.

John Smith, *Poems upon Several Occasions*. A mixture of odes, songs, ballads, epistles, anacreontics, dialogues, and occasional or nonce poems. Smith imitates Butler ('A Rhapsody upon a Lobster'), puts into ballad form the story of Hans Carvel (from Ariosto, Smith claims, though La Fontaine's and Prior's versions were available), adapts two of Horace's odes, and translates Chaucer's 'Miller's Tale.' His variety and cosmopolitanism, and range of tones and styles including the 'metaphysical' (as in the fine song 'I saw Lucinda's bosom bare'), are quite normal for this eclectic period.

Anne Finch, Countess of Winchilsea, *Miscellany Poems on Several Occasions*. In her early fifties when her only collection of verse appeared, Lady Winchilsea resigned herself to the lesser role allotted women: 'How are we fallen,' she asks in 'The Introduction,' 'fallen by mistaken rules?/And education's more than nature's fools.' Her poems do not venture into the ambitious, by deliberate and somewhat embittered self-restriction, except perhaps with the Pindaric 'Upon the Hurricane in November 1703.' The quality of her minor verse – of love and retirement, along with fables and songs – and of some experiments, like 'Fanscomb Barn' (in blank verse), make one wish she had risked more. Her intelligence is clear in her versions of common genres and subgenres: the fable in 'The Young Rat and His Dam,' the session of the poets in 'The Circuit of Apollo,' and the night piece in 'A Nocturnal Reverie.'

1714

Daniel Burgess, *Psalms, Hymns, and Spiritual Songs.* Homely language and a quiet, happy faith mark this large collection from various biblical texts.

John Gay, *The Fan.* A mock-heroic about the divine making of a fan, like Achilles' shield in Homer, to serve in love combats.

John Gay, *The Shepherd's Week.** Rustic pastorals that at once spoof and enjoy the materials of rural life.

Alexander Pope, *The Rape of the Lock.** The five-canto expansion of the version in two cantos, written in 1711 and published in 1712.

Edward Young, *The Force of Religion, or Vanquished Love.* The two books in heroic couplets about the tragic anguish of Lady Jane Grey, full of tears and self-abnegation, draw on an ethos best exploited by the 'she tragedies' of Nicholas Rowe, who was to produce a play on this subject in 1715, of Ambrose Philips, of Edmund Smith, who at his death in 1710 was planning a tragedy about Lady Jane, and of John Banks, whose late seventeenth-century 'she tragedies' still held the stage. This ethos may be particularly associated with the group surrounding Addison; Pope's *Eloisa to Abelard* (1717), which draws on and very much complicates the ethos, was based on a translation of Abelard's text by John Hughes (1713), a contributor to the Addison-Steele periodicals and later a tragedian.

1715–19 The Jacobite Rebellion of 1715, in favor of the would-be James III (the Old Pretender), was put down; leading Tories were impeached or effectively exiled. In 1716 the Whig Parliament passed the Septennial Act, giving themselves and future parliaments a life of seven instead of the previous three years. Tory acts to secure Anglicanism were repealed and dissenters were given new protection.

1715

Sir Samuel Garth, *Claremont.* Despite the prefatory suggestion that this is a topographical poem and the indignant satire on flattery in the opening verse paragraphs, *Claremont* is a panegyric on the Earl of Clare (later Duke of Newcastle) through evocations of a Golden Age and Ovidian narrative. (Garth was then occupied on a joint translation of the *Metamorphoses*, to be published in 1717.)

Alexander Pope, tr., *The Iliad of Homer.* Pope's translation (1715–20) remained the only full one from the 1670s to the 1790s. It gave Homer a dignity and splendor denied him even by Dryden's bumptious version of Book I, and provided rich annotation from scholarly sources so as to illuminate Homer's culture and art. A rival translation published in 1715 by Thomas Tickell, perhaps at the urging of Addison (and perhaps with his help), challenged Pope's at the outset but, like the work of most of Pope's foes, has been remembered only because of its connection with him.

Edmund Spenser, *The Works*, ed. John Hughes. Hughes's edition, prefaced and lengthily annotated, testifies to the increasingly acute historical consciousness of early eighteenth-century readers as well as to the breadth of their tastes. A useful bibliographical aid to the influence of Spenser and his contemporaries is to be found in Earl Wasserman, *Elizabethan Poetry in the Eighteenth Century* (1947).

1716

[Edward Baynard], *Health, . . . Showing How to Keep and Preserve It*. There were repeated editions of this collection of medical advice from a well-known doctor, with its admonitions against drunkenness.

John Gay, *Trivia, or The Art of Walking the Streets of London*. In Gay's burlesque of Virgil's *Georgics*, the rhythms and majesty of nature are replaced by the hazardous haphazardness of urban life. As is common in his work, a variety of perspectives and tones – satiric, celebratory, sympathetic, mock-formal – enriches and complicates the poetic texture. *Trivia* easily exceeds the merit of its predecessors, like Ned Ward's tours, and its successors, like the anonymous *St. Paul's Cathedral* (1750).

Lady Mary Wortley Montagu, *Court Poems*. Lady Mary suffered the piracy here of three of the 'town eclogues' written in 1715–16 with varying degrees of help from Gay and published as a full set of six in 1747. These employ the mode of pastoral dialogue for pointed satire on society foibles; the relation to Gay's *Shepherd's Week* and *Trivia* is obvious. Witty, polished, well-modulated to catch both heroic rhythms and those of speech, these are very good poems of their kind.

[John Thornycroft], *Military and Other Poems upon Several Occasions*. Twenty-five years' worth of odes, pastorals, epistles, (very proficient) ballads and songs, political poems, fables, and translations are collected here. In a lengthy elegy for Queen Mary (died 1694), one can see clearly how typical panegyric imagery was inverted for elegy, for instance in 'The lovely she, thus like a winter's sun,/Should lose her light ere half her race was run.'

1717

Elijah Fenton, *Poems on Several Occasions*. Fenton, best known as one of Pope's helpers with the *Odyssey* and as the editor of Waller (1729), wrote original poems including odes, translations, a Chaucerian imitation (like Pope and Prior before him), and 'An Epistle to Mr. Southerne,' with a versified history of English poetry.

[Giles Jacob], *The Rape of the Smock*. In this loose (in every sense) imitation of Pope's poem, Philemon sees Celia undressing, steals her smock, and trades it back to her for a night together.

George Markland, *Pteryplegia, or The Art of Shooting Flying*. Even this poem, written (one presumes) by a hunter in colloquial, jovial couplets about being a sportsman in shooting birds, manifests some of the ambiguity of feeling about the hunt which one finds in *Cooper's Hill, Windsor Forest,* and *Rural Sports.*

Thomas Parnell, tr., *Homer's Battle of the Frogs and Mice*. Of the four versions of this pseudo-Homeric poem between *The Dispensary* and the *Dunciad* – Samuel Parker's (1700), Parnell's, the younger Samuel Wesley's (1726), and H. Price's (1736) – this is the best and best-known; it is annotated in the Scriblerian manner, suitable for a mock-heroic.

Alexander Pope, *The Works*. The most important new works in this collection were two exercises in pathos, 'Verses to the Memory of an Unfortunate Lady,' a theatrical monologue, and *Eloisa to Abelard*. If one likes this sort of poem, one will like Pope's; eighteenth-century readers certainly did, as indicated, for example, by the at least half-dozen replies written entitled *Abelard to Eloisa*.

Thomas Tickell, *An Epistle from a Lady in England to a Gentleman from Avignon*. The epistle is political satire, like Tickell's similarly popular *An Imitation of the Prophecy of Nereus* (1715), on the enemies of George I. The Jacobite lady begins by bolstering the spirits of her exiled fiancé, telling him that all the women favor the Pretender, but as she goes on to imagine the Papist Stuarts she progressively shifts allegiance to the Hanoverians and ends by urging the exile to return to her and to an England governed by a heaven-appointed race. The *Imitation* and the *Epistle* are politically and poetically shrewd, skillful poems. Most of Tickell's non-satiric ambitious poems, like *Oxford* (1707), *To . . . the Lord Privy Seal on the Prospect of Peace* (1713), and *Kensington Garden* (1722), are in a panegyric mode that only first-rate poets could handle with wit and intelligence; Tickell cannot offer more than dignity and deftness.

1718

Matthew Prior, *Poems on Several Occasions*. For this, Prior's most important publication, he meticulously revised texts and prepared copy. The volume includes the first publications of Prior's two most ambitious poems, *Solomon on the Vanity of the World* and *Alma, or The Progress of the Mind*. The former synthesizes traditional wisdom in heroic couplets, arguing that human knowledge (Book I), pleasure (Book II), and power (Book III) are all vain, as *Ecclesiastes* tells us, and that only in divine knowledge and power can the spirit have pleasure and rest. Too resolutely grave for its own good (despite such lines as 'could they think the new-discovered isle/Pleased to receive a pregnant crocodile?'), *Solomon* still profits enough from a style at once so terse and easy that it remains quite readable, even for those who relish sententiousness less than eighteenth-century readers did. *Alma* is thoroughly delightful: in Hudibrastics, it makes fun of philosophical systems, especially Descartes's and Locke's, as it rambles through the whims and quirks of the mind.

Nicholas Rowe, tr., Lucan, *Pharsalia*. Replaced Thomas May's translation (1627) and remained standard throughout the century.

1719

'Joseph Gay,' *Miscellanies upon Several Subjects*. The unimpressive collection includes
'The Petticoat,' a shortened version of the (also unimpressive) *The Hoop-Petticoat*
(1718), both of them mock-heroics with various debts to *The Rape of the Lock* and
to John Gay's *The Fan* – the pseudonym, shared by John Durant Breval and
Francis Chute, may as Pope suggested be an attempt to capitalize on John Gay's
reputation. The *Miscellanies* also contain 'Ovid in Masquerade,' a burlesque of
Metamorphoses XIII, and dramatic and prose works.

George Sewell, *Poems on Several Occasions*. A short volume of panegyrics, prologues
and epilogues, and translations.

1720–4 From the speculator's crash of 1720 (the South Sea Bubble) and the
deaths of the Earls of Stanhope and Sunderland, who had been leading ministers,
emerged the power of the greatest English politician of the first half of the century,
Sir Robert Walpole. Coarse, cynical, penetrating, and principled more as to ends
than to means, he was master of the Commons, trusted advisor of George I and II,
and undisputed prime minister from the early 1720s to 1742. The beginning of his
ministry was devoted to putting national finances in order and to encouraging
industry.

1720

Nicholas Amhurst, *Poems on Several Occasions*. A medley mostly made up of light
verse, competently written in a variety of forms.

Samuel Croxall, *The Fair Circassian*. A rewriting of the Song of Solomon as a verse
dialogue, several times reprinted with added miscellaneous poems of Croxall's.

John Gay, *Poems on Several Occasions*. Gay revised, sometimes drastically, some
previously published poems, like *Rural Sports, The Fan*, two physicotheological
poems of 1714 ('A Thought on Eternity' and 'A Contemplation on Night'), *The
Shepherd's Week*, and *Trivia* for the first volume of *Poems*. The second volume
included much new material, such as four burlesque eclogues ('The Birth of the
Squire . . . in Imitation of the *Pollio* of Virgil' is the most memorable), 'An Elegy
on a Lap Dog,' and a popular ballad—one of Gay's great talents was ballad-
writing – 'Sweet William's Farewell to Black-Eyed Susan.'

John Hughes, *The Ecstasy*. In this ode, the speaker rises above earth to survey the
ruins of empire, the devastations of war and of natural disaster, and the glories of
the heavens; in transit he meets Newton's soul, a 'pointed flame' that commutes
'daily . . . /In search of knowledge for mankind below.' The ode is of interest for
not only its Newtonian panegyric but also its imitation of one of the odes of the
Polish Jesuit Casimir Sarbiewski, whose Horatian odes (in Latin, published in
the 1620s) were admired, translated, and influential. Hughes, who wrote many
odes, panegyric or musical, adapts the modern classic in exactly the way he
adapted ancients like Horace.

1721

[Giles Jacob], *Human Happiness . . . with Several Other Miscellaneous Poems.* The title
poem, in stodgy heroic couplets, moralizes about honesty and recommends
retirement. Among Jacob's others is a Spenserian fragment, 'The Funeral of
Chloe.'

Bezaleel Morrice, *An Essay upon the Poets.* Parts or all of a number of poems include
general critical precepts and specific comments on the line of English poets:
Morrice has the precepts in his preface and the lists of commendable ancients
and moderns in the heroic couplets of his verse, where he metes out praise and
blame to Milton (in blank verse), Spenser, Shakespeare, Waller, Cowley,
Dryden, Rochester, and Oldham. His earlier *Three Satires* (1719) had shown the
same kind of judicial zeal, in their attack on Pope's Homer for too much
fashionable polish (as against Tickell's translation). Morrice's miscellaneous
work, retirement and love poetry mostly, is to be found in his still earlier
Miscellanies or Amusements in Verse and Prose (1712), a volume that is miscellaneous
but not very amusing.

Jonathan Smedley, *Poems on Several Occasions.* Light verse, including political
ballads and two or three attacks on Swift ('The Ode-Maker,' 'Fixed on a
Church Door').

1722

[Matthew Concanen], *Poems upon Several Occasions.* There are the usual claims that
the poems are juvenilia, this time truthful, and the usual poems to justify the
need for the claims. 'A Letter to a Critic in Vindication of the Modern Poets'
praises a miscellaneous lot – Southerne, Congreve, Eusden, Pope, Swift,
Granville, Young, Ambrose Philips, Steele, Sewell, and Gay – in objecting to a
bias for the old poets. *A Match at Football* is a lamely done mock-heroic in Gay's
manner.

Thomas Parnell, *Poems on Several Occasions.* This posthumous volume – Parnell
died in 1718 – was edited by Pope, the subject of Parnell's reverential 'To Mr.
Pope.' The verse is minor but – elegiac, lyric, narrative, or calmly
reflective – engaging and well-executed. 'A Night Piece on Death' is an early
example of 'graveyard' verse; 'Elysium' sounds the themes of Ovid's *Heroides*
and of 'she tragedies'; and the religious verse, if not inspiring or inspired, rings
true.

[Elizabeth Thomas ('Corinna')], *Miscellany Poems on Several Subjects.* A woman of
dubious character and strong mind, Thomas shows some of the latter in the
epistles, rather less in the odes found in this volume. She endorses feminism both
here and in her 'Verses to Dr. Swift' in *The Metamorphosis of the Town* (1730).

1723

David Mallet, *William and Margaret.* A pathetic ballad of a false lover's penitence over the bereft maiden's grave; considerable popular success.

Allan Ramsay, *The Tea-Table Miscellany*. Volume 1 of five in this collection of songs, especially Scots songs with traditional tunes. There were numerous editions, and imitators like William Thomson's *Orpheus Caledonius* (1726, 1733) and David Herd's *The Ancient and Modern Scots Songs* (1769, 1776). In the same year, 1723, appeared an English equivalent, *A Collection of Old Ballads*, perhaps edited by Ambrose Philips.

1724

Henry Needler, *The Works*. Published six years after Needler's death (at twenty-eight), the volume is of greatest interest for its reflection of contemporary attitudes regarding the importance of commerce ('A Sea Piece,' 1711), physicotheology ('To Sir Richard Blackmore' and the verse in the letter to Mr D., 16 August 1711), and science ('Of the Causes of Dreams').

Allan Ramsay, ed., *The Ever-Green*. A two-volume collection of older Scots poetry which made available much verse written before 1600.

1725–9 Walpole survived the change of Kings at the death of George I (1727) but his concentration of power began to draw increased opposition from a broad-based (Whig, Hanoverian Tory, Jacobite Tory) group of self-styled 'patriots' whose organ was the periodical the *Craftsman*, started in 1726. Frederick, Prince of Wales, and, gradually, the most important literary figures in England joined this opposition.

1725

John Glanvill, *Poems, Consisting of Originals and Translations*. Numerous translations from Latin poets; and forty years' culling of originals, including some eighty-three pages of panegyric poems (in couplets and Pindarics) and love poems and songs of some merit.

Christopher Pitt, tr., *Vida's Art of Poetry*. Vida's *De arte poetica* (1527) was the third of the three such canonical guides, the others being by Horace and Boileau, to be translated in the period. Pitt's, the earliest English translation of the poem, remained standard till the end of the century.

Alexander Pope, tr., *The Odyssey of Homer*. With the substantial help of William Broome and Elijah Fenton, whose eight and four books respectively Pope revised as well, of course, as translating the other twelve books himself, the *Odyssey* appeared in 1725–6. This was the only translation between two dubious ones of the Restoration – Ogilby's (1665) and Hobbes's (1675) – and Cowper's (1791).

Edward Young, *The Universal Passion*.* The first four of the seven satires collected in 1728 as *The Love of Fame*.

1726

John Dyer, 'Grongar Hill'. A charming landscape poem made more charming when Dyer substituted for his first attempt, in Pindarics, another in octosyllabics (actually two versions of this exist). By tossing aside the lumber of sublimity, Dyer gave up its effects for an unpretentious pleasure in walking and moralizing quite different from the grandeur of Thomson's *Winter* the same year. Robert Aubin's *Topographical Poetry in Eighteenth-Century England* (1936) provides detailed finding lists of such poems.

Jonathan Swift, *Cadenus and Vanessa*. This apology in verse to the rejected, bitter Esther Vanhomrigh was probably written for her eyes alone in 1713, the year before her death. Pirated in 1726, it was published by Swift in the *Miscellanies* of 1727. In the poem the exquisite Vanessa (Esther) falls in love with the lukewarm middle-aged Cadenus (Swift; 'cadenus' is an anagram of Latin *decanus* = dean). The placatory function of the poem is obviously individual, but as an exploration of a love at once desirable and deceitful, *Cadenus and Vanessa* is in keeping with a whole flock of earlier eighteenth-century poems, some of them, like *Eloisa to Abelard*, markedly different in tone and style.

James Thomson, *Winter*. The first version of the first poem in what was to become *The Seasons*.* *Summer* appeared in 1727, *Spring* in 1728, *Autumn* with the complete, revised *Seasons* of 1730. *The Seasons* was again significantly revised in 1744 and slightly so for the final version of 1746. These revisions, many of which suggest Thomson's mode of reexploring his subject matter, provide great insight into his method of seeing nature and reading poetry.

1727

Richard Collins, *Nature Displayed*. Explanations of the contexture of the body and sense organs and of the body-soul relationship in the expression of the passions – the poem, in poor pentameter couplets, has its only interest in connection with the history of ideas. These sorts of discussions fascinated eighteenth-century scientists and, in popular form, color the assumptions of much literature.

John Gay, *Fables*. In a century when scores wrote fables, Gay's were deservedly most popular, both these, published five years before his death, and the posthumous *Fables. Volume the Second* of 1738, 'mostly on subjects of a graver and more political turn' (as the 'Advertisement' says). The first set were ostensibly written for a child, the future Duke of Cumberland, and despite their excellence they tend to lack the power and sophistication of Gay's superb, Swiftian fables of 1738.

William Somervile, *Occasional Poems*. Many of the occasions were panegyric, which Somervile handled well; his songs, translations, stanzaic poems, fables, and tales make very pleasant reading.

Jonathan Swift, Alexander Pope, *et al.*, *Miscellanies in Prose and Verse*. Swift's contributions include three 'progress' poems of note: 'Phillis, or The Progress of Love,' in which disaster falls on a runaway heiress; 'The Progress of Beauty,' about the decay of a whore; and 'The Progress of Poetry,' about fat and lean times for a writer.

James Thomson, *A Poem Sacred to the Memory of Sir Isaac Newton*. A superb elegy in blank verse, describing Newton's comprehensive eye, mind, and physico-theological piety. The scientific imagination is to Thomson, as it was to other such writers, not opposed to but like the imagination of poets and prophets, responding to and being responded to by a universe created by divine imagination, idea made substance.

1728

John T. Desaguliers, *The Newtonian System of the World the Best Model of Government*. Himself a scientist, Desaguliers here compares the English Constitution to the integrated Newtonian system, in which solar gravitation (government) corrects and yet gives full play to individual inertial movement (liberty).

Samuel Edwards, *The Copernican System*. A discussion of the system, with tributes to Thomson and Newton, ending with a patriotic finale.

David Mallet, *The Excursion*. Mallet's imaginative prospect poem in two books of blank verse is marked by pictorial effects, 'sublime' descriptions of an earthquake and a volcanic eruption, and a physicotheological survey of the heavens. Mallet and Thomson, then at work on *Summer*, were in frequent correspondence during the writing of *The Excursion*, and the two men encouraged each other in creating grandiose effects. Thomson was in his mid-twenties and Mallet in his early twenties, when extravagance of scene and feeling must have seemed wonderfully enticing.

William Pattison, *Poetical Works*. In the two posthumous volumes from the year after Pattison died, aged twenty-one, are 'A Session of the Cambridge Poets,' Ovidian love epistles, and the common fare of occasional and gallant verse.

Alexander Pope, *The Dunciad*.* The earlier version of the poem in three books. For the *Dunciad Variorum* (1729) Pope added the Scriblerian notes and other apparatus.

Richard Savage, *The Bastard*. Savage's most popular poem is autobiographical and self-celebrating; it deals with the joys and woes of the claimed bastard son of the Countess of Macclesfield.

1729

[James Bramston], *The Art of Politics*.* A clever application of Horace's *Ars poetica* to politics.

Henry Carey, *Poems on Several Occasions*. In this much enlarged third edition (earlier ones in 1713 and 1720), much of the verse is designed with music in mind

198

and is therefore simple, though often slangy, in diction. Carey's output includes satires on Methodism ('The Methodist Parson'), taste ('A Satire on the Luxury and Effeminacy of the Age'), and Ambrose Philips's children's verse ('Namby-Pamby'); there are also, as one often finds along with satire, retirement poems. As a poet – Carey also wrote plays – he was best known for his songs and ballads.

James Ralph, *Miscellaneous Poems*. The volume groups, separately paginated, *Night* (1728), an anticipation of *The Seasons* in blank verse; *Clarinda, or the fair Libertine* (1729), a satire with strong kinship to *The Rape of the Lock* (sylphs and coquette – in this case a seduced coquette); the three books of the short (2000 lines) epic *Zeuma*, in blank verse, about Montezuma (1729); and a blank verse ode, *The Muses' Address to the King* (1728).

Richard Savage, *The Wanderer*. Savage tries for grandeur and pathos – and achieves melodrama and the slightly macabre – in this visionary prospect poem in couplets, with scenes of nature, a moralizing and misery-struck hermit (who dominates three of the five cantos), and allegorical figures.

[James Thomson], *Britannia*. Peace and commerce are praised in this anti-Walpole poem for the sake of rousing young Britons to manliness (avoiding luxury), love of liberty, and, if necessary, arms.

1730–4 Walpole took over the management of foreign as well as domestic policy in 1730, trying to keep various brewing national antipathies from exploding into war. In general his domestic procedures – strikingly like eighteenth-century procedures in science, philosophy, and poetics – were to codify, and thereby often to revise, the understandings of common law into written form, so as enlarge central control over them. Implicit in these procedures is a threat of despotism, and it was to this that the Opposition reacted, handing him in 1733 his first serious defeat over a plan to regulate and improve trade by extending excise taxes and the scope of those who would enforce these taxes.

1730

Stephen Duck, *Poems on Several Subjects*. The best-known of the natural, untutored poets so fussed over in the eighteenth century – those who 'proved' by their example that poetry was the result of a glorious spirit, not acquired polish – Duck was a thresher who came to public notice in 1730 and met with great success and patronage even from the Queen. He also met with mockery, as in 'Arthur Duck's' *The Thresher's Miscellany* (1730), a partly salacious collection imitating the format of Duck's *Poems*. Duck's verse, though often metrically crude or tiresome and highly imitative in phraseology, is rarely contemptible, from his early, naive, autobiographically descriptive 'The Thresher's Labour' on. He avoids affected simplicity or ponderousness, both of which one would expect to have tempted him.

Walter Harte, *An Essay on Satire*. Harte's best-known poem, with discussions of epic satire, the history of satire, and the need for proper satire, takes the *Dunciad* as an ideal; and Harte himself imitates Pope, as in his portrait of a hack writer: 'His pride, a pun; a guinea his reward;/His critic, Gildon; Jemmy Moore, his bard.' Among Harte's earlier poems (1727) are 'An Essay on Painting' (on the rules thereof), and classical adaptations. Forty years later (1767), he published *The Amaranth, or Religious Poems*, in parables, fables, and visions. The 'Advertisement' to 'Religious Melancholy' has a discourse on neologisms in poetry, and – as with several poets of the 1760s – Harte moves to a more Drydenian use of couplets, for instance in 'The Vision of Death,' where he blames Pope's 'overscrupulous regularity.'

John Loyd, *A Satire on the Times*. A denunciation of four allegedly lewd or distasteful modern plays and their audiences.

Joseph Mitchell, *Poems on Several Occasions*. These two extremely various volumes include mock-heroics, biblical paraphrase, odes, love poems, and numbers of sometimes amusing pleas for patronage. 'The Doleful Swains' is in Scots dialect and Mitchell's Latin ode (with English translation) on Buchanan has Scotophiliac comments on poetry. Mitchell's interest in art emerges in his *Three Poetical Epistles to . . . Masters in the Art of Painting* (1731).

Allan Ramsay, *Collection of Thirty Fables*. The fullest collection of Ramsay's shrewd, charming fables in Scots dialect. Ramsay was a prolific poet in many genres, writing both English and Scots, and best in comic or lightly satiric work, where his openness and geniality are great virtues; some of his songs, too, are very agreeable.

James Thomson, *The Seasons*. The first edition of all four poems together.

George Woodward, *Poems on Several Occasions*. Aside from addresses to Chloe, Phoebe, and the rest, the volume contains an ode on the weakness of human reason (a recurrent theme); 'An Evening Slumber,' with novel incantatory effects from repetition and alliteration; 'The Pindaric,' a satire on that form, with its long lines of 'rumbling stuff' interspersed with short ones that 'must in softer accents squeak'; 'A Sonnet Imitated from Spenser,' uncommon for 1730; and 'A Hymn to the Creator' in imitation of Milton.

1731

[James Miller], *Harlequin-Horace, or The Art of Modern Poetry*, The *Ars Poetica* stood on its head to satirize the farcical chaos of fads in modern verse.

Matthew Pilkington, *Poems on Several Occasions*. In a 'session of the poets,' which joins his mediocre pastorals and odes, Pilkington singles out for praise the sublimity and pathos of Pope, as in *Windsor Forest* and *Eloisa*, perhaps as a counterpoise to the rise of Thomson and his fellows.

Alexander Pope, *An Epistle to . . . Burlington*.* The earliest published of Pope's four moral epistles. The others first appeared 1732–5.

Isaac Thompson, *A Collection of Poems*. Minimal talent is shown in the poems but the preface about the pastoral (before Thompson's examples of it) has some interest, as does – for its orthodoxy about the balance between genius and art, poetic fire and the rules, free variety and directed economy of writing – his 'Essay upon the Art of Poetry' (1728).

Henry Travers, *Miscellaneous Poems and Translations*. The original work of this Cambridge poet, besides elegies and epistles, includes a poem on the barrenness of the fens, their natural and political history (including learned notes on icy volcanos and the antiquity of mosquito nets), and Ely Cathedral.

1732

Thomas Chaloner, *The Merriest Poet in Christendom, or Chaloner's Miscellany, Being a Salve for Every Sore*. The salve had a short shelf-life: an unimpressive collection of juvenilia, impromptu light verse, and other trivia.

George Granville, Lord Lansdowne, *Genuine Works in Verse and Prose*. Granville, born 1667, published his first collection of poems in 1712, and the rather elegant, rather empty poems of love and flattery in Volume 1 (Volume 2 contains plays) presumably represent over forty years' work.

William King (of Oxford), *The Toast*. Augmented at various times during the 1730s, this elaborate, obscene satire on some of King's personal enemies – the heroine, forbidden male lovers because of excess, is turned into a hermaphrodite and eventually a eunuch – claims to be a translation by one Peregrine O'Donald of an original rhymed Latin poem by a Scandinavian. King also provided an apparatus, including the Latin poem, annotations, and appendices.

George, Lord Lyttelton, *The Progress of Love*. Four eclogues – 'Uncertainty,' 'Hope,' 'Jealousy,' and 'Possession' – mark the stages of love between Damon and Delia with the usual paraphernalia of pastoral attending them.

John Milton, *Paradise Lost*, ed. Richard Bentley. The great classical scholar amended Milton's text freely and brought derision upon himself; he both exemplified and stimulated the crowd of Miltonic commentators, like Zachary Pearce (1732), Jonathan Richardson father and son (1734), and Thomas Newton (1749), whose important and often reprinted edition drew on a variety of printed and manuscript commentaries.

Jonathan Swift, *The Lady's Dressing Room*. This is the earliest of Swift's group of 'scatological' poems (1732–4). The idealistic Strephon is appalled by the filth and excrement in Celia's private chamber, a theme Swift reworked in 'Strephon and Chloe' and 'Cassinus and Peter.' *A Beautiful Young Nymph Going to Bed* shows a whore stripping herself of the prosthetics that make her seem lovely.

John Whaley, *A Collection of Poems*. A medley of fables, biblical and classical paraphrase, epistles, tales, and so forth, in Hudibrastics, heroic couplets, anapaestic couplets, stanzas, and blank verse. Not all are by Whaley. The most noteworthy poems are two on art, 'An Essay on Painting' and 'The Two

Statues' (about a rough-hewn one that looks better atop a temple than a highly polished one), and 'An Epistle to Mr. Pope' which advises him to give up satire for 'the flowery paths of Pindus' and praise the England of George II and Walpole (to whom there is a panegyric ode).

1733

John Bancks, *Poems on Several Occasions*. Bancks insists that his verse is occasional and amateur, as it is, like inferior Prior, quite pleasant and often somewhat racy. Stephen Duck's vogue was such that in his first volume, *The Weaver's Miscellany* (1730), Bancks had claimed to be a poor Spitalfields weaver - in fact he had been apprenticed to one before becoming a bookseller – but his poems do not read like those of Duck.

Samuel Bowden, *Poetical Essays on Several Occasions*. Two volumes (1733, 1735) of the usual variety, better than run-of-the-mill, include a prospect poem with a rhapsody to trade and commerce ('Antiquities and Curiosities in Wiltshire and Somerset'), an elegy to Newton on the splendor of a world informed by human knowledge and therefore more esthetic because more comprehensibly complex, and 'The Earth: A Philosophic Poem,' which makes an analogy between the earth and man's body. Bowden demonstrates here and in his *Poems on Various Subjects* (1754) a belief in an 'anima mundi' or 'plastic mind,' and a related tendency to multiply analogies.

[James Bramston], *The Man of Taste*. Through an oafish persona, Bramston satirizes everything that passes for modern taste in social behavior, gardening, and dress. A sequel is [Thomas Newcomb's] *The Woman of Taste* (1733), a somewhat better poem, on the model of the *Ars poetica*, with the same cluster of satiric targets. In their belittling the self as socially perceived and contrived, these poets reflect the same ethos that informs serious meditative and introspective verse, with its focus on spiritual self-improvement.

David Mallet, *Of Verbal Criticism*. With Bentley's Milton (1732) as his special butt, Mallet satirizes pedants and commentators on literature.

[Thomas Newcomb], *The Manners of the Age*. These thirteen long satires in heroic couplets are unusual in being pro-Walpole even though they attack the pervasive affectations and corruptions of the age. Newcomb writes capably but produces flat poems because he lacks singleness of theme and discernable order to discipline his comprehensive indictment.

[Alexander Pope], *An Essay on Man*. Pope's attempt to present man within cosmic, social, and individual orders, in four epistles (1733–4) – the fundamentally ethical design of this poem, like the esthetic design of *An Essay on Criticism*, demands not a single system but an equilibrium among various forces. This equilibrium, ratified divinely in the Great Chain of Being (Epistle 1), becomes a non-reductive principle to make the argument of the whole *Essay* coherent.

Alexander Pope, Horatian poems.* From early 1733 to 1738, Pope published imitations of five epistles, four satires, and two odes of Horace's, together with a two-part *Epilogue to the Satires*. The magnificence of his achievement here in appropriating these texts is beyond cavil.

Jonathan Swift, *On Poetry: A Rapsody*. With particularly savage energy, Swift offers 500 lines of sarcastic recipe for succeeding as a poet by flattery, hypocrisy, and pretense. He similarly produced a sample (parodic) amorous poem, 'A Love Song in the Modern Taste' (1733) and treated the subject of 'the heroic style' whimsically and personally in *An Epistle to a Lady Who Desired the Author to Make Verses on Her* (1733; title page dated 1734).

1734

Henry Baker, *The Universe: A Poem Intended to Restrain the Pride of Man*. A physicotheological and astrotheological poem in heroic couplets, with similarities to Pope's *An Essay on Man* in wording, though Baker's is the far more religious poem. Reprinted several times in the course of the century, *The Universe* enjoyed more popularity than Baker's two volumes of *Original Poems* (1725–6), mostly short conventional forms (anacreontics, lyrics, meditations) about conventional subjects.

Mary Barber, *Poems on Several Occasions*. Clever, amusing occasional verse, written in part to instruct Barber's son.

Isaac Hawkins Browne, *On Design and Beauty*. An epistle of more critical than poetic interest, about the relation of natural and artistic order, the harmonious interdependence of the parts of a work of art, and similar topics.

1735–9 To charges of corruption, absolutism, and ruthlessness were added those of cowardice for Walpole's reluctance to prosecute war; he was forced into the War of Jenkins' Ear, based on national pride and economic advantage over the Spanish, in 1738. The long fight for dominion effectively continued, despite interruptions, till 1763, with the leading voice for high-minded conquest being that of the magnificent orator but erratic politician William Pitt. During these years another sort of orotund high-mindedness also gained a following: the evangelistic Methodism of John Wesley and George Whitefield.

1735

Henry Brooke, *Universal Beauty*. Brooke's debts are to *An Essay on Man* and *The Seasons* in the six books of this exhaustive, windy, exclamatory survey of nature, physical, divine, and human. Scientific explanations in the text (written in Latinate heroic couplets, thereby joining Pope with Thomson in style) and the annotations argue physicotheology; but Brooke also embraces allegory, as in Book 5, where the change from tadpole to frog is taken not only as a providential fact but also – according to the note to verse 243 – as 'representative of the present state of man and his future hopes.' We have here a double pattern

203

common in much poetry of the period, in which natural facts scientifically explained through reason point to the greater reason of God's design, and in which the same facts taken as emblems to stimulate moral reflection point us to truths about everyday life.

Hildebrand Jacob, *Works*. Jacob wrote a good bit of reasonably able light verse, some of which was more salacious than was usual in 1735. Besides criticism in prose the volume also contains a poem on human pride, 'Bedlam.' Later in 1735 Jacob published part of an epic, *Brutus, the Trojan Founder of the British Empire*, a theme on which Pope also had epic designs.

Alexander Pope, *An Epistle to Dr. Arbuthnot.* Pope's apologia for himself as a satirist. He also published the second of his revisions of two satires by Donne, the first having appeared in 1733.

Richard Savage, *The Progress of a Divine*. Savage's best verse satire, a violent, frank, at times oversensational portrait of a priest out for preferment.

William Somervile, *The Chase*. A didactic descriptive poem in four books on hunting; the shorter (under 300 lines) *Field Sports* (1742) is a descriptive sequel on hawking. Somervile sounds Thomsonian themes, for example in his closing request that he be given 'to know wise Nature's hidden depths' and in his discussions of animal instinct (Book 2). He follows Denham, Dryden, and Pope in, for example, his symbolic treatment of savage hounds who 'with one mutual cry insult the fallen!/Emblem too just of man's degenerate race,' his parallel between the hunt and political oppression (Book 2), and his pathetic treatment of the stag (Book 3). Like all these predecessors, too, he engages in historical digressions and considers his subject worthy of a high style, even of passionate sublimity at times.

James Thomson, *Liberty*. A long, rather dull blank-verse poem (1735–6) that tries to 'trace Liberty from the first ages down to her excellent establishment in Great Britain.' This politicized, anti-Walpole history turns on the analogy between Britain and Rome, once great and now ruined.

1736

John Armstrong, *The Economy of Love*. A rather startlingly frank discussion in Latinate verse of such subjects as nocturnal emission, menstruation, masturbation, and pubic hair, among others. Later editions were expurgated by Armstrong himself, as the rashness of his twenty-fifth year became clearer to the physician nearing sixty.

Isaac Hawkins Browne, *A Pipe of Tobacco*. Six masterful parodies of Cibber, Ambrose Philips, Thomson, Young, Pope, and Swift as they would write about a pipe.

Bevil Higgons, *A Poem on Nature in Imitation of Lucretius*. Physicotheology in 330 lines of heroic couplets, fathoms below Lucretius.

Jonathan Swift, 'The Legion Club.' Perhaps Swift's most violent poem, this invective, naming names, treats the Irish House of Commons as a madhouse.

1737

Albania. An enthusiastic blank-verse tribute to Albania, the Genius of Scotland, with the praise of liberty and the proudly invidious contrasts with other lands – no 'ruthless panthers' or 'tarantula [that] exerts its charm' in Caledonia! – that are staple in the patriotic verse of the period.

James Barber, *Poetical Works*. Four satires, mock-heroic and topical.

Richard Glover, *Leonidas*. This twelve-book epic in laconic blank verse about the battle of Thermopylae was much praised in its own time for its noble sentiments about bravery and freedom – implicit slurs at Walpole's pacific policies – but is too prosy and sententious, with too much plastered-on emotion, to be read with pleasure.

Matthew Green, *The Spleen*. A clever poem, like all of those in Green's small corpus, which was published posthumously in the year of Green's death, *The Spleen* is his only long poem (over 800 lines) and the only one anybody remembers. It is about avoiding and curbing one's irritable gloom through exercising the body and keeping the mind tranquil, and thus has affinities with the poems of retirement and of achieving happiness which were current in the period.

Jabez Hughes, *Miscellanies in Verse and Prose*. Most of the verse in this volume, published six years after Hughes's death, is translation, most interestingly Cornelius Severus's (?) first-century 'sublime' poem *Aetna*, which tries to offer scientific explanations for spectacularly described volcanic eruptions – the poem is obviously a predecessor of Thomson's and Mallet's work of the 1720s and 1730s. Hughes's volume also includes panegyrics, Pindarics, and songs.

William Shenstone, *Poems upon Various Occasions*. This earliest volume of Shenstone's includes the earliest version of his best-known poem 'The Schoolmistress,' much expanded in 1742 and again in 1748. A gently amusing, sentimental account of a country school, the poem uses Spenser's style for both comic distance and naive tenderness.

Benjamin Stillingfleet, 'An Essay on Conversation.' A well-written preceptive epistle, relating manners to human needs and human nature in a harmony of paradoxical demands; why one *must* suffer follies (if not fools) gladly.

John and Charles Wesley, *A Collection of Psalms and Hymns* (American edition; English edition, 1741). Wesleyan hymns spread in popularity with repeated publications and enlargements of this volume and the Wesleys' others, like *Hymns and Sacred Poems* (1739): they were responsible for some thousands of hymns.

1738

[Robert Dodsley], *The Art of Preaching*. A close, earnest, and capable though not witty adaptation of Horace's *Ars poetica* for the pulpit.

Samuel Johnson, *London*. Johnson imitates Juvenal's Third Satire, in which a

205

speaker flees the corrupt, lengthily indicted town for the country; and directs his indictment of the age, as expectable in the late 1730s, against Walpole.

1739

Daniel Bellamy (the elder and the younger), *Miscellanies in Prose and Verse*. The verse, in Volume 1, principally consists of two quite competent, amusing mock-heroics, one a markedly elaborated translation of Holdsworth's *Muscipula* (1709) and the other, 'Backgammon, or The Battle of the Friars.'

Samuel Boyse, *Deity*. Despite Boyse's uneven, disconnected work, several eighteenth-century editions appeared of this group of eleven rhymed poems, each of about fifty or sixty lines on divine attributes: eternity, unity, spirituality, omnipresence, immutability, omnipotence, wisdom, providence, goodness, rectitude, and glory.

Moses Browne, *Poems on Various Subjects*. The more usual range of styles, tones, and genres are supplemented by 'piscatory eclogues' (preceded by a defense of the genre and annotated for references to natural history), a physicotheological 'Essay on the Universe,' and Welsh and Irish dialect poems; an interesting collection.

Richard Glover, *London, or The Progress of Commerce*. Descriptive and allegorical blank-verse tribute to commerce and to the British arms that visit 'the hideous waste of ruthless war' on those – 'the servile pupils of tyrannic Rome' – who try to interfere with English trade.

[Richard Powney], *The Stag Chase in Windsor Forest*. The most elaborate working out of the kind of hunting sequence initiated in *Cooper's Hill*: here a whole series of emblematic moralizations of the hunt are used to praise Frederick, Prince of Wales, with the hunters representing British valor (to be used to fight the French) and the stag a pathetic victim of political faithlessness. As in Denham, Dryden, Pope, Gay, and Somervile, the point of view is multiple rather than simple; but here implied political rhetoric – Frederick was anti-Walpole, valorous warriors suggest the mean-spiritedness of Walpole's peace policy, and political faithlessness may accuse a 'court party' such as Walpole's – reconciles the multiplicity.

Elizabeth Rowe, *Miscellaneous Works in Prose and Verse*. This posthumous collection two years after the death of a poet who began publishing in 1696 mostly contains lyrics and religious poetry, but also adaptations and translations from the Italian and, surprisingly, an imitation of Michael Drayton. Rowe's poetry shows especially clearly the tendency of early eighteenth-century serious verse to forego interesting imagery and modifiers in favor of those that reinforce or integrally qualify common nouns: from two of her hymns, for example, one gets 'crystal streams,' 'flowery fields,' 'blessed retirement,' 'rosy dawn,' and 'gloomy night.'

Jonathan Swift, *Verses on the Death of Dr. Swift*. Finished in 1732, this partially boastful, partially ironic elegy for Swift presents the world as soon forgetting him and even his eulogist as distorting his achievements. The world around Swift and even, more lightly, he himself appear dominated by self-interest. The tone of the poem is so complex as to have led to a remarkable variety of interpretations.

1740–4 Walpole fell in 1742 and the erstwhile 'Patriots' began a scramble for power that disillusioned many of their naive adherents. Eventually a stable, 'broad bottom' ministry took over, calming some domestic factionalism if not the animosity long felt by Englishmen toward their Hanoverian King with his German mistresses and electorate. Even his military victory at Dettingen (1743) was soured by reports of his partiality for his Hanoverian troops. With Walpole's departure, though, the Opposition lost its focus, and intellectuals, including poets, turned from politics.

1740

[Sarah Dixon], *Poems on Several Occasions*. In these competent retirement and love poems, with some religious verse, Dixon shows a range of classical allusion that one might not expect from a female poet denied proper education, but that in fact is not surprising in eighteenth-century women's verse. She is capable too of mordant and striking lines, as in the beginning of 'The Returned Heart': 'It must be mine! no other heart could prove/Constant so long, yet so ill-used in love.'

John Dyer, *The Ruins of Rome*. Dyer reflects on imperial decline and fall as he walks through the ruins; a favored subject among English moralists with classical educations, who could enjoy being sententious, elegiac, and anti-papist in viewing the collapse of the empire whose dominance they expected their nation to emulate.

Richard Glover, *Admiral Hosier's Ghost*. As England engaged with Spain in war, Glover inflamed spirits with this pathetic ballad about the death of Hosier in 1727 at the hands of the Spanish.

[James Miller], *Are These Things So?* A widely-read accusation of wickedness in Walpole's government; many responses were elicited.

Christopher Pitt, tr., Virgil, *The Aeneid*. Pitt had earlier (1728, 1736) published parts of his slightly stiff translation; the now complete version was to share with Dryden's the honor of being considered standard. After 1753, Pitt's *Aeneid* appeared with Joseph Warton's translations of Virgil's other poems, and Warton's notes on the whole Virgilian corpus.

William Somervile, *Hobbinol, or The Rural Games*. After a short preface on burlesque come three cantos of burlesque Miltonics about the tragedy of Hobbinol, arrested for breach of promise by the mother of his two children, Mopsa, just as his triumph in brawling and his sweetheart Ganderetta's in racing at May Day games seem to have brought these two lovers together. This moderately amusing poem may owe something to Butler's descriptions of the rustics who battle Hudibras; along these lines, Somervile has a short poem in both Butler's and Milton's styles, called 'Hudibras and Milton Reconciled.'

Horace Walpole, *An Epistle from Florence*, The epistle, not printed till 1748 in Dodsley's *Collection*, attacks dry book-learning and (especially popish) oppression. The praise of liberty – a bit odd in 1740 from the son of Sir Robert Walpole, whose enemies so often evoked that ideal – sounds a familiar note in the xenophobic verse of the 1730s and 1740s.

1741

[Thomas Catesby, Lord Paget], *Miscellanies in Prose and Verse*. Lord Paget's verse, able and commonsensical, is that of a squire rather than a literary man, and harks back to a tough cynicism more of the Restoration – Paget was born in 1689 – than the 1740s. 'An Essay on Human Life' in heroic couplets and other poems in Hudibrastics aim to show 'that Fortune rules the roost,/And favours fools and knaves the most.'

1742

William Collins, *Persian Eclogues*. These four love poems in couplets, written when Collins (born 1721) was seventeen or eighteen, make a thin attempt at the exotic wildness of Oriental color. Each corresponds to a different time of day and a different mood, as do Pope's pastorals, and each mixes passion and subjective moralizing in the established pastoral manner.

Thomas Cooke, *Original Poems*. After this collection of some twenty years' worth of verse, Cooke's poetical efforts went largely into (undistinguished) odes (1749–55) and the four epistles of *Immortality Revealed* (1745). This volume prints some nineteen odes among its medley of generic verse, but its most intriguing piece is the revised version (1729) of *The Battle of the Poets* (first version, 1725), revised so as to revenge Cooke's inclusion in the *Dunciad*. Pope and Swift are made to battle with–and lose to–Tickell, Theobald, Philips, and Dennis.

Alexander Pope, *The New Dunciad*. Book IV of the revised work.

Edward Young, *The Complaint, or Night Thoughts on Life, Death, and Immortality*.* Young began publishing his blank-verse poem (1742–5).

1743

Robert Blair, *The Grave*.* Moral, mortal, evangelical meditations in dramatic blank verse.

Philip Francis, tr., *The Odes, Epodes, and Carmen Saeculare of Horace*. The standard translation for the rest of the century, an annotated bilingual version completed with the Satires and the Epistles in 1746.

[James Hammond], *Love Elegies, Written in the Year 1732.* Hammond's elegies were written when he was young (twenty-two) and published when he was dead; despite their several times being reprinted, Dr Johnson hits the mark: 'He produces nothing but frigid pedantry. It would be hard to find in all his productions three stanzas that deserve to be remembered.'

Alexander Pope, *The Dunciad in Four Books.**

1744

Mark Akenside, *The Pleasures of Imagination.* The first version – later extensively changed – of a long didactic poem in blank verse about the imagination and its operative principles as works of nature and art are perceived. Akenside discusses greatness, novelty, and beauty as they affect the mind; connections between the esthetic and the moral; the passions; taste; and ridicule. The texture of the poem itself is varied by description and allegory, a political excursion in Book 2 (in line with Akenside's long-standing, obligatory – for an up-to-date poet – opposition to Walpole), and paeans to divine order. In the revision, incomplete when Akenside died in 1770, he responds to new tastes in style (simpler, more archaic), politics (more Tory), philosophy (more skeptical about human reason), and criticism (changed classifications of esthetic categories, interest in original genius); the new version also pays more attention to concrete detail.

John Armstrong, *The Art of Preserving Health.* This frequently reprinted preceptive poem adapts the instructive georgic mode to Air, Diet, Exercise, and the Passions. Armstrong's two best-known later poems are both verse epistles, also instructive in their own way, on subjects much in vogue near mid-century, *Of Benevolence* (1751) and *Taste* (1753) – the latter is the more interesting.

Jane Hughes Brereton, *Poems on Several Occasions.* This posthumous collection – Brereton died in 1740 – contains pleasant, unimpressive verse. In 'The Dream,' an imitation of part of Chaucer's *House of Fame,* she apologizes for her poetic incapacity as a woman but then proceeds not only to imitate Chaucer but also to indicate some knowledge of astronomy, mythology, classical history, and Boethius's work.

William Collins, 'A Song from Shakespeare's *Cymbeline.*' Published with Collins's second, revised edition of *Verses . . . to Sir Thomas Hanmer,* Shakespeare's editor (1743). The *Verses* praise Shakespeare with historical comparisons (the classics, Shakespeare's contemporaries, the French) and imagined tableaux from the plays. The 'Song' then imitates a Shakespearean lyric, the dirge for Imogen, with the pictorial imagination, the natural setting, and the appeal to the passions that Collins has eulogized in the *Verses.*

Edward Moore, *Fables for the Female Sex.* Each fable in this exceptionally popular collection begins by establishing an occasion – the hasty marriage of an adolescent, the negligent dowdiness of a woman who has secured a husband – to which an ensuing fable is apposite. Since most of Moore's other poetry is light, complimentary, occasional verse, the fables channeled what was obviously a temperamental preference for ease and charm into a more lasting form.

Joseph Warton, *The Enthusiast, or The Lover of Nature*. The lover of nature writes blank verse, praises nature above art, idealizes a primitive Golden Age, idolizes Shakespeare, and spurns 'the far-fetched cates of luxury' – *The Enthusiast* is a *locus classicus* for this collection of attitudes. Warton's having written a well-done Popean satire, 'Fashion,' at about the same time suggests the affinity between pastoral and retirement poetry (of which *The Enthusiast* is plainly a variant) and the 'times' satire of the 1730s and later, where social values are unthinkingly modish and corruptible.

Paul Whitehead, *The Gymnasiad*. This Scriblerian presentation of a boxing match followed several other satires of Whitehead's on the model of Pope's: *The State Dunces* (1733), *Manners* (1739), and *Honour* (1747) all share Pope's political views, his aphoristic couplets, and his presentation of himself as proud, honest, and independent. They do not share Pope's skill but they are adept.

1745–9 The Young Pretender, Bonnie Prince Charlie (the would-be Charles III), took advantage of troop diversion for foreign wars to launch an invasion of England in 1745. He came close to London but he and his Scots army were driven back and eventually demolished by forces under the Duke of Cumberland – 'Butcher' Cumberland, as his remorselessness led him to be dubbed – at Culloden in 1746. Pitt joined the ministry and won great praise for his lack of venality in office. In 1748 came peace or, rather, effective truce in Europe. The English were then engaged in colonial wars in India, successfully so after command was given to Robert, Lord Clive.

1745

Mark Akenside, *Odes on Various Subjects*. After *The Pleasures of Imagination*, Akenside's poetry was almost entirely lyrical, including odes of the 1740s and 1750s, a fine *Hymn to the Naiads* (written 1747), and other hymns and inscriptions. His political interests appear in several odes, especially 'To Curio,' revised from his indignant attack in couplets on his erstwhile 'Patriot' comrade William Pulteney, Earl of Bath, *An Epistle to Curio* (1744), but also in 'On Leaving Holland,' *To the . . . Earl of Huntingdon* (1748), and the spirited *To the Country Gentlemen of England* (1758).

John Brown, *An Essay on Satire*. Prompted by Pope's death, Brown tries to provide a history of satire, rules for writing it, and purposes it serves; he produced a well-written preceptive poem, full of orthodoxy on its subject.

William Meston, *Poetical Works*. This collection is listed here since the earliest extant edition, that of 1767, claims to be the sixth; Meston died in 1745. His *Works* include the anti-Presbyterian *The Knight* (1723) in the manner of

Hudibras; the moral and political *Old Mother Grim's Tales* (1737); and some Latin and some Jacobite poems.

Samuel Say, *Poems on Several Occasions*. A posthumous collection – Say died in 1743 – including some love poetry of about 1701 together with moral verse, biblical paraphrases, and classical translations, none of which is so interesting as the two long prose essays on metrics.

William Thompson, *Sickness*. This highly allusory, sometimes allegorical poem, with debts to Spenser and Milton, depicts Thompson's bout with smallpox and his deep religious feelings as a result. His only other noteworthy poem is *A Hymn to May* (1740), a Spenserian imitation of sorts in the seven-line stanza (ababccc) of Phineas Fletcher's *The Purple Island* (1633). The *Hymn*, about 500 lines long, is in the rapturous descriptive vein, with panegyric digressions and mythological coloring.

John Whaley, *A Collection of Original Poems and Translations*. This potpourri includes work by others, such as Peter Layng's 'To Alexander Pope, Esq., On His Essay of [sic] Man' (urging a Christian continuation of that poem) and 'Abelard to Heloisa, by a Lady.' Whaley contributes a 'Rhapsody to Milton,' a praise of Sir Robert Walpole's estate at Houghton, and a poem to Vacuna, the goddess of indolence.

1746

Thomas Blacklock, *Poems on Several Occasions*. The first publication of the blind Scots poet, a competent minor writer, includes odes, elegies, and classical and biblical imitations and paraphrases.

William Collins, *Odes on Several Descriptive and Allegoric Subjects*.* Twelve consecutive odes on poetry and patriotism.

Aaron Hill, *Free Thoughts upon Faith, or The Religion of Reason*. Hill argues in exceptionally tough, dense blank verse on the roles of faith and reason in religion, insisting on the weakness of reason and dogma.

J. Phelps, *The Human Barometer, or Living Weather-Glass*. Phelps deals with that central eighteenth-century concern, the relations among body, soul, and physical environment (especially the climate). He connects health and virtue, offers medical details, and discusses psychosomatic disorders.

[James Ruffhead], *The Passions of Man*. The poem is an offshoot of *An Essay on Man*, with strong emphasis on benevolence and almost none on Christianity.

Tobias Smollett, *Advice*. This and its companion in raging satire, *Reproof* (1747), use the Horatian mode of dialogue between 'Poet' and 'Friend' which Pope developed in the 1730s: Friend prudently or complacently tries to soften Poet's attack, while Poet proves his satiric case by citing multiple examples of vice and refusing to grant facile praise. These indictments and the bitter ode 'The Tears of Scotland' (after the carnage at Culloden) are Smollett's earliest published work.

Joseph Warton, *Odes on Various Subjects*. Pictorial odes filled with personification, the collaboration of natural scenes and allegorical imagination.

1747

Thomas Gilbert, *Poems on Several Occasions*. Heavily in debt to Pope, Gilbert is best in his political verse of the 1730s, reprinted here with some songs, epistles, and 'Wandering Thoughts on the State of Man.' 'A Satire' has a defense of naming culprits instead of masking them with pseudonyms or keeping only to type characters – this was an ethical and tactical question debated throughout the period.

Thomas Gray, *Ode on a Distant Prospect of Eton College.** The first of Gray's English poems to be printed, probably written in 1742, like 'Ode on the Spring' (published anonymously in Dodsley's *Collection*, 1748), 'Sonnet on the Death of Mr. Richard West' (first published 1775), and 'Ode to Adversity' (first published 1753). In 1747, Gray wrote the last of these early odes, 'On the Death of a Favourite Cat,' published by Dodsley in 1748. This burlesque elegy is the best of many mock-elegies written for animals – and many real elegies written for them – both before and after mid-century. Three of the other poems, like the 'Ode on the Death of a Favourite Cat,' turn on the difference between an unthinking response and a deeper one. The unthinking boys of Eton enjoy the illusory safety of youth, unlike the pensive speaker. West's mourner pushes aside, by his use of stale poetic diction, the sun and birds insensible to his deep personal loss. And the poet's stock moralizing on spring makes the sportive insects turn to pity him, 'a solitary fly' whose 'sun is set [and whose] spring is gone' while they, the insects, seize the chance to frolic in May. The thrust of each of these poems is different; and the 'Ode to Adversity' treats the theme in still another way, by asking for disillusionment through pain so that the poet can be a better man.

[Charlotte Ramsay Lennox], *Poems on Several Occasions*. Lennox is best when knowingly tongue-in-cheek, as in 'The Art of Coquetry,' but her pastorals are sometimes unintentionally funny, as when she lets sensibility flower in a biblical garden: 'A Pastoral from the Song of Solomon' indulges in the romantic ('on that lovely face/Let me with fond ecstatic rapture gaze') and the melodramatic (the blood runs freezing to my panting heart').

George, Lord Lyttelton, *To the Memory of a Lady Lately Deceased, a Monody*. This lament for Lady Lyttelton struck his contemporaries as harmonious, tender, and sincere, suitably personal and suitably adorned with pastoral and mythological allusion to give it dignity; an admired and imitated piece of work.

David Mallet, *Amyntor and Theodora, or The Hermit*. Blank-verse narrative of the Hebrides: lovers reunited, long-lost father found in three cantos.

William Mason, *Musaeus: A Monody to the Memory of Mr. Pope, in Imitation of Milton's Lycidas*. Pope's mourners include Chaucer, speaking what purports to be Middle English; Spenser in the stanzas of *The Shepheardes Calendar* (about Pope's pastorals) and *The Faerie Queene*; and Milton, in blank verse.

Josiah Relph, *A Miscellany of Poems*. Published four years after Relph's death, this volume is noteworthy for its pastorals and classical imitations in Cumberland dialect; those who like Keats may be interested in one comic dialect poem, 'St. Agnes' Fast, or The Amorous Maiden.' Other poems are in more usual literary English.

Thomas Warton, *The Pleasures of Melancholy*. The nineteen-year-old poet's raptures, in Thomsonian blank verse (with inspiration from *Il Penseroso*), over the appropriate works of art (Spenser, Shakespeare, Otway) and nature, and the ruins or Gothic vaults that combine both.

1748

Adollizing. An allegedly true narrative about a young man's sexual satisfaction with a nubile doll on which he successively fixes heads resembling the reigning beauties of the town. This somewhat scabrous tale treats a theme, the relationship between love and the lover's fantasies, that recurs in verse as well as in such contemporary works as *Clarissa* and *Tom Jones* (1748, 1749).

Robert Dodsley, ed., *A Collection of Poems by Several Hands*. The most important poetic miscellany of the century, Dodsley's appeared first in three volumes, then (1749, 1755) in four, and finally (1758 and, with revisions, thereafter) in six. Others, especially George Pearch, extended the collection. Dodsley's volumes kept readers up to date, especially with the shorter pieces of a wide range of poets newly prominent in the 1740s. Some of Gray's earlier odes, and verse by Fawkes, Cambridge, Grainger, Jago, and the Wartons first appeared here. In general, the number of miscellanies and editions of miscellanies suggests how central they were during the whole period, 1660–1780, in the spread of different kinds of verse; see Arthur E. Case, *A Bibliography of English Poetical Miscellanies, 1521–1750* (1935).

William Hamilton (of Bangour), *Poems on Several Occasions*. Hamilton's best-known work is the Scots ballad 'The Braes of Yarrow'; his other poems include Horatian and other classical imitations, odes, and miscellaneous shorter verse (mostly epistles, lyrics, and epitaphs).

James Thomson, *The Castle of Indolence*. A Spenserian narrative, brilliantly successful in some parts (the amusing and descriptive) and wearisomely preachy in others, about men set free by the Knight of Arts and Industry from the Castle of Indolence, where they lounge in self-indulgent, luxurious ease. Thomson sometimes takes imitation to the edge of deliberate burlesque, genially playing with Spenser's style in a way perfectly suited to the sensibility, at once moral and comfortably nostalgic, that informs this poem about progress and modernity. As becomes progressively less true in the eighteenth century, poetic excellence here ebbs and rises together with complexity of reaction. (By contrast, a ballad is likely to try to establish esthetic merit on simple intensity of reaction.)

Thomas Warton (the elder), *Poems on Several Occasions*. In this posthumous

213

volume – Warton died in 1745 – the poet's sons added their own material to their father's, so that runic materials and the like lie next to moral epistles and satires in the manner of Edward Young. Except for love poetry, which is lacking, the volume has the usual variety of styles and mixture of original, imitated, and translated or paraphrased verse – it is just updated by filial interference.

1749

William Collins, *Ode Occasioned by the Death of Mr. Thomson*. This lovely, simple tribute in quatrains to Thomson, who died in 1748, is built on the double movement of the darkening day and the speaker as he glides down the Thames in a boat. This *Ode* was possibly Collins's last completed poem; his 'Ode to a Friend' may have been completed in 1750 but remained unpublished till 1788, when it appeared as 'An Ode on the Popular Superstitions of the Highlands of Scotland, Considered as the Subject of Poetry.' The 'sublime' evocation of Scotland and the musical variety of the poem make this ode one of Collins' most striking.

Samuel Johnson, *The Vanity of Human Wishes*.* Elegiac imitation, with Christian coloring, of Juvenal's Tenth Satire.

Henry Jones, *Poems on Several Occasions*. This bricklayer-turned-poet wrote literate, refined poems in celebratory modes and that of *An Essay on Man*. 'Philosophy' contains a panegyric of science; 'Rath-Farnham' preaches the Great Chain of Being; and 'An Essay on the Weakness of Human Knowledge and the Uncertainty of Mortal Life' and 'On the Vain Pursuits and Imperfect Enjoyments of Human Life' make one think of both Pope and Johnson.

Thomas Warton (the younger), *The Triumph of Isis*. A satire on Cambridge ('Still let her senates titled slaves revere,/Nor dare to know the patriot from the peer') as a loyal Oxford response to William Mason's *Isis*, which accused Oxford of seditious Jacobitism (1749).

Gilbert West, tr., *The Odes of Pindar*. A powerful, though slightly too wordy and artificial translation of a poet whose works West's father Richard had edited (1697). Pindar had remained untranslated in England till Ambrose Philips (1748) and West published volumes devoted to him; eight other translations of single poems or groups of poems appeared 1750–1800. Given the popularity of the Cowleyan Pindaric in the Restoration, these facts suggest the linkage, clear in Gray, between the 'primitive' in the real (rather than the Cowleyan) Pindar and in the Welsh, Scandinavian, and medieval poets whose works had begun fascinating the poets of mid-century.

1750–4 Domestic matters dominated these years: the adoption of the Gregorian Calendar in England, with the 'loss' of eleven days (1752); a controversial Act regulating marriages (1753); and another, so controversial that it had to be repealed in the same year, permitting Jews to become naturalized citizens (1753).

The death of Frederick, Prince of Wales, removed the leader of opposition to George II (1751), but after the death of Henry Pelham (1754) the ministry became somewhat less stable. New rumblings began abroad, this time with France in the New World.

1750

Christopher Smart, *On the Eternity of the Supreme Being.* Smart won the Seatonian Prize in 1750, 1751, 1752, 1753, and 1755 with five blank-verse poems on divine attributes, eternity, immensity, omniscience, power, and goodness. His repeated winning suggests the competence of his verse, but these essays lack the distinction and individuality that mark his later religious poetry.

Isaac Thompson, *Poetic Essays on Nature, Men, and Morals.* Includes a specimen of an 'Essay on Providence and Virtue,' which lacks esthetic and moral order.

Robert Upton, *Poems on Several Occasions.* Mainly rural retirement and amorous pastoral verse, like 'On Retirement: A Miltonic Essay.'

1751

Richard Owen Cambridge, *The Scribleriad.* This mock-epic was the first poem in English published by Cambridge during the 1750s, his period of poetical activity in a life that lasted till 1802, when he was eighty-five. The initial writing dates from the mid-1740s, when the revised *Dunciad* stimulated a satire on false taste and false science. The plan of the poem, in which Scriblerus's 'curious soul' drives him 'Insatiate, endless knowledge to obtain,' and its execution are unexceptionable, but the results are not very entertaining. Cambridge's miscellaneous verse, like *The Scribleriad,* is accomplished rather than excellent, most of it short, occasional, and/or classical imitation, and none of it serious.

John Free, *Poems and Miscellaneous Pieces.* These poems, written over a period of at least two decades, might have been called 'Poems Light and Loyal,' the later group including 'Stigand, or The Antigallican,' which identifies an unrhymed Miltonic style with versificatory and sociopolitical freedom.

Thomas Gray, *Elegy Written in a Country Churchyard.**

Gilbert West, *Education.* Like West's earlier *On the Abuse of Traveling* (1739), this is a well-done Spenserian narrative with room for a continuation which West never wrote. Travel can be abused, in West's former poem, by letting luxurious and despotic foreign lands tempt one from love of one's own; education involves battles with the giant Custom and spurning vain amusements for knowledge and virtue.

1752

Soame Jenyns, *Poems.* Now known largely from Johnson's murderous review of a metaphysical and ethical work of his, Jenyns was also a writer of respectable

215

verse, including a pair of energetic social satires, *The Modern Fine Gentleman* (1746) and *The Modern Fine Lady* (1751), and an ingenious adaptation of Horace's *Epistle* 2 : 1.

J.M., *The Scale, or Woman Weighed with Man.* Three cantos in heroic couplets in defense of woman's virtue, benevolence, and common sense, though arrogant man derides and victimizes her in sexual and connubial relationships.

[Moses Mendez], *The Seasons, in Imitation of Spenser.* Mendez's decision to challenge comparison with Spenser and Thomson was ill-advised. Still, he tried again with another Spenserian imitation, *The Squire of Dames* (published 1758).

Christopher Smart, *Poems on Several Occasions.* A collection of early verse, omitting a great deal of periodical material; the only ambitious poem included is Smart's georgic, *The Hop-Garden.*

1753

Robert Dodsley, *Agriculture.* This blank-verse georgic was to have been Book 1 of a three-book poem, *Public Virtue,* but Dodsley got no further than three cantos of advice on husbandry with scientific explanations in verse.

[James Fortescue], *Essays Moral and Miscellaneous.* These two dull, feeble volumes (1753, 1754), along the lines of Fortescue's earlier moral platitudes in *A View of Life* (1749), expand on Solomon ('The Speech of Wisdom'), offer standard preachments ('On the State of Man, His Passions, Their Objects and End'), and summarize, as best Fortescue could, religious and natural knowledge ('Science').

Thomas Hamilton, Earl of Haddington, *Forty Select Poems.* Like 'G——e P——e's' often reprinted *The Festival of Love,* these bawdy tales in tetrameter couplets, with no detailed obscenity or many obscene words, suggest the tameness of most later eighteenth-century bawdy. John Wilkes's *An Essay on Woman* and related poems (written in the 1750s, made public in 1763) are an exception that led to a *cause célèbre.*

Christopher Smart, *The Hilliad.* This successful short lampoon, still worth reading, attacks John Hill, a pamphleteer and self-claimed expert on a variety of subjects, through a Scriblerian satire with 'Notes Variorum' to a mock-heroic text. As usual, the choice of mock-heroic proceeds from the victim's puffed sense of his due, so that Hill is 'Damned to the scandal of his own applause.'

1754

John Duncombe, *The Feminiad.* Despite the '-iad,' this poem commends rather than satirizes some fifteen or so women authors.

George Jeffreys, *Miscellanies in Verse and Prose.* A rather agreeable collection of the short verse of a long lifetime (1678–1755).

James (Dance) Love, *Poems on Several Occasions.* Fables, songs, epigrams, prologues and epilogues; a jocular mock-heroic 'Cricket' in Gay's manner with Scriblerian notes; and a satire on modern corruptions of taste (harlequin performances, opera, the theatrical shows of Samuel Foote) in 'The Stage.'

Elizabeth Tollet, *Poems on Several Occasions*. This posthumous collection has odes, songs, epistles, pastorals, epigrams, and biblical and classical paraphrases dating back at least as far as 1717; it also has a physicotheological poem, 'The Microcosm,' and one vigorous feminist poem, 'Hypatia.'

1755–9 With hostilities toward France rapidly kindling, Pitt formed his first ministry, which he led till 1761. 'The Great Commoner,' as he was known, directed world-wide military operations against the French, with great success in 1758–9. Through the succession of wars in mid-century, England was beginning to demonstrate a military and economic dominance to match her position, since 1715, as the most important intellectual center in Europe, a position she maintained till 1780 with the necessary help of a brilliant, cosmopolitan Scots culture.

1755

[George Colman and Bonnell Thornton, eds], *Poems by Eminent Ladies*. Of particular note among the selections from eighteen female poets are the very skillful moral epistles, in the manner of Pope, by Mary Jones (and also her 'Elegy on a Favourite Dog,' which beautifully captures a mock-heroic rueful tone), and some of Mary Leapor's poems. Some of the poets in these two volumes, like Constantia Grierson and Mary Masters, were published on their own as well as in this edition; others, like Letitia Pilkington, were hardly 'eminent.'

Samuel Derrick, *A Collection of Original Poems*. Derrick says that some were written by a 'man of fashion whom I am not permitted to name' and that his own are mostly juvenilia; the apologetic beginning is deserved for these songs, simple odes, cantatas, and social verse.

1757

Cornelius Arnold, *Poems on Several Occasions*. In one way or another typical of the interests and/or modes of the period are 'Commerce,' a blank-verse poem on trade, 'Distress,' a blank-verse poem on melancholy, 'The Mirror for the Year M.DCC.LV' in Spenserian stanzas that describe Death's whisking off mortals of various character types, and 'London,' about leaving the city, in the manner of Johnson's poem of the same name. There are also tales and dialogues, songs, fables, poems of rural retirement, and even an acrostic.

William and John Duncombe, eds, *The Works of Horace in English Verse*. Two volumes of translations and imitations by various hands (1757, 1759).

John Dyer, *The Fleece*. A georgic devoted to one of England's great native industries.*

Thomas Gray, *Odes.** The two magnificent Pindarics, 'The Progress of Poesy' and 'The Bard'.

William Whitehead, *Elegies, with an Ode to the Tiber.* During the 1740s Whitehead, who became Poet Laureate this year, wrote well but not very well in the style of Pope: *The Danger of Writing Verse* (1741), *An Essay on Ridicule* (1743), and *On Nobility* (1744) are moral epistles; *Anne Boleyn to Henry the Eighth* (1743) imitates the *Heroides* like *Eloisa to Abelard; Atys and Arastus* (1744) is a pathetic tale not in the manner of Pope but of Dryden's *Fables.* During the 1750s, he took up the newer styles as in *A Hymn to the Nymph of Bristol Spring* (1751) and in these elegies, though Whitehead remained civil and preceptive rather than enthusiastic, pictorial, and imaginative. The *Elegies* and *Ode*, all written in France or Italy, rehearse the moral, elegiac themes so common among Englishmen who reflected on history and lost empire.

William Wilkie, *The Epigoniad.* This nine-book epic in couplets follows certain Homeric figures after the Trojan War. Despite an interesting preface on the epic and much learning in the poem, Wilkie is likely to convince readers that writing epic in Pope's style requires Pope. There was only one edition, 1769, after the first of 1757. Wilkie's *Fables* (1768) are dull.

1758

Thomas Edwards, *The Canons of Criticism.* This edition, published the year after Edwards's death, contains some fifty of his sonnets, thirteen of which had earlier appeared in Dodsley (1748). The impulse behind the sonnets is largely Miltonic.

William Hawkins, *Dramatic and Other Poems.* This collection of miscellaneous verse by the sometime Professor of Poetry at Oxford (1751–6) includes an expanded version of his mock-heroic *The Thimble* (1743–4), a polished but too trifling combination of the style of *The Rape of the Lock* and the Scriblerian annotation of the *Dunciad* – Hawkins was not alone among poets of the 1740s and 1750s in combining these. 'An Essay on Genius' deals with the relations between body and soul, and women and men, with the roster of English poets, and with climate; it remains commonplace.

Edmund Spenser, *The Faerie Queene.* As Newton's edition of Milton (1749–52) brought together a wealth of eighteenth-century scholarship on that poet, so the editions of *The Faerie Queene* by John Upton and by Ralph Church update Hughes's Spenser (1715) with a better text and notes collected from scholars and critics.

1759

Samuel Butler, *Genuine Remains*, ed. Robert Thyer. An annotated edition of numbers of Butler's hitherto unpublished works, chosen for merit and lack of indecency, this volume made available much significant poetry, like 'The Elephant in the Moon' and several topical satires.

1760–4 The death of George II in 1760 brought to the throne his grandson, George III, whose inexperience, hostility toward those whom the old King had trusted, and faith in his overweening Scots advisor, Lord Bute, rapidly created trouble. A period of ministerial instability followed, and shortly after the Peace of Paris (1762–3) put an end to the Seven Years' War, Bute had to resign under a shower of vilification. In the same year the radical demagogue John Wilkes was prosecuted for libel in his paper *The North Briton* on such dubious legal grounds that a hue and cry arose about freedom of the press and freedom of British subjects from arbitrary arrests. The ensuing controversy brought to light an obscene poem of his (maybe of his friend Thomas Potter's), *An Essay on Woman*, which led to Wilkes's flight to France and subsequent outlawry.

1760

George Keate, *Ancient and Modern Rome*. Keate's first published poem gives the key to his career: it copies the mode of Dyer's *The Ruins of Rome* (1740). Similarly *The Alps* (1762) draws on Thomson and *The Ruins of Netley Abbey* (1764) on the 'graveyard' school. *Ferney* (1768) joins a chorus of Englishmen in defending Shakespeare against Voltaire ('Above control, above each classic rule,/His tutress Nature and the world his school'). Of Keate's poems, only his prologues and epilogues give pleasure.

Robert Lloyd, *The Actor*. Lloyd and Charles Churchill, friends, had similar careers, in each case beginning with a poem on the stage which made his reputation; both wrote satire; both died late in 1764. But while Churchill strove to be sublime, Lloyd was content to be frisky and facile. *The Actor*, which praises Garrick and mocks stage affectations, is quite good in this vein, and the *Two Odes* (1760), written with George Colman in mockery of Gray's and William Mason's loftiness, are very good in another. Lloyd's verse is often engaging, in particular *The Poet* (1761) and 'On Rhyme,' both of them epistles to friends.

James Macpherson, *Fragments of Ancient Poetry Collected in the Highlands of Scotland*. Macpherson was already the author of a six-canto heroic poem in couplets about ancient Scots history, *The Highlander* (1758), which smacks of a cross between Pope's *Iliad* and Macpherson's own 'Ossianic' verse. The *Fragments* – simple, spontaneous (as 'fragments'), set in wild nature, abrupt, passionate – startled contemporary readers with their style. See pp. 113–15 above.

'Porcupinus Pelagius' (Macnamara Morgan?), *Satires on Several Occasions*. There are seven, mostly on public issues and mostly in anapaestic couplets. Among satiric butts are the 'broad bottom' ministry that replaced Walpole ('The Triumvirade'), 'sublime' poetry ('The Porcupinade,' in blank verse), and the quacks and false literati of London ('The Pasquinade') – some of these borrow openly from the *Dunciad* in devices and Scriblerian annotations.

1761

Charles Churchill, *The Rosciad*. Churchill launched his career with this poem, a satiric consideration of the current actors and actresses, and also in 1761 with *The Apology*, a satire on critics. Each poem went through five editions within the year.

David Garrick, *The Fribbleriad*. The great actor and capable playwright was also exceptionally adroit at light verse with a satiric bite, combining ease and energy of line and diction, for example in his songs, prologues, and epilogues. *The Fribbleriad* is his best longer poem, a mock-heroic attack on the allegedly hermaphroditic Thaddeus Fitzpatrick, a theatrical rioter.

1762

Elizabeth Carter, *Poems on Several Occasions*. Carter's only extensive collection of poems contains largely moral and religious verse some of which shows the poet's extensive learning but not great poetic talent.

Charles Churchill, *The Ghost*. These four books of tetrameter couplets (1762–3) center on a ghost scare in Cock Lane but ramble digressively; they are now best known for their attack on Dr Johnson.

Mary Collier, *Poems on Several Occasions*. Collier, a washerwoman who hoped to tread in Stephen Duck's footsteps – her 'The Woman's Labour' (1739) responds to his 'The Thresher's Labour' – provides insights into the life of poor rural women, resentful of men of their own class and of the upper classes generally. Unsurprisingly, poems about things she experienced are better than her elegies, biblical paraphrases, and other conventional poems.

William Falconer, *The Shipwreck*. Falconer's long narrative (made a good bit longer in 1764) in heroic couplets, mixing love and nautical description, sublimity, and pathos, was irresistible to many readers of the 1760s but is more resistible now.

James Macpherson, *Fingal, an Ancient Epic Poem*. The six martial books of *Fingal* and a number of shorter poems involving heroic exploits, the supernatural, rescued maidens, noble heroes, and Celtic bards were collected in the first considerable body of 'Ossianic' verse. Macpherson wrote historical annotations and offered parallel passages in Homer, Virgil, and even the Bible to show how the primitive epic imagination of the blind bard Ossian worked.

John Ogilvie, *Poems on Several Subjects*. An interesting critic, Ogilvie was not a poet of distinction. His odes, as in this volume, are excellent examples of the highly figured style, using cinematic effects of swooping toward and away from described objects for strong visual and kinesthetic impressions. Filled with adjectives and insistent on bringing the subject within the reader's experience (a function of, for instance, the dream vision), these odes and 'The Day of Judgment' (in heroic couplets) seem to be written to the specifications of Ogilvie's criticism, with its emphasis on the dramatic and the psychological. His slightly later *Providence* (blank verse; 1764) tries to make thought sensory through allegory as the poem moves through the natural world, history, and the moral world.

1763

John Brown, *The Cure of Saul*. 'The heaven-forsaken monarch' is cured by music, the effects of which Brown tries to imitate in verse as Dryden had in *Alexander's Feast*. Brown's ode has some power, but it huffs and limps its way into all the pitfalls that Dryden avoided.

Charles Churchill, *The Prophecy of Famine*. A violent, well-sustained attack on the Scots, this poem marked Churchill's debut as a political poet allied with John Wilkes and the anti-Bute radicals. His next poem of the year, *An Epistle to William Hogarth*, heaped contempt on the artist as envious and senile (for having dared to support Bute and caricature Wilkes); and two more, *The Conference* and *The Author*, proclaimed Churchill's own fearless independence and uprightness, in contrast to other political and poetic figures.*

John Hoole, tr. Torquato Tasso, *Jerusalem Delivered*. In this first complete translation since Fairfax's (1600), Hoole was so successful that he went on to Metastasio (1767) and Ariosto's *Orlando Furioso* (1783; replacing the translation of 1755 by William Huggins, which in turn had been the first since the 1590s). Revived interest in these Italian chivalric romances obviously accords with other examples of the new zest for olden times in the 1760s.

James Merrick, *Poems on Sacred Subjects*. Mostly paraphrases.

Christopher Smart, *A Song to David*.* Smart's long, elaborate ode of praise. By this time Smart had presumably stopped work on the collection of fragments of antiphonal rejoicing published in 1939, *Jubilate Agno*.*

Sir Charles Hanbury Williams, *A Collection of Poems*. Numbers of Sir Charles's poems had been published separately or anthologized in the 1740s, but after his death in 1759, six eighteenth-century editions appeared, with a complete edition in 1822. This popularity is the more impressive because almost all the poems are occasional, sometimes serious ('An Ode to . . . Stephen Poyntz,' amorous poems to the actress Peg Woffington) but most often satirical, like his excellent political ballads. By and large, within their limits, they justify Horace Walpole's praise: 'If Sir Charles had many superiors in poetry, he had none in the wit of his poetry.'

1764

Charles Churchill, *Gotham*. In this year of his death, Churchill continued making direct political attacks prompted by specific incidents (*The Duellist*, *The Candidate*) and self-defense (*The Farewell*, *Independence*). He also wrote *The Times*, with a focus on sexual behavior, particularly homosexuality. *Gotham* differs from the others in being far more fanciful and relaxed, although it too contains the

221

common political and personal themes as Churchill makes himself, poetically, a kind of patriot king.

[Dorothy Dubois (or Dubourg?)], *Poems on Several Occasions*. The volume opens, as women's often do, with a slightly pert apologetic poem about the author's sex, and goes on with undistinguished, facile narratives, elegies, fables, and short poems (like 'Extempore on Thought,' which begins, fatally, 'I'll think no more; it wearies me to think').

William Falconer, *The Demagogue*. An attack in Churchillian vein on Churchill's political leader, Pitt; too relentlessly ferocious to be clever.

Oliver Goldsmith, *The Traveller, or A Prospect of Society*. In this combination of the verse epistle and the prospect poem, the traveler surveys various powerful nations of Europe, finds all lacking, and realizes that 'bliss . . . centres in the mind.' The forward movement of the poem and the surges of feeling are beautifully balanced by the analogical, antithetical structure, just as the energy of the heroic couplets is balanced by their epigrammatic syntax.

James Grainger, *The Sugar Cane*. Aside from his translation of Tibullus (1759), Grainger's only poem of note is this West Indian georgic in four books of blank verse. The cultivation of the cane, the natural disasters to which it (and the lovers so drearily obligatory since Thomson) is prey, and the exoticism of the West Indies in general make up the poem. Passages sympathetic to blacks in Book 4 are unsurprising in a poem of the 1760s.

William Shenstone, *The Works in Verse and Prose*. The verse, in the first of these two volumes printed the year after the poet's death, includes elegies (with a prose essay on the genre) and short poems, serious and amusing, from about 1737 on. Apart from 'The Schoolmistress,' the best known is *The Judgment of Hercules* (1741) – Hercules chooses virtue – and the mildly scatological 'Inscription' is the funniest. Shenstone was a gentleman poet, easy, genteel, well turned out, and minor.

John Wilson, *Clyde*. In a long descriptive poem about the scenes along the course of the river Clyde, the poem celebrates Scots heroes, activities (including the hunt, with the usual ambiguity of feeling), and landscape.

1765–9 Without adequate parliamentary leadership, George III sent for Pitt, who outraged his admirers by accepting both the ministry and a peerage. As the Earl of Chatham he lost his audience in the Commons, and found himself so isolated that he withdrew into the gloomy, imperious, hypochondriacal egoism that was his native mode; and this at a time when obvious difficulties were increasing between England and the American colonies. Wilkes returned from exile and was denied election to Parliament despite an overwhelming majority of votes in his borough. The grave constitutional issue posed was meat to many writers, especially the pseudonymous satirist 'Junius' (1767–72).

1765

Thomas Percy, ed., *Reliques of Ancient English Poetry*. Largely a collection of ballads and metrical romances, Percy's volumes made available a wealth of 'primitive' narrative, annotated and expounded upon, to an audience eager for such material. He had earlier (1753) published *Five Pieces of Runic Poetry Translated from the Icelandic*; several Scots were reviving their national 'ancient poetry' in the 1760s and 1770s, and Evan Evans had offered *Some Specimens of the Poetry of the Ancient Welsh Bards* (1764). The *Reliques* are not all ancient, since Percy included poems by Mallet, Tickell, Glover, Shenstone, Hamilton, and Grainger; and he did not hesitate to alter texts somewhat or to compose 'The Friar of Orders Gray' by joining selected fragments from Shakespeare with 'a few supplemental stanzas' of his own. This admixture of the modern only added to the influence enjoyed by the collection.

Christopher Smart, *A Translation of the Psalms of David.**

William Stevenson, *Original Poems on Several Subjects*. Original but unoriginal: Stevenson's six books of *Vertumnus, or The Progress of Spring* is shrunken Thomson in heroic couplets, and 'The Progress of Evening, or The Power of Virtue' scoops together in two short pages all the clichés of the meditative ode or elegy: the bat on leathern wings, the wheeling insect with its dull drone, the moon as a pale empress, the stars with silver lamps in the blue vault, the owl as a 'melancholy bird of woe,' a 'tottering tower, with ivy overgrown,' and of course 'enthusiastic rapture [that] thrills the breast.'

1766

Christopher Anstey, *The New Bath Guide*. Epistolary social satire; see pp. 133–4 above. Anstey vainly tried to recapture his success, especially in *An Election Ball . . . in the Zomersetshire Dialect* (1776). He also wrote other light verse, occasional satire, and serious elegy. *On the . . . Death of the Marquis of Tavistock* (1767) is noteworthy for its dropping rhyme and smooth metre for dramatic effects.

Richard Graves, ed., *The Festoon: A Collection of Epigrams Ancient and Modern*. A good collection, beginning with 'An Essay on the Nature of the Epigram,' *The Festoon* has historical interest because of the tendency of so much Restoration and eighteenth-century verse to strive for the conditions of the epigram, by which I do not mean the quip or the maxim but the pointed and unified expression of principal thoughts, for panegyric, satiric, amorous, or humorous ends. More attention should be given, I suspect, to the role of Martial, with his keen observation and condensed expression, in forming eighteenth-century poetic style; he was exceptionally popular, and of course has a place of honor in *The Festoon*.

Evan Lloyd, *The Methodist*. Slashing attack on religious fervor, in terms of equations familiar from attacks on Puritans in the last century and on Methodists – even in *The New Bath Guide* – during this: pride, lust, and greed masquerade as a demotic, irrational religion.

George Meen, *Happiness*. Blank verse, 450 lines, combining the examination of states of life (as in *Rasselas*) and a dream vision with allegorical figures like Beauty, Love, Piety, and Liberty.

Anna Williams, *Miscellanies in Prose and Verse*. Thirty years' accumulation of rather grave but not dreary or pretentious poems, a few of them by other people, like Williams's friend Samuel Johnson. One can guess their nature by their titles, such as 'Verses Addressed to Mr. Richardson, on His History of Sir Charles Grandison' (which sneers at Fielding), 'Reflections on a Grave Digging in Westminster Abbey,' 'The Happy Solitude, or The Wished Retirement,' and 'Rasselas to Imlac.'

1767

William Dodd, *Poems*. The usual range of odes, tales, elegies, sonnets, mock-heroics, and especially pastorals – the preface to the 'Moral Pastorals' has critical material of some interest. 'To the Author of *Tristram Shandy*' has some ironic biographical amusement: Parson Sterne is scolded for immoral writing by Parson Dodd who ten years later was to be hanged for forgery.

Charles Ingram, *The Rise and Progress of the Present Taste in Planting*. The poem provides precepts about the natural garden and its parts, along with a history of parks and gardens, with accounts of true and false taste: the false is seen in 'Trees clipped to statues, monsters, cats, and dogs,/And hollies metamorphosed into hogs,' the true in a kind of edenic wildness which conceals art to reveal 'nature only more improved.'

Richard Jago, *Edge Hill, or The Rural Prospect Delineated and Moralized*. The prospect lies where Oxfordshire meets Warwickshire, the delineation is in tableaux corresponding to different times of day, and the moralizing comes in digressions and episodes after Thomson's manner. These four books in blank verse are Jago's only ambitious poetic work; he also wrote shorter poems, mostly light verse of the 1750s.

Edward Jerningham, *Poems*. *The Nunnery* (1762) has the distinction of being a serious parody of Gray's *Elegy*:

> The glistening eye, the half-seen breast of snow,
> The coral lip, the blush of Nature's bloom,
> Awaits alike the inevitable foe:
> The paths of pleasure lead but to the tomb.

Jerningham's other modish experiments in pathos and his panegyrics (in later editions of his *Poems*) tend to use this same elegiac stanza, and do so about this well.

William Julius Mickle, *The Concubine*. A Spenserian narrative, the title of which was later chastened to *Sir Martyn*, about a knight's lapse into and recovery from dissipation.

1768

Hugh Downman, *The Land of the Muses*. The volume has miscellaneous verse and the title poem, all quite undistinguished in quality. *The Land of the Muses* is written as if to be inserted in Book 2 of *The Faerie Queene*, betweeen cantos 11 and 12. As a close Spenserian imitation (later, however, rewritten in couplets) it differs from Downman's irregular, free-flowing treatment of that other stanzaic form typically borrowed from earlier English poets, the sonnet. A physician by trade, Downman later (1774–6) wrote a didactic poem called *Infancy*, on maternal care and the management of children.

William Kenrick, *Poems Ludicrous, Satirical, and Moral*. Kenrick was known for scurrility, none of which appears in this volume with its various political satires (anti-Pitt), literary-artistic satires (against 'graveyard' poets), and philosophizing (on the weakness of human understanding, moral sentiment, relativism of values, and various religious topics). These last are of some interest for what one might call the journalism of ideas.

Alexander Ross, *Helenore, or The Fortunate Shepherdess*. A very long pastoral tale in broad Scots, mostly colloquial but with calculated effects of tonal range, like 'Now when the morn was gilt wi' Phoebus' beams,/And reek in streaming tow'rs frae lum-heads leams. . . .'

John Hall Stevenson, *Makarony Fables*. Like *Fables for Grown Gentlemen* (1761, 1770), this is witty, jaunty Aesopianism. Stevenson's verse is almost all light, except for some of his imitations of Horace's odes. Some of it is political – anti-Tory, anti-Scots – and some, like *Crazy Tales* (1762), leaps gleefully into the bawdy Boccacciesque. Much of this verse is charming with dashes of absurdity.

1769

Thomas Gray, *Ode for Music*. A panegyric ode for the installation of the Duke of Grafton as Chancellor of Cambridge University; Gray's last poem. His political sympathies – Grafton was Prime Minister – had earlier led to one of the deadliest political satires after Pope, 'On Lord Holland's Seat near Margate, Kent' (written 1768, printed in a miscellany, 1769).

[Brockhill Newburgh], *Essays Poetical, Moral, and Critical*. Includes poems dating from at least 1743, with both light and religious verse, translations and adaptations of the classics, an attack on rhyme ('To the Honourable Lieutenant General Cholmondoley'), and some mock-heroic.

1770–5 Ministerial instability ended with the administration of Lord North (1770–80), who dealt well with a crisis in India (1773) but badly with the more important one in America. The Boston Tea Party (1773) was only one episode in a history of pamphleteering, civil disobedience, harassment, and some violence since the mid-1760s. In early 1775, shots had been fired at Lexington and by the middle of that year, the American Revolution was well under way.

1770

Michael Bruce, *Poems on Several Occasions*. After Bruce's death (in 1767, aged twenty-one), his old schoolmate John Logan undertook this edition of his poems; some of the poems were not Bruce's, and some of Bruce's poems – one of which Logan was accused of having appropriated – were not in the volume. Logan may well have tampered with the texts of those poems he printed. What we have is attractive, simple, and harmonious descriptive and elegiac verse without any real pressure of intelligence, imagination, or convincing feeling behind it.

Oliver Goldsmith, *The Deserted Village*. About the destruction of an idealized, fondly remembered village through rural depopulation. 'Luxury' is the villain as 'trade's unfeeling train/Usurp the land and dispossess the swain.' The eloquence of Goldsmith's poetry almost makes the sentimental nostalgia of this pastoral elegy convincing. He moves from the tender to the plangent, from the plain to the moral and imaginative sublime with sureness and power. For those to whom politics can best be understood through human interest stories, *The Deserted Village* may have a social effect beyond that of personal lament for the fantasies of one's youth.

James Robertson, *Poems*. Robertson's career was essentially one of the 1770s and 1780s, with short narrative poems, some moral, some attempting tragic scenes (like the sorrow of a mad lover, a sort of Eloisa to Abelard from Bedlam), some amusing. The amusing ones work best. Robertson wrote anti-Methodist poems, including a parody of a Wesleyan hymn; 'On Our Modern Comedies' (1768), against the 'sentimental' mode; and other satires as well.

[Edward Thompson], *The Court of Cupid*. These poems represent Thompson's work as a young man during the early and mid-1760s, when he was in his twenties: they are almost all merry and coy – rather than actionable – bawdy verse, including 'Cooper's Well' (an obscene full-scale parody of Denham) and satiric epistles to town whores ('The Meretriciad,' 'The Courtesan,' 'The Demi-Rep'). Thompson's verse of the later 1770s includes some popular sea songs, an offshoot from his lifelong career in the navy.

William Woty, *Poetical Works*. In this collection and his *Poems on Several Occasions* Woty shows himself skilled at elaborated light verse (on wigs, corkscrews, tobacco stoppers, and that sort of thing) and mild satire, like 'The Auctioneers' (on modern taste in gardens, pictures, and *objets d'art*), *The Graces* (1774; a satire on Chesterfield's letters to his son), and 'Fashion' (1767; a denunciation of fashion and luxury). He wrote pleasant epistles and other verse that smacks of being designed for periodicals.

1771

James Beattie, *The Minstrel*. The first of two books of this widely read, influential poem (1771–4) in Spenserian stanzas, tracing – so Beattie says – 'the progress of a poetical genius, born in a rude age, from the first dawning of fancy and reason till . . . [he can appear] in the world as a minstrel.' The portrait of this stock character, drawn from Percy's *Reliques*, is leavened with autobiographical reminiscences and personal sentiments. *The Minstrel* lacks plot; it is, as Beattie wrote to a fellow Scot, a 'philosophical or didactic [rather] than a narrative poem.' Little Edwin communes with Nature and moralizes, listens to folk tales and moralizes, and visits with a moralizing hermit who recommends Science and Philosophy to him. All work and no play makes Beattie a dull poet, here and in most of his other original verse, largely odes, epistles, and elegies. An exception is his broad Scots poem 'To Mr. Alexander Ross.'

1772

Catherine Jemmat, *Miscellanies in Prose and Verse*. Politely conventional light and more serious verse (elegies, epistles, odes, paraphrase of a psalm 'in imitation of Milton's style' – this last being preceded, in the manner so typical and admirable in eighteenth-century collections, by 'The British Pickled Herring and Anchovy').

Sir William Jones, *Poems, Consisting Chiefly of Translations from the Asiatic Languages*. The distinguished orientalist included a number of his classical imitations along with his adaptations of the Near Eastern poets. His critical essays are intriguing, his renderings of the oriental poems very much in the florid manner developed from the mid-century ode.

William Mason, *The English Garden*. Four books (1772–81) in blank verse for a preceptive poem which, 'painting nature as scorning control, should employ a versification for that end as unfettered as nature itself' (Mason's preface). In this most ambitious gardening poem of the century, Mason cannot resist a Thomsonian digression to the tedious and dismal love story of Alcander and Nerina in Book 4, but otherwise he avoids narrative and keeps in view his preceptive ends – admonitions to be 'natural' – and his pictorial means.

[Thomas Mercer], *The Sentimental Sailor, or St. Preux to Eloisa*. Mercer frames the epistle to display a wide range of states of emotion, and in the notes to numerous classical and modern poets implies the degree to which the passion of St Preux is archetypal, both individual and universal. Mercer's later *Poems* (1774) also includes annotated descriptive and dramatic poems ('Arthur's Seat,' a topographical poem; and 'Elysium: A Dream,' a Virgilian visit to the underworld), as well as 'Of Poetry: An Epistolary Essay' which professes the same values – 'glowing rapture,' 'enlivening soul' – that the introduction to *The Sentimental Sailor* advocates.

Samuel Whyte, *The Shamrock, or Hibernian Cresses*. In 500 pages appear two decades' worth of Whyte's verses in practically every genre but satire and Thomsonian prospect poetry, even rebuses, enigmas, and Spenserian allegory.

1773

Anna Laetitia Aikin (Mrs Barbauld), *Poems*. Mrs Barbauld's collection includes odes, elegies, epistles, hymns, and occasional verse, nothing more expansive except for *Corsica* (1768), a blank-verse celebration of 'the flame of Liberty' burning amid the 'rocky, deep-indented shores/And pointed cliffs'; panegyrics to 'generous Boswell' and much more to the Corsican patriot Paoli are also part of this quite competent, wholly conventional poem – like all Barbauld's work before 1780.

Thomas Blacklock, *A Panegyric on Great Britain*. A 'times' poem satirizing British learning, political life, and vice.

John Byrom, *Miscellaneous Poems*. Volume 1 is mostly secular, with much extremely competent light verse; Volume 2 is mostly religious, with what I think is the only genuinely interesting body of eighteenth-century religious verse, in colloquial language, defending an enthusiastic and at times mystical religion, with careful delimiting of the areas of the senses, reason, and revelation. There are also hymns and pious reflections. The secular poems include philosophical arguments (in the metre of *The New Bath Guide*), some Jacobite poems (a few in Lancashire dialect), 'Thoughts on Rhyme and Blank Verse,' and an 'Epistle on the Art of English Poetry.'

Andrew Erskine, *Town Eclogues*. Poems, allegedly written eight to ten years earlier 'to expose the false taste for florid description which prevails so universally in modern poetry.' Moderately funny dialogues present streetwalkers relating their pastoral seductions – they are Amaryllis and Daphne – with a mixture of pathetic and low imagery; harlequins and undertakers are used to satirize modern fashions; one hangman tells the other, 'Sure if in transmigration truth there be,/The great Caligula revives in thee.'

Robert Fergusson, *Poems*. The only collection published in the short lifetime (1750–74) of the fine Scots poet. Fergusson's poems are typically in Scots dialect, flexible and colloquial. Among his best are a description of Edinburgh's urban scene, 'Auld Reikie'; 'The Farmer's Ingle'; and a protest 'To the Principal and Professors of the University of St. Andrews, on Their Superb Treat to Dr. Samuel Johnson.' More limited in range than Burns, Fergusson bears comparison with him in the sort of poem they both wrote, and presumably would have continued to grow as a poet.

[William Mason], *An Heroic Epistle to Sir William Chambers*. An exceedingly popular satiric epistle about the fashion for oriental gardening, with a general assault on many other targets; almost equally popular was a sequel, *To the Public, an Heroic Postscript* (1774).

[Percival Stockdale], *The Poet*. The ideal of this figure, with much about feeling ('soar[ing] . . . on fancy's wings,' souls that 'revibrate' the poet's songs) and the genesis of poetic ideas ('Ideas rising on ideas throng;/His working bosom teems with embryo-song'). Stockdale, despite these 'romantic' biases, in fact praises Pope, Johnson, and Savage, and criticizes Macpherson.

1774

John Bennet, *Poems on Several Occasions*. Like Duck and Collier, Bennet was a workman, in this case a journeyman shoemaker who rose from dust to the poetic empyrean; but not very far, since his poems are the usual unremarkable assortment of short tales, songs, and moralizing, with the rustic subjects obligatory for untutored genius included, but treated rather starchily.

Thomas Blacklock, *The Graham*. In this 'heroic ballad,' the Scots leader Graham comes to rescue his English love Anna Howard from her family and precipitates a great battle, ending in peace and reconciliation.

Oliver Goldsmith, *Retaliation*. Unfinished at the time of Goldsmith's death, the poem consists of good-humoured but sometimes barbed epitaphs for those of Goldsmith's friends who had teased him – months before he died, of course – by writing mock-epitaphs for him. The wit of *Retaliation* least clear to modern readers is in its toying with the idealization and taboos of panegyric and specifically of the epitaph, a genre in itself during the eighteenth century.

John Langhorne, *The Country Justice*. Part I (of three; the poem was completed 1775–7) of a varied, digressive, skillfully written mixture of the moral, the pathetic, the humane, and the satiric – the poem, in rhyme, is about the offices of a rural justice of the peace. Langhorne is one of the more capable minor poets of the 1760s and 1770s, though too often wordy, stale, and simpering to be more than that. His sonnets, fables, odes, elegiac poems, and long narrative ballad *Owen of Carron* (1778) do well with the genres in vogue; but the less conventionally generic *The Country Justice* is the best of his work.

John Tait, *The Cave of Morar*. Tait's three volumes of the mid-1770s nicely exemplify some of the new fashions in poetry. *The Cave of Morar* is a narrative in quatrains, with a Scots heroine (Emma) and hero (Edgar) united despite feuds; Morar, an old hermit who pours out his woes, turns out to be Edgar's father. *The Land of Liberty* (1775) is an allegory in Spenserian stanzas, with the visionary processional common both because of Spenser's own example and because the ceremonious stanza allowed the poem to be conceived as a series of expatiatory units. Here a dream vision of demonic Monarchy and Ambition (English vices) and Discord (anarchic American democracy) realizes a battle in which the English Constitution defeats evil Faction. The American war also recurs in Tait's *Poetical Legends* (1776), in which two Yankee lovers, Henry and Jessy, are spared by British military mercy ('The American Captive'); this poem and 'The Fatal Feud' are once more narratives in simple quatrains.

1775

George Crabbe, *Inebriety*. A cheerful and delightful poem, with smatterings of mock-heroic and burlesque of Pope, about drunkenness.

Anne, Lady Miller, ed., *Poetic Amusements at a Villa near Bath*. The first offering of verse contributed at Lady Miller's society salon. Although some writers of mild distinction – Anstey, Garrick, Richard Graves, Anna Seward – dropped their verses along with the others into the urn Lady Miller had ready for those who joined her poetical competitions (for a myrtle crown), most of the versifiers and still more of the verse were happily forgettable. Her circle amused itself and – at its expense – many readers, like Richard Tickell, who in *The Wreath of Fashion, or The Art of Sentimental Poetry* (1778) singles out its 'Sonnets, odes, acrostics, madrigals' as 'A motley heap of metaphoric sighs,/Laborious griefs and studied ecstasies.'

Mary Robinson, *Poems*. If Robinson had been talented enough to write well, the volume would suffer from its restriction to topics and types thought suitable to ladies, such as pastorals, little odes to charity, and the like.

William Bagshaw Stevens, *Poems, Consisting of Indian Odes and Miscellaneous Pieces*. The Indian odes include Brahmin chants, war songs, and love songs – the sublime ones are more irregular in stanzas and metres than the soft. Some of Stevens's miscellaneous poems imitate or translate ancient Western poems, both primitive and classical. Others practice well-worn current genres.

1776–80 In these years, the American colonies were lost, though peace did not come till 1782. France and Spain, which had sided with the colonies, worried English forces in Europe; the Irish had to receive concessions; and in 1780 the Commons approved Dunning's resolution 'that the influence of the Crown has increased, is increasing, and ought to be diminished.' The sense of threat and of governmental impotence helped produce the anti-Catholic Gordon riots of 1780, a week of arson and looting during which there were over 450 casualties in London.

1776

Richard Graves, *Euphrosyne, or Amusements on the Road of Life*. Volume 1 this year, Volume 2 in 1780: a collection of small verses, occasional, panegyric, epistolary. In general Graves is an amusing light versifier, and some of the poems on gardening and those that make reference to the powers of the imagination are of interest to the historian of ideas.

William Julius Mickle, tr., Luis de Camoens, *The Lusiad*. One imperial nation's interest in another, particularly in a 'discovery of India'; the land of Anson and Cook turning its eyes on Vasco da Gama; a poetic tradition that doted on epic narrative – the success of the well-done Mickle translation, so long after Fanshawe's (1655) was predictable.

Hannah More, *Sir Eldred of the Bower*. The paragon Sir Eldred, overcome with sudden jealousy, stabs the handsome stranger hugged by his new bride Birtha; the victim is Birtha's long-lost brother Edwy, whose death causes in turn the deaths from grief of Birtha and her old father Ardolph. Heavily moralized, in ballad quatrains, this 'legendary tale' was published with another, of a jilted nymph who turns to stone (at her own plea), causing her perfidious lover's suicide and herself to be wounded – despite her petrifaction – and thus becoming 'The Bleeding Rock' that is the poem's title.

William Hayward Roberts, *Poems*. This mediocre collection includes a denunciation of rhyme ('A Poetical Epistle to Christopher Anstey') and several poems in rhyme. There is also a long blank-verse poem on the existence, attributes, and providence of God and an epistle on English poetry (Philips, Thomson, Somervile, Young, Akenside, Glover, Mason, Gray, and others).

William Whitehead, *Variety.* Whitehead's popular narrative in tetrameter couplets, like his *The Goat's Beard* (1777), imparts to married couples wholesome advice with twinkling condescension: be sensible, loving, content in your own place.

1777

Thomas Chatterton, *Poems.* * Seven years after the death of Chatterton (1752–70), this collection gave to the public the allegedly medieval verse that had hardly been sampled in print by readers during the poet's lifetime. His career had two phases: from mid-1768 to mid-1769, Chatterton elaborated the 'Rowley' poems, and from early 1769 to the autumn of 1770, he both extended the medieval exotic to other 'primitive' kinds, 'Ossianic' and African, and pulled back into satire. The later phase was, of course, the more conventional. 'An Excellent Balade of Charitie' and 'Englysh Metamorphosis, Book I' are the most admirable examples of the 'Rowley' mode. 'The Consuliad' will do to exemplify the satiric, with its embracing of Churchill's style – the more Shandean parts of that style are typified in 'February: An Elegy' with its mixture of tones and its self-consciousness.

[William Combe], *The Diaboliad.* The devil, needing a successor, sends imps to England to find willing, suitable candidates; they present their claims in the 'session of the poets' mode. This witty, angry personal satire – Combe names names – elicited several imitations, like the feminine version *The Diabo-lady*, and another five associated satires by Combe himself within the next two years.

William Roscoe, *Mount Pleasant.* A prospect poem in couplets on the beauties of nature and commerce around Liverpool, with rebukes for avarice and – an increasingly common topic – the slave trade.

Elizabeth Ryves, *Poems on Several Occasions.* Unremarkable verse crammed with allegorical entities, whether abstractions or gods; when sexed, Ryves's speakers are feminine, but otherwise the volume does not differ from those written by men at about the same time.

[Alexander Crowcher Schomberg?], *Bagley, A Descriptive Poem, with the Annotations of Scriblerus Secundus.* * *Bagley* is a superb caricature of poetic modes popular in the 1770s; very funny, if slightly less good, is Schomberg's *Ode on the Present State of English Poetry*, published as by Cornelius Scriblerus Nothus.

1778

John Bampfylde, *Sixteen Sonnets.* * Most of the sonnets are emblematic, for example, a description of sea prospects leading to a moral conclusion. The conclusions are compelled by the poet's notion of the genre rather than by any internal logic or rationale of development within the poem. Some simply come inconclusively to an end. The antique language ('yclad,' 'irksome thrall') and the discrepancy between the form of the poem (quatrains) and the movement of thought are typical of the 1770s. Bampfylde, twenty-four when the sonnets appeared, was a young man of considerable talent, but he spent the remainder of his life in prison or a madhouse.

Henry Brooke, *A Collection of the Pieces*. Besides *Universal Beauty*, calendared in 1735 above, the four volumes contain fables, a Chaucerian imitation, and an Irish epic song in Ossianic style ('Conrade, a Fragment'), among many other things.

Richard Cumberland, *Miscellaneous Poems*. A thoroughly conventional, innocuous collection, mostly of the stanzaic forms popular in the 1770s.

Robert Holmes, *Alfred, an Ode, with Six Sonnets*. The ode celebrates a Saxon King in the form of 'The Bard'. The sonnets are Italian in form but they do not use the breaks between octet and sestet for breaks of thought nor do they propel an argument with the *when*s and *if*s common in sixteenth- and seventeenth-century sonnets. Typically for their time, they are essentially each a single statement.

Sir John Henry Moore, *Poetical Trifles*. A miscellany with a parody of Gray's *Elegy* and serious elegies of its own; the volume contains verses closely resembling Byron's *Don Juan* in style and a very good mock 'Palinode to the Reviewers.'

1779

William Cowper, *Olney Hymns*. Sixty-seven hymns, most in quatrains, with considerable sense of personal passion informing them. Cowper's self-dramatization seems expressive rather than – as in Isaac Watts – persuasive and communal. Published with a large number of hymns by John Newton.

C. Lyster, *Summer Trifles*. An 'olio,' as Lyster says, of the usual kinds, including love poems and a biblical paraphrase; contains parodies of Gray and Anstey.

1780

George Crabbe, *The Candidate*. A finely-written, funny plea for a degree of indulgence from the critics of the *Monthly Review*.

Anne Steele ('Theodosia'), *Poems on Subjects Chiefly Devotional*. Hymns and other devotional forms, 'sincere' and dull.

Appendix 2: Poets Laureate

1638–68   Sir William Davenant
1668–88   John Dryden (deposed at the time of the Revolution)
1688–92   Thomas Shadwell
1692–1715 Nahum Tate
1715–18   Nicholas Rowe
1718–30   Laurence Eusden
1730–57   Colley Cibber
1757–85   William Whitehead

Index

The index lists writers and – for periodical and anonymous works – titles cited in the text and Appendix 1, the Chronology beginning on p. 166.

237

242

DATE DUE

HIGHSMITH 45-102   PRINTED IN U.S.A.